# TERROR IN THE BALANCE

# TERROR IN THE BALANCE

## SECURITY, LIBERTY, AND THE COURTS

ERIC A. POSNER

ADRIAN VERMEULE

UNIVERSITY PRESS

2007

# OXFORD
## UNIVERSITY PRESS

Oxford University Press, Inc., publishes works that further
Oxford University's objective of excellence
in research, scholarship, and education.

Oxford   New York
Auckland   Cape Town   Dar es Salaam   Hong Kong   Karachi
Kuala Lumpur   Madrid   Melbourne   Mexico City   Nairobi
New Delhi   Shanghai   Taipei   Toronto

With offices in
Argentina   Austria   Brazil   Chile   Czech Republic   France   Greece
Guatemala   Hungary   Italy   Japan   Poland   Portugal   Singapore
South Korea   Switzerland   Thailand   Turkey   Ukraine   Vietnam

Published by Oxford University Press, Inc.
198 Madison Avenue, New York, New York 10016

www.oup.com

Oxford is a registered trademark of Oxford University Press

Library of Congress Cataloging-in-Publication Data
Posner, Eric A.
Terror in the balance : security, liberty, and the courts /
Eric A. Posner, Adrian Vermeule.
ISBN-13 978-0-19-531025-2
ISBN 0-19-531025-X
1. War and emergency powers—United States.
2. National security—Law and legislation—United States.
3. Civil rights—United States.  I. Vermeule, Adrian, 1968–  II. Title.
KF5060.P67 2007
342.73'0412—dc22        2006007848

1 3 5 7 9 8 6 4 2

Printed in the United States of America
on acid-free paper

# ACKNOWLEDGMENTS

This book is the fruit of years of collaboration during which we benefited from many conversations with friends, colleagues, and family, to whom we are very grateful. We cannot mention all of them here, but we would like to extend special thanks to Geoffrey Stone, with whom we have had numerous conversations about these topics in the course of teaching a joint seminar, and to Jack Goldsmith, Richard Posner, John Yoo, and six anonymous referees, who read the entire manuscript and provided helpful comments on it. We presented versions of the book at Columbia University, Duke Law School, the University of Pennsylvania Law School, and the University of Delaware; we owe thanks to the participants at those events, and particular thanks to Jon Elster and Jeremy Waldron, who provided detailed and challenging comments on parts of the manuscript. Abigail Moncrieff and Michelle Ognibene provided excellent research assistance and technical support.

We would also like to thank the various journals in which earlier versions of some of the chapters appeared, as follows: Eric A. Posner and Adrian Vermeule, *Accommodating Emergencies*, 56 STANFORD LAW REVIEW 605 (2003); Adrian Vermeule, *Libertarian Panics*, 36 RUTGERS LAW JOURNAL 871 (2005); Eric A. Posner and Adrian Vermeule, *Should Coercive Interrogation Be Legal?* 104 MICHIGAN LAW REVIEW 671 (2006); Eric A. Posner, *Terrorism and the Laws of War*, 5 CHICAGO JOURNAL OF INTERNATIONAL LAW 423 (2005); Eric A. Posner, *The Design of Political Trials*, 55 DUKE LAW JOURNAL 75 (2005); Eric A. Posner and Adrian Vermeule, *Emergencies and Democratic Failure*, 92 VIRGINIA LAW REVIEW 1091 (2006).

# CONTENTS

# TERROR IN THE BALANCE

# INTRODUCTION

When national emergencies strike, the executive acts, Congress acquiesces, and courts defer. When emergencies decay, judges become bolder, and soul searching begins. In retrospect, many of the executive's actions will seem unjustified, and people will blame Congress for its acquiescence and courts for their deference. Congress responds by passing new laws that constrain the executive, and courts reassert themselves by supplying relief to anyone who is still subject to emergency measures that have not yet been halted. Normal times return, and professional opinion declares that the emergency policies were anomalous and will not recur, or at least should not recur. Then, another emergency strikes, and the cycle repeats itself.

One can identify roughly six periods of emergency during American history, each with its own paradigmatic instance of alleged executive overreaching.[1] The undeclared war with France at the end of the eighteenth century produced the Sedition Act, which permitted Federalist authorities to lock up Republican critics of the John Adams administration. The Civil War from 1861 to 1865 produced Lincoln's suspension of habeas corpus and imposition of military rule, which included prosecutions of war critics. World War I and the Red Scare generated Espionage Act prosecutions of war critics and the harassment of immigrants and aliens. World War II produced the internment of Japanese Americans. The early cold war saw prosecutions of communists. The post-9/11 emergency resulted in an array of aggressive security measures, including detention without trial of members of al Qaeda and reliance on coercive interrogation. One might also include the period of civil unrest during the Vietnam War, which led, arguably, to political prosecutions of draft-card burners and others. On the other side of the ledger is the War of 1812, which is perhaps the only emergency where the executive was not accused of overreaching and indeed was condemned for its passivity.

Two opposite lessons may be drawn from this history. The weight of academic commentary argues that the history is one of political and constitutional failure. The emergency causes panic; the public characteristically misunderstands the source of the emergency, blames local groups which are conveniently within range of law enforcement but are essentially harmless, at the same time uses the emergency as a pretext to grab the property of those groups, and demands decisive action, including symbolic action, from the authorities. Political leaders also panic, and they implement irrational policies without sufficient deliberation; or, if they do not, they take advantage of the public's confusion in order to implement policies that the public rejects when it is calm and unafraid. Everyone undervalues the policies and values on which the long-term health of the nation depend—equality before the law, democratic deliberation, due process, political freedom—and places exaggerated weight on security. Policies justified on the basis of the emergency become entrenched and persist even after the emergency ends, resulting in long-term loss of freedom for Americans.

A different view, however, is that the history is largely one of political and constitutional success. The essential feature of the emergency is that national security is threatened; because the executive is the only organ of government with the resources, power, and flexibility to respond to threats to national security, it is natural, inevitable, and desirable for power to flow to this branch of government. Congress rationally acquiesces; courts rationally defer. Civil liberties are compromised because civil liberties interfere with effective response to the threat; but civil liberties are never eliminated because they remain important for the well-being of citizens and the effective operation of the government. People might panic, and the government must choose policies that enhance morale as well as respond to the threat, but there is nothing wrong with this. The executive implements bad policies as well as good ones, but error is inevitable, just as error is inevitable in humdrum policymaking during normal times. Policy during emergencies can never be mistake-free; it is enough if policymaking is not systematically biased in any direction, so that errors are essentially random and wash out over many decisions or over time. Both Congress and the judiciary realize that they do not have the expertise or the resources to correct the executive during an emergency. Only when the emergency wanes do these institutions reassert themselves, but this just shows that the basic constitutional structure remains unaffected by the emergency. In the United States, unlike in many other countries, the constitutional system has never collapsed during an emergency.

The two views of history have opposite normative implications. Those who hold the first view devote their energies to persuading Congress and judges to scrutinize executive actions during emergencies. The simplest view, which we label the *civil libertarian view*, holds that courts should be willing to strike down emergency measures that threaten civil liberties to the same extent that they strike down security measures during normal times; perhaps courts should be even less deferential during emergencies, given that emergencies create new opportunities for taking advantage of the public. Some scholars who are sympathetic to the civil libertarian view, but who do not go so far, think that courts should be more deferential during emergencies than during normal times; but these scholars also think that the judges should assert themselves more than they have historically and that the judges should wield constitutional doctrines that require the executive to work in tandem with Congress. Except when the context requires greater precision, we will refer to both types of scholars as civil libertarians.

The second view of history suggests that the traditional practice of judicial and legislative deference has served Americans well, and there is no reason to change it. This view reflects the collective wisdom of the judges themselves, and although no one doubts that injustices occur during emergencies, the type of judicial scrutiny that would be needed to prevent the injustices that have occurred during American history would cause more harm than good by interfering with justified executive actions. Those who hold this view usually have little confidence in congressional leadership and argue that Congress should defer to the executive as well.

This book argues for the latter view. We maintain that the civil libertarian view, in any version, rests on implausible premises and is too weak to overcome the presumptive validity of executive action during emergencies.

Our argument has two components. First, the *tradeoff thesis* holds that governments should, and do, balance civil liberties and security at all times. During emergencies, when new threats appear, the balance shifts; government should and will reduce civil liberties in order to enhance security in those domains where the two must be traded off. Governments will err, but those errors will not be systematically skewed in any direction and will not be more likely during emergencies than during normal times, in which governments also make mistakes about quotidian matters of policy. Second, the *deference thesis* holds that the executive branch, not Congress or the judicial branch, should make the tradeoff between security and liberty. During emergencies, the institutional advantages of the executive are enhanced. Because of the importance of secrecy, speed, and flexibility, courts, which are slow, open, and rigid, have less to contribute to the formulation of national policy than they do during normal times. The deference thesis does not hold that courts and legislators have no role at all. The view is that courts and legislators should be more deferential than they are during normal times; how much more deferential is always a hard question and depends on the scale and type of the emergency.

To that extent, we agree with the subset of civil libertarians who concede that courts and legislators should defer somewhat more during emergencies than during normal times. Nonetheless, even these civil libertarians criticize the courts and Congress for their excessive deference during emergencies. We agree with the descriptive premise, but not the normative one. Courts and legislators are far more deferential during emergencies than any civil libertarians would have them be, but we think this is good and, for the most part, inevitable. Accordingly, we will argue for a much higher degree of deference than any version of the civil libertarian view permits. In our view, the historical baseline of great deference during emergencies is also the right level of deference.

To be clear, we do not argue that government always acts rationally, or with public-regarding motivations, nor that it always strikes the correct balance between security and liberty. Our two theses are just two halves of our central claim, which is about the comparison of institutional performance during normal times, on the one hand, and during emergencies, on the other. Our central claim is that government is better than courts or legislators at striking the correct balance between security and liberty during emergencies. Against the baseline of normal times, government does no worse during emergencies, or at least its performance suffers less than that of courts and legislators. By contrast, the institutional structures that work to the advantage of courts and Congress during normal times greatly hamper their effectiveness during emergencies; and the decline in their performance during emergencies is much greater than the decline in governmental performance. Therefore, deference to government should increase during emergencies.

Chapter 1 introduces the affirmative arguments for both the tradeoff thesis and the deference thesis. We focus on judicial deference to the executive, but in some places (particularly in chapters 1 and 5) we bring in the legislature; in those cases, the deference thesis means that legislatures as well as courts do and should defer to the executive. The remaining chapters of part I address the main systemic arguments of the civil libertarians. They argue that the executive chooses bad policies during emergency because of panic, a failure to perceive the long-term costs of policies that limit civil liberties, and political failure generally. We argue that all of these claims are unpersuasive, for many overlapping reasons.

Part II traces the consequences of these arguments for a range of policy controversies. We emphasize that, as lawyers, we do not have any expertise regarding optimal security policy, and so we do not try to argue for or against any particular policy. Instead, we seek to show that the typical lawyers' arguments mustered by civil libertarians against standard emergency measures are not persuasive. These lawyers' arguments stress the legal and institutional damage that emergency policies might cause. Part II addresses, among other things, emergency framework statutes, coercive interrogation, military trials, censorship laws, and reduction of process protections in trials of terrorists.

Although our argument proceeds at an abstract level, we will anchor the argument by discussing a range of security policies adopted after the terrorist attacks of September 11, 2001, including the following:

*Military action.* The president has sent troops to Afghanistan, Iraq, the Philippines, and other countries with orders to capture or kill members of al Qaeda and to provide military and civil assistance to friendly governments. The president has claimed this power to authorize counterterrorism operations under the commander-in-chief power of the U.S. Constitution; he has also received congressional approval. The Authorization for Use of Military Force issued shortly after 9/11 provides authority to capture and detain members of al Qaeda.

*Detention of enemy combatants outside the theater of hostilities.* Armies customarily detain enemy soldiers until the end of hostilities. Citing this authority, the president has claimed the power to detain indefinitely members of al Qaeda wherever captured, including those captured on American soil. Although these actions are not unprecedented, they have been controversial. In other Western countries, detention without charges has been used as well, but as a part of regular law enforcement and subject to limits of a few days or weeks. After an adverse ruling by the Supreme Court, the United States now gives detainees the opportunity to challenge the determination that they are enemy combatants before a military tribunal.

*Heightened search and surveillance powers, including intelligence sharing.* The PATRIOT Act, which was passed shortly after the 9/11 attacks, permits law enforcement agencies and intelligence agencies to share information and expands the search and surveillance powers of law enforcement agencies. For example, the law makes it easier for law enforcement agencies to seize records related to a terrorist suspect from third-party custodians, such as libraries, and to obtain nationwide eavesdropping warrants. The Bush administration also authorized the National Security Agency to perform warrantless wiretaps of overseas communications, including those originating or termi-

nating in the United States, when it believes that one party is associated with Islamic terrorist organizations. This action arguably con-
flicted with statutes and customary practices that required warrants,
although the administration argues that it is authorized by the president's executive powers and by the Authorization for Use of Military
Force (a joint resolution, which has the legal force of a statute).[2]

*Ethnicity-based search and surveillance.* The U.S. government denies that it
engages in ethnic profiling, but it is hard to believe that law enforcement agencies, acting on their own discretion, stop and search iden-
tifiable Arabs and Muslims at the same rate that they stop and search
the rest of the population. The immigration sweeps (see below)
were explicitly based on country of origin, and after 9/11, the FBI
targeted Arab and Muslim residents and Arab Americans for volun-
tary interviews.

*Coercive interrogation.* Press reports suggest that the U.S. government has
used aggressive interrogation measures, including water-boarding,
which is a technique that induces the sensation of drowning, against
members of al Qaeda. The U.S. government denies that it engages
in torture; at the same time, the Bush administration has opposed a
congressional proposal to forbid American officials to engage in torture, suggesting that it wishes to retain flexibility. In addition, American authorities turn over captured members of al Qaeda to friendly
countries that are likely to interrogate them using torture.

*Immigration sweeps and surveillance.* After the 9/11 attacks, American
authorities detained large numbers of aliens from Arab and Muslim
countries. Although these aliens had problems with their documen-
tation, it is clear that they were targeted because of their race or
religion, since undocumented aliens from other countries were not
targeted in these sweeps. Many were deemed to be terrorist threats
and deported.

*Terrorism and material support statutes.* American law prohibits terrorism,
including all of the crimes that individually make up terrorism, such
as murder, conspiracy, and material support of terrorism. The last
two provide prosecutors with a great deal of authority to prosecute
people who are only peripherally involved in terrorist activity, such
as people who contribute money to Islamic charities with a connection to a terrorist organization.

*Military trials.* The Bush administration has begun trying members
of al Qaeda before military commissions. These commissions are

staffed by soldiers, and the defendants have limited process rights. The commissions are used to try enemy combatants who have been accused of committing crimes, including war crimes, but have not been used against Americans, who so far have been detained and released or turned over to the criminal justice system. Although there is precedent for such commissions, they remain controversial, and the Supreme Court recently limited their use in certain respects.

*Censorship.* The United States has not passed censorship laws, but other countries have. Notably, British law currently prohibits people from advocating terrorism.[3] Under current constitutional understandings, such a law would be unconstitutional if passed in the United States—although those understandings are liable to change rapidly during emergencies.

These measures, taken together, are less aggressive than those taken during prior emergencies. Martial law, which was used during the Civil War and World War II, dispenses with civil liberties altogether, leaving the decisions on how to investigate crimes, try suspects, and punish criminals almost entirely within the discretion of the military. The internment of Japanese Americans during World War II was the result of a military order. Many people think these earlier actions were mistaken; others might think that even if they were justified in the past, they are not justified today. Unfortunately, it is extremely difficult to evaluate whether these measures were justified or not; with the benefit of hindsight, we lose the ability to see events through the eyes of those who made the decisions. It is also difficult to evaluate the post-9/11 measures. Whether the government justifiably detains al Qaeda suspects without charging and trying them depends to a large extent on the magnitude of the threat, the importance of secrecy, and other factors that few people outside of government are in a position to evaluate.

For this reason, we have no opinion about the merits of particular security measures adopted after 9/11, as noted above. We hold no brief to defend the Bush administration's choices, in general or in any particular case. Many or most of its policies may or may not be wrong. Our point is that we are not well positioned to judge the merits of those policies, nor are the civil libertarian critics of those policies.

Rather, our focus is on the institutional allocation of authority to evaluate such policies. For example, suppose that ethnic or racial profiling during emergencies does not increase security, or even reduces it; if it does not increase security, then it is all cost and no benefit, and thus a bad policy. We call this a *first-order* question and bracket such questions to the extent possible. We focus instead on the *second-order* institutional and legal challenges—such as the arguments that ethnic profiling is inevitably a pretext for the scapegoating of minorities or that it irreversibly expands government power. Our basic concern is to rebut a common set of second-order arguments that courts should be skeptical of executive action during emergencies. Arguing on this plane is attractive to civil libertarians; it allows them to avoid evaluating the merits of policies about which lawyers know little, policies that fall within the expertise of security professionals. But, as we show, these arguments are flimsy.

# PART I

## CONSTITUTIONAL LAW
## AND THEORY

In this part, we lay out our affirmative view of emergency powers and critique the leading alternatives. Our view is that judges deciding constitutional claims during times of emergency should defer to government action so long as there is any rational basis for the government's position, which in effect means that the judges should almost always defer, as in fact they have when emergencies are in full flower. In times of emergency, judges should get out of the government's way, because sometimes government will choose good emergency policies, and even when it does not, judicial intervention may only make things worse, not better. Throughout, we discuss the effect of emergencies on both governmental decisionmaking and judicial review. Our argument is in the alternative: government functions no worse during emergencies than during normal times, and even when government makes mistakes during emergencies, judicial intervention cannot improve matters.

The basic argument for this view is laid out in chapter 1. There is a straightforward tradeoff between liberty and security. We define a "security-liberty frontier" akin to the Pareto frontier, which is familiar in welfare economics. At the security-liberty frontier, any increase in security requires a decrease in liberty; a rational and well-functioning government will already be positioned on this frontier when the emergency strikes and will adjust its policies as the shape of the frontier changes over time, as emergencies come and go. If increases in security are worth more than the corresponding losses in liberty, government will increase security; but if reductions in security will produce greater gains from increased liberty, government will relax its security measures. A "rational" and "well-functioning" government here is one that makes no systematic errors of cognition, that is motivated to maximize the welfare of the whole polity, and that is as willing to increase liberty after an emergency has passed as it is willing to increase security when an emergency arises. Given the tradeoff thesis, judicial review in times of emergency cannot improve matters, because there is no reason to think that courts possessing limited information and limited expertise will choose better security policies than does the government.

The succeeding chapters of part I explain, and rebut, the leading criticisms of the tradeoff thesis. These arguments either suggest that government systematically malfunctions in times of emergency, or suggest that judicial intervention can have net benefits, or both. In chapter 2, we consider the "panic theory" of governmental decisionmaking in times of emergency. On this theory, government officials panic or implement the panicked views of the populace, and the panic causes officials systematically to overestimate the benefits of increased security and to underestimate the costs of reduced liberty. We criticize the panic theory on several grounds. Fear can improve decisionmaking as well as hamper it, because fear supplies motivation that can overcome pre-existing inertia. In some circumstances, fear can even sharpen the assessment of threats. Cognitive failings and social influences have no inherent valence; although they are capable of generating *security panics*, which cause government to supply excessive security, they are equally capable of generating *libertarian panics*, which cause government to supply inadequate security measures. In any event, there is no class of decisionmakers who can be insulated from panic at acceptable cost, not even judges.

In chapter 3, we consider the "democratic failure theory." This account differs from the panic account because it accepts that government officials are rational and act as agents for a majority of citizen-voters, who are also rational. On this picture, citizen-voters are not only rational, but self-interested, and this causes their governmental agents to supply security policies that benefit the majority at the expense of political, ideological, or ethnic minorities. Government chooses security policy rationally, but its goal is to maximize the welfare of current democratic majorities, rather than the overall welfare of the polity. We argue that the democratic failure theory fails on several counts. The structures of voting and representation that are said to produce democratic failure are the same in both emergencies and normal times; there is little evidence and no theoretical reason to believe that democratic failure is more likely in emergencies. It is equally consistent with the democratic failure theory that majorities will cause government to supply excessive liberty, rather than excessive security, and the costs of the searching judicial review recommended by the theory increase during emergencies, to unacceptable levels. The judges know all of this, which is why they defer heavily to government in times of emergency, even with respect to policies that democratic failure theorists find, in hindsight, to be infected with animus or opportunism.

In chapter 4, we consider the "ratchet theory" of emergencies, which suggests that there is a systematic bias in governmental moves along the security frontier: government will increase security and decrease liberty during emergencies, but will never readjust by increasing liberty after the emergency passes, or at least will do so less than it should. In a closely related version of this theory, policies that increase security in one domain will spill over into other domains. In either case, the ratchet theory predicts a long-term trend toward an oppressively authoritarian regime. But the ratchet theory fails as well. Ratchet accounts typically lack any mechanism that makes policies spill over into new areas or that makes them stick after the emergency has passed; there is no evidence for ratchets in the history of American security policy;

and it is unclear what judges, who must decide one case at a time, could do about such long-term trends anyway.

What these arguments have in common, and what makes them attractive to many civil libertarians, is that they seem to be more sophisticated grounds for constraining emergency power than does a brute appeal to rights. These arguments posit interesting mechanisms of governmental failure or complex, second-order effects of security policies in times of emergency. Unfortunately, for all of their intrinsic interest, these mechanisms and effects are too precious, too fragile, or too speculative to provide convincing grounds for impeaching governmental decisionmaking during emergencies. Nor do these mechanisms support a robust role for judicial review during emergencies, because judges are often subject to the same distortions of cognition or motivation, and because judges lack the information necessary to sort good governmental choices from bad ones.

# CHAPTER ONE

# Emergencies, Tradeoffs, and Deference

In this chapter, we lay out two basic views of the relationship between constitutional law and emergencies: a civil libertarian view, which typically advocates robust judicial review of governmental decisionmaking in times of emergency, and our view, which advocates strong judicial and legislative deference to government decisionmaking in times of emergency. We articulate a tradeoff thesis about security and liberty; defend the tradeoff thesis against critiques; and articulate the deference thesis, which complements the tradeoff thesis by claiming that judges and legislators should defer to government's balancing of security and liberty during emergencies. For the most part, we focus on judicial deference, although we bring in legislators later in the chapter and elsewhere. Our larger aims are to clarify our premises and the limits of our project and to indicate the line of argument we will take in later chapters.

We will begin by laying out the structure of the tradeoff thesis and considering some critiques. We then turn to defining two components of the theory: "emergencies" and "government."

## STRUCTURE OF THE THEORY

### Emergencies and the Constitution: Two Views

There are two main views about the proper role of constitutional law during national emergencies. We label them the "deferential" view and the "civil libertarian" view. The *deferential view* is that judicial review of governmental action, in the name of the Constitution, should be relaxed or suspended during an emergency. During an emergency, it is important that power be concentrated. Power should move up from the states to the federal government and, within the federal government, from the legislature and the judiciary to the executive. Constitutional rights should be relaxed so that the executive can move forcefully against the threat. If dissent weakens resolve, then dissent should be curtailed. If domestic security is at risk, then intrusive searches should be tolerated. There is no reason to think that the constitutional rights and powers appropriate for an emergency are the same as those that prevail during times of normalcy. The reason for relaxing constitutional norms during emergencies is that the risks to civil liberties inherent in expansive executive power—the misuse of the power for political gain—are justified by the national security benefits.

This deferential view describes the law as it has actually operated in our courts. Conventional wisdom among constitutional lawyers fits this picture; it holds that courts defer heavily to government in times of emergency, either by upholding government's action on the merits, or by ducking hard cases that might require ruling against the government.[1] The basis for this deference is not any explicit provision in the Constitution. Although Article 1, section 9, of the U.S. Constitution authorizes Congress to suspend the privilege of habeas corpus "when in Cases of Rebellion or Invasion the public Safety may require it," this emergency power was pointedly vested in the legislative branch rather than the executive, and in any event it has rarely been invoked in formal terms. The real cause of deference to government in times of emergency is institutional: both Congress and the judiciary defer to the executive during emergencies because of the executive's institutional advantages in speed, secrecy, and decisiveness. We document this claim throughout the succeeding chapters.

The second major view about emergencies, the *civil libertarian view*, is that constitutional rules should not be relaxed during an emergency, or at least should not be relaxed as far as courts actually have. Civil libertarians do not usually claim that nothing should change during emergencies; constitutional doctrine already provides that the level of protection for civil liberties depends on the interest of the government. Consider, for example, "compelling interest" standards used to evaluate laws that discriminate against protected classes. When an emergency exists, the government has a compelling interest in responding to it in a vigorous and effective way. Yet civil libertarians believe that emergency power has gone too far. On this view, the record of history is one of bad policymaking during emergencies and of excessive judicial deference. Panicky or ill-motivated governments have unnecessarily restricted civil liberties; excessively compliant courts have rubber-stamped these policies.

Although the civil libertarian view and the deferential view can be given different doctrinal formulations, what interests us is not the nominal legal rules but rather the degree of operational deference that courts give the executive during an emergency. Let us stipulate that judges could provide "high" or "low" deference during emergencies, where high deference permits some aggressive executive actions that are prohibited by low deference. High deference could be implemented through a threshold test: courts will apply strict scrutiny unless they first find that an emergency exists, in which case they will permit any executive action that has a rational basis. High deference could also be implemented through a relaxed version of the ordinary compelling-interest test, where judges find that the government's interest becomes more compelling whenever an emergency occurs, whether or not there is a formal declaration (by courts or other officials) that an emergency exists. An example discussed in chapter 3 is that the Supreme Court afforded the government great operational deference in the *Korematsu* decision[2] upholding the internment of Japanese Americans during World War II, even though the Court nominally employed "strict scrutiny." Correlatively, low deference could result from the refusal to treat constitutional rights differently during emergencies and normal times, or it could result from the use of a strict compelling-interest test.

Whatever the doctrinal formulation, the basic distinction between the two views is that our view counsels courts to provide high deference during emergencies, as courts have actually done, whereas the civil libertarian view does not. During normal times, the deferential view and the civil libertarian view permit the same kinds of executive action, and during war or other emergencies, the deferential view permits more kinds of executive action than the civil libertarian view does. We assume that courts have historically provided extra deference during an emergency or war because they believe that deference enables the government, especially the executive, to act quickly and decisively. Although deference also permits the government to violate rights, violations that are intolerable during normal times become tolerable when the stakes are higher. Civil libertarians, on the other hand, claim either that government action is likely to be worse during emergencies than during normal times, or at least that no extra deference should be afforded to government decision-making in times of emergency—and that therefore the deferential position that judges have historically taken in emergencies is a mistake.

The deferential view does not rest on a conceptual claim; it rests on a claim about relative institutional competence and about the comparative statics of governmental and judicial performance across emergencies and normal times. In emergencies, the ordinary life of the nation, and the bureaucratic and legal routines that have been developed in ordinary times, are disrupted. In the case of wars, including the "war on terror," the government and the public are not aware of a threat to national security at time 0. At time 1, an invasion or declaration of war by a foreign power reveals the existence of the threat and may at the same time cause substantial losses. At time 2, an emergency response is undertaken.

Several characteristics of the emergency are worthy of note. First, the threat reduces the social pie—both immediately, to the extent that it is manifested in an attack, and prospectively, to the extent that it reveals that the threatened nation will incur further damage unless it takes costly defensive measures. Second, the defensive measures can be more or less effective. Ideally, the government chooses the least costly means of defusing the threat; typically, this will be some combination of military engagement overseas, increased intelligence gathering, and enhanced policing at home. Third, the defensive measures must be taken quickly, and—because every national threat is unique, unlike ordinary crime—the defensive measures will be extremely hard to evaluate. There are standard ways of preventing and investigating street crime, spouse abuse, child pornography, and the like; and within a range, these ways are constant across jurisdictions and even nation-states. Thus, there is always a template that one can use to evaluate ordinary policing. By contrast, emergency threats vary in their type and magnitude and across jurisdictions, depending heavily on the geopolitical position of the state in question. Thus, there is no general template that can be used for evaluating the government's response.

In emergencies, then, judges are at sea, even more so than are executive officials. The novelty of the threats and of the necessary responses makes judicial routines and evolved legal rules seem inapposite, even obstructive. There is a premium on the executive's capacities for swift, vigorous, and secretive action. Of course, the judges know that executive action may rest on irrational assumptions, or bad motivations, or may otherwise be misguided. But this knowledge is largely useless to the judges, because they cannot sort good executive action from bad, and they know that the delay produced by judicial review is costly in itself. In emergencies, the judges have no sensible alternative but to defer heavily to executive action, and the judges know this.

## Minimalism: A Third Way?

Cass Sunstein advocates judicial "minimalism," both generally and with particular application to judicial review of constitutional claims in times of war and emergency. *Minimalism* is the idea that judges should proceed "one case at a time," issuing rulings that are both narrow as opposed to broad and shallow as opposed to deep. Such rulings leave many things undecided, keeping judicial options open for the future.[3] In the emergency setting, minimalism is conceived as an alternative both to "national security fundamentalism"—what we call the deferential view—and to "liberty perfectionism," what we call the civil libertarian view.[4] Minimalist judges do not defer to unilateral presidential action, instead requiring presidential action to be authorized by statute; where it is so authorized, however, minimalist judges will reject or disfavor civil liberties claims based on rights.[5]

Minimalism is a valuable perspective on constitutional adjudication generally, but it is not an alternative to the choice between deferential review and civil libertarian review. Sunstein has introduced an issue that is actually unrelated to the issue of deference versus nondeference; the tangential issue is whether judges should proceed through wide and deep rulings or through narrow and shallow ones. Sunstein thinks the latter are generally best, but such rulings might either be deferential or not. In the narrowly crafted decisions in the case at hand, both judges who defer to government and those who override government action are good minimalists. In this one-case-at-a-time sense, minimalism is a strictly procedural recommendation that does not engage the debate between national security fundamentalism and liberty perfectionism.

The further idea that judges should require statutory authorization for executive action does engage that debate. That idea, however, is not minimalist in any distinctive sense; it has nothing to do with the procedural issue of whether judges should proceed one case at a time. A requirement of statutory authorization for executive action takes sides on the deference question by splitting the baby down the middle and is in that sense a moderate option, but it is not minimalist except by stipulation. An authorization requirement might or might not be a good idea, and might or might not be a good description of judicial practice. The idea of proceeding one case at a time, however, is not relevant to those questions.

Overall, Sunstein has lashed together two different senses of minimalism, but the two have no necessary connection to each other. Later, when we define "government" for purposes of the tradeoff thesis, we will argue that the requirement of statutory authorization lacks either descriptive or normative appeal. For now, the relevant points are that procedural minimalism is not a third way between the deferential view and the civil libertarian view and that a requirement of statutory authorization must be defended on its own terms, rather than as an implication of minimalism.

## Emergencies, Politics, and Judicial Review

What considerations or arguments arbitrate between the deferential view and the civil libertarian view? In very general terms, one needs both a theory of emergency politics and a theory of judicial review during emergencies. A *theory of emergency politics* assesses whether governmental decisionmaking is better or worse, according to some normative standard, during emergencies than in normal times. Of course, we mean to include here the possibility that the relevant normative standard could be multidimensional, in which case governmental decisionmaking during emergencies might be both better in some respects and worse in others than during normal times. A *theory of judicial review during emergencies* assesses whether such review is likely to improve government's decisions or make them worse. Civil libertarians tend to believe that governmental decisionmaking is worse during emergencies than during normal times; they also tend to believe that nondeferential judicial review during emergencies would make things better, not worse. By contrast, we believe that government decisionmaking is not systematically worse during emergencies; at a minimum, governmental performance declines less during emergencies than does that of courts. Accordingly, judicial review of the security–liberty tradeoffs that government makes during emergencies is affirmatively harmful.

In principle, either the theory of emergency politics or the theory of judicial review during emergencies might be detached from the other and offered separately. First, civil libertarians need not, as a logical matter, hold that governmental decisionmaking is worse in times of emergency. They might simply hold that, even if governmental decisionmaking is identical in emergencies and in normal times, nondeferential judicial review can produce net benefits during times of emergency. We criticize this view in chapter 3. In many cases, however, civil libertarians praise judicial review precisely because they hold a certain theory of emergency politics: they believe government decisionmaking is especially bad in times of emergency, so that in comparative terms even judges of limited institutional competence can improve matters through nondeferential judicial review. It is thus an important part of our project to critique the civil libertarian account of emergency politics. As we shall see in chapter 2, for example, many civil libertarians believe that governmental decisionmaking during times of emergency is panicky, much worse than during normal times, and thus they advocate an increased role for judicial review during emergencies. We deny both the panic thesis and the institutional conclusion that judges can improve upon government's panicky decisionmaking.

Second, and conversely, some civil libertarians offer an account of emergency politics that does not culminate in praise for judicial review. In principle, and sometimes also in practice, civil libertarians might distinguish between constitutionalism outside the courts and judicially enforced constitutionalism. They might say that nonjudicial actors, such as legislators and executive officials, should protect civil liberties more vigorously than they historically have, even if the judges should not attempt to improve upon government's emergency policies. On this version, the civil libertarian advances a theory of emergency politics but does not advocate increased judicial review during emergencies. In chapter 5, for example, we will see Bruce Ackerman's view of emergencies: Ackerman's diagnosis is the usual one of panicky politics, but his prescription is for a novel form of legislative remedy, rather than for judicial oversight. Ackerman's theory fails, however, partly because the diagnosis is unpersuasive (as discussed in chapter 2) and partly because if the diagnosis is correct then the prescription is doomed to failure (as discussed in chapter 5). Overall, even if politics and judicial review can be pried apart at the conceptual level, there are institutional, empirical, and psychological links between the two subjects. For completeness, then, we will argue in the alternative, contesting the civil libertarian view of both emergency politics and judicial review during emergencies.

We also emphasize, to forestall misunderstanding, that in the following chapters we emphatically do not attempt to offer general theories of politics or of judicial review. Our claims are strictly comparative in character; they are about the differences between emergencies and normal times and the effect of those differences on the relative performance of government and courts. As for politics, we do not assume that government always chooses good policies; obviously, it does not. What we argue is that governmental decisionmaking is not systematically worse during emergencies than during normal times. In chapter 3, for example, we critique the idea that government "scapegoats" minorities during emergencies; the problem with the idea is that government often scapegoats or oppresses minorities during normal times as well. Similarly, where judicial review is at issue, we do not assume that judicial review never improves governmental policymaking. What we argue is that judicial review is especially likely to prove counterproductive or even futile during emergencies, due to factors that are unique to emergencies. Thus, we assume, as a baseline, that there will be robust judicial review during normal times.[6] Our suggestion is that the rules should change during emergencies.

## The Tradeoff Thesis

The general framework for our position is the *tradeoff thesis*. With other scholars, we argue that there is a tradeoff between security and liberty. The basic idea of the tradeoff is not original with us;[7] indeed, it is one of the oldest theories of emergency powers. Our contribution is to analyze the comparative statics of institutional performance, of both government and courts, in striking the security-liberty balance during both emergencies and normal times. We pursue the tradeoff thesis to its ultimate conclusions without flinching at its implications, particularly its implications for judicial review of government action in times of emergency.

The tradeoff thesis can be stated in simple terms. Both security and liberty are valuable goods that contribute to individual well-being or welfare. Neither good can simply be maximized without regard to the other. The problem from the social point of view is to optimize: to choose the joint level of liberty and security that maximizes the aggregate welfare of the population. Liberty, of course, has many different strands—there are many different kinds of negative and positive freedom—but those complexities are not material to our approach. As political theorist Jon Elster puts it, "[t]he metric for security can be established as the risk of harm. The metric for liberty is more difficult to determine, since the value includes such disparate components as freedom of speech, freedom of association, due process, and privacy. To get around this problem we basically have to ignore it, by stipulating that we have some way of aggregating the components of liberty into an aggregate measure."[8] In our view, any conceptual imprecision that arises from this aggregation does not affect the lower-level institutional problems we will discuss.

To motivate the tradeoff theory, consider the wide range of real-world settings in which security and liberty, in its various aspects, trade off against one another:

> *Security and privacy.* Under the USA PATRIOT Act, passed in 2001 and renewed in 2005 and 2006, executive officials may inspect records held by businesses and other institutions, including the records held by libraries and bookstores about the activities of their patrons. As a doctrinal matter, such records do not carry a "reasonable expectation of privacy" sufficient to trigger the Fourth Amendment's protections against unreasonable searches and seizures. Nonetheless, civil libertarians have protested that this provision of the USA PATRIOT Act goes too far in authorizing governmental intrusion on personal information and chills the exercise of free speech.
>
> *Security and due process.* After the 9/11 attacks, President George W. Bush issued an executive order that created military commissions to try noncitizen detainees charged with being enemy combatants. The order granted defendants some procedural protections but far fewer than would be afforded in ordinary criminal trials; most nota-

bly, the fact finder is not a jury but a panel of military officers, and proof is by a less stringent standard than that used in criminal trials, which require proof beyond a reasonable doubt.[9] Recently, the Supreme Court invalidated, on statutory grounds, part of the administration's scheme. Apart from trials before military commissions, the president has also claimed the authority to detain citizen or noncitizen enemy combatants for the duration of hostilities. A decision by the Supreme Court, *Hamdi v. United States*,[10] placed some procedural restrictions on executive detention of enemy combatants but left open the possibility that military tribunals charged with reviewing combatant status, rather than judicial hearings, will satisfy those restrictions. In these respects, the law of military detention and military commissions sacrifices due process protections to expedite the handling of suspected enemy combatants.

*Security and free speech.* In the United Kingdom, after the July 7, 2005, attacks on the London bus and train system, Parliament enacted major legislation, the Terrorism Act 2006, that curtails speech in the name of security. Among other broad provisions, the law prohibits statements that directly or indirectly encourage terrorist acts and proscribes organizations that glorify terrorism.[11] At the same time, however, the U.K. government has also sought to restrict speech along another margin, by prohibiting "hate speech" directed against Muslims.[12] We return to the latter point in chapter 3. These proposals build on existing laws,[13] enacted after 9/11, that have allowed the conviction of radical Muslim clerics for inciting "racial and religious hatred" and violence.[14] In the United States, a similar (albeit much more tentative) reform involves changes in FBI guidelines, after 9/11, that permitted agents to enter public places—including mosques—to monitor possible terrorist activity.[15]

*Security and nondiscrimination.* After 9/11, federal agencies engaged in the profiling of possible terrorists on racial, ethnic, national, and religious grounds. Examples include the special registration program, now defunct, which required aliens in the United States from a designated list of (almost exclusively) Muslim nations to register with the Immigration and Naturalization Service (INS); the Absconder Initiative, under which aliens from nations with substantial al Qaeda presence were targeted for removal; and Operation Liberty Shield, which subjected asylum applicants from such nations to mandatory detentions.[16] These were explicit policies;

some critics have also claimed that federal officials have engaged in covert ethnic or racial profiling in airport screening and other security-related searches.[17]

These are examples in which government has curtailed civil liberties or civil rights, as compared to some baseline set by preexisting rights or by the ordinary legal system, in the name of increased security during an emergency. Of course, nothing so far said shows that these policies are good, that these restrictions of civil liberty really have increased security, or that judges should uphold the relevant policies. They do show, however, that in many domains government officials believe or at least say that an increase in security requires restricting liberty.

It is occasionally suggested that some examples of this sort involve tradeoffs within the domain of security, rather than between security and liberty. If government officials take intrusive action in order to fight terrorism, this can cause a kind of insecurity to those affected. But putting the problem this way does not eliminate the tradeoff; it just relabels it. We might then speak of a tradeoff between "security type 1"—the social good that is increased to the extent that the terrorist threat is reduced—and "security type 2"—the social good that is reduced by governmental measures aimed at reducing the terrorist threat. It is not clear what this relabeling accomplishes, so we will stick with the conventional terms.

The claim that security and liberty trade off against one another implies that respecting civil liberties often has real costs in the form of reduced security. Sometimes civil libertarians deny this; below, we offer an interpretation of that position. It is clear, however, that sometimes tangible security harms do in fact occur when claims of civil liberties are respected. Consider the following examples:

*9/11 and the Intelligence Wall*  In 1978, Congress passed the Foreign Intelligence Surveillance Act,[18] creating procedures for judicial oversight of searches and wiretaps in cases involving foreign agents and intelligence. The act provided that the "primary purpose" of the surveillance must be to gather foreign intelligence information. By a complex process of institutional change, the provision came to be interpreted—probably erroneously[19]—as having created a "wall," or barrier, to information sharing between intelligence and law enforcement. The rationale for the wall was civil libertarian, resting on fears that law enforcement would exploit intelligence information to bring ordinary criminal prosecutions; it was never clearly explained why such a practice would be bad. By the late 1990s, the prevailing understanding was that the wall was quite thick. This was itself an erroneous construal of internal Justice Department guidelines issued in 1995; but it was predictable that the guidelines would be misinterpreted by field agents in the FBI and elsewhere, as the guidelines had been made extremely complex and refined, in an effort to show punctilious respect for civil liberties.[20]

Although counterfactuals are uncertain, it is plausible that, absent the wall, the 9/11 attacks would have been thwarted—as the 9/11 Commission found.[21] The commission documented a series of instances in which the CIA possessed information that would have helped the FBI, whose agents were intermittently on the trail of the 9/11 attackers. At crucial junctures, the wall blocked information sharing between these agencies.

*Screening and Profiling* The 9/11 Commission also found that the attacks could have been prevented by more aggressive screening and profiling at immigration points. "More than half of the 19 hijackers were flagged by the Federal Aviation Administration's profiling system when they arrived for their flights, but the consequence was that bags, not people, were checked."[22] The commission urged both a more systematic combination of immigration enforcement functions with counterterrorism functions and expanded discretion for line officials to use discretionary, intuitive judgment to screen out threats.[23] These two reforms—combination rather than separation of functions and increased discretion for executive officers—are the sort of adjustment that governments routinely make during times of emergency and that are hallmarks of the administrative state where economic regulation is concerned, but that civil libertarians resist.

*Coercive Interrogation* Statutes and treaties prohibit torture by the U.S. government; although the term is narrowly defined, the so-called McCain Amendment, enacted in 2006, also prohibits "cruel, inhuman and degrading" treatment.[24] The civil libertarian arguments for such prohibitions are obvious, and we evaluate them in chapter 6. Here, we merely note strong evidence that coercive interrogation, in both its stronger and weaker forms, saves lives (that could not be saved through other means at acceptable cost). The director of the Central Intelligence Agency has stated that coercive interrogation has produced actionable intelligence that has helped to thwart terrorist attacks;[25] in chapter 6, we recount evidence from Israel to the same effect and rebut critiques of that evidence. Quite probably, respecting the civil liberties of those who would otherwise be subject to coercive interrogation effectively causes the deaths of some unknown and unidentifiable set of terrorism victims.

*Free Speech (and Democracy)* Consider the striking finding that press freedoms are positively correlated with greater transnational terrorism; nations with a free press are more likely to be targets of such terrorism.[26] Correlation is not causation, but there are obvious mechanisms that might explain this, such as the ability of terrorists to exploit free media coverage to spread fear and dramatize their cause and the freedom of the press to reveal security secrets. According to the 9/11 Commission's report, "al Qaeda's senior leadership had stopped using a particular means of communication almost immediately after a leak to the *Washington Times*."[27] The Bush administration says that the *New York Times*'s leak of the National Security Agency's surveillance program has alerted terrorists that the United States is monitoring communications they may have believed were secure. And the British government believes that fundamentalist mullahs used sermons to recruit terrorists and encourage terrorism.[28] More broadly still, democracies in general are more often subjected to suicide attacks[29] and terrorism of all sorts, both domestic and transnational, while authoritarian regimes suffer much less from these harms.[30]

Of course, not every issue of security policy presents such a tradeoff. At certain levels or in certain domains, security and liberty can be complements as well as substitutes. Liberty cannot be enjoyed without security, and security is not worth enjoying without liberty. And, in some circumstances, it is possible that there are policies, other than the ones that government adopts, that would increase both security and liberty. In some situations, rational policymakers can increase security at no cost to liberty, or increase liberty at no cost to security. But it is plausible to assume that advanced liberal democracies rarely overlook such opportunities, as we discuss shortly. Only a very dysfunctional government would decline to adopt policies that draw political support from both proponents of increased security and proponents of increased liberty.

## The Security-Liberty Frontier

All of this implies that there is what we might call a *security-liberty frontier*. In welfare economics, the Pareto frontier, or contract curve, identifies a range of points at which no win–win improvements are possible: any change in policies that makes A better off must make B worse off. A similar frontier can be defined for liberty and security (see figure 1.1).

At the security–liberty frontier, any increase in security will require a decrease in liberty, and vice versa. The problem from the social point of view

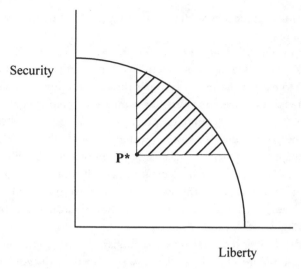

FIGURE 1.1

is one of optimization: to choose the point along the frontier that maximizes the joint benefits of security and liberty. Neither security nor liberty is lexically prior; no claims of the type "liberty is priceless" or "security at all costs" will be admitted.

Of course, the frontier itself conveys no information about where the optimal tradeoff point lies. There is no general answer to the question, which depends entirely on the values or preferences of the people in the relevant society. Whether a given increase in security is worth a given decrease in liberty depends upon what people want. Rather, the frontier represents a constraint on the opportunities available to governments. One might wish it otherwise, but beyond some point, increasing security simply does require decreasing liberty.

Crucially, the shape of the security-liberty frontier changes over time. In many settings, as we shall see throughout the chapters that follow, the important question for constitutional law is not the absolute level of the frontier but how its shape changes as emergencies come and go. As threats increase, the value of security increases; a rational and well-motivated government will then trade off some losses in liberty for greater gains in increased security. This does not mean, of course, that the overall level of social welfare remains unchanged before and after the emergency; social welfare declines because the existence of a terrorist threat makes the polity worse off. What it means

27

is that government increases welfare to the highest level that it can, given the new constraints.

The significance of change over time cannot be overstated. We will see, at many points, a civil libertarian argument that whatever package of civil liberties happens to exist at the time a terrorist threat arises must be maintained as is; adjustments that reduce liberty are bad even if they produce greater gains in security. This is a virulent form of the fallacy of the status quo—that whatever exists must be good—and can be the product of hindsight bias,[31] as we shall explain in chapter 5. In fact, the balance between security and liberty is constantly readjusted as circumstances change. A well-functioning government will contract civil liberties as threats increase. A government that refuses to adjust its policies has simply frozen in the face of the threat. It is pathologically rigid, not enlightened.

The tradeoff thesis rests on a series of standard assumptions. Here and later, we bracket and ignore all of the well-known problems with aggregative social welfare functions that compare goods across persons. An assumption of the tradeoff thesis is that security and liberty are comparable, meaning that people can make judgments about the relative worth, to them, of increases (decreases) in security that produce a concomitant decrease (increase) in liberty. Moreover, we also assume that security and liberty are *interpersonally* comparable, meaning that a loss in liberty (security) for Jack can be compared to a greater gain in security (liberty) for Jill, allowing us to make meaningful claims about whether overall social welfare has increased or decreased as a result of government policies. Economists sometimes urge that interpersonal comparisons are either unscientific or conceptually meaningless; but security policy is not a scientific subject, and meaningful interpersonal comparisons are made in many policy domains.

None of this need imply the stronger claim that security and liberty are commensurable along a monetary metric, although it is consistent with that additional assumption. Economists typically assume that an analysis of costs and benefits must proceed by consulting people's willingness to pay to reduce terrorist threats. For any given policy proposal, if the benefits, so measured, exceed the costs, also so measured, then the policy should be adopted. Willingness to pay, however, need not and often does not track welfare, principally because of the declining marginal utility of money: rich people may be willing to pay more than poor people for some good, even if poor people would derive more welfare from that good.[32] When we refer to "costs" and "benefits," we will use the terms in a relaxed sense that refers to gains and losses in terms of welfare, rather than to willingness to pay. Later in this chapter, we discuss the significance and limits of our welfarist premises.

## Policymaking at the Frontier

Given the existence of the security-liberty frontier, what follows? We begin by setting out a baseline picture of policymaking at the security-liberty frontier. In a strong version, government chooses policies optimally in light of the preferences of the population and as circumstances change over time. In a weak version, which is the one we will advance, government does not always choose policies optimally, but it does choose accurately on average. On this view, government makes no systematic errors; there is no systematic bias or skew in governmental moves along the frontier.

This baseline picture is a heuristic and expository device, not an empirical claim about security policy. Our claim is not that, in fact, governmental choices about security policy are invariably accurate on average. Rather, we aim to clarify the points of disagreement between our view and standard civil libertarian views. Civil libertarians who believe that security policy is systematically flawed, or that judges can improve matters through constitutional review, or both, must be rejecting the baseline picture in one of several well-defined ways, which we will review in chapters 2, 3, and 4. Once the disagreements are clarified, our affirmative view is an argument from relative institutional competence, comparing emergencies and normal times. The argument is that there are few or no domains in which it is true both that (1) government choices about emergency policies are not accurate (on average) *and* that (2) judicial review can make things better. Conversely, it is almost always the case either that (1) government makes accurate (on average) policy choices during emergencies policy *or* that (2) constitutional review by judges cannot systematically improve upon those choices. Civil libertarians who subscribe to vigorous judicial review in times of emergency—and this is the dominant mode of thought among civil libertarians—need to identify a large and important set of cases in which government blunders or acts opportunistically during emergencies *and* in which judges can improve matters. In our view, any such set is trivially small.

This baseline picture assumes—again, as a strictly expository device—that government is both rational and well motivated. *Rational* here just means that the government makes no systematic errors in its empirical estimates and causal theories when assessing the likely effects of increases or decreases in security and liberty. Although government makes mistakes, those mistakes are randomly distributed; thus government's assessments are correct on average. This assumes that government officials, and the voters and citizens who are their principals, implicitly use accurate probability distributions to estimate the likelihood of uncertain outcomes. The methodological assumption is obviously strong; the justification is that errors are symmetrical and wash out so that aggregate behavior obeys accurate probability distributions even if individual behavior deviates in both directions.

On this picture, governments act as rationally during emergencies as during normal times. The decision to infringe on civil liberties for security purposes may be right or wrong, but it is no more likely to be right or wrong than the quotidian decision to construct a highway or to reduce funding for education. There is no reason to think that the government will systematically undervalue civil liberties or overvalue security during emergencies nor that it will systematically overestimate the magnitude of a threat, compared to its behavior during non-emergencies. Instead, the government will attach the same weights to these goods as it does during normal times; it will also on average accurately estimate the magnitude of the threat.

*Well-motivated* here means that the government acts so as to maximize the welfare of all persons properly included in the social welfare function. This formulation is deliberately vague because we bracket for now the problem of whose welfare, exactly, should enter into the social welfare function. In chapters 3, 5, and 8, we examine more and less expansive views on this question: perhaps the welfare only of citizens should be taken into account, or of citizens plus resident aliens, or of all persons affected by government policies wherever they reside. Whoever is properly included, a well-motivated government is one that does not display either systematic agency slack or systematic majoritarianism. Officials do not systematically act as agents either for a majority or for a minority. Rather, government impartially maximizes the welfare of all whose interests and preferences should count.

Given these two conditions, how will a rational and well-motivated government respond to terrorist threats? As the benefits of security increase due to exogenous threats such as terrorism, a well-functioning government will supply more security and less liberty because the value gained from the increase in security will exceed the losses from the decrease in liberty. Again, government may make mistakes, but it is no more likely to make mistakes about security policy than about more routine business, and there will be no predictable or systematic skew in governmental decisionmaking.

## A COMPARATIVE INSTITUTIONAL CLAIM

As a matter of fact, this baseline picture is almost certainly incorrect. Government does not always act rationally; sometimes government officials enjoy agency slack and use it to engage in self-dealing, opportunism, or other welfare-reducing actions; sometimes government officials act as tightly constrained agents for the majority and enact policies that oppress minorities. But the baseline picture helps us to clarify the position we will defend: government is not more likely to do these things during emergencies than during normal times, whereas courts are less able to police such behavior during emergencies than during normal times. This is an empirical and institutional claim, which we shall support in every succeeding chapter, not a conceptual claim. If courts were perfectly informed and well motivated, then they might weed out bad emergency policies chosen by irrational or ill-motivated governments. But we just do not have courts of that sort. In particular cases, judges may do better than government at assessing the relative likelihood of threats to security and liberty or the overall costs of particular policies. But this will be wholly fortuitous, and judges who think they have guessed better than government may guess worse instead. Judges are generalists, and the political insulation that protects them from current politics also deprives them of information,[33] especially information about novel security threats and necessary responses to those threats. If government can make mistakes and adopt unjustified security measures, then judges can make mistakes as well, sometimes invalidating justified security measures.

On this comparative institutional view, there is no general reason to think that judges can do better than government at balancing security and liberty during emergencies. Constitutional rules do no good, and some harm, if they block government's attempts to adjust the balance as threats wax and wane. When judges or academic commentators say that government has wrongly assessed the net benefits or costs of some security policy or other, they are amateurs playing at security policy, and there is no reason to expect that courts can improve upon government's emergency policies in any systematic way.

## COST-BENEFIT ANALYSIS, SECURITY POLICY, AND CONSTITUTIONAL LAW

Before proceeding to discuss critiques of the tradeoff thesis and its corollary, judicial deference, we need to be clear about its relevance to our project. Our basic project, and the point of the tradeoff thesis, is to set a baseline against which to assess the civil libertarian position on constitutional law. That position typically rests on the twin claims that governmental decisionmaking is systematically worse during emergencies than during normal times and that judicial review of government policymaking during emergencies should be stricter than non–civil libertarians advocate and stricter than it historically has been.

Implicit in the foregoing are some qualifications and limits on our project, which we will indicate explicitly. First, our project is *not* to evaluate, on the merits, whether particular antiterrorism policies pass or fail cost-benefit analysis. That is the province of experts in terrorism policy, econometrics, and empirical research. When we discuss particular policies in part II, we do so to illustrate and argue for a position about constitutional law and adjudication, one that falls within our expertise as lawyers: other lawyers who are no more expert in antiterrorism policy than we are, namely, the judges, should defer to government policies. Second, the tradeoff thesis does not set out an empirical claim about governmental motives or behavior. The tradeoff thesis is an expository device that allows us to clarify the grounds on which civil libertarians advocate more expansive or intrusive judicial review of government policymaking during emergencies.

In both parts I and II, we will criticize civil libertarians for advancing empirical and institutional claims that lack supporting evidence. Yet we will not attempt to provide systematic, rigorous empirical evidence for our claims either, although we do draw upon history, case studies, and other informal evidence. There is no inconsistency in this posture, because the burden of uncertainty in evaluating politics and judicial review during times of emergency falls on the civil libertarians. We will show that, historically, constitutional law during emergencies has been extremely deferential; indeed the principal impetus for the civil libertarian position has been to criticize the record of supine judicial review during emergencies. Given this status quo, it is incumbent upon civil libertarians to show that adopting their recommendations would represent an improvement. Absent a showing of this sort, there is no reason for the judges to change what they do during emergencies, which is mostly to uphold what government does.

## CRITIQUES OF THE TRADEOFF THESIS

Let us turn to some general critiques of the tradeoff thesis. We begin with arguments that deny that security and liberty trade off against each other at the margins on which government usually operates. In every case, these arguments turn out to be parasitic on the theory that government decisionmaking during emergencies is irrational (what we call the panic theory) or the theory that government does not act to maximize overall welfare during emergencies (what we call the democratic failure theory). Both theories are discussed in subsequent chapters. We then turn to some philosophical critiques of the tradeoff idea itself.

## Policymaking below the Frontier?

Sometimes civil libertarians say that government adopts policies that can be bettered on both the dimension of security and the dimension of liberty. In our terms, this means that government has chosen policies below the security frontier—for example, at the point marked P* in figure 1.1. A range of moves to the frontier would produce both greater security and greater liberty. An analogue to this in constitutional doctrine is the idea of the "least restrictive alternative."[34] Roughly, the idea is that government should not burden liberty unnecessarily; it should adopt the least possible restriction on liberty that suffices to move security to a desired level.

It is certainly possible that policy might be stuck below the frontier. Imagine that, in the face of a policy of ethnic profiling at airports to catch terrorist suspects, terrorist groups adapt by sometimes recruiting or coercing light-skinned and non-Arab suicide bombers or hijackers. Suppose then that a switch to random searches, without profiling, would improve security; that a switch to random screening would also represent an increase of liberty, somehow defined; and that government does not change its policy of racial profiling, perhaps because of racial animus. In such circumstances, a political coalition of libertarians and the security-minded might form to advocate policy change. Whether or not such a coalition forms, judges might improve upon government's decisionmaking by invalidating the racial-profiling policy, if government's second choice would be random screening.

Real-world examples are few and far between, however. One does not often see a coalition between the American Civil Liberties Union and equivalent pro-security groups to oppose government policies. The reason is probably that most liberal democratic governments are not so dysfunctional as to adopt or retain policies that are unanimously opposed by groups on all sides of security debates. Ordinary politics will usually move government to or near the security frontier, rather than producing policies that fail to exploit mutual gains. Why exactly would government adopt a policy, from among the alternatives, that places unnecessary restrictions on liberty? Perhaps the implicit claim is that government is acting irrationally, out of panicky overreaction (as discussed in chapter 2), or opportunistically, to oppress minorities (as discussed in chapter 3). If so, then the idea of policymaking below the frontier is parasitic on one of these other claims about emergency politics and lacks independent significance.

To be sure, even where a policy is unanimously condemned by both civil libertarian groups and pro-security groups, bargaining failure might occur. Starting from point P*, there is more than one point on the frontier that will improve both security and liberty relative to the status quo policy (the set of all such points lies in the shaded region in figure 1.1). Each point produces a different mix of security and liberty, and the political coalition may splinter over which point to advocate. But this is equally possible in ordinary times for ordinary policies, having nothing to do with security and liberty. The presumption is that the political system, run by officials who if nothing else are expert bargainers, will usually overcome such obstacles to find a negotiated solution.

We may add to these points about emergency politics some points about judicial review during emergencies. In the rare cases where policymaking gets stuck below the frontier, judicial intervention can do little to improve the situation, for two reasons. One reason is that intervention may be affirmatively harmful. The rare cases in which policies are stuck below the frontier do not come labeled as such. Civil libertarians claim, in many cases, that the government's policies are bad for security as well as bad for liberty or that there is a less restrictive alternative to the policy the government has chosen. But usually the government disagrees, and the judges know that they may do great harm if they erroneously side with the civil libertarians, especially in times of emergency. The second reason is that judicial intervention may simply be futile, even if not counterproductive. If government really is so dysfunctional that policy gets stuck below the frontier, it may ignore a judicial remedy or substitute a new policy that is also below the frontier. We expand upon these points in chapter 3.

Sometimes, the point about less restrictive alternatives is put in temporal terms. On this version of the idea, "[r]estricting civil liberties should be a last not a first resort,"[35] and government should show—to citizens or judges or both—that it has exhausted all other measures before curtailing liberty. The thought seems to be that if government restricts civil liberties before experimenting with alternatives, it might miss out on less restrictive alternatives and choose a policy below the frontier. This view, however, essentially attaches zero weight to the opposite risk: an obligation to exhaust all alternatives might cause great interim harm before government is allowed to adopt a liberty-restricting policy that is, indeed, located at the frontier. The hard question is what the interim policies should be while government searches for optimal policies, and it begs the question to say that the interim policy must be a regime that does not restrict civil liberties. If the risk of interim harm is sufficiently great, it is hardly obvious why this should be so.

The same point holds if the focus is on judicial review rather than non-judicial politics. The hard case, for judges, arises when government claims that time is of the essence, that experimentation with alternatives would be foolhardy, and that the interim risks are sufficiently great that restrictions of liberty are warranted. It would be a bold judge who would require the government to exhaust all other alternatives in such a posture, and quite sensibly our judges have not been so bold. In such cases, civil libertarians seem to presume that governmental claims of urgency arise from irrational panic or opportunism, but this just means that the temporal version of less restrictive alternatives is also parasitic on one of the modes of governmental failure addressed in later chapters.

## Security, Liberty, and Budgets

Sometimes, civil libertarians suggest that the security-liberty tradeoff is illusory because government can increase security, without any reduction in liberty, simply by increasing funding for security measures. Government might, for example, adopt more elaborate screening procedures at airports that do not require racial profiling, and yet also do not unduly delay travelers, because government allocates enough personnel to the program to minimize delay. This is akin to the claim that government has chosen a policy below the security-liberty frontier in that security might be increased with no reduction in liberty, but this argument adds a twist: by supposing that funding for security can be increased, the argument in effect pushes the frontier of opportunities farther out.

But this kind of argument makes things too easy by supposing that free lunches can be had. Throughout the following chapters, we assume a budget constraint. We assume, in other words, that the courts cannot simply order the government to spend more money in order to enhance liberty without reducing security. The justification for this assumption is twofold, resting on a point about nonjudicial politics and a point about judicial review.

On the political level, security and liberty are goods, but there are other goods as well. Absent some ambitious global theory suggesting that government has not allocated funds optimally across categories of programs—a theory the civil libertarians do not advance—the presumption should be that the interests reflected in other domains, having no bearing on liberty or security, make the same marginal contribution to social welfare. As for judicial review, the judges do not order government to increase spending on security programs during emergencies. Courts either recognize that more expensive measures are not politically feasible, so that the actual effect of such an order would be to reduce security, or recognize that they might err in their assessments of budgetary priorities, causing greater welfare losses by transferring money away from other programs. The allocation of funding across government programs requires a systemic perspective that courts lack and for the most part know that they lack. Moreover, government might simply ignore the order, putting courts to the difficult remedial task of affirmatively reallocating government funding across programs through coercive injunctions. These points do not apply to civil libertarian proposals that are centered on legislative reform through framework statutes and other nonjudicial devices. Those proposals, however, fail on other grounds, as discussed in chapters 3 and 5.

## Objections: Philosophical and Institutional

We may generalize some of the foregoing points by examining a prominent argument by legal philosopher Jeremy Waldron, who worries that the tradeoff thesis—what he calls "the image of balance"—will produce excessive dilution of civil liberties.[36] We will suggest that Waldron alternates between two very different ways of criticizing the tradeoff thesis, that this is typical of civil libertarian analysis of security policy, and that the alternation results from an intellectual dilemma that civil libertarians face.

Waldron begins by raising "concerns about consequentialism"[37] based on the familiar ideas that rights might trump other considerations or that rights are side constraints that have lexical priority over aggregate welfare. This rights talk, however, is paired with a different mode of analysis—a "call for care and caution"[38] that is itself consequentialist, based upon a series of ways in which the security-liberty tradeoff might go wrong. Security gains might be strictly "symbolic" because people "lash out, or they want their government to lash out and inflict reprisals."[39] The distribution of liberties matters as much as their aggregate level; the concern is that the "security-gains for most people are being balanced against liberty-losses for a few"[40] and that a democratic government responsive to the preferences of a majority will fail to account for the losses that fall upon minorities. Waldron implies that if this occurs, excessive security will be the result. Another concern is that granting government more power to implement security measures, as threats increase, also increases the risk of authoritarian abuses by government.[41] To be clear, Waldron is not making empirical claims. He is indicating causal and institutional mechanisms that might cause the security-liberty tradeoff to be done erroneously, principally in the sense that security might be given excessive weight.

What sort of critique is this? An external critique of the tradeoff thesis, let us say, would simply claim that the package of civil liberties that government affords at some particular point on the security frontier is inadequate according to some independent theory. The basis for an external critique might be, for example, some nonconsequentialist theory of rights, holding that some aspect of liberty has lexical priority and cannot be traded off against security (unless perhaps the costs of respecting that aspect of liberty would be "catastrophic," as we discuss shortly). An internal critique of the tradeoff thesis, on the other hand, would say that if government attempts directly to strike the optimal balance between security and liberty, it will systematically get the balance wrong. Problems of cognition and emotion, agency slack between government officials and the population, majoritarian oppression, or second-order effects, such as ratchets, will cause government officials to curtail liberty too hastily or too broadly. In this sense, the objections to the tradeoff thesis discussed in chapters 2, 3, and 4 are all internal critiques of the tradeoff thesis.

Although Waldron's initial rights talk suggests an external critique of the tradeoff thesis, his concrete concerns are all internal critiques. The worry that people or officials lash out, producing restrictions of civil liberties that are not cost justified, is a version of the panic argument discussed in chapter 2, according to which panic will produce excessive levels of security. The worry that the majority will increase its security without taking account of the minority's lost liberty is the democratic failure argument discussed in chapter 3; here too, the concern is that security will be supplied at excessive levels from the standpoint of a social welfare function that takes into account the minority's interests as well as the majority's. The worry that increases in security will produce authoritarian abuses identifies a cost of increasing security, one that is itself folded into the tradeoff thesis, which (it bears repeating) does *not* hold that security should simply be maximized. In this last setting, Waldron fleshes out his concern with the possibility that increasing security may often produce a slippery slope toward ever-greater authoritarianism, an idea that also carries undertones of the ratchet position. We critique the slippery slope idea and the ratchet idea in chapters 4 and 6.

In general, Waldron's concrete worries are internal to the tradeoff thesis. Although Waldron's expertise is in jurisprudence and political theory, his concerns about the tradeoff thesis are not conceptual in character and are not derived from that expertise. Rather, they rest on implicit institutional and causal hypotheses about political psychology and its effects on policymaking, about the structure of political representation, and about the second-order consequences of recognizing expanded governmental powers in times of emergency. Throughout, we will suggest that all concerns of this nature just identify potential costs of alternative policies and are thus more grist for the tradeoff thesis's mill. Most important, neither philosophers nor generalist judges should be at all confident that their ability to assess institutional and psychological questions of this sort is superior to that of the government officials whose work they would either evaluate or review.

Waldron, like other theorists we shall encounter in later chapters, alternates between external and internal critiques of the tradeoff thesis. The dilemma that produces this two-pronged approach is both intellectual and rhetorical. External critiques risk being, and seeming, extremist and impractical. Internal critiques, on the other hand, seem more plausible, yet require empirical and institutional predictions about the effects of alternative antiterrorism policies. The latter requirement puts civil libertarian theorists—who are usually philosophers or constitutional lawyers rather than terrorism experts—in the position of offering hypotheses, speculations, or empirical claims well outside of their domain of expertise.

## A Note on Carl Schmitt and Weimar

The philosopher-jurist most often invoked in discussions of emergencies is Carl Schmitt. A Weimar era academic and Nazi fellow-traveler, Schmitt articulated some famous ideas about emergency powers, including the claims that whoever has the power to declare emergency exceptions to standard legal rules is the true sovereign and that the liberal legalist ambition to subject emergencies to procedural oversight is futile. Political theorists interested in emergency powers, and some academic lawyers as well, are much taken with Schmitt; nearly every discussion of emergencies pores over the canonical texts yet again.[42] This focus on old texts may just be the very enterprise of political theory, as distinct from political philosophy, but the centrality of Schmitt is plausibly part of a broader phenomenon, which is the tendency to discuss emergency powers through the lens of Weimar historiography and politics. The specter of Weimar's collapse, in which repeated invocations of emergency powers were followed by an authoritarian takeover, looms ominously in the civil libertarian imagination.

Our procedure is to extract the marrow from Schmitt and then throw away the bones for the professional exegetes to gnaw. In modern terms, Schmitt has a few useful points—most important, that emergencies are hard or even conceptually impossible to define ex ante, that emergencies must be governed by ex post standards, rather than by ex ante rules, and that liberal legalists are addicted to process but tend to ignore or to underestimate the costs of process, including the opportunity costs of forgone government action in emergencies. We deploy these points throughout, most centrally in chapter 5, when we examine Bruce Ackerman's proposal for a framework statute governing emergencies. The conceptual analysis with which Schmitt embroiders these ideas, however, strikes us as largely unhelpful, and we will ignore it.

More generally, Weimar has received too much attention in this setting. Civil libertarians invoke the shadow of Weimar to imply, and occasionally say, that expanding government's powers during emergencies will produce another Hitler. It will not, in today's liberal democracies anyway; and if it did, there would be nothing that civil libertarian judges could do about it. Emergencies always pose novel challenges; information about the new post-emergency conditions is at a premium, so the value of historical analogies is low. Weimar was an unconsolidated and institutionally shaky transitional democracy extant some three-quarters of a century ago; its relevance for emergency politics in consolidated modern democracies is not obvious, and we will see evidence that transferring large chunks of power to the executive during emergencies need not, and usually does not, end in dictatorship. The real risk is that civil libertarian panic about the specter of authoritarianism will constrain government's ability to adopt cost-justified security measures. We return to these points throughout.

## Rights, Consequences, and Welfare

To clarify some of these points, one might find it helpful to distinguish some different ways of evaluating security policies. At the highest conceptual level is the choice between consequentialist and nonconsequentialist accounts. The former stipulates that a policy is good just insofar as its consequences are good, while the latter stipulates that a policy might have intrinsic merits or demerits. Within consequentialism, there is a further choice between welfarist and nonwelfarist theories. The former stipulates that consequences matter only if they affect human well-being in some form, whereas the latter stipulates that consequences might be good or bad even apart from their welfare effects—an example being the idea that rights violations might count as bad consequences, regardless of welfare.[43] At both levels, an important wrinkle is the distinction between exclusive and inclusive criteria of evaluation. The difference is between saying that consequences or effects on welfare are relevant and saying that consequences or effects on welfare are all that matters. Even if one believes that consequences or welfare effects are relevant to assessing policies, one might believe that other things are relevant too.

The tradeoff thesis is both consequentialist and welfarist. External critiques of the tradeoff thesis are nonconsequentialist or nonwelfarist or both, whereas internal critiques of the tradeoff thesis are also consequentialist and welfarist; they just attach different probabilities and weights to various consequences. We have seen that Waldron, while purporting to question the very "image of balance" itself, actually cycles between the external and internal modes of critique. As we will see throughout, this is typical of civil libertarian theorists, who alternate between contesting the tradeoff thesis and identifying ways in which the tradeoff might be done incorrectly. Few civil libertarians really want to defend an absolutist view of rights as side constraints—even with respect to coercive interrogation or torture, as we discuss in chapter 6.

There are two common alternatives. One strategy is to defend a view of rights as deontological constraints which can, however, be overcome if a threshold of catastrophic consequences is reached—the standard case involves torturing a suspect to prevent a bomb from going off. The other strategy is to segue, often imperceptibly, from a conceptual analysis of security policy into an institutional and empirical analysis that tries to identify costs internal to the tradeoff thesis—even if the civil libertarian thereby steps beyond his domain of expertise. We saw Waldron do this, and the phenomenon recurs throughout, especially in the various critiques of coercive interrogation canvassed in chapter 6.

Civil libertarian theorists fear that consequentialism is insufficiently protective of rights; on a consequentialist analysis, all rights are contingent and are in principle hostage to what the facts show. The dilemma for civil libertarians, however, is that each of the other two positions—rights absolutism and threshold deontology—has intellectual and rhetorical disadvantages. The absolutist rights-based position attracts very few defenders, in part because it seems fanatical and thus threatens to marginalize its proponents. In the face of hypotheticals or actual cases, like the ticking-bomb scenario, rights absolutists must deny that such hypotheticals are realistic or at least deny that legal rules should be organized around them; such responses are not wholly convincing in an era in which ticking bombs do, with some frequency, go off. The threshold deontology position compromises with such concerns, and thus seems more plausible, but the price is a reduced theoretical coherence and an arbitrary flavor. A standard question for threshold deontologists is why, exactly, the threshold should be set at catastrophic harm rather than simply harm that exceeds the benefits of respecting the relevant constraints. As we will see in chapter 6 and elsewhere, threshold deontologists typically premise their arguments for a given threshold on muted institutional and empirical claims that are unpersuasive when amplified.

In what follows, we will generally ignore approaches to evaluating security policies either that are strictly nonconsequentialist or that posit absolutist theories of rights. We will suppose, at a minimum, that consequences for human welfare are relevant to evaluating policies, even if nonwelfarist considerations are relevant too. Those who believe that welfare is not the exclusive basis for policy evaluation can at least find the tradeoff thesis of interest insofar as they find welfare relevant.

Those who think that consequences generally or welfare specifically are irrelevant to policy evaluation will balk at our premises. Fortunately, however, we believe that the philosophical debates over consequentialism, welfarism, and their competitors will often make no difference to the institutional and policy issues we discuss. Although welfarism excludes theories that attach intrinsic value to rights, quite apart from the effect of rights on human well-being, adopting welfarist premises makes no difference to our conclusions in many cases. We are interested in institutional questions, principally the comparison of governmental decisionmaking and judicial review in times of emergency. High-level philosophical questions, such as the choice between consequentialism and nonconsequentialism or between welfarist and nonwelfarist theories of rights, often turn out to have no cutting power at this level. Many governmental decisions and judicial approaches will be bad on both welfarist and nonwelfarist views, while others will be good on both welfarist and nonwelfarist views. Conclusions about the low-level questions tend to turn instead on empirical and institutional assessments of competing policies and of the comparative competence of executive officials, legislators, judges, and other legal actors. In such cases, welfarism is merely an expository convenience; all or most of what we say could be rewritten in nonwelfarist terms without changing the substance of the analysis.

## DEFINING EMERGENCIES AND GOVERNMENT

The tradeoff thesis is a theory of governmental decisionmaking during times of emergency; the theory implies a deferential role for constitutional law during emergencies. Both *emergency* and *government* are protean words, however. Here we offer working definitions of these terms.

## Emergency

What is an emergency? Who decides when an emergency exists?

As to the first question, we will follow Elster by distinguishing three categories of emergencies: those brought about by intentional human action (such as a large-scale terrorist attack), those that are the product of human action but not of human design (such as an economic crisis or Chernobyl), and those caused by nature.[44] These categories are fuzzy at the boundaries—for example, the harms created by "natural" disasters are the joint product of nature and of earlier human action—but are adequate for our limited purposes. We focus throughout on the first category, with comparisons to the second to illuminate the analysis of the first; we largely ignore the third.

As far as the first category is concerned, the logic of our view is that emergencies lie on a continuum, or sliding scale. At one end are routine domestic policies adopted in peacetime, where bureaucracies churn out incremental policy changes, judges repeatedly see similar issues and become familiar with the costs of blocking or permitting government action, and the stakes of particular judicial decisions are low. At the other end are policies adopted in times of full-blown crisis, when it might be reasonable to believe that serious harms threaten the nation, as in the immediate aftermaths of Pearl Harbor or 9/11. Novel threats, heightened public concern, and deaths arising from hostile attacks typify these situations; the ordinary routines of bureaucratic policymaking are suspended, and elected officials quickly intervene to redirect resources and reorient policies. Time is of the essence, the stakes of blocking necessary government action are possibly catastrophic, and uncertainty reigns. In between are situations in which government policy is unusually consequential for foreign policy or for national security, but where some or all of the features that describe a full-blown emergency are absent.

Moreover, emergencies have a half-life and will decay over time, both because the emotional responses produced by the emergency decay, and because the government rationally updates its beliefs as new information is acquired; if no new attacks occur, the government will downgrade its threat assessment, and judges will worry less and less about the harms of blocking emergency measures. As time elapses from the beginning of the emergency, and as enemy attacks or other catastrophic harms dwindle away or stop altogether, judges will defer less. In what follows, we will argue both that judges defer heavily during times of emergency and that judges tend to reassert themselves as the emergency decays, as though emerging from a burrow after the storm has passed. We will see that in the recent *Hamdan* case, for example, the Supreme Court for the first time squarely invalidated a government policy adopted after 9/11, in part because there have been no successful attacks on U.S. soil in that period and the sense of crisis has ebbed. Before *Hamdan*, however, the Court's rulings were largely civil libertarian in rhetoric but largely deferential in substance, or so we will claim. The post-9/11 emergency illustrates the usual cycle, with *Hamdan* marking the beginning of the inevitable judicial reaction against post-9/11 policies.

Quite obviously, this analysis does not pinpoint with any precision when emergencies begin and end. Schmitt seems to have thought that it was conceptually impossible to define emergency, at least before the fact. That claim is too strong, because emergencies may be defined by paradigm cases and family resemblances rather than conceptually. A weaker form of the claim, however, is surely plausible. Emergency is a continuous variable, and can be more or less serious; the boundary between emergency and non-emergency is so fuzzy and indistinct that no one can be severely faulted for failing to specify where it lies. As explained shortly, we will focus on core cases in which emergency is undisputed—the first few years after Pearl Harbor or after 9/11.

The answer to the "who decides" question is: it depends. Often, all branches of government will agree that an emergency exists, and the "who decides" question does not arise. World War II, the immediate aftermath of 9/11, and the early cold war illustrate this case. We emphasize that this is the core case we address, throughout the book. In this core, there is no doubt of the existence of a serious emergency. Because the events that gave rise to the emergency are observable by all—consider the fall of the World Trade Center, or the loss of an American fleet—the executive has no private information about those events, and there is no real risk that the executive is falsely claiming an emergency in order to expand its powers. Although it is characteristic of emergencies that political actors will be uncertain of the emergency's scope and duration, the principal question for judges is not whether an emergency exists, but which policy instruments the executive should be allowed to use to meet it—instruments that would be off-limits during normal times.

The most difficult questions arise when we move outside the core—when the executive claims there is an emergency and the judges disagree. But, we will argue in chapters 2 and 3, this case will be rare, because judges who are aware of their limited capacity to evaluate the executive's claims will usually defer, although the pressure to defer tends to diminish as the observable events that gave rise to the emergency recede. If the executive branch and the judiciary do disagree, then, as always is the case with a constitutional crisis, the outcome depends on whether the public, the elites, or the military have confidence in the executive or the judiciary. For example, Abraham Lincoln prevailed over Justice Roger Taney at the outset of the Civil War, by defying Taney's habeas corpus order,[45] but the executive branch acquiesced in the judiciary's skepticism about emergency measures in the second decade of the cold war.

In short, we propose that in the core cases, the "who decides" question is irrelevant, because all institutions agree; and that outside the core, judges will and should defer less as the events that gave rise to the emergency fade (assuming that no new attacks occur). We cannot supply any precise answer about exactly where, on the continuum between core emergencies and ordinary times, judges will and should stop deferring to the executive. But no one else can answer that question with precision either, and in any event our main concern is with the core cases. Even in those cases, civil libertarians want judges to restrict the executive's choice of measures for meeting the emergency. Consider the public letter signed by over 700 law professors on December 13, 2001, just three months after the 9/11 attacks, that criticized an executive order establishing rules for military tribunals in terrorism cases.[46] This sort of civil-libertarianism, which applies even when the emergency is red-hot and indisputable, is our principal target.

Throughout, our argument presupposes that judges are capable of making a second-order determination whether conditions are such that their own first-order judgments are likely to be informed and valuable rather than uninformed and irrelevant.[47] Cases where judges determine that their own involvement would not be valuable are common; the political question doctrine, under which judges refuse to intervene in (for example) disputes between the executive and legislative branches, is the conventional illustration. An implication of this view is that the judges themselves will calibrate deference as events move along the continuum between normal times and full-blown emergencies. As the urgency of government action increases, the stakes grow higher, and the costs of frustrating needed security measures grow ever more daunting, the judges will be more constrained to defer. Increased deference to government is inevitable in time of emergency, because the judges know that the stakes are high and that their information is limited; we will see that the judges have often been quite candid about these constraints. Conversely, as the emergency decays, the judges will move back to a less deferential stance. We document this pattern in later discussion.

All of this is quite conventional, because constitutional law already requires judges to determine whether emergency conditions exist, with the most prominent special case of emergency being war. Consider doctrines holding that contract and property rules may be abrogated or limited in times of emergency,[48] doctrines that grant government heightened "war power,"[49] and doctrines that grant the president "protective" powers when Congress is not in session, or emergency legislation has not yet been put in place, or existing law somehow contains gaps that have been exposed by novel threats. The questions of what is an emergency and who decides are questions to which constitutional law already provides answers.

## What Is Government?

So far, we have spoken generally of "government" and have stated the thesis—to be supported throughout the later chapters—that courts both do and should defer more heavily to government in times of emergency than in normal times. A wave of recent scholarship, however, makes a valuable contribution by suggesting that government should be disaggregated. On this view, courts deciding cases during emergencies afford more deference to executive action that is authorized by congressional statute than to free-standing executive action, and rightly so.[50] We will call this the *authorization requirement* and express skepticism about it on both normative and descriptive grounds. Descriptively, courts typically defer to the executive branch in times of emergency, not to Congress-plus-the-executive or to Congress in its own right. Normatively, the authorization requirement is ambiguous; requiring legislative approval for executive action in times of emergency will often make things worse, not better. In the following chapters, then, *government* means the executive branch. We will suggest that, in times of emergency, courts should defer even to free-standing executive policies that restrict civil liberties to promote greater gains in security or that target dissenters or racial and ethnic minorities on the same grounds—although we will also claim that there will rarely be any such free-standing policies, because the same emergency circumstances that produce the policies also tend to produce statutory authorization for the policies.

We begin with the normative questions. On the view we will lay out in later chapters, the expected costs of judicial review rise sharply in times of emergency, because erroneous judicial invalidation of new security policies can produce large harms. How can we interpret the authorization requirement here? The most straightforward interpretation is that the requirement reduces the expected costs of judicial review, because congressional involvement reduces the number of objectionable policies that are adopted. Congress, on this view, is a more deliberative institution than is the executive, and this deliberation will tend to weed out laws that are bad—either in the sense that they are panicky or irrational (chapter 2), or in the sense that they are ill motivated, failing to take into account the welfare of minorities (chapter 3), or in the sense that they have long-term ratchet effects that the executive does not take into account or affirmatively welcomes (chapter 4).

The idea that Congress will, on net, weed out bad policies rests on an institutional comparison. The president is elected by a national constituency on a winner-take-all basis (barring the remote chance that the Electoral College will matter), whereas Congress is a summation of local constituencies and thus affords more voice to political and racial minorities. At the level of political psychology, decisionmaking within the executive is prone to group polarization and other forms of groupthink or irrational panic,[51] whereas the internal diversity of legislative deliberation checks these forces. At the level of political structure, Congress contains internal veto gates and chokepoints—consider the committee system and the filibuster rule—that provide minorities an opportunity to block harmful policies, whereas executive decisionmaking is relatively centralized and unitary.

The contrast is drawn too sharply, because in practice the executive is a they, not an it. Presidential oversight is incapable of fully unifying executive branch policies, which means that disagreement flourishes within the executive as well, dampening panic and groupthink and providing minorities with political redoubts.[52] Where a national majority is internally divided, the structure of presidential politics creates chokepoints that can give racial or ideological minorities disproportionate influence, just as the legislative process does. Consider the influence of Arab Americans in Michigan, often a swing state in presidential elections.

It is not obvious, then, that statutory authorization makes any difference at all. One possibility is that a large national majority dominates both Congress and the presidency and enacts panicky policies, oppresses minorities, or increases security in ways that have ratchet effects that are costly to reverse. If this is the case, a requirement of statutory authorization does not help. Another possibility is that there are internal institutional checks, within both the executive branch and Congress, on the adoption of panicky or oppressive policies and that democratic minorities have real influence in both arenas. If this is the case, then a requirement of authorization is not necessary and does no good. Authorization only makes a difference in the unlikely case where the executive is thoroughly panicky, or oppressively majoritarian, while Congress resists the stampede toward bad policies and safeguards the interests of oppressed minorities.

Even if that condition obtains, however, the argument for authorization goes wrong by failing to consider both sides of the normative ledger. As for majoritarian oppression, the multiplicity of veto gates within Congress may allow minorities to block harmful discrimination, but it also allows minorities to block policies and laws which, although targeted, are nonetheless good. As for panic and irrationality, if Congress is more deliberative, one result will be to prevent groupthink and slow down stampedes toward bad policies, but another result will be to delay necessary emergency measures and slow down stampedes toward good policies. Proponents of the authorization requirement sometimes assume that quick action, even panicky action, always produces bad policies. But there is no necessary connection between these two things; expedited action is sometimes good, and panicky crowds can stampede either in the wrong direction or in the right direction. Slowing down the adoption of new policies through congressional oversight retards the adoption not only of bad policies, but also of good policies that need to be adopted quickly if they are to be effective.

Overall, adding congressional involvement increases the costs of adopting new emergency policies, and thus has several cross-cutting effects. It reduces the number of laws that embody unjustified discrimination against democratic minorities, which is good, but it also reduces the number of laws that embody justified security measures targeted against minorities, which is bad, and it retards panicky measures by adding delay to the system, which is especially dangerous in times of emergency. To be sure, the worry that Congress will block needed security measures is just a possibility, not a systematic empirical finding. Democratic failure theorists, however, provide little systematic evidence for the assumption that requiring authorization improves outcomes, on net, because Congress blocks unjustified security measures. As a normative matter, the requirement of authorization is simply ambiguous.

The concern we have just articulated, that Congress will block or delay justified security measures, itself explains congressional practice. Legislators themselves know that Congress is not well suited for emergency action. Rather than trying to legislate for emergencies during emergencies, legislators act beforehand, authorizing the president and executive agencies to act if an emergency arises and generally granting them massive discretion.[53] Legislative action during emergencies consists predominantly of ratifications of what the executive has done, authorizations of whatever it says needs to be done, and appropriations so that it may continue to do what it thinks is right. Aware of their many institutional disadvantages—lack of information about what is happening, lack of control over the police and military, inability to act quickly and with one voice—legislators confine themselves to expressions of support or concern.

The historical record of emergency-driven ratifications, authorizations, and appropriations does not show that the deliberative processes of Congress have been engaged. The more plausible explanation is that Congress, knowing itself helpless before the emergency, looks to the executive for leadership, gratefully defers to its judgment, and provides it with any legislation that it may desire. On this view, unauthorized executive action ought to be rare—and indeed it is, as we shall note below. When it does occur, one does not know whether to blame the executive for acting hastily or Congress for failing to overcome its institutional disabilities despite an emergency.

Does the authorization requirement explain judicial practice? The problem with this claim is that there is little truly unilateral executive action. Qualitative legal analysts observe that the authorization thesis "fits" a large number of Supreme Court cases decided during wartime.[54] The observation is quite correct, but the comparison group is too small; we just have too few cases in which the judges were forced to decide squarely whether statutory authorization is necessary for emergency action by the executive.[55] Part of the problem is that authorization is an endogenous product of the president's decision to adopt a given policy, which will often produce authorization from a cooperative or supine Congress. Consider the Japanese internment policy, which was initially based upon an executive order but received statutory ratification from Congress a month later;[56] or Lincoln's emergency policies, undertaken without statutory authorization in the early months of the Civil War, which were later ratified by statute.[57]

More simply, the massive number and scope of statutory delegations since the New Deal, especially in areas impinging upon national security and foreign policy, means that there is almost always a statute lurking somewhere in the picture. Judges have considerable discretion to read statutes more or less broadly, or at higher or lower levels of generality, so as to suggest that Congress has authorized the executive action. Consider the plurality opinion in *Hamdi v. United States*,[58] which arguably stretched a general congressional authorization to use military force by reading it to authorize detention of U.S. citizens alleged to be enemy combatants, despite the presence of an earlier statute requiring that detention be specifically authorized.[59] A similar example is *Hamdi*'s predecessor, *Ex parte Quirin*,[60] in which the Court relied upon a general and nonexplicit statutory provision to find congressional authorization for the president to try by military commission U.S. citizens accused of being enemy combatants. Clearest of all is *Dames & Moore v. Regan*,[61] which threw a set of largely inapposite statutes into a blender and mixed up an authorization for the president to suspend claims pending in the U.S. courts against a foreign nation. Many other cases touching on war, the military, or foreign affairs are similar.[62] As political scientists Terry Moe and William Howell put it:

The Court can issue rulings favorable to presidents, but justify its
decisions by appearing to give due deference to the legislature. . . .
Congress's collective action problems, combined with the zillions
of statutes already on the books, make it entirely unclear what the
institution's "will" is—and this gives the Court tremendous scope
for arguing that, almost whatever presidents are doing, it is consistent with the "will of Congress." . . . [E]ven when presidents are quite
vague (as they frequently are) about the constitutional and statutory
provisions that supposedly justify their unilateral actions, the courts
have actively sought out and creatively construed justifying provisions
in the law, provisions that presidents did not even employ on their
own behalf.[63]

If judges strain to find statutory authorization for executive action in times
of emergency, why do they do so? As we explain in subsequent chapters, there
is an institutional dilemma facing judges who must review the executive's
emergency policies; the problem is that the judges lack the competence to
evaluate those policies. The judges know that the executive might be acting opportunistically or from bad motives, but they also know that the policy
might be a vitally necessary security measure, or was not authorized because
Congress moved too slowly. Worst of all, the judges know that they do not
know which of these possibilities is actually the case; they cannot sort opportunism from executive vigor. In a situation of this sort, the judges will be pow-
erfully tempted to defer, while also finding some relevant statute to suggest
that Congress too has approved the policy. The finding of statutory authorization, however strained, is largely costless to the judges, reassures the public by
denying that the executive is running around without a leash, and preserves
the principle of statutory authorization for a future day on which the judges
might rouse themselves to apply it seriously. The point is not that judges are
acting out of disreputable motives: quite the opposite. On our view, judges
tend to defer because there is usually little else that even the most public-spir-
ited of judges can do. The stakes are too high and the judges' information is
too poor.

In decisions of this sort, the statute is not really a moving part, although
later commentators may correctly point out that the judges referred to the
statute as authority for the executive action. Here, the famous *Korematsu* decisions in 1943,[64] which upheld the internment of Issei and Nisei (first-genera-
tion and second-generation Japanese immigrants, many of whom were citizens) is a good example. Although Franklin D. Roosevelt's internment order

was ratified by a later statute, and although the Court mentioned the statute in passing, the Court was candid that the basis for deference was simply that the conditions under which the internment order was issued allowed no other course of action:

> Congress, reposing its confidence in this time of war in our military
> leaders—as inevitably it must—determined that they should have the
> power to [order internment]. There was evidence of disloyalty on
> the part of some, the military authorities considered that the need for
> action was great, and time was short.[65]

Note the suggestion, very damaging to the authorization requirement, that the Congress too has little real choice but to defer to the executive in times of crisis. If this is so, then we are back to the initial point that statutory authorization or ratification will predictably be forthcoming during emergencies, making a judicial requirement of statutory authorization rather hollow.

This is hardly the whole picture. There are cases in which the Court has construed statutes narrowly to deny the executive authority in quasi-military or quasi-emergency settings.[66] On one interpretation, this is especially likely where the president acts contrary to accepted historical practices and traditions,[67] whatever the statutory texts say, which suggests that statutory authorization is a placeholder for an inquiry that the judges conduct by using extrastatutory heuristics or rules of thumb. There are also a very few cases in which the Court seems to have actually taken risks by holding that a sitting president was adopting emergency policies without statutory (or constitutional) authority. The *Youngstown* case,[68] in which the Court invalidated Harry S Truman's order to take control of production at the nation's steel mills to prevent a threatened strike, is a possible example, albeit a slightly muddy one, because the decision came late in a stalemated foreign war (the Korean War) conducted by a deeply unpopular president, rather than in the heat of a genuine emergency.[69] *Youngstown* thus rests on an unusual confluence of factors;[70] at most, *Youngstown* illustrates our previous point that, as the cycle of emergency decays and the potential security costs of judicial intervention decline, judges will rediscover their courage.

The *Hamdi* decision, on the other hand, is not a real example of judicial courage, because the decision may well turn out to have been largely costless to the government. The Court's holding that the government must afford some review of citizens' detentions has yet to be cashed out and might amount to little if review is very deferential, on the merits, and if military tribunals (the so-called Combatant Status Review Tribunals) can do the reviewing. We discuss this point at length in chapter 8. Suffice it to say here that commentators who celebrate *Hamdi* as an important example of judicial protection for civil liberties during emergencies[71] are paying too much attention to the decision's rhetoric and not enough to its opaque and possibly inconsequential substance.[72] As Geof Stone, a noted civil libertarian, suggested *before* the cases were decided, *Hamdi* and its companion cases were a judicial "freebie," lacking "immediate consequences"[73]—which in our view makes *Hamdi* a cheap victory for civil liberties.

The most recent decision, *Hamdan v. Rumsfeld*, held[74] that (1) the trial by military commission (not proceeding according to the rules governing courts-martial) of an enemy combatant on a charge of "conspiracy" was not authorized by domestic statutes or by the international common law of war, and also that (2) the military commissions were procedurally defective under the binding treaty obligations of Common Article 3 of the Geneva Conventions, themselves incorporated by reference into domestic statutes. The first holding is in tension with *Hamdi*'s holding that detention of enemy combatants is authorized by the AUMF. Although the two can nominally be reconciled by saying that detention of illicit combatants, but not military trial for conspiracy, was traditionally permitted under the laws of war, it is quite clear that the earlier case takes a more capacious view of the executive's traditional war powers than does the later one.

What matters for present purposes is that *Hamdan*, like *Youngstown*, does provide a clear example of a judicial finding of lack of statutory authorization. There is also a broader political similarity: *Hamdan*, like *Youngstown*, illustrates the tendency of judges to pile on a politically weakened president after the heat of the emergency has cooled. It is an irony that the heat of the emergency may cool precisely because a president's earlier emergency measures have been successful (although we are agnostic about whether that is in fact true in the case of the Bush administration), and have received deference from the judges. Part of what drives the cycle of emergencies is the self-undermining character of successful precautions: the security guard whose presence deters robbers from even attempting their crimes runs the risk of being dismissed as useless, because no crimes are ever observed. This interpretation of *Hamdan* fits perfectly with the cyclical account of emergencies; the decision thus confirms our overall thesis. Where emergencies have sufficiently decayed, perhaps because earlier emergency measures have succeeded, judges reassert themselves.

It is not here a legitimate complaint that the cyclical thesis is "unfalsifiable" because emergencies lie on a continuum, making it unclear exactly when emergencies decay and pass into history. The complaint fails on three grounds. First, as we have mentioned, emergencies are well-defined by paradigmatic instances and core cases, even if not conceptually. The cycle thesis would be untenable if the Court had overridden executive emergency measures six months after Pearl Harbor or six months after 9/11. That such a course of action was and remains unthinkable suggests the powerful pressure on judges to defer in the heat of emergency. Second, the authorization thesis, which we are criticizing, is no more falsifiable than our denial of it. As a descriptive claim the authorization thesis says that judges put special emphasis on statutory authorization for executive action *during emergencies*. This view builds in precisely the same fuzzy reference to emergencies that underpins the cycle thesis.

Third, falsifiability is a criterion that is impossible to fulfill in this setting in any event. There are simply too few relevant cases, too many degrees of freedom to allow rigorous testing of causal hypotheses. This is a standard problem in law and social science; not every question can be addressed by the methods of large-number empiricism. Under conditions of this sort, descriptive claims are still possible, but they must rest on interpretive case studies, and on tracing the actual processes by which particular decisions were reached. That is the sort of descriptive claim we have offered here, and the authorization thesis is exactly the same sort of claim. Both claims must be judged on their own terms, not on irrelevant large-number grounds.

To sum up the methodological and legal issues: there is a smallish set of cases that do squarely support the authorization thesis, but there is also a smallish set of cases that squarely contradict it. The clearest is *In re Debs*, in which the Court granted the president an injunction to continue the operation of the railways in the face of a massive strike, despite the lack of any statutory authorization at all.[75] *Debs* is a stark contrast to *Youngstown* and *Hamdan*. The point, of course, is not to tote up cases on either side, but to emphasize how few cases squarely put the authorization thesis to the test. In times of emergency, executive action and statutory authorization correlate tightly, although not perfectly.

This makes it difficult to falsify our view that statutory authorization is not decisive in most emergency cases, but it also makes it difficult to falsify the authorization thesis, because we rarely observe unauthorized executive action. Recall the conventional wisdom among constitutional lawyers that the courts defer heavily to government in times of emergency. Our suggestion here is that the deference runs mostly to the executive, not to Congress. The observation that the authorization thesis fits most of the cases is too fragile to show the contrary, because a finding of authorization may often be a rationalization of the judges' decision rather than a causal factor in the judges' decisionmaking, and there are too few cases to discriminate between the two possibilities.

As an alternative to the hypothesis that congressional approval validates executive action and justifies judicial deference, while congressional silence justifies judicial scrutiny, we propose the hypothesis that courts *and* Congress defer to the executive during emergencies because their institutional advantages during normal times are overwhelmed by the executive's advantages during emergencies. When the executive acts without statutory authorization, this may say more about congressional incapacity than executive overreaching, and thus courts have no reason to treat congressional silence as a signal that the executive action is suspect.

## EXECUTIVE DESPOTISM?

We have said that government, for the purposes of the tradeoff thesis, means the executive branch, directed by (though not fully controlled by) the president. In some quarters, the topic of emergency powers causes a reflexive concern about executive abuses. Presidents or executive officials use emergency powers opportunistically, to increase their power; the result is violation of civil liberties, perhaps even culminating in widespread oppression or a police state. As we suggested above, civil libertarians are obsessed by the shadow of Weimar, in which constitutional failure culminated in executive dictatorship.

We must distinguish here between two versions of the civil libertarian concern. The first is a concern about agency slack, or presidential opportunism and power grabbing that violates the preferences of democratic majorities. A different version is that democratic majorities will themselves prefer to oppress minorities, that this preference increases during emergencies, and that the executive during emergencies will be the instrument of majoritarian oppression. We take up the second version at length in chapter 5; for the reasons given there, it is the more serious of the two concerns.

As for the agency-slack version of the thesis, we will take up the topic at several points in what follows. Chapter 3 argues that presidential opportunism is constrained by politics and that judges can do little to prevent it in any event; chapter 4 argues that the expansion of executive authority during emergencies has no long-term, ratchet-like consequences; and chapter 5 suggests that a general fear of executive despotism is unfounded in advanced liberal democracies. Here, we will simply summarize, for later reference, our grounds for skepticism about the agency-slack idea.

Four points are critical, and they suggest that the concern is either greatly overblown or does not support civil libertarian prescriptions, or both: presidential or executive preferences need not systematically favor increased executive power during emergencies; political constraints will rule out abuses that the politically engaged public does not favor; even if increased executive power in emergencies creates abuses, the security gains may be greater still; and in any event civil libertarian judicial review is a feeble bulwark against a truly imperial executive.

First, the executive-despotism concern supposes that executive officials desire, above all, to maximize their power. As Daryl Levinson has emphasized, both for officials generally and for executive officials in particular, it is hardly obvious that this is so, at least in any systematic way.[76] Lower-level executive officials and administrative agencies have many other possible goals or maximands, including the desire to enjoy leisure or to advance programmatic or ideological goals—goals which will usually be orthogonal to the tradeoff between security and liberty and which might even include the protection of civil liberties. The same is true for presidents: some have been power maximizers; some have not. Moreover, even with respect to power-maximizing presidents, critics fail to distinguish the man from the office. Presidents as individuals do not internalize all of the gains from expanding the power of the presidency as an institution, because those gains are shared with future presidents and senior executive officials.[77] Conversely, presidents as individuals do not fully internalize harms to the institution and may thus acquiesce in limitations on executive power for partisan or personal advantage. The latter point may be more pronounced in emergencies than in normal times, because emergencies shorten the relevant time horizon; policymaking for the short run looms larger than in normal times. (We bracket for now the question of whether this is bad, an issue taken up in chapter 2.) Emergencies thus increase the divergence between the utility of individual officeholders and the institutional power of their offices, which extends into the remote future, beyond the horizon of the emergency.

Second, whatever the intrinsic preferences of presidents and executive officials, politics sharply constrains their opportunities for aggrandizement,[78] especially in times of emergency. The president is elected from a national constituency (ignoring the low probability that the Electoral College will make a difference). A first-term president who seeks reelection to a second term, or even a second-term president who seeks to leave a legacy, will try to appeal to the median voter, or at least to some politically engaged constituency that is unlikely to be extremist in either direction. If the national median or the political center favors increased executive authority during emergencies, then the president will push the bounds of his power, but if it does not, then he will not; there is no general reason to think that national politics will always push executive authority as far as possible, even during emergencies.

Of course, during emergencies, the public will often favor increased executive power, and this may be fully sensible, given the executive's relative decisiveness, secrecy, centralization, and other advantages over Congress and other institutions. Note, in this connection, the important finding that political constraints on the executive are associated with increased terrorism;[79] shackling the executive has real security costs. The critics of executive power typically assume that executive power not only expands during emergencies, but expands too far. However, the critics supply no general reason to think this is so; they systematically conflate increases in executive power with "aggrandizement," a normatively loaded concept which connotes an unjustified increase. We return to this point shortly. Here, the point is just that the expansion of presidential power during emergencies may reflect nothing more than the demands of the politically effective public, rather than intrinsic opportunism.

The political constraints on the executive branch and the president are partisan as well as institutional. The president is the leader of a political party but is also beholden to it. The party constrains the president in various ways, and it is not necessarily in the interest of a single party to enhance the power of the executive during emergencies. For one thing, the president's party may not win the next presidential election; for another, his party may have many other bases of power, including Congress, the judiciary, and local institutions. Expanding the president's personal or institutional power need not be in the interests of partisan politicians who govern behind the scenes. Opposition parties, of course, have powerful incentives to criticize the expansion of presidential power during emergencies, portraying small adjustments to the legal rules as omens of a putsch. In emergencies, partisan criticism can make the political constraints on presidents even tighter than during normal times, a point we emphasize in chapter 5. Governmental decisionmaking is often more visible during emergencies than during normal times; emergency policymaking is more centralized, even within the executive branch, and more closely associated with the president; the resulting policies often present a larger target for political attack.

Third, the critics of executive power in emergencies are usually unclear about their normative premises. Suppose that executive power increases during emergencies and that this results in abuses. In terms of the tradeoff thesis, however, such abuses are just a cost to be measured against the benefits of increased security, given the finding, reported above, that a constrained executive is associated with higher levels of terrorism.[80] If the gains on the security margin exceed the costs, then the expansion of executive power improves social welfare overall, and no special opprobrium should attach to the executive's behavior, although it would be nice to also prevent the abuses if possible. The critics treat executive abuses of civil liberties as something to be minimized, down to zero. But this is quixotic, and even if it were feasible, it would not be desirable. Some rate of abuse is inevitable once an executive branch is created, and an increase in abuses is inevitable when executive discretion expands during emergencies, but both shifts may be worth it; the critics fail to account for the gains side of the ledger.[81] Granting the executive extensive powers during emergencies has many benefits, about which the critics are often silent.

Concerns about increasing executive power often rest on an implicit status quo bias, or naturalistic fallacy. The assumption is that the scope or level of executive power before the emergency was optimal. But this need not be so, and there is no general reason to think it will be so; consider the finding that the 7/7 attacks in London went unprevented because the United Kingdom's intelligence services, who knew something about the plotters, had too few resources to investigate them adequately.[82] Emergencies may release the polity from a sclerotic equilibrium in which executive power was too feeble to meet new challenges, as we illustrate in chapter 4. One interpretation of history is that emergencies allow presidents to obtain powers that are necessary to cope with new problems. Our original constitutional structure, with a relatively weak presidency, reflects the concerns of the eighteenth century and is not well adapted to current conditions.

Finally, to the extent that the critics of executive power envision judicial review as the solution, they are whistling in the wind, especially during times of emergency. The critics envision an imperial executive, who is either backed by a sustained national majority or else has slipped the political leash, and who enjoys so much agency slack as to be heedless of the public's preferences. In either case, it is not obvious what the critics suppose the judges will or can do about it. As we will recount in more detail in later chapters, the judges proved largely powerless to stem the tide of the New Deal, in conditions of economic emergency, or to stop Japanese internment during World War II, or to block aggressive punishment and harassment of communists during the cold war. What is more, many of the judges had no desire to block these programs. Judges are people too and share in national political sentiments; they are also part of the political elite and will rally 'round the flag in times of emergency just as much as others do.[83]

Critics of executive power implicitly appeal to a slippery-slope argument: once executive power is increased to meet an emergency in a manner that is necessary and reasonable, it will unavoidably expand beyond what is necessary and reasonable. As we emphasize in chapters 4 and 5, the problem with this argument is that there is no evidence for it and no mechanism that generates such a slope. The critics focus obsessively on pathological polities like Weimar, ignoring that current well-functioning liberal democracies do not present the same conditions that led to dictatorship in 1933. More recent work in comparative politics suggests that grants of emergency powers or of decree authority to executives do not systematically end in dictatorship.[84]

## CONCLUSION

So far we have set out the structure of the tradeoff thesis, rebutted some external critiques, defined the crucial terms *emergency* and *government*, and rebutted some common but ill-formed arguments for concern about executive power during emergencies. We now turn to the internal critiques of the tradeoff thesis, starting with one of the most common: the idea that, during emergencies, the cognition or emotional reactions of officials or voters are somehow distorted, resulting in panicky policies that produce excessive levels of security.

# CHAPTER TWO

# The Panic Theory

Many accounts of emergency emphasize the Constitution's role in limiting the impact of fear on government policy. The *panic thesis* argues that because fear causes decisionmakers to exaggerate threats and neglect civil liberties and similar values, expanding decisionmakers' constitutional powers will result in bad policy. Any gains to national security would be minimal, and the losses to civil liberties would be great. It follows that enforcing the Constitution to the same extent as during periods of normalcy would protect civil liberties at little cost, and therefore the civil libertarian view is superior to the deferential view.

The panic thesis is a staple of both academic[1] and popular[2] discussions of emergency powers. It has not, to our knowledge, ever been subject to a full-fledged critique in the academic literature.[3]

We argue that the panic thesis is wrong and does not support the civil libertarian position. We make four points. First, fear does not play an unambiguously negative role in decisionmaking. Against the standard view that fear interferes with decisionmaking, we argue that fear has both cognitive and motivational benefits. Second, even if fear did play a negative role, it is doubtful that fear, so understood, has much influence on policy during emergencies, or that it has more influence on policy during emergencies than it does during normal times. Third, even if fear did play a negative role in decisionmaking and played a greater role during emergencies than during normal times, it is doubtful that these effects could be mitigated, at an acceptable cost to national security, through constitutional adjudication. Fourth, even if fear did play a greater negative role during emergencies than during normal times, it does not necessarily have a pro-security valence; fear could lead to libertarian panics as well as security panics. All four of these points, individually and in the aggregate, suggest that the civil libertarian view will not improve policy choices by restricting the influence of fear.

## PRELIMINARIES

Fear can influence government action in two ways. First, government officials might feel fear. Second, even if government officials do not feel fear, the public might feel fear, and government officials might feel compelled to act on the public's fears, lest they be turned out of office for being insufficiently responsive to the public's concerns. In the second case, it is a useful simplification to assume that government officials, by acting as honest agents, act as if they were themselves afraid; thus, the two cases can be treated as though they were the same. Later in this chapter, we consider another possibility, one in which only the public feels fear and government officials are insulated from popular pressure.

To understand how fearful government officials might make decisions, one can profitably begin by considering the rational actor model as a baseline. The rational actor model assumes that people implicitly use accurate probability distributions to estimate the likelihood of uncertain outcomes. The methodological assumption is obviously strong; the justification is that although errors occur in both directions, aggregate behavior obeys accurate probability distributions. If government agents are rational actors in this sense, then governments act as rationally during emergencies as during normal times. The decision to infringe on civil liberties for security purposes may be right or wrong, but it is no more likely right or wrong than the everyday decision to raise the sales tax or open government land for logging. There is no reason to think that the government will systematically undervalue civil liberties or overvalue security during emergencies, or that it will systematically overestimate the magnitude of a threat, compared to its behavior during normal times. Instead, the government will attach the same weights to these goods as it does during normal times; it will also on average accurately estimate the magnitude of the threat.

The rational actor model does not clearly support either the deferential view or the civil libertarian position. The critic of the deferential view can argue that a rational executive will disregard civil liberties similarly during emergencies and during normal times; therefore, constitutional enforcement should be similar as well. Courts can protect civil liberties while permitting emergency measures by requiring that the government show that infringements on civil liberties serve the compelling interest in national security. The defense of the deferential view rests not on the rational actor model, but on an empirical claim about relative institutional competence: courts are in a bad position to evaluate the executive's emergency measures. Secrecy is more important than during normal times; so are speed, vigor, and enthusiasm. The characteristics of judicial review—deliberation, openness, independence, distance, slowness—may be minor costs, and sometimes virtues, during normal times, but during emergencies they can be intolerable.

The panic thesis argues that the problem with emergency measures is not that they may be rational but objectionable infringements on civil liberties, but that they are frequently irrational, and thus infringe on civil liberties without also creating sufficient national security benefits. During emergencies, panic interferes with the rational assessment of risks. The distortion can take a number of forms: exaggeration of the probability or magnitude of the threatened harm or, what amounts to nearly the same thing, neglect of competing values, such as privacy and equality. As a result, government interests will not usually be as compelling as many people think they are, and government policy, if not constrained, will unnecessarily interfere with civil liberties. Although this argument is conventionally advanced by civil libertarians concerned by wartime restrictions, it also underlies a popular view about the effectiveness of terrorism: that it "trap[s] the authorities into brutal repression and over-reaction which then alienates the public and drives them into tacit or active collaboration with the terrorists."[4] The claim is not that the government rationally curtails civil liberties in order to combat the terrorist threat, but that the government overreacts and that the public tolerates a rational response but not an overreaction. The source of the overreaction could only be fear or some other emotion, such as anger or outrage.[5] On this view, the civil libertarian rejection of the deferential view has two virtues: preservation of civil liberties, a good in itself, and preservation of the government against its own bad judgment.

This argument, at its base, holds that the government's policy will not reflect accurate probability distributions, or else that a rational government will take advantage of the public's inaccurate probability distributions so that it can accomplish ends denied to it during normal times. Fear displaces the rational assessment of the risks at one level or the other. Is this view accurate?

## TWO VIEWS OF FEAR

The civil libertarian view depends heavily on a particular theory of fear, a theory that implies that fear interferes with cognition and judgment. However, fear is a complex emotion, and generalizing about its relationship to cognition is hazardous.

Fear is in part a purely physiological response to a threat, a response that is outside of conscious control.[6] When a person comes upon a tiger in a jungle, he or she undergoes certain physiological changes—the chemistry of the blood changes, the heartbeat increases, certain areas of the brain are stimulated—which result in an urge to flee that can be overcome only with difficulty. One interesting aspect of this phenomenon is that panic responses appear to be asymmetrically distributed: false positives are more likely than false negatives. A person is more likely to flee from a shadow that looks like a tiger than to fail to run from a tiger that looks like a shadow.[7] Evolutionary psychologists argue that the asymmetry of responses is the result of an asymmetry in the payoffs. A person who is attacked by a tiger is less likely to reproduce than a person who unnecessarily runs away from a shadow. Thus, the noncognitive aspect of fear has two immediate implications: people do not think about threats and react to them "rationally," and the automatic reaction to threats reflects long-gone evolutionary pressures rather than the needs of an agent in modern society.

This story yields two opposing approaches to the role of fear in decision-making. The first, simple view is that fear interferes with cognition: the person who feels fear reacts to the threat instinctively rather than deliberatively and in a way that is biased rather than neutral. Fear of air travel causes people to drive, which is riskier than flying; fear of pesticides, toxic waste, and genetic engineering causes people to endorse expensive and ineffective policies that cause more harm than good.[8] This fear-interferes-with-cognition view has deep roots in the Western philosophical tradition, a long-running theme of which is the opposition of reason and passion.[9] Passions interfere with reason, and the rational person attempts to suppress or harness them. When one is motivated by a passion, it means that one's choices are unlikely to be good ones.

The second view is that fear does not interfere with cognition, or if it does, the interference contributes to good action.[10] There are two related points here. First, fear enhances the senses: the person who feels fear is attuned to the threat and alert to every nuance of the environment. Second, fear provides motivation. Where a fully rational person spends time deliberating, the fearful person acts quickly. Both of these factors suggest that fear can play a constructive role during emergencies.

How does fear enhance the senses? Although the fearful person may make the characteristic mistake of seeing a tiger in a shadow, the other side of this error is the sensory arousal that allows the person to pick out in the environment threats that would otherwise be invisible. It has been said that after 9/11, airplane passengers and security officials paid much more attention to other passengers and were more ready to alert authorities or to intervene personally if they saw something suspicious. This alertness resulted in many false positives: conversations were misinterpreted, conclusions were drawn from swarthy complexions, and harmless objects were confiscated as weapons. But in a few cases, hijackings or bombings were, or may have been, prevented. Do the lives saved justify the inconvenience to all passengers and Arabs and Muslims in particular? Civil libertarians might say yes or no, but one's position on this question is not the issue. What recent experience has shown is that fear has generated cognitive gains as well as losses, and part of the reason is that the asymmetry between gains and losses that underlies the evolutionary story may apply to a world threatened by terrorism as well, however imperfectly. The simple story—that fear means error—is too simple.

The motivational benefit of fear for individuals is that it enables a rapid response to a possible threat that, if real, would not give individuals time to deliberate about available options. To the drafter of a rule that constrains the curtailment of civil liberties, or to the judge who seeks to enforce that rule or the general civil libertarian position, the decisionmaker always has a powerful argument: "your rational assessments—even if they are not clouded by your remoteness from the current emergency—may have resulted from a kind of clear thinking but are fatally compromised by your motivational remoteness. If you did not feel fear, then you cannot have put in the necessary effort to make the right decision." Fear compels people to devote resources to solving a problem that for a dispassionate and uninvolved person may be interesting but not compelling. In this way, fear motivates not only action but deliberation. Having perceived a threat, and felt fear, people will work hard to think of ways to address it. They are more likely to discard old assumptions and complacent ways of thinking and to address problems with new vigor.

The second, complex view of fear does not deny the insights of the first view; it incorporates them into a more nuanced account. Fear will produce choices that are different from those that will be made by a person who does not feel fear, but these choices may be better or worse, depending on the context. The argument here mirrors an increasingly influential psychological and philosophical literature on the passions, a literature that stresses the constructive role of the passions in judgment.[11] "Emotions provide the animal [including the human] with a sense of how the world relates to its own set of goals and projects. Without that sense, decisionmaking and action are derailed."[12] Disgust involves a form of magical thinking that causes people to avoid objects or persons who are harmless, but it also reflects moral judgments and motivates the condemnation of morally offensive behavior.[13] Anger can magnify slights and provoke unreasoned violence, but it is also a response to an offense against one's dignity or person and can motivate legitimate protest.[14] The passions do not always inhibit reason; they also inform reason and provide the motivation for necessary action.

Against the view that panicked government officials overreact to an emergency and unnecessarily curtail civil liberties, we suggest a more constructive theory of the role of fear. Before the emergency, government officials are complacent. They do not think clearly or vigorously about the potential threats faced by the nation. After the terrorist attack or military intervention, their complacency is replaced by fear. Fear stimulates them to action. Action may be based on good decisions or bad: fear might cause officials to exaggerate future threats, but it also might arouse them to threats that they would otherwise not perceive. It is impossible to say in the abstract whether decisions and actions provoked by fear are likely to be better than decisions and actions made in a state of calm. But our limited point is that there is no reason to think that the fear-inspired decisions are likely to be worse. For that reason, the existence of fear during emergencies does not support the civil libertarian theory that the Constitution should be enforced as strictly during emergencies as during normal times.

## THE INFLUENCE OF FEAR DURING EMERGENCIES

Suppose now that the simple view of fear is correct and that it is an unambiguously negative influence on government decisionmaking. Critics of the deferential view argue that the supposed negative effect of fear justifies skepticism about emergency policies and, therefore, about the deferential view. The problem with this argument is that it implicitly assumes that fear has more influence on decisionmaking during emergencies than on decisionmaking during normal times. This assumption is not plausible.

The panic thesis holds that citizens and officials respond to terrorism and war in the same way that an individual in the jungle responds to a tiger or snake. The national response to an emergency, because it is a standard fear response, is characterized by the same circumvention of ordinary deliberative processes: (i) the response is instinctive rather than reasoned, and thus subject to error; and (ii) the error will be biased in the direction of overreaction. While the flight reaction might have been a good evolutionary strategy on the savannah, in a complex modern society the flight response is not suitable and can only interfere with judgment. Its advantage—speed—has minimal value for social decisionmaking. No national emergency requires an *immediate* reaction, except by trained professionals, such as soldiers or police officers, who execute policies established earlier. Instead over days, months, or years people make complex judgments about the appropriate institutional response. And the asymmetrical nature of fear guarantees that people will, during a national emergency, overweight the threat and underweight other things that people value, such as civil liberties.

But if decisionmakers rarely act immediately, then the tiger story cannot bear the metaphoric weight that is placed on it. Indeed, the flight response has nothing to do with the political response to the bombing of Pearl Harbor or to the attacks on September 11. The people who were there—the citizens and soldiers beneath the bombs, the office workers in the World Trade Center and the Pentagon—no doubt felt fear, and most of them probably responded in the classic way. They experienced the standard physiological effects and (with the exception of trained soldiers and security officials) fled without stopping to think. It is also true that in the days and weeks after the attacks, many people felt fear, although not the sort that produces an irresistible urge to flee. But this kind of fear is not the kind in which cognition shuts down. Some people did have more severe mental reactions and, for example, shut themselves in their houses, but these reactions were rare. The fear is probably better described as a general anxiety or jumpiness, an anxiety that was probably shared by government officials as well as ordinary citizens.[15]

While, as we have noted, there is psychological research suggesting that normal cognition partly shuts down in response to an immediate threat, we are aware of no research suggesting that people who feel anxious about a medium-term or long-term threat are incapable of thinking, or thinking properly, or that they systematically overweight the threat relative to other values. Indeed, it would be surprising to find research that clearly distinguished "anxious thinking" and "calm thinking," given that anxiety is a pervasive aspect of life. People are anxious about their children, about their health, about their job prospects, about their vacation arrangements, about walking home at night.[16] So it is hard to see why anxiety about more remote threats, from terrorists or unfriendly countries with nuclear weapons, should cause the public or elected officials to place more emphasis on security than is justified and to sacrifice civil liberties unnecessarily. Quite the contrary, a standard view is that people ignore low-probability risks and that elected officials with short time horizons ignore remote ones; on this account, government will probably do too little to prevent terrorist threats, not too much.

Fear generated by immediate threats, then, may cause instinctive responses that are not rational in the cognitive sense, not always desirable, and not a good basis for public policy, but it is not this kind of fear that leads to restrictions of civil liberties during wartime. The internment of Japanese Americans during World War II may have been due to racial animus, or to a mistaken assessment of the risks; it was not the direct result of panic. Indeed, there was a delay of weeks before the policy was seriously considered.[17] The civil libertarians' argument that fear produces bad policy trades on the ambiguity of the word *panic*, which refers both to real fear that undermines rationality and to collectively harmful outcomes that are driven by rational decisions, such as a bank panic, in which it is rational for all depositors to withdraw their funds if they believe that enough other depositors are withdrawing funds. Once we eliminate the false concern about fear, it becomes clear that the panic thesis is indistinguishable from the argument that during an emergency people are likely to make mistakes. But if the only concern is that during emergencies people make mistakes, there would be no reason to demand that the Constitution be enforced normally during emergencies. Political errors occur during emergencies and during normal times; once the panic thesis is rejected there is no reason to think that political errors occur at a higher rate during emergencies such that judicial scrutiny should be heightened, despite all of the disadvantages described in chapter 1.

In sum, the panic thesis envisions decisionmakers acting immediately when in fact government policymaking moves slowly even during emergencies. Government is organized so that general policy decisions about responses to emergencies are made in advance, and the implementation of those policies during an emergency is trusted to security officials who have been trained to resist the impulse to panic. The notion of fear causing an irresistible urge to flee is a bad metaphor for an undeniable truth: during an emergency, the government does not have as much time for making decisions as it usually does, and as a result will make more errors than it usually does. But these errors will be driven by ordinary cognitive limitations and not the pressure of fear; thus, the errors will be normally distributed. It is as likely that the government will curtail civil liberties too little as too much.

## A NOTE ON COGNITIVE PANICS

It is possible that civil libertarians' worry about the influence of fear is not based on any assumption about emotions per se, but is based on concerns about cognition. Their theory might be that, during emergencies, individuals, whether as voters or as decisionmakers, are more likely to make cognitive errors than during normal times. Something about emergencies causes cognition to falter. This view, by itself, would not justify the civil libertarian view. If individuals make more errors during emergencies than during normal times, they are just as likely to err in favor of too much liberty as to err in favor of too much security. As we emphasize below, "libertarian panics" would occur to the same extent that "security panics" occur. The civil libertarian view would, by reducing only the errors in favor of security, create an overall policy bias against security. The civil libertarian view would be justified only if an additional assumption is made, namely, that errors are biased in favor of security in the first place.[18]

Clearly, this is what civil libertarians must think. People worry that, after a terrorist attack, the public will overreact and demand unnecessary restrictions on civil liberties. No one seems to worry that, after abuses by the police come to light, the public will overreact and demand unnecessary restrictions on policing. But no one has explained why cognitive error would be biased against civil liberties in this way. The public cares about national security and about civil liberties; why should its errors be biased against only the latter?

An instructive analogy is Timur Kuran and Cass Sunstein's argument that environmental disasters distort regulation because of their "availability." Because environmental disasters are salient, they engage the availability heuristic, which causes people to overestimate the probability of recurrence and demand regulation that is not cost justified.[19] Unfortunately, the evidence for this argument is only anecdotal. We know that many environmental regulations are not cost justified, but we do not have enough data to subject the Kuran-Sunstein hypothesis to a statistical test.

But even if Kuran and Sunstein are correct about environmental regulation, there is an important difference between environmental regulation and security policy. If environmental disasters are salient, the cost of overregulation—lost consumer surplus resulting from inflated production costs—does not have salience. This asymmetry in the availability of the costs of underregulation and overregulation could result in overregulation, as Kuran and Sunstein argue. By contrast, the government's violation of civil liberties—mass internments, torture, and so forth—are just as salient as the terrorist attacks that provoke them. The availability heuristic therefore can work its ill effects on both sides of the problem: terrorist attacks cause people to overestimate the probability of further terrorist attacks, but civil liberties infringements also cause people to overestimate the probability of further infringements. Nondeferential constitutional adjudication would prevent the first error from leading to overregulation, but it would not prevent the second error from leading to underregulation. Therefore, courts influenced by the civil libertarian view would bias policy against security.

The availability heuristic is not the only cognitive process that can lead to misperception of risks; indeed, those who argue that the government overreacts to threats frequently invoke other heuristics and biases—a "confirmation trap bias" and an "overconfidence bias," for example—that, they claim, bolster the possibility of overreaction.[20] But there are cognitive processes on the other side. Kip Viscusi and Richard Zeckhauser, for example, conducted an empirical study that suggests a "hindsight-choice bias": people update their beliefs about the risks of terrorism after a terrorist attack but they fail to realize that they have done so. As a result, they believe that the pre-attack security measures were adequate for the risk, and object to rational changes in security policies in response to the attack.[21]

This balancing of cognitive problems has an air of unreality. The real problem here is that the availability heuristic is poorly understood. No one knows what makes one event psychologically salient and another event psychologically inert, and for that reason it is hard to talk productively about the extent to which availability on one side of an issue can cancel the effects of availability on the other side of the issue. The availability heuristic and similar cognitive mechanisms provide a flimsy basis for departing from the deferential view, which assumes that errors occur but that the distribution of errors is unbiased.

## INSTITUTIONAL PROBLEMS

So far, we have argued that citizens and officials are no less capable of good judgment during emergencies than during normal times. By this we mean that decisionmakers make no more errors during emergencies than during normal times (although the errors might matter more during emergencies) and that even if they do make more errors during emergencies, they are no more likely to make errors that are systematically biased in favor of security, at the expense of civil liberties, during emergencies than during normal times. We now consider the panic thesis on its own terms, and we assume for the sake of argument that people predictably panic during national emergencies while remaining calm at other times and that the panic has unambiguously negative consequences for decisionmaking.

The civil libertarian view—that the Constitution be enforced as strictly during an emergency as during a non-emergency—depends on citizens, executive officials, or judges having the ability to enforce the Constitution strictly despite their own fear-addled judgment that a policy is justified by a threat to security. Is this assumption realistic? How can one bind oneself against one's own bad judgment? We examine three mechanisms: (i) intrapersonal self-restraint; (ii) reliance on rules; and (iii) insulation of decisionmakers. The first two assume that the decisionmakers must constrain themselves—for example, that an executive branch official who feels fear must find some way to avoid the ill effects of this emotion. Civil libertarians do not normally make this argument and instead rely on judges to constrain officials, but nonetheless it is productive to consider the case where judges are not available to constrain decisionmakers. The third mechanism relies on institutional devices to ensure that the officials who make decisions during emergencies are either not likely to panic or are constrained by other officials who are not likely to panic, including judges. In our evaluation of this third mechanism, we will directly confront the arguments of the civil libertarians.

## Intrapersonal Self-Restraint

The panic theory, which assumes that fearful officials make worse judgments than do calm officials, is not the same as the civil libertarian view. The panic theory is just one rationale for the civil libertarian view; we discuss other rationales in other chapters. Indeed, the panic theory is broader than the civil libertarian view: it holds that officials in a state of fear should always discount their own risk assessments, whereas the civil libertarian view refers to one particular circumstance, that of emergency. We might therefore ask: if the panic justification for the civil libertarian view is correct, why not constrain policy choices whenever officials are panicked, not just when there is an emergency, and give calm officials free rein, even if there is an emergency? Officials could be made to understand that whenever they feel fear, they are likely to discount civil liberties and exaggerate the threat.[22] When they know themselves to be afraid, they should engage in a kind of intrapersonal overcompensation and assume that their own estimate of the threat is too high. Having pushed down a risk assessment that they know to be high, they can make a rational decision even when afraid.

This *panic rule*, as we will call it—discount your own estimate of a threat if you feel fear—captures the panic theory more precisely than the civil libertarian view does. The panic rule is, in legal parlance, a *standard*; its contours are those of the underlying normative goal: prevent fear from interfering with decisionmaking. Thus, the panic rule tells officials to discount their risk assessments if and only if they feel fear. The civil libertarian position is a rule: it tells officials to discount their risk assessments if and only if there is an emergency. The fact of emergency serves as a proxy for the normative concern, that of fear.

The benefit of the panic rule is that it allows the Constitution to accommodate calm officials and requires careful constitutional scrutiny only of the decisions of those who panic. The problem is its psychological unrealism. To see this problem, suppose that third-party enforcement of the Constitution is not feasible: the officials who determine policy or law in a state of fear are the same as the officials charged with enforcing or respecting the Constitution. Executives who know that judges will defer to their foreign policy are nonetheless expected to obey the Constitution. And judges themselves may feel fear to the same degree as the decisionmakers whose laws are being reviewed in court. The panic rule asks these officials to discount their own threat assessments whenever they feel fear.

The problem with this rule is that it assumes that fearful decisionmakers can accurately determine the conditions under which they should not trust their own judgment. Suppose that some event, such as a terrorist attack, occurs, and then the question facing decisionmakers is whether to use ethnic profiling in order to attempt to prevent further attacks. If, as we must assume, the decisionmakers are afraid, then they will overestimate the probability of another terrorist attack and thus be more likely to infringe on civil liberties than they would if they were calm. Self-restraint could occur only if decisionmakers could also realize that they overestimate the risk because they are afraid. But this is psychologically unrealistic: either decisionmakers are afraid and exaggerate the risk, or they are not afraid and assess the risk accurately or with normal, unbiased error.[23]

The contrary view would have one think that officials could both believe that a threat exists and, knowing that they are afraid, doubt their own belief. But if officials take the existence of fear as an indication that they should discount their own beliefs, then why should they credit the belief that there is a threat in the first place?[24] People feel fear because they perceive a threat; they cannot step outside of themselves and doubt their own beliefs just because they know that fear can interfere with cognition. The aspiration that people should "proceed with skepticism and restraint when we know for certain that we do not know enough *and that our judgment is skewed by fear*" is at least difficult to meet and may be a psychological impossibility.[25]

## Rules

The psychological unrealism of the panic rule might be avoided through the use of a more rule-like rule, one that does not require a decisionmaker to hold incompatible beliefs. People have foresight and can design rules and institutions that will dampen the influence of panic on political outcomes. People might be able to design a rule that provides that when some event associated with panic occurs, decisionmakers should be cautious about passing laws or endorsing other political actions. The mechanism involves a distinction between the identification of conditions that can be accurately perceived and acted upon even when the subject is emotionally aroused, and the exercise of good judgment, which the emotional state precludes. Decisionmakers would, even in their fear-clouded minds, realize that they are afraid because a significant event has occurred, and thus that they should discount their own judgments or at least delay acting on them.

The condition or proxy could be an emergency described in relatively clear terms: an invasion or attack by foreign soldiers, a natural disaster, a spike in the death rate, a severe economic downturn. When these events occur, people could feel themselves committed to discounting their own assessments of risk. The rule might say that, after a terrorist attack, one should divide one's updated probability assessments by two. If people think that a subsequent attack is certain, they should discount that to 50 percent; if they think the second attack will kill millions, they should cut the estimate in half. As a result, people will be less willing to permit police to single out Arabs or Muslims for suspicion, shut down the airports, and eavesdrop on telephone calls. We will call this type of rule an *emergency rule*. It differs from the panic rule by telling officials to alter their decisionmaking processes during an emergency (which is assumed to be roughly correlated with panic) rather than telling them to alter their decisionmaking processes whenever they are in the grip of fear.

The argument depends on several assumptions, all of them troublesome. First, it must be the case that decisionmakers can, while panicking, accurately identify the conditions under which they panic, that is, they must be able to determine that their current probability estimates are made under the relevant conditions and not independently of these conditions. Decisionmakers must think "because there was a terrorist attack six months ago, my current predictions are inaccurate" and not "the terrorist attack occurred long enough ago for me to have recovered my cognitive abilities." Second, the conditions must actually be correlated with panic. If the rule is "discount one's assessment of the risks if a terrorist attack occurred within two (four? ten?) years," then it must be the case that people's assessments are exaggerated within that time frame and to a sufficient extent, and are not reasonably accurate in a substantial portion of the cases. Third, the conditions must be capable of being specified in advance with reasonable accuracy and must generate more benefits than costs. People must be able to know what kinds of events are likely to generate fear and thus interfere with probability estimates, as well as the time frame during which the effect lasts: airplane crashes, terrorist attacks, military interventions, and the like, all with their own associated time frames. If the conditions are incorrectly specified, then the rule will result in people discounting their own beliefs when they are accurate and thus failing to deliver an adequate response to an authentic emergency. But because we have so little information about how people exaggerate risks when afraid, and how much of a discount is appropriate, it is hard to believe that any rule would improve behavior.

The emergency rule also does not fully escape the psychological unrealism of intrapersonal self-restraint, which was the main flaw of the panic rule. People in the grip of fear will rationalize their decisions on the basis of their exaggerated assessment of the threat. Because the threat is significant, they will think, a compelling government interest justifies intrusions on civil liberties. Although it is possible that they choose less restrictive laws than they would under the deferential view, we doubt that officials in the grip of fear are capable of making such fine distinctions. Fear, according to the simple view endorsed by the panic thesis, focuses attention on the threat and away from civil liberties. Officials will reach for any policy that addresses the threat and are likely to find a compelling government interest in the fact of the emergency. This is the lesson of history. One can say in favor of the emergency rule that it is, with respect to psychological realism, superior to intrapersonal self-restraint. Intrapersonal self-restraint requires people to discount their own judgments, whereas the emergency rule appears to tell them to act the same—or not too differently—during emergencies as otherwise. But it is not much of an improvement.

In addition, like all rules, the emergency rule reduces decision costs through overinclusion. As well as applying to those who panic, the emergency rule applies to officials who remain calm despite the emergency, and prevents them from implementing rational policies. It also applies to fearful officials whose policies might be based on exaggerated notions of risk but still are better policies than those available under the Constitution strictly construed. A policy of detaining certain aliens, for example, may be based on an exaggerated notion of the threat but still be preferable to the status quo. If unconstrained officials choose policies that are biased against civil liberties, it remains unlikely that strictly enforcing the Constitution according to the civil libertarian view, rather than being deferential, will ensure that policies that reflect the optimal balancing of liberty and security will be chosen.

The panic rule and the emergency rule reflect different tradeoffs between discretion and overinclusion, but neither is satisfactory. The emergency rule does not, in the end, escape the charge of psychological unrealism. Both rules require people to act as if they did not believe their own judgments—the first, by recognizing that fear may hamper their judgments; the second, by recognizing relatively objective conditions associated with fear that may hamper their judgments. The first vests too much discretion in the person who, by hypothesis, cannot trust his own judgment. The second reduces discretion but then relies on the wholly unsupported claim that the objective conditions under which fear interferes with decisionmaking can be identified and specified in advance and are sufficiently correlated with periods of public and official fear.

## Insulation of Decisionmakers

The third mechanism vests emotionally disciplined people with political authority and insulates them from popular opinion. Emotionally disciplined people are less likely to panic than normal people are and thus are more likely to choose good policies if unconstrained by popular opinion; but they might rationally implement policies demanded by a panicking citizenry if the alternative is ejection from office. There are two versions of this argument. One possibility is to reduce popular accountability at all times, so that political leaders will be insulated when an emergency occurs. The other possibility is to vest authority in particular individuals when an emergency is identified or declared; for example, the president could declare an emergency, and the military would then have temporary police powers.[26] Both versions assume that the people in leadership positions—ordinary politicians in the first case, and the president (at the point of declaring the emergency) and military officials (after the emergency is declared) in the second case—will actually be calmer during an emergency than will the public. Both versions also assume that the insulation cannot be pierced by public sentiment.

These assumptions are all questionable. The U.S. Constitution already insulates political officials from popular pressures to some extent—more so than a direct democracy, for example—and it is probable that executive officials, who are constantly exposed to crises large and small, do not panic as frequently as ordinary people do. But the usual fears about relaxing constitutional protections during emergencies are based on the assumption that elected officials do panic sometimes; so the fact that they are insulated already is no comfort. Insulating them further would be perverse: it would make officials less accountable during normal times so that they would be less likely to be influenced by panicking citizens during emergencies. But that just means that civil liberties will be violated more often during times of calm. Civil libertarians don't want to reduce civil liberties during times of calm; they want government officials to respect normal constitutional barriers during emergencies.

If government officials are not willing to do that—either because they are panicking or because they need to respond rationally to a threat—then giving them greater insulation against popular fears will not improve their decisions.

It also is questionable whether elected officials can resist political pressures when citizens panic. A large part of dealing with a national emergency is to calm the fears of citizens. Government's usual response is to channel and dam up these fears rather than dismiss them as irrational. If the public believes that a threat exists, official assurances to the contrary do no good—instead, it is evidence to the public that the government is unprepared and insufficiently vigorous—and waving the Constitution at the public will not help when the public believes that the Constitution itself is being threatened.

Finally, the public does not usually choose officials on the basis of their ability to stay calm during emergencies. There are too many other relevant considerations. Most politicians are elected on the basis of their ability to deliver the goods during ordinary times. Although sometimes a politician's background contains indications of emotional discipline, the latter is not a salient issue in political contests.

What can be said for the insulation method is that it is psychologically realistic. If emotionally disciplined people can be identified in advance and given positions of authority, then it is not psychologically unrealistic to assume that they will make decisions in a calm way. Along the dimension of psychological realism, then, the insulation method dominates the other two rules. But the insulation method does much worse on the cost-benefit dimension. Insulated officials are not democratically responsive and lack essential information. This means that they are not likely to make good policy choices and that the public will not trust them with significant power. Insulation also may require constraints on the activities of the relevant officials, as we will discuss.

Federal judges are highly insulated officials in the American constitutional system. For this reason, civil libertarians argue that judges are well positioned to guard civil liberties against the excesses of panic during wartime and other emergency periods. One might argue that judges are more likely to be calm during emergencies than are officials in the political branches because of the nature of adjudication. Cases come to judges only after a time lag during which emotions may cool. Adjudication puts a premium on argument and deliberation, whereas executive officials are not compelled to deliberate and may simply issue orders. And because judges are removed from the centers of power, they might not feel as anxious about the consequences of their decisions and may therefore be able to think more clearly about the problem.

All of this might be right to some extent, but the advantages of insulation come at a very high price. Making a decision after a long delay just means that the emergency is not dealt with in a timely fashion; it would be absurd to require the political officials to wait six months before making decisions, and yet that is the effect if they must wait six months or more for judges to affirm or reject their decisions. Judges may feel less anxious because they are not fully responsible for bad policy, but this means that they may have less of an incentive to make correct decisions.

Judges themselves appear to accept this pessimistic view. American judges have almost always deferred to the executive during emergencies. The reason is apparently that the judges have done the cost-benefit balancing that the civil libertarians have neglected, and found themselves wanting. If insulation gives them the advantage of calm, the price is lack of information and lack of power. Judges do not have the information that executives have, and are reluctant to second-guess them.[27] They also do not have access to the levers of power, so they can only delay a response to an emergency by entertaining legal objections to it. They do not have such access because such power cannot be given to people who are not politically accountable. Finally, the assumption that judges are less swayed by passion than are elected officials is not obviously correct; Justice Robert H. Jackson thought that judges are equally vulnerable.[28] All of this explains why, during emergencies, judges rarely feel that they have their ordinary peacetime authority to interfere with executive decisionmaking.

Indeed, the champions of civil liberties during emergencies in American history have usually been officials in the executive or legislative branches, not the justices of the Supreme Court. During the Palmer raids, the attorney general's agenda was resisted by the acting secretary of Labor, whose approval was needed for deportations.[29] The Labor Department, unlike the Supreme Court, had the political power to block or delay deportations because its expertise about, and authority over, the regulation of immigration, gave it legitimacy. During World War II, many members of the Roosevelt administration opposed the internment of Japanese Americans, and though they could not prevent the military's decision, they ensured that the internment was carried out in as humane a fashion as possible.[30] Also, it was the Justice Department that opposed Roosevelt's schemes to squelch dissent.[31] During the cold war, although neither Truman nor Dwight D. Eisenhower took brave public stands against Senator Joseph McCarthy, they criticized his methods and tried to undermine his influence, and he was eventually defeated by opposition from high-level appointees in the executive branch and elected officials in the legislative branch. The Supreme Court was, throughout these events, largely passive, barring occasional efforts to trim the rough edges of anticommunism through indirect procedural rulings and narrow statutory construction. It did not have the political authority to oppose the executive or legislative branches during emergencies, and so it did little. The justices could not have made the case that they understood the nature of the emergency better than executive officials did. Only officials within the political branches, who could make a credible case that they had better information and motives than the opponents of civil liberties and had the proper institutional responsibility for handling the emergency, had the necessary public legitimacy.

## FEAR AND PRECOMMITMENT

The civil libertarian view relies on a simple and much criticized theory that constitutional or other rules can be properly thought of as rational (good) precommitments against emotional (bad) decisions. The old metaphor is that of Ulysses being tied to the mast so that he would not yield to the songs of the Sirens. But the analogy does not hold, as a recent literature has emphasized.[32] Because the Sirens were both irresistible and unambiguously bad, prior commitment to stay on the ship was an unambiguously good choice. In addition, Ulysses could trust his crew. Fear, though, plays a valuable role as well as a negative role; and no commitment device can be designed in advance to prevent fear from influencing behavior, nor is there reason to think that broad constitutional restrictions on executive power would produce good outcomes by reducing the influence of fear. It is perverse for a government to commit itself not to respond vigorously to emergencies. A purely rational response to a crisis sounds good in the abstract, but some motivational oomph is necessary as well, and when fear is needed to supply that motivation, constitutional restrictions on its influence can do much harm.

Legal scholars dwell on the many historical events in which fear appeared to produce bad policy choices. These are the Red Scares, the banking panics, and so forth. But there are also many cases where the absence of fear may have resulted in policies that were weak when they should have been vigorous. Here, we count the failed Weimar government before Hitler[33] and the Kerensky government before Lenin. Conventional wisdom blames unpreparedness for the 9/11 attacks not on lack of information but on bureaucratic inertia. Leading officials assessed the risks correctly but could not summon the necessary political will. Fear changed this instantly. In the United States before World War II, public complacency about American security between two oceans hamstrung public officials who were better informed. Roosevelt sought to stir up fear so as to motivate the war effort, by contrast to his effort to suppress fear during the early years of the Great Depression. His contrary actions just show how fear has both good and bad effects, and fear that can be disabling in one context may provide needed motivation in another.

## LIBERTARIAN PANICS

Earlier, in our discussion of Kuran and Sunstein's argument, we claimed that a cognitive theory of panic does not imply that security panics are differentially likely to occur; indeed, we argued that the availability heuristic could just as likely lead to libertarian panics, in which voters overestimate the threat of civil liberties violations and underestimate the security benefits of governmental policies. A similar point can be made about the noncognitive theory of panic. If people see government encroachment on their liberties as the threat—as the shadow of the tiger—they are just as likely to overreact, both in the sense of exaggerating risks and in the motivational sense. Panic can produce a widespread and unjustified suspicion of governmental responses to genuine security risks.

Overall, the mechanisms of panic have no systematic relationship to the tradeoff between security and liberty. The standard analysis observes that the mechanisms of panic may cause a society to purchase too much security and too little liberty, but the opposite is also possible and equally likely, at least in the abstract. A corollary is that a given society at a given time can undergo both security panics and libertarian panics. The former will increase the perception of risk, while the latter will reduce trust in government to prevent those risks; the net result is unclear, and it will be a sheer fortuity if the two effects cancel each other out. Although it is possible in principle that the very same institutions or social groups might undergo a security panic and a libertarian panic simultaneously, it is more likely that both types of panics occur at the same time but among different institutional or social sectors. Pointing to the existence of a security panic in one sector is not even prima facie inconsistent with the possibility of a libertarian panic in other sectors. If legislators are in the grip of a security panic, judges may be in the grip of a libertarian panic, or vice versa. We will examine these institutional implications below.

### Libertarian Panics in America

Nothing in the mechanisms of panic suggests any systematic tilt toward security panics, as opposed to libertarian panics. But do libertarian panics actually occur? We cannot offer a full historical treatment, for lack of expertise. Instead, we will briefly consider both the founding era and the period after 9/11, merely to provoke ideas and to generate plausible hypotheses for further research.

*Colonial America*  Bernard Bailyn describes the atmosphere of public opinion in colonial America after 1763 in the following terms:

> [The colonists] saw about them, with increasing clarity, not merely mistaken, or even evil, policies violating the principles upon which freedom rested, but what appeared to be evidence of nothing less than a deliberate assault launched surreptitiously by plotters against liberty both in England and in America. . . . This belief transformed the meaning of the colonists' struggle, and it added an inner accelerator to the movement of opposition. For, once assumed, it could not be easily dispelled: denial only confirmed it, since what conspirators profess is not what they believe; the ostensible is not the real; and the real is deliberately malign.

It was this—the overwhelming evidence, as they saw it, that they were faced with conspirators against liberty determined at all costs to gain ends which their words belied—that was signaled to the colonists after 1763, and it was this above all else that in the end propelled them into revolution.[34]

Bailyn emphasizes that this widespread, and wildly overheated, suspicion and mistrust of the British colonial administration "rose in the consciousness of a large segment of the American population before any of the famous political events of the struggle with England took place." The 1763 Stamp Act was "a danger signal":

> For though it could be argued, and in a sense proved by the swift repeal of the act, that nothing more was involved than ignorance or confusion on the part of people in power who really knew better and who, once warned by the reaction of the colonists, would not repeat the mistake—though this could be, and by many was, concluded, there nevertheless appeared to be good reason to suspect that more was involved.[35]

If Bailyn is right, then the very American Revolution itself[36] might be described as the consequence of a widespread and sustained libertarian panic, or perhaps a wave of serial panics. Bailyn does little to identify the mechanisms that produced the founding era libertarian panics; of course, that is not his chief concern. It takes little imagination, however, to see the mechanisms of panic at work. A social-scientific version of Bailyn's treatment might suggest that the colonists focused obsessively on highly salient or available episodes of government oppression, whether or not those episodes were representative of British policy; neglected the probabilities of an antilibertarian conspiracy, focusing solely on what consequences it would have if it did materialize; and polarized, through group discussion and other social mechanisms, toward an extremist libertarian viewpoint.

*The PATRIOT Act Panic* Let us provide a bookend to the founding era by examining the reaction, particularly among intellectuals and other segments of the elite public, to statutes and administrative policies created after 9/11 to reduce terrorism risks. The subject is heterogeneous; for convenience, we will focus on the most salient component of terrorism policy, the USA PATRIOT Act of 2001, though we should also mention the overreaction to revelations that the National Security Agency (NSA) wiretaps communications between Americans and suspected terrorists abroad: 21 percent of Americans believe it very likely or somewhat likely that the NSA has listened in on their telephone conversations.[37] As for the PATRIOT Act, many civil libertarians denounced it in apocalyptic terms. Since 9/11, some 360 local communities and 4 states have passed ordinances calling the act a fundamental retrenchment of American civil liberties.[38] Much popular and academic commentary takes an equally lurid line.[39]

Many of these claims can only be described as ignorant; many are also irrational, even hysterical. The most common mistake is a sort of baseline error. Civil libertarians ascribe to the PATRIOT Act "deprivations" of civil liberties as measured from some baseline set of entitlements that either never existed, or that was changed in the relevant respects long before the PATRIOT Act was passed.

Here are some examples of baseline error. First, consider one of the act's most controversial provisions, the so-called sneak-and-peek provision (section 213). The provision allows the required notice to the target of a search warrant to be delayed for a reasonable period, if a court finds reasonable cause for doing so. Local ordinances and public statements by libertarian advocacy groups have denounced the provision as a fundamental curtailment of civil liberties;[40] the ACLU claimed that it marks a "sea change in the way search warrants are executed in the United States."[41] The problem is that the provision merely codifies preexisting settled law. As of 1979, the Supreme Court had already described the argument that notice could not be delayed as "frivolous."[42]

Second, consider section 215 of the act, which allows and indeed requires courts to issue subpoenas for business records in national security investigations. Many have denounced the provision as a mechanism of governmental oppression. Yet the provision codifies a power that grand juries (typically dominated by prosecutors) have long exercised without judicial oversight. Measured from that baseline, as opposed to some imaginary libertarian one, the addition of judicial subpoenas looks no worse, and possibly better, from the point of view of targets and defendants.

The most critical example of baseline error, however, involves the complaint that the PATRIOT Act authorizes the Orwellian electronic surveillance of persons who are suspected of posing a threat to national security.[43] The problem is that this practice predated the act by more than a quarter century. Before 1978, security agencies engaged in electronic surveillance of suspected national security threats without any judicial restriction. The Foreign Intelligence Surveillance Act of 1978 (FISA) provided that security agencies would have to apply to the courts for wiretap warrants, but the applications were secret, and the FISA left in place the standard rule that warrant applications would proceed ex parte, without notice to the person under surveillance.[44] The PATRIOT Act's only significant contribution to the law in this area is section 218, which eliminated administrative and judicial interpretations of the FISA that had created a wall of separation between the information held by counterintelligence officials and that held by law enforcement officials. But most of the FISA was in place long before the PATRIOT Act; and the FISA itself represents a libertarian, rights-protective regime, relative to the pre-1978 legal baseline.

Overall, then, the reaction to the PATRIOT Act among journalists, public commentators, and academics was grossly out of proportion to its real effect. The next question is why such a systematic error of public perception has occurred. Future sociological work might trace and specify the mechanisms that have created this libertarian panic. In addition to individual-level cognitive failures, such as baseline error, it seems plausible to hypothesize that social mechanisms have been in play, including various forms of polarization, herding, and cascades among the state governments, legal elites, and libertarian intellectuals who have condemned the PATRIOT Act in strong terms.

## A Note on Domestic Surveillance

Relevant in this connection is the widespread legislative and public criticism of the Bush administration's domestic surveillance program, under which the National Security Agency monitored international communications to or

from the United States initiated by suspected members of al Qaeda and affili-
ated terrorist organizations.[45] The program, when discovered, was instantly
denounced by critics. The problem is that it is hardly clear that the program
is illegal at all; the issues are difficult. The president claimed that this category
of communications was enemy "signal intelligence" and its interception an
ordinary and traditional incident of warfare, in which case the surveillance
was arguably authorized by the post-9/11 joint resolution (the "Authorization for Use of Military Force" or AUMF) authorizing the use of all "necessary and appropriate" force against al Qaeda. That argument is supported by
the holding in *Hamdi* that the AUMF authorizes detention of enemy combatants as a traditional executive power under the laws of war, but it is also
undermined by Justice Stevens's holding in *Hamdan* that the AUMF does not
authorize military commissions to try charges of conspiracy, in part because
such charges were historically unprecedented in the laws of war. *Hamdi* and
*Hamdan* are in tension on this point; if they can be reconciled it is with the
claim that the AUMF authorizes all and only those implicit executive powers
that are traditional under the laws of war, which might well include signal
intelligence.

To be sure, even if interception of signal intelligence is authorized by the
AUMF, it might be prohibited by some other law. However, the statute supposed by critics to prohibit the program, the Foreign Intelligence Surveillance
Act, is complex and contains gaps that might be used to support the program
or some of its components. Here much depends on factual details about how
exactly the surveillance is carried out, details that are not public and perhaps
could not be made public without destroying the intelligence value of the
program itself. Even if the program is barred by FISA, the administration has
argued that the AUMF might be taken to have implicitly repealed FISA on
this point, although a similar argument was made and rejected in *Hamdan*.
Apart from precedent, the critics say that the more specific provisions of FISA
restricting surveillance trump the general provisions of the AUMF, but the latter is actually more specific on another dimension: it only applies to al Qaeda
and other individuals or groups who have helped al Qaeda, and thus can reasonably be understood to implicitly repeal FISA in that limited setting. Finally,
even if FISA bars the program and has not been implicitly repealed, lower-
court case law might reasonably be taken to suggest that FISA might then be
unconstitutional as a violation of the president's constitutional powers.[46] The
Fourth Amendment arguments are also unclear, for both sides.

The legal issues are murky, and reasonable people can disagree, despite the
critics' overheated denunciations. What is striking, however, is the genuine

perception in some quarters that the program was a blatant violation of law.[47] The perception stoked the opposition to the PATRIOT Act's renewal. We conjecture that the ominous, Nixonian overtones of surveillance and wiretapping contributed to a public perception that the program was far more sinister, and far less legitimate, than it actually was. This is another example of a consequential libertarian panic.

## How Frequent Are Libertarian Panics?

We have not attempted to show either that libertarian panics are frequent in American history, or that they are as frequent as security panics. A full historical investigation, equal in scope and detail to Geoffrey Stone's indispensable history of security panics,[48] would be needed to document either of those claims. What we have attempted to show is that libertarian panics (1) are conceptually possible and (2) have occurred at important moments of our history.

It remains possible that security panics occur more frequently, and more intensely, than libertarian panics; the issue is empirical and cannot be resolved through a priori reasoning. People panic easily at the thought that terrorists are trying to kill them, but they also panic easily at the thought that jack-booted government thugs are coming for them. It bears emphasis, moreover, that no conclusions about optimal institutional design are possible without estimating the relative frequency and gravity of both security panics and libertarian panics. The civil libertarian view cannot be justified simply by documenting a long history of security panics. Unless and until an equally thorough history of libertarian panics is done, we just do not know the relative expected magnitude of the two effects, and the institutional-design assumptions of the standard model are unjustified.

## Law and Institutions

Suppose there are libertarian panics. What follows? The risk of security panics is said to justify legal doctrines or institutional arrangements that place a drag on liberty-restricting governmental action. These rules act as second-best constraints that limit the frequency and gravity of unjustified restrictions on liberty. If there are libertarian panics, however, then the legal and institutional calculus is more complicated. In addition to unjustified restrictions on liberty, we must be concerned about inadequate restrictions on liberty. The very legal rules and institutional arrangements that minimize the first type of error will exacerbate the second type of error. The net result depends on facts about the relative risks and magnitudes of the two types of error, and we can say little about this in the abstract. It seems clear, however, that optimal legal rules and institutional arrangements will certainly be less libertarian than they would be if security panics were the only type of panic in the picture.

## Second-Best Libertarianism

Let us turn to the role of security panics in the security-liberty tradeoff that we introduced in chapter 1. In the most sophisticated version of the argument, decisionmakers who are subject to security panics ought not to engage directly in balancing that attempts to strike the optimal tradeoff between liberty and security. Those decisionmakers will predictably skew their judgments in favor of security, resulting in excessively restrictive policies ("excessively" from the standpoint of the social welfare function that defines the optimal tradeoff).

The institutional solution, on this view, is to deny frontline decisionmakers the authority to engage in direct or first-order balancing of liberty and security. The preferred alternative is second-order balancing, under which civil liberties are overprotected through second-best rules that mitigate the risk of error in the first-order calculus.[49] Consider the Court's development of overprotective restrictions on government's ability to punish political speech. An all-things-considered first-order optimization or balancing approach to political speech that threatens social harms would "ask whether the gravity of the evil, discounted by its improbability [*sic*], justifies such invasion of free speech as is necessary to avoid the danger."[50] Doctrines holding that legislation must be content neutral, and that government may only punish political speech that "imminently" incites unlawful action,[51] build in a skew that compensates for predictable decisionmaker error in the application of the first-order balancing test. As the example shows, the argument for second-order balancing goes beyond an abstract claim that rules may correct for the errors that decisionmakers commit under first-order balancing. In this setting, the argument for second-order balancing is an argument not only for rules, but for rules with a distinctly libertarian slant—a kind of *second-best libertarianism*. The idea is to build into the second-order rules a skew in favor of liberty that will compensate for predictable pressures toward overweighting security—pressures such as security panics.

## Two Types of Errors

Given the possibility of libertarian panics, second-best libertarianism is simplistic. Doctrines and institutions that compensate for the distorting effect of security panics (relative to the optimum that a perfect first-order balancer would identify) will exacerbate the distorting effect of libertarian panics. The argument for second-best libertarianism focuses exclusively on one type of error—excessive security induced by security panics—and ignores another type of error, excessive liberty induced by libertarian panics.

Consider two institutional solutions for the problem of security panics.[52] The first suggestion involves internal congressional procedures intended to create a barrier against panicky legislation restricting civil liberties. For example, "Congress could enact a rule prohibiting it from enacting wartime legislation without full and fair deliberation."[53] The second suggestion is for a "protocol [that] might require any wartime legislation limiting civil liberties to contain a 'sunset' provision."[54] The assumption common to such suggestions is that "[a]nything that slows the process, allows for greater deliberation, and limits the potential scope and impact of hastily enacted legislation limiting civil liberties is salutary."[55] In chapter 5, we will examine proposals by Bruce Ackerman, along similar lines, for framework legislation to govern future emergencies.

There are many possible lines of objection here. Such protocols, which are not entrenched in the Constitution, may themselves be overridden by panicked legislators so, given the diagnosis of security panics, the remedy may be a nonstarter.[56] And the two suggestions are in some tension with each other, as the knowledge that a given law contains a sunset proviso lowers the stakes of enacting it and may thus detract from the very legislative deliberation that the first protocol is meant to encourage.[57]

The possibility of libertarian panics supports a different objection, however. To the extent that libertarian panics occur, then the danger is that the political system will produce too little legislation restricting civil liberties, rather than too much. Institutional protocols or arrangements that further raise the cost of enacting restrictions on civil liberties will push the system further away from the optimum, not (as the assumption runs) closer to it. Legislators forced by internal protocols to enact less liberty-restricting legislation than they otherwise would will merely underprotect security all the more, from the standpoint of the social optimum.

To be sure, the precise shape of the optimal institutional rules will depend upon the relative frequency and gravity of the two types of errors. If libertarian panics are rare and mild, a diluted second-best libertarianism might still be appropriate. But if libertarian panics are as frequent and powerful as security panics, then the optimal rules will be those suggested by first-order balancing; there will be no reason to introduce a second-order skew to compensate for errors in either direction. We can even imagine, on certain facts, a case for *second-best authoritarianism*: if libertarian panics are more frequent and powerful than security panics, then second-order institutional design would do well to build in a compensating skew that would push outcomes in the direction of less liberty and more security.

## CONCLUSION

The theory that emotion, and especially fear, interferes with government decisionmaking is an important one, and it has not received sufficient attention in the academic literature. There are many difficult issues. First, fear may improve decisionmaking, or it may worsen it, or it may do both, in different circumstances. No one knows what the truth is. Second, even if fear interferes with the judgment of ordinary people, including voters, government officials may be experienced enough to overcome fear and decide rationally and to resist political pressure by fearful citizens to implement bad policy. Third, even if fear influences both government officials and ordinary people, and results in bad policy, the bad policy is not necessarily inconsistent with civil liberties. There may be libertarian panics as well as security panics. Fourth, even if the bad policy is consistently antilibertarian, it is doubtful that institutional fixes—such as judicial enforcement of constitutional rights—can halt bad policy without also interfering with good policy.

All of this raises the question of why so many people insist that government actions during emergencies reflect fear rather than rational judgment under conditions of great uncertainty, and to such an extent that they believe that constitutional adjudication would improve emergency-related security measures. One reason might be that governments often seem to take draconian measures during emergencies and then pull back subsequently, as though to acknowledge that the original measures were erroneous. But it is not clear that this is a good description of history: did the U.S. government overreact to Pearl Harbor or underreact to the earlier invasion of Manchuria? Did it overreact to the September 11 attacks, or did it underreact to the earlier embassy bombings in Africa? Even if it is a good description, error does not imply irrationality or emotion or bias, any more than it implies nefarious motives, as Bailyn's colonists thought. It may well be rational for governments to react harshly at the start of an emergency, and then to adjust policies as time reveals whether the original reactions were warranted.[58] With the benefit of hindsight, the early reactions might seem inexplicable except as the result of panic. But this does not do justice to the problem that the government faces at the time of emergency, when uncertainty is great and the consequence of error may be catastrophic. That such adjustments occur does not show that the original reactions were unjustified nor that, looking forward, we should try to prevent our government from vigorous reactions to future emergencies.

Another reason is that there is no doubt that during emergencies the emotions of the public are heightened. But, as we have explained, it is a mistake to equate heightened public anxiety with panic. An emotionally aroused public may be a better, rather than worse, monitor of the government.

Civil libertarians, like Bailyn's colonists, seek hidden explanations for governmental action that they do not like and understand. The colonists indulged in conspiracy theories and found their explanation for the mild British infringements on civil liberties in a theory of tyrannical intentions—what we would today describe as excessive agency slack and executive despotism. But today, Americans live in a democracy; executive power is constrained by politics in important ways (as we discussed in chapter 1); and it is hard to accuse officials of a tyrannical agenda when their security measures are endorsed by the public. Thus, the explanation for these measures seems to require a theory of mass hysteria. But this explanation does not turn out to be plausible.

# CHAPTER THREE

# The Democratic Failure Theory

In this chapter, we consider a central theme of the civil libertarian view of emergencies. The argument is that malfunctions in the political system will cause emergency policies to systematically harm the interests of political, ethnic, or ideological minorities. Of course, in a partially majoritarian democracy, minorities will often lose. Yet those who advance this argument have something more specific in mind. Self-interested majorities will cause government policy to provide too much security, relative to an impartial baseline somehow defined, because those majorities do not bear the full costs of increased security. Rather, democratic majorities partially externalize the costs of increased security onto minorities. "[A]s almost always happens, the individuals whose rights are sacrificed are not those who make the laws, but minorities, dissidents and noncitizens. In those circumstances, 'we' are making a decision to sacrifice 'their' rights—not a very prudent way to balance the competing interests."[1] We dub this view and its variants the *democratic failure theory*.

In chapter 1, we suggested that rational and well-motivated governments will provide more security as threats increase. On what grounds might one want constitutional rules to block this shift? Here, we bracket the possibility, discussed in chapter 2, that governments will act irrationally due to panic or other decisionmaking pathologies that afflict officials or voters. A different class of arguments, which is our focus here, suggests that government will act rationally, but not to maximize the welfare of the whole polity. Government will wholly or partially externalize the costs of security onto nonvoters or other politically unrepresented groups. The structure of representation will thus cause government to provide too much security, from the social point of view.

On several counts, however, the democratic failure theory is puzzling, and our aim here is to express skepticism about it. First, it is not clear what the account has to do with emergencies. The structures of voting and representation that are said to produce democratic failure are the same in both emergencies and normal times. Perhaps an emergency causes a loss for society as a whole. But it is still unclear why the new, post–emergency equilibrium will be relatively worse for the minority than was the old, pre–emergency equilibrium; the minority should get the same proportional slice of the social product it had before, albeit from a smaller pie. The possibility that a majority will externalize costs onto nonvoters or other minorities is just a general structural charge against democratic decisionmaking, one that can apply at any time, not merely in times of emergency or terrorist threat. There is little evidence, and no theoretical reason to believe, that democratic failure is more likely in emergencies. Indeed, there is some evidence that minorities fare especially well in times of emergency, because government has more need of their contributions. Emergencies have often been an engine of progressive government and policy reform.

Second, just as the democratic failure theory is not really tied to emergencies, so too it does not necessarily imply that government will provide excessive security. Political distortions may arise whenever the majority does not bear the full costs of its policies; when this occurs, public goods will be supplied at the wrong levels. But security is just one public good among others. Another such good is liberty, which depends upon government provision of the public goods that protect liberty, such as law enforcement.[2] It is equally consistent with the democratic failure theory that majorities will cause government to supply excessive liberty—insufficient regulation of terrorist threats—when majorities do not bear the full expected costs of terrorism, perhaps because those costs are concentrated in particular areas. Majorities may externalize the costs of liberty as well as the costs of security.

The best construal of the democratic failure theory is that it is not really about security policy in times of emergency. On this version, the account just applies during emergencies the standard approach of representation-reinforcing judicial review, derived from the Supreme Court's famous *Carolene Products* opinion[3] and the work of John Hart Ely.[4] Courts should presumptively require government to proceed through general laws and policies, as opposed to narrowly targeted ones. Government action directed against dissenters, the disenfranchised, or discrete and insular groups among the citizenry should be strictly scrutinized to smoke out animus or opportunistic scapegoating of ideological, political, or ethnic minorities, and this is true in both emergencies and normal times.

We will suggest, however, that the *Carolene Products* framework misfires during times of war or other emergency, whatever its value in ordinary settings. Here, aliens and citizens present different cases. Where resident aliens and other de jure nonvoters are concerned, there is a serious problem, well known in democratic theory and elsewhere, that affects the democratic failure theory. Why should the interests of resident aliens be included in the social welfare function that, in the democratic failure theory, provides the baseline for measuring political distortion? After all, many governmental decisions affect the interests of residents of Canada, or China, despite their lack of representation in the American political system. The puzzle is why the interests of resident aliens should be deemed to be as weighty as those of citizens, while the interests of nonresident aliens need not be. These problems exist during normal times, but are much accentuated during times of emergency, when the status and regulation of aliens become a more pressing problem.

Where political or ethnic minorities among the citizenry are concerned, the problem of defining the scope of the demos does not arise, but other problems remain. When faced with government action during emergencies, the costs of the searching judicial review recommended by *Carolene Products* increase, often to unacceptable levels. Smoking out government animus or opportunism requires information that the judges do not have in times of emergency; the costs of judicial mistakes are higher, because judicial invalidation of a policy necessary for national security may have disastrous consequences; and the sheer delay created by vigorous judicial review is more costly as well, because in emergencies time is at a premium. The judges know all of this, which is why they defer heavily to government in times of emergency, even with respect to policies that democratic failure theorists find, in hindsight, to be infected with animus or opportunism.

The upshot is that the *Carolene Products* approach should neither be accepted nor rejected wholesale; much depends upon the political setting and upon the nature of the groups and interests at issue. Emergencies strain the *Carolene Products* framework, and in some places the framework cannot hold up. At the retail level, we will propose the following views: (1) we will accept for the sake of argument that *Carolene Products* is a sensible approach to judicial review of laws affecting citizens in normal times; (2) we suggest that *Carolene Products* cannot justify genuine heightened scrutiny—nondeferential review—of laws affecting citizens in times of emergency and that the judges will predictably refuse to engage in such scrutiny even if it were desirable; and (3) we are skeptical that *Carolene Products* can coherently be applied to laws affecting aliens and other persons who are not members of the political community, either in times of emergency or in normal times. The problem of the boundaries of the political community is, however, most serious in times of emergency, when the regulation of aliens becomes a more pressing issue.

We will begin with some conceptual preliminaries. We define *democratic failure* and contest the assumption, common to the theories we examine, that there is a necessary link between democratic failure and excessive security. We suggest that the democratic failure theory cannot uniquely predict excessive government provision of security; self-interested majorities may also provide excessive levels of other public goods, including liberty. Just as political distortions in normal times cause government to supply inadequate regulation of firearms and other dangerous goods, so too in times of emergency political distortions may cause insufficient protection of minorities' security, perhaps by the inadequate regulation of terrorist threats whose expected costs fall disproportionately on minorities.

We then examine two different versions of the democratic failure theory, which hold different views about the relationship between democratic failure and emergencies. In the first version, democratic failure is especially likely in times of emergency. We question this view. Even on the internal logic of the theory, democratic failure is not more likely in times of emergency. If the structure of voting and representation causes government to act on behalf of a majority rather than on behalf of all, this is equally true during normal times and during emergencies. An emergency is just an exogenous shock that reduces the size of the social pie but that need not change the proportions of the pie that are enjoyed by different groups. There is little historical evidence that democratic failure is especially likely in times of emergency; to the contrary, emergencies have often bettered the position of minorities, because government has greater need of their political, economic, and military contributions.

We then turn to a different (and, in our view, better) version of the democratic failure theory. On this version, democratic failure is no more likely in emergencies than in normal times, but no less likely either. The same *Carolene Products* framework that applies during normal times applies during emergencies. General laws are presumptively valid, because they force majorities to internalize the social costs of their actions, but policies or laws that target racial, ethnic, or political minorities should be given strict scrutiny and are presumptively invalid.

As against this view, we suggest that the standard *Carolene Products* approach comes unglued during times of emergency. Judges face a risk of committing errors in two directions: they may erroneously validate policies that stem from democratic failure, or they may erroneously invalidate measures necessary for national security. The risks and costs of the first type of error are constant across both normal times and emergencies, but in emergencies the risks and costs of the second type of error spike upward. In times of emergency, the judges' information is especially poor, their ability to sort justified from unjustified policies especially limited, and the cost of erroneously blocking necessary security measures may be disastrous. Included among those costs is the cost of delay, which amounts to a temporary blockage of new policies and which is especially serious during emergencies, where time is all. In general, the difference in the stakes between emergencies and normal times makes the limited capacities of judges decisive. Historically, the judges themselves have recognized this, remaining quiescent until the emergency decays and passes by. In times of emergency, judicial deference is both desirable and predictable, given the high stakes and the judges' limited information and competence.

These institutional points apply to both citizens and aliens, but we will also consider the distinctive problems that resident aliens pose for the democratic failure theory. We suggest that resident aliens are, if anything, less likely to be subjected to arbitrary discrimination than are discrete and insular subgroups among the citizenry. If aliens lack the vote, they possess an exit option that citizens realistically do not; the structure of the international order will constrain majoritarian oppression of aliens; and aliens' welfare will itself be a component of the majority's welfare, which government is assumed to maximize on the democratic failure theory.

## THE DEMOCRATIC FAILURE THEORY

The democratic failure theory differs from the panic account, considered in chapter 2. The democratic failure theory accepts that government officials are rational and that they act as agents for a majority of citizen-voters, who are also rational. (Later, we expand upon our discussion of executive despotism in chapter 1 by discussing the possibility that officials enjoy agency slack.) What is distinctive is a further assumption: the citizen-voters are not only rational, but self-interested, and this causes their governmental agents to supply security policies that benefit the majority at the expense of political, ideological, or ethnic minorities. Government chooses security policy rationally, but its goal is to maximize the welfare of current democratic majorities, rather than the overall welfare of the polity. From the social point of view, government acts rationally but not in a well-motivated fashion.

There are several important variants of this theory. One dimension of variation involves the identity of the relevant majorities and minorities. Sometimes, "the majority" refers to political majorities: citizens who are also voters make up the majority, and those who cannot vote make up the minority. Although the class of nonvoters includes some citizens, such as children and (in some states) ex-felons, the emphasis in this version is typically upon resident aliens, illegal immigrants, and other outsider groups who are formally barred from the franchise. Here, an important claim is that security policy after 9/11 has imposed large and differential burdens upon aliens and immigrants; according to this view, the disenfranchisement of these groups ensures that majoritarian politics will not adequately represent their interests. The voting majority instead externalizes all or part of the costs of security. For example, consider the detention of illegal immigrants on security grounds; the presidential order establishing military commissions, which applied only to noncitizens; the PATRIOT Act's special provisions for noncitizens; and the treatment of aliens detained at Guantanamo Bay.

In another version, "minority" refers to some ethnic or racial minority, such as Arab Americans, and "majority" refers (usually implicitly) to whites. Here, the claim, although usually implicit, is that ethnic minorities are formally entitled to vote, but they lack effective political power, ensuring that democratic decisionmaking will not adequately weigh their interests. After 9/11, on this view, new security policies have imposed differential burdens on minorities. Consider the possibility that federal officials have been engaging in ethnic profiling in airport screenings and other security-related searches, or the FBI's program of interviewing noncitizen ethnic Arabs who might pose security risks. The sometime emphasis on ethnic minorities blurs the boundaries between the panic account and the democratic failure theory. To the extent that security policies such as ethnic profiling are said to embody invidious discrimination, rather than statistically rational discrimination, democratic failure may stem from irrational standing passions and ethnic animus.

There is some overlap between these two versions of the democratic failure theory. Important policies after 9/11 have applied only to noncitizens, yet within that category have focused on ethnic minorities. Examples, some of which we have previously touched upon, include the special registration program, now defunct, which required aliens in the United States from a designated list of (almost exclusively) Muslim nations to register with the INS; the Absconder Initiative, under which aliens from nations with substantial al Qaeda presence were targeted for removal; and Operation Liberty Shield, which subjects asylum applicants from such nations to mandatory detentions.[5] Such programs combine the selective regulation of noncitizens with the selective regulation of Arabs or Muslims or both.

If the diagnosis is democratic failure, what is the prescription? Either in the case of noncitizen nonvoters, such as resident or temporary aliens, or in the case of dissenters or ethnic minorities among the citizenry, the democratic failure theory applies or adapts to emergencies the idea of representation-reinforcing judicial review of democratic decisionmaking, stemming from *Carolene Products*. If government cannot be trusted to engage in the ordinary balancing of security and liberty, because systematic distortions produce excessive levels of security, judges should develop rules that produce a kind of second-order balancing. The aim of these second-order rules is to push governmental decisions on the security-liberty tradeoff back toward the optimum. One prescription is the prophylactic overprotection of free speech, although this is typically tied to the panic account, which supposes that emergencies will produce a "pathological perspective"[6] that causes government officials to overregulate political speech. For the democratic failure theory, the crucial prescription is *generality*: laws must apply generally to all affected classes of citizens or persons, in order to ensure that majorities do not impose selective burdens that voters would be unwilling to bear themselves. In Justice Jackson's words, "there is no more effective practical guaranty against arbitrary and unreasonable government than to require that the principles of law which officials would impose upon a minority must be imposed generally."[7] In our terms, generality ensures that democratic majorities internalize the costs of government policies.

It is not clear, however, what the *Carolene Products* framework has to do with emergencies; it is a standard framework for judicial review in normal times on purely domestic issues. Theories of democratic failure often leave the connections among emergencies, democracy, and *Carolene Products* review unspecified or opaque. We may distinguish three possible views, as follows:

1. Judicial review should be stricter in emergencies than in normal times. This is a straightforward entailment of the panic account, which theorists frequently run together with the democratic failure theory. In the pure form of the democratic failure theory, however, it is unclear why democratic failure should be more worrisome in times of emergency. The basic mechanism of democratic failure— the mismatch between formal voting rights or de facto political influence, on the one hand, and the population whose welfare government should promote, on the other—exists both in emergencies and in normal times. Democratic failure theorists seem to worry that majorities will scapegoat minorities during emergencies or seize on an emergency to harm minorities in opportunistic fashion, but that worry lacks a direct connection to the mechanisms of distortion that these theorists typically adduce. We expand upon these puzzles below.

2. Judicial review should be equally strict in emergencies and in normal times. This does not follow from the panic view, which supposes that governmental decisionmaking suffers from special distortions in times of emergency. The democratic failure theory might best be understood to adopt this position, however; the account would cheerfully concede that there is nothing special about emergencies. It is just that the same representation-reinforcing approach still applies in times of emergency. We suggest below that this is the best version of the democratic failure theory. But if it is, then democratic failure is not a distinctive lens through which to view security policy.

3. Judicial review should be less strict, more accommodating, or more deferential in emergencies than in normal times. Courts cannot systematically improve upon government's first-order balancing of security and liberty. Whatever hope they have of doing so in normal times, as in ordinary criminal settings where security and liberty trade off against each other, is dramatically attenuated during times of emergency, because the judges' information is especially poor and the costs of judicial mistakes are especially high.

Our view is that position 3 is correct and that positions 1 and 2 are wrong. One might claim that this view attacks a straw man. On this claim, even the most vociferous critics of judicial passivity during emergencies agree that judges should be more deferential during emergencies than during normal times; the critics' complaint is only that judges go too far and are more deferential than circumstances warrant. We agree that this is a possible reading of the critics, though they are hardly clear on this point. However, their relentless assault on the history of judicial deference during emergencies suggests that, if they do think that judges should be more deferential during emergencies than during normal times, then they believe that emergency-level deference should still be low. Our view, by contrast, is that emergency-level deference should be high, as high as it has in fact been. It is impossible to quantify this difference or describe it with specificity, of course; but the practical implications are clear. The critics think that history shows that judges have exercised too much deference; we think that history shows that judges have acted correctly. The critics urge judges to strike down post-9/11 Bush administration policies; we think that judges should defer, as they always have done, though we have no view about whether these policies are correct.

Note that the strictness of judicial review refers to the actual level of deference to government that judges afford, rather than to the nominal rules of scrutiny that judges employ. We may illustrate with the case of nongeneral laws that impose differential burdens on ethnic minorities or aliens. Suppose that judges apply some form of strict or at least heightened scrutiny to such laws in normal times, but admit an exception for cases in which government has an especially important or compelling interest. In times of emergency, judges might say either that nongeneral laws receive reduced scrutiny, or that nongeneral laws are to receive the "same" heightened scrutiny that they would receive in normal times. But even the latter position could be compatible with increased deference to government, if judges recognize a broader range of compelling government interests in emergencies than in normal times. In what follows, we will focus solely on the operational level of judicial deference to government (as we discussed in chapter 1), which may be either high or low, rather than on the nominal rules.

For completeness, we will mention several further complications surrounding the democratic failure theory. The first issue involves the standard question of whether democratic failure should be measured against a welfarist baseline or against some nonwelfarist theory of rights. For the reasons discussed in chapter 1, we will state the democratic failure argument in welfarist terms. This need not be a sectarian or contentious assumption, nor does it produce a major distortion of the arguments. For one thing, rights are themselves an important component of welfare; more important, the differences between welfarist and nonwelfarist accounts of rights are not relevant to the issues we discuss. Differences between foundational theories of rights rarely make a difference to the institutional issues surrounding emergencies and democratic failure, so our welfarist statement of the theory is just an expository convenience.

Second, the democratic failure theory is sometimes combined with a concern about the ratchet effects of security policies. "The argument that we are only targeting aliens' rights, and therefore citizens need not worry, is in an important sense illusory, for what we do to aliens today provides a precedent for what can and will be done to citizens tomorrow."[8] We critique ratchets and some related ideas in chapter 4 and ignore the issue here.

Third, some strands of the democratic failure theory emphasize that laws and policies should be "general." Is this the same as the *Carolene Products* approach? We will treat praise for generality as a minor variant of *Carolene Products*. Generality cannot be taken literally; a statute that applies only to a very small class C is fine, not even presumptively bad, so long as there is some normatively valid reason to target C. The rationale for the classification is still general, in the sense that it would apply to anyone similarly situated. (The Supreme Court once said that a statute applying only to Richard

Nixon defined "a legitimate class of one."[9]) Generality, by itself, has no normative appeal: "[r]acial, religious and all manner of discrimination are not only compatible [with] but often institutionalized by general rules."[10] The question is what counts as a valid reason for targeting or selectively burdening a subgroup, and the appeal to generality does not help with that question. The real worry is that the relevant class will be defined along prejudiced or invidious lines, according to some entirely independent theory of prejudice or invidiousness. A theory of judicial review under which judges should ensure the generality of laws and policies is either untenable or else morphs into a theory of judicial review that aims to weed out prejudiced or invidious laws and policies. That is the core of the *Carolene Products* enterprise, which we examine below.

Fourth, we will assume that *Carolene Products* review applies equally to statutes and to executive action under constitutional or statutory authority. *Carolene Products* is concerned with a form of majoritarian distortion; it is not concerned with whether the source of the distortion is an elected legislature or an elected executive. For historical reasons the main focus of *Carolene Products* theory has been majoritarian distortions arising in representative legislatures, but this is inessential; the same arguments apply, with appropriate modifications, to executive action. Indeed, in our system, the presidency is in one sense more majoritarian than Congress; the latter is an aggregation of local majorities, whereas the president is (barring the low chance that the Electoral College affects the outcome) elected by a national majority.

Finally, the democratic failure theory can be combined with a concern about agency slack between voting majorities and government officials. Instead of emphasizing cost externalization by self-interested majorities acting through tightly constrained agents, one might emphasize the risk that officials who enjoy agency slack will opportunistically promote their individual or institutional interests; perhaps such officials would even use their freedom to harm political or ethnic minorities. Here, too, it is not clear how much this variant adds. If the principal worry is that autonomous officials will scapegoat minorities to augment their individual or institutional power, then the presupposition must be that there is some preexisting susceptibility to political or ethnic hatred among the population, and it does not very much matter whether that hatred vents itself through majorities acting through their agents or through autonomous officials generating or exploiting the hatred for self-interested reasons. Either way, excessive security is the problem, not the precise mechanism that produces it; and in any event the focus on popular emotions shades into the panic account again. In what follows, we will note these shadings and variants when relevant, but will focus on the most straightforward version of the democratic failure theory, under which rationally self-interested officials act as agents for rationally self-interested majorities.

## WHAT IS DEMOCRATIC FAILURE?

What exactly is a "democratic failure"? Here, we will begin by offering a simple definition that is presupposed by the theories we examine. We then suggest that democratic failure theories focus too narrowly on the risk that government will excessively reduce the liberties of minorities while providing too much security to the public. In fact, the democratic failure theory does not necessarily predict that government will supply too much security. It is equally possible, given the theory, that a government pandering to self-interested majorities will supply minorities with too much liberty or inadequate security.

### Democratic Failure: A Definition

To identify a democratic failure, one needs to know what counts as a "democratic success." In welfarist terms, the following benchmark is common. Imagine a society with a political system that implements policies that affect the welfare of citizens. Certain policies would, if implemented, be Pareto improving: they would make at least one person better off while making no one else worse off. The political system either does or does not implement these policies. If it does, there is a democratic success; if it does not, there is a democratic failure.

The Pareto standard is too austere for a real government, however. Virtually no policy can survive that standard. We might, then, define success more loosely: a *democratic success* occurs when laws are passed that enhance overall welfare. A *democratic failure* occurs when such laws are not passed, or when laws are passed that reduce overall welfare. Defining a social welfare function that aggregates across persons is notoriously difficult—that is why the conceptually simpler Pareto standard is usually used—but we will stipulate, roughly, that overall welfare increases when a project makes nearly everyone better off and virtually no one worse off, or when a project makes a substantial number of people significantly better off at the expense of a relatively small number of people who are made only trivially worse off.

Why might a political system implement a policy that fails to maximize overall welfare or that even reduces overall welfare? There are many possible answers to this question. One answer focuses on the risks of majoritarianism: if the government is elected by majority rule, and wishes to be reelected by the same majority, it will be in the interest of the government to pass laws that benefit the majority, even if those laws inflict greater harms upon the minority. But there are other theories of democratic failure as well. Above, we mentioned agency slack theories, which hold that governments—including both elected officials and bureaucrats—choose policies that favor their own interests or ideologies, or the interests of their supporters, at the expense of the majority; because the majority cannot perfectly monitor the government's activities, the government has the freedom to use public resources for private interests. These theories come in many different flavors. Some arguments emphasize the perverse incentives of bureaucracies. Others suggest that governments favor organized interest groups, such as trade organizations and unions, at the expense of the majority; these groups pool resources to lobby the government, while the majority is diffuse and unorganized. There are also various theories that focus on the difficulties of aggregating preferences in a way that produces consistent, nonarbitrary social choices.

These theories have had less influence on the mainstream constitutional law literature than has the majoritarian version of democratic failure theory. There are two reasons for this. First, as we suggested in chapter 1 for the special case of presidential agency slack, the agency cost theories lack solid theoretical or empirical foundations and have ambiguous implications for evaluation of law and policy.[11] Second, the theories do not imply that judges, even well-motivated judges who seek to act in the public interest, can solve the democratic failures that the theories identify.

The second problem is the one upon which we focus. Even if judges are well motivated, it is unlikely that they have the institutional capacity to correct the failures predicted by agency cost theories. Consider, for example, the interest group approach, which suggests that virtually all laws reflect the influence of interest groups. The implication of the theory is that courts should scrutinize all laws to smoke out socially harmful rent seeking, a task that modern courts are unwilling and unable to execute, and have not since the New Deal. Courts might restrict the influence of interest groups by employing proxies, such as a rule of thumb that laws providing concentrated benefits and dispersed costs harm diffuse majorities more than they benefit well-organized minorities and therefore should be struck down. Yet the proxy is too crude. Laws that provide concentrated benefits and dispersed costs will often increase overall welfare, if the beneficiaries of the redistribution have a

higher marginal utility for income than does the majority, or if the beneficiaries are being given incentives to provide social goods. Laws and projects
as diverse as Social Security (which benefits the elderly) and the funding of
basic research (which benefits universities) would be suspect. Experience has
taught us that courts are in no position to evaluate such laws for impermissible interest group influence. The same reasoning applies to the other types
of agency slack theory.

As for the social choice paradoxes, they are mostly a theoretical possibility; it is not at all clear that they materialize in real-world legislative institutions.[12] Whatever the case, the problem with these theories is that they either
suggest that government policy cycles arbitrarily, in which case a court could
do nothing to improve the situation, or that policies will be dictated by a self-
interested agenda setter, which is just a version of the agency slack theory. For
these reasons, we will downplay the competing accounts of democratic failure
and confine our attention to the most straightforward, majoritarian version of
democratic failure theory.

For all of its problems, the majoritarian version of the democratic failure
theory—the *Carolene Products* version—does not seem as vulnerable to objection as the agency cost and social choice versions. The reason is probably that
the majoritarian version is compatible with a moderate role for the courts,
one to which we are accustomed. Not all laws are the result of democratic
failures; thus courts need not scrutinize every law that is passed. Only certain
types of laws—those that are not general but that target a discrete and insular
minority—need to be scrutinized. The burden placed on courts thus seems
reasonable. In addition, the theory seems plausible—or, at least, has been considered plausible by many constitutional law scholars—even if it relies on a
simplistic conception of democratic politics, as we discuss below. The notion
that majorities exploit minorities has an extremely long intellectual pedigree,
is reflected in American constitutional history going back to the founding,
and, in particular, seems to have been spectacularly confirmed by the history
of race relations in the United States. For all of these reasons, we will focus, for
the most part, on the majoritarian version of the democratic failure theory.

## Democratic Failure, Security, and Liberty

If there is a democratic failure of the majoritarian sort, how will the majority
accomplish its ends? Here, we suggest that the democratic failure theory has
no intrinsic connection to security. In particular, the theory cannot uniquely
predict that government will provide excessive security and insufficient liberty.

Given the structural premises of the account, it is equally possible that government will provide minorities with inadequate security or excessive liberty.

Recall the simple view sketched in chapter 1, according to which government supplies some mix of security and liberty. Failure theorists emphasize the risk that majorities will cause government to supply too much security, because they do not bear the full costs of security. But the mechanism of democratic cost externalization is pitched at too high a level of abstraction to produce the conclusion that failure theorists want to reach. If the structure of the political system allows democratic majorities to externalize costs onto minorities and outsiders, they may externalize any sort of cost, not merely the costs of purchasing security. In particular, it is quite possible that democratic majorities will externalize the costs of *liberty* onto minority and outsider groups, purchasing too little security because majorities do not bear the full costs of insecurity.

Majority-dominated governments have a range of policy instruments at their disposal: direct regulation, taxation, and spending, among others. Theorists of democratic failure focus on the dangers of regulation, in particular the danger that regulation will impose excessive security restrictions on minorities in order to benefit majorities. Yet when other instruments are brought into the picture, it is clear that majorities can exploit minorities, in the sense of exploitation we have defined above, through other instruments as well and in ways that need not yield excessive security. In addition to regulation, taxation might explicitly or implicitly take from minorities to benefit majorities. Less intuitively, majorities might exploit minorities through regulation or spending that insufficiently protects minorities' security, relative to the welfarist baseline.

We may begin with some analogies from normal times and from purely domestic policy settings. Consider the claim, in debates over criminal justice policy, that the political system invests too little in protecting minority communities from crime, especially in urban areas:

> [T]o the extent that crime victims, or those who live in fear of
> becoming crime victims, are diffuse and poorly organized, and to
> the extent that a large part of the population need not share the fear
> that these victims bear, crime losses may be undervalued by local and
> state authorities, and are certainly undervalued by federal government
> officials.[13]

The costs of crime are borne disproportionately by minorities who live in urban areas. Yet those minorities lack a full measure of political influence, as compared to affluent libertarians who support expansive definitions of constitutional rights—rights that protect the criminals who prey upon minority communities. The affluent libertarians do not bear the full costs of crime, and thus support a more expansive scheme of civil liberties than would be produced if poor minority communities had proportionate influence in the political system.

Government (under)regulation of firearms might count as another example. Rural voters who use firearms for hunting and other purposes might object to government regulation of firearms even if increased regulation would be beneficial from the social point of view. The rural voters who block firearms regulation do not bear the full social costs of gun violence, which are partially externalized onto city dwellers. This is not solely a just-so story; there is some evidence that, whatever the prevalence of symbolic politics in other domains, voters act in strictly self-interested fashion where firearms regulation is concerned,[14] and voters in rural areas of southern and western states are much more likely to oppose gun control than are urban voters in states such as California and New York.[15]

The common theme in these examples is that the political system shoves off the costs of liberty onto a subset of the community that lacks a full share of political power. The same mechanism might operate in the terrorism context. Consider the possibility that majorities who live outside of the large urban areas that are the best targets for terrorism will cause the political system to invest too little in terrorism prevention, because they do not bear the full expected costs of terrorist threats. One possibility is that voters from largely rural states who supported the Republican party in 2000 and 2004 might cause the national political process to provide inadequate security for urban centers dominated by Democrats. Consider that a large share of federal block grants for terrorism prevention go to rural western states.[16] Too little is spent on security in the most threatened areas, and too much in the least-threatened areas.

The misallocation of terrorism funding no doubt represents an example of the allocative distortions produced by the Senate's geographical basis of representation. But that is the point: if the structure of Senate representation causes political distortions, those distortions have no particular valence with respect to the tradeoff between security and liberty. Political distortions may produce excessive liberty in some domains as well as excessive security in others. There is no general reason to think that cost externalization systematically tilts in the direction of producing too much security, rather than too much liberty. Security is a public good. But there are many other public goods, including freedom from private violence, which must be protected and supported by government expenditures on security and order. Whatever the optimal supply of public goods at a given time, and whatever political forces produce the actual supply at a given time, the appeal to democratic cost externalization is compatible with insufficient as well as excessive security.

We have not yet said anything about judicial review, a topic we defer to later discussion. Suppose that democratic failure can produce either excessive security or excessive liberty; perhaps it even produces both, at different times, in different places, or on different policy dimensions. Democratic failure theorists can sensibly say that courts should police both forms of democratic failure. Courts should police the excessive provision of security by government, when that occurs; it is neither here nor there that government may also supply inadequate protection to minorities. Courts might also police the latter, perhaps under the rubric of "equal protection of the laws," whose core historical meaning encompasses governmental failure to protect minorities from third-party harms.

In practice, however, it is striking that democratic failure theorists say little or nothing about the problem of excessive liberty. No theorist, as far as we are aware, has suggested that courts should reallocate antiterrorism appropriations to beef up the security apparatus where it is most needed, or that courts should second-guess the government's policies for protecting ports from terrorist attack when the ports are located in urban states that lack political power during Republican administrations. The reason, presumably, is that judicial review of this sort would prove infeasible and possibly counterproductive. Courts might suspect democratic failure in the underprovision of security to minorities, but would be hard pressed to know what the optimal arrangements would be and hard pressed to enforce those arrangements even if they were known; government might circumvent the courts' decisions by reallocating funding on other margins, or simply by ignoring them.

There are two lessons here. First, the same problems of judicial capacity that constrain judicial review of inadequate security also constrain judicial review of excessive security. The courts' institutional capacities are the same, whatever the mechanism of democratic failure. Thus, if critics of judicial deference do not believe that courts should scrutinize laws that enhance liberty during times of emergency—such as the provisions of the PATRIOT Act that strengthen privacy protections—they need to explain what it is about security-enhancing laws that justifies special judicial scrutiny. Second, systemic effects and dynamic governmental responses also undercut judicial review of policies that impose excessive security. If courts police policies that produce excessive security but not policies that produce excessive liberty, government may tend to substitute the latter type of exploitation for the former. Here, we merely note these problems of judicial capacities and systemic effects. Later, we arrange these points into an argument against *Carolene Products* review during times of emergency.

## DEMOCRATIC FAILURE AND EMERGENCIES

We turn now to a critique of the two main versions of the democratic failure theory. Here, we criticize the version which holds that democratic failure is more likely, or more damaging, in emergencies than in normal times, so that judicial review must be more strict during emergencies. Below, we turn to the view that democratic failure is equally likely in normal times and in emergencies, so that judicial review must at least be equally strict in both settings. We also give affirmative arguments for our alternative view, which is that judicial review should be more deferential in emergencies than in normal times, even where facially discriminatory laws are at issue.

We will begin with the principal approach to judicial review that democratic failure theorists endorse: the *Carolene Products* theory. Surprisingly, the literature is barren of efforts to model *Carolene Products* review. Thus, we will confine ourselves to some conceptual observations that set up the subsequent analysis. We suggest that neither democratic failure theory generally, nor *Carolene Products* review in particular, can logically be tied to emergencies. The structural mechanisms that are said to produce failures, primarily the structures of voting and representation, operate equally in emergencies and in normal times; nor is there historical evidence that democratic failures are systematically more likely, or more harmful, in emergencies. To the contrary, we examine mechanisms and evidence suggesting that emergencies often improve the political and economic position of minorities.

### The *Carolene Products* Theory

The *Carolene Products* theory, unlike the agency cost theories of democratic failure canvassed above, appears to have straightforward normative implications and straightforward implications for the role of courts. If majorities exploit minorities by enacting laws that target the minorities, then courts should have a preference for general laws, which require the self-interested majority to internalize the costs. Courts should be less deferential toward targeted laws than toward general laws.

But the concern that self-interested majorities will impose excessive costs on targeted minorities is itself ambiguous. Virtually all laws, taken in isolation, harm a minority of the population: gas taxes save energy but hurt poor people who drive a great deal; gun control laws save lives but harm people who need guns to protect themselves; environmental laws protect the environment but may harm people who hold certain jobs; and so forth. Thus, the *Carolene Products* theory assumes that a law cannot be evaluated in isolation. A law that benefits a majority while injuring a minority may be acceptable as long as it is not the case that the political process generates only (or mostly) laws that have a similar effect. Rather, a well-functioning political process sometimes produces laws that benefit any given minority. Because different coalitions assemble on different issues, there are no groups that are repeat losers or structurally disfavored minorities.

This is why *Carolene Products* refers not to any minority, but to (1) a "discrete and insular minority" that (2) is historically oppressed because of (3) "prejudice."[17] The people who belong to a discrete and insular minority that is historically oppressed are likely to be in the political minority always or almost always, rather than in a political minority sometimes but in a political majority at other times. The *Carolene Products* theory imagines that majority prejudice bars minorities, especially African Americans, from joining the winning coalition on issue after issue—tax policy, education policy, defense policy, and so forth. We can say that a law reflects a democratic failure when (1) the benefit to the majority is less than the loss to the minority, or (2) the benefit to the majority is more than the loss to the minority on a particular law, but the members of the minority rarely find themselves in winning coalitions, so that their losses from the political process over some lengthy period of time exceed their gains.

*Carolene Products* does not say that courts will evaluate every law, and reject all laws that are democratic failures as defined above. The problem is one of institutional capacity: courts are not in a good position to evaluate the gains and losses from a law. In a world in which African Americans are poorer on average than whites, any nonprogressive form of taxation might be said to be a democratic failure, according to our revised definition; determining whether this is the case would require a very complicated evaluation of people's preferences, people's views about the proper distribution of wealth, and other factors.

Given their limited capacities, courts cannot conduct such an analysis. Rather, they presume that laws that explicitly burden African Americans are democratic failures, and laws that do not are not democratic failures. The implicit logic is that facial discrimination is a proxy for democratic failure. When there is no facial discrimination, and no other obvious indication of discrimination, such as evidence of overt racial animus in the legislative history, most of the time no democratic failure has occurred. The distinction between general and targeted laws is a rough-and-ready means to measure whether the majority shares in the law's burdens and thus internalizes the law's social cost.

There are many standard criticisms of the *Carolene Products* approach, even in ordinary times. First, its assumption that majorities exploit minorities, in the sense of exploitation defined above, does not have a sound theoretical foundation. As we mentioned above, a contrary thesis is that minorities exploit majorities. Public choice theory suggests that interest groups sometimes cause governments to adopt policies that transfer wealth from the diffuse and unorganized majority to a well-organized minority. Public choice theory has many problems, but it surely reflects an important truth, especially when minorities are in a defensive rather than offensive position and can benefit from blocking legislation that would benefit the majority even more. Similarly, we might expect discrete and insular minorities to organize and form groups that exercise disproportionate political power.

Second, *Carolene Products* assumes that the majority is monolithic, when in fact policy is created by shifting majorities that comprise diverse groups. The *Carolene Products* theory implicitly assumed a very crude story, in which a majority of whites oppresses a minority of African Americans. This story simplifies unacceptably. White liberals, workers, government employees, and urban dwellers often find themselves in coalitions with African-American civil rights proponents, workers, government employees, and urban dwellers, because their interests converge with respect to discrete issues. But if the story did contain some truth in the past, it is even less plausible in the present and in the context of the 9/11 emergency. Jose Padilla is Hispanic, yet there was no effort to target Hispanics after his arrest, in part because Hispanics as a group have shown no general disposition to support al Qaeda, but also because Hispanics have considerable political power. So do Arab Americans, especially those who reside in a swing state in presidential elections.

Third, *Carolene Products* assumes that people in the majority do not care about the well-being of people in the minority. This assumption may, again, have been a rough truth in the past, when whites and African Americans were segregated and mutually hostile. But, today, thanks in part to civil rights laws and perhaps even to the *Carolene Products* line of cases, the population is much more integrated. Although residential segregation persists, there is much more intermarriage between whites, on the one hand, and Hispanics, Asian Americans, and even African Americans, on the other hand. Educational, class, and wealth differences do not overlap with racial and ethnic differences to the extent that they once did. African Americans remain a special case, but no one thinks that post-9/11 emergency regulations should target African Americans. If people are less likely to support laws that discriminate against their spouses, children, relatives, coworkers, and neighbors, then the risk of democratic failure at the expense of ethnic or racial minorities is lower than it used to be. On this picture, judicial review according to *Carolene Products* may itself have undermined the very conditions that originally made it an attractive approach.

Our purpose here, however, is not to criticize *Carolene Products* generally, but to focus on the relationship between democratic failure and emergencies. We thus bracket these standard criticisms of *Carolene Products* and focus on the special case of the emergency. Critics of the 9/11 emergency policies argue that judicial review should be enhanced during an emergency because the probability of democratic failure increases during an emergency. We are now in a position to see why this argument is unsound.

## The *Carolene Products* Theory and Emergencies

We said in chapter 1 that emergencies and the threat of terrorism produce a social loss. The government must invest in prevention, repair, intelligence, policing, and military activity; society as a whole is worse off than before the emergency. None of these characteristics are related to the concerns reflected in the *Carolene Products* theory. The shrinking of the social pie is something that happens all the time due to random exogenous shocks, such as an economic downturn or a bad crop season. The majority's reaction to such losses will often be facially neutral policies that may or may not burden a minority. Under the *Carolene Products* theory, these polices will not be checked by courts even if they may cause a disparate impact. In the case of a recession, the policy may be a reduction of interest rates and the creation of jobs programs. In the case of an emergency, the policy may be the sealing of borders and the introduction of new security procedures in airports. Analytically, we have the same case: a policy in response to a threat.

Crucially, the structures of voting and representation remain the same as they were before the emergency. The political constraints need not shift, even if society as a whole is poorer than before. The majority has no greater ability to impose costs on a minority in the emergency case than in the non-emergency case. The structural mechanisms of voting and representation that are said to produce democratic failure operate the same way both in emergencies and in normal times. Suppose that the structures of voting and representation allow a 60% majority to take 80% of the social pie. If an emergency shrinks the pie, the structure of voting does not change, and the minority will still get its 20%, just of a smaller pie. Perhaps some more elaborate account of democratic failure might predict that the minority's *share* would itself shrink; but any such account would require a theory running well beyond the simple voting mechanisms that are the stock-in-trade of the democratic failure theory.

## Emergencies and Opportunism

Some theorists emphasize the worry that officials, particularly executive officials, will seize on an emergency to implement policies that were blocked by political constraints before the emergency. Thus, Mark Tushnet argues that "emergencies may matter because they alter the constraints under which decisionmakers operate,"[18] although the emergency does not necessarily alter the preferences or evaluations of decisionmakers. Consider again the 9/11 attacks. Prior to those attacks, most decisionmakers knew that foreign terrorists posed a threat to Americans on American soil, and although they did not anticipate the form of the 9/11 attacks, they did have equally horrific, indeed more horrific, possibilities in mind, such as the use of biological or chemical weapons, which could kill tens of thousands of people. At the same time, these decisionmakers also might have valued civil liberties less than most Americans do: they simply did not think that dissent and privacy are preeminent values. Prior to 9/11, they could not implement their policy preferences because many or most Americans would not tolerate them, and it is always hard to change the status quo. After 9/11, they took advantage of the more fluid political environment in order to enact their preferences as law.

Tushnet seems implicitly to be supposing here that the relevant officials will seize upon the emergency to implement policies that the public does not want. This is an account based on agency slack between voters and officials, rather than majoritarian oppression; as such, it is vulnerable to all of the problems with agency failure accounts of executive opportunism that we discussed in chapter 1 and above. During emergencies, the executive receives more discretion from the legislature and the voters, but this may just be because the legislature and the voters think that this is the best way to respond to the emergency, and tolerate or even welcome the shift of policies toward the executive's preferences. Partisan politics constrain the executive even during emergencies; although the opposition will initially rally around the flag, this effect is short-lived, and political criticism will be all the more

fierce as the policy stakes increase. Indeed, in some respects, the political constraints on executive action during emergencies may be tighter than during
normal times. Some policies adopted during emergencies are more visible to
engaged publics, including officials from the opposing political party, journalists, civil libertarians, and watchdog groups, than are policies churned out by
bureaucrats who fly below the public radar during normal times. We return
to this point below.

Moreover, Tushnet's normative assumptions are obscure. Suppose Tushnet
is right that during emergencies the boundaries of the politically possible
change. Are the changes for good or for ill? Tushnet emphasizes the down-
side risks, suggesting that in the more fluid environment created by an emergency, politicians will exploit cognitive biases among the populace in order
to "achieve their policy goals in the face of opposition."[19] Tushnet does not
explicitly say that these policy goals are bad, as do the theorists of panic we
critiqued in chapter 2, but his emphasis on the cognitively disreputable genesis
of the new policies suggests that he is suspicious of their merits. Tushnet, that
is, shares with the panic theorists an ingrained pessimism about politics during emergencies.

Against this, there are two points. First, as we emphasized in chapter 1,
even granting Tushnet's premises, the executive abuses produced by increased
agency slack during emergencies are just a cost. That cost must be weighed
against the security benefits of affording executive officials increased discretion
during emergencies; in any given case, the security benefits may outweigh the
harms to civil liberties. Tushnet here falls into the civil libertarian assumption
that executive abuses should be minimized and, if possible, eliminated, rather
than optimized. If abuses are the inevitable by-product of increased discretion
that is desirable on other grounds and produces net benefits overall, however,
then this is a mistake.

Second, consider a more optimistic contrary view: emergencies and war
spur nations to high achievements and progressive social change. Consider the
two greatest emergencies in American history: the Civil War and the period
extending from 1929 to 1945, encompassing the Great Depression and World
War II. To the emergency policies implemented during the Civil War, we owe
the emancipation of the slaves and the Civil War amendments to which it led;
the modernization of the U.S. Army; the beginnings of centralized monetary
policy; and the first glimmer of federally operated social welfare agencies (the
Freedmen's Bureau, Civil War pensions, and so forth). To the policies implemented in the wake of the Great Depression, we owe Social Security, Medi-
care, labor regulation, and the administrative state. If we consider World War
I an emergency, we can add the creation of the income tax during that war

and the enfranchisement of women in its wake. We might even call the found-ing period an emergency and attribute all of our constitutional institutions to policies created while the nation was in political crisis.

Several mechanisms produce this connection between emergencies and beneficial change. Emergencies may force governments to adopt policies that unsettle the status quo or that liberate citizens from adaptive preferences; where the status quo was unjust or harmful to a broad class of citizens, the disruption produced by emergencies is good. Consider that the need to staff crucial industries during World War II led government to encourage the entry of women into the labor force, with massive consequences for gender relations in the postwar period. More generally, war often loosens the grip of interest groups and has a democratizing effect. The franchise frequently expands dur-ing or after wars, in response to soldiers' unanswerable claim that they ought to be able to vote if they are expected to fight for the nation. And elites who need a broad base of taxation and public support to fight other elites are repeatedly forced to make political concessions to the populace. The overall picture is that, during wars and other emergencies, the interests of elites and populations converge or overlap far more than in normal times. The result is something like a common concern for common interests, or even for the common good. Emergencies can even produce something like a constitutional moment, in which collective deliberation about the overall good of the polity temporarily replaces, or at least supplements, ordinary distributive politics.

The Bush administration has not used the 9/11 emergency as an excuse for implementing progressive domestic policies, but many commentators have noticed the similarity between Bush's idealistic goal of spreading democ-racy and the progressive foreign policy of Woodrow Wilson. Both presidents assumed that Americans would be willing to make sacrifices in order to spread democracy to foreign countries. But both presidents needed an emergency before they could motivate support for their idealistic aims.

Civil libertarian arguments about emergency policies typically claim that because of the emergency, policies and laws proposed by the government are more likely to be bad than during normal times. As we have argued, this is a mistake. At a minimum, we think that the policies are no likely to be worse; and we also suggest that in a broad range of cases the policies are likely to be better, because emergencies tend to unsettle an unjust or harmful status quo ante, and because individuals are more likely to attend to the common good. To be sure, disagreements about policy will persist; indeed, these disagree-ments will be heightened because so much more is at stake during an emer-gency than during normal times. But the disagreements may be more elevated, and more principled, than during normal times.

## Emergencies and Scapegoating

An important variant of the opportunism idea is the worry that minorities will be subject to scapegoating during emergencies. The scapegoating concern is a hybrid of rational and nonrational accounts of democratic failure, or else equivocates between the two; it also equivocates among various possible assumptions about the motives of officials and about the agency slack that officials hold. Sometimes, the picture is of a majority actuated by standing passions or animus against minorities, animus that remains latent during normal times but that becomes overt during emergencies, particularly if minorities are aliens from a country or group that has become an enemy by virtue of the emergency. Sometimes, the picture is that majorities or interest groups harbor a desire to expropriate the assets of minorities, a desire that is constrained by politics during normal times but that can be satisfied during emergencies, for unclear reasons. On either picture, officials implement the majority's non-rational animus or self-interested aims through emergency policies. On yet another picture, self-interested officials seize upon emergencies to scapegoat minorities, as a pretext to expand their own power; in this version, latent animus present in the population is whipped up by officials who enjoy some agency slack.

In any of these versions, there is further a question about which groups can be made into scapegoats. *Carolene Products* assumes that some set of discrete and insular minorities can be identified. Talk of scapegoating sometimes makes it sound as though the choice of targets is entirely unconstrained, so that political entrepreneurs can define new target groups as emergencies arise, even if the target groups have no relation to the source of the emergency. It is obvious that there must be some constraints on the choice of targets—could the class of all left-handed people be made into scapegoats?—but these constraints are never clearly specified. It is hard to evaluate the scapegoating idea, which is vague about the mechanisms at work and which supports no clear predictions about which groups can be scapegoated, under what conditions.

Whatever sense one attaches to the idea, it is dubious that scapegoating increases during emergencies. Minorities undoubtedly are scapegoated during emergencies, but they are during normal times as well, albeit in less visible ways; it is not clear that emergencies change anything other than the rhetoric or rationalizations surrounding the majority's actions. Indeed, as against the view that scapegoating increases during emergencies, emergencies actually enhance the political position of minorities in several ways. First, because emergencies capture the attention of the public, it will be more difficult for the government to conceal oppressive or redistributive policies, making it easier for minorities to mobilize opposition to such policies. Second, because redistributive policies create deadweight costs, they become less attractive during emergencies. When the survival of the pie is at stake, only the most dysfunctional government will further endanger it by adopting bad policies that ensure that the majority gets a disproportionate slice. A respectable body of thought holds that nations are most likely to adopt efficient macroeconomic policies during financial emergencies and most likely to adopt inefficient redistributive policies when the nation's finances are not in crisis.[20] Above, we suggested that emergencies do not change the political constraints under which majorities and officials operate. Here we suggest, alternatively, that even if the boundaries of the politically possible do shift, the shift can often help minorities rather than hurt them. We provide evidence for this suggestion below.

Are there other possible mechanisms that could cause unjustified discrimination against minorities to increase during emergencies? No author has concretely identified such a mechanism; the literature is almost entirely conclusory. To be sure, such mechanisms could exist. Perhaps emergencies enable groups that compete for resources during normal times to create temporary majority coalitions because an emergency-related minority is a focal point that they can rally around. Perhaps emergencies raise public awareness and increase public monitoring of politics, so that minorities find it more difficult to exercise influence to protect themselves behind the scenes. Perhaps emergencies increase the power of the executive because the legislature rationally delegates power to it, and then the executive uses its power to exploit minorities. Perhaps emergencies—in extreme cases—directly interfere with the political process by shutting down courts, preventing citizens from casting votes, or hindering elected officials from congregating, whereupon residual power holders exploit minorities. We suggest these possibilities to improve upon the extant arguments, not because we think they are plausible. All of these theories leave open the possibility that a minority will itself exploit an emergency by joining the winning coalition (perhaps with other minorities), rather than being exploited. We suggest these theories as examples of the type of argument that the critics must come up with before they can be taken seriously.

So much for theory; what of the evidence? Have democratic failures occurred more often during emergencies than during normal times? This question is extremely difficult to answer because of the difficulty of identifying democratic failures and emergencies in a noncontroversial way. But a few observations can be made.

If we think of democratic failures from the *Carolene Products* perspective as large-scale, systematic transfers of wealth from minorities to majorities, then the most plausible examples of democratic failure in American history are the transfers of land from American Indians to whites, often in violation of treaties, throughout the nineteenth century (and earlier); Jim Crow laws and other racial structures or policies targeted against African Americans (especially) and various immigrant minorities, such as the Chinese of the West Coast; and the repression of religious minorities, such as the Mormons prior to their migration to Utah. None of these policies was based on an emergency, or justified by reference to an emergency, unless we define emergency in an implausibly broad sense. In some of these case, interested parties justified discriminatory policies by appealing to security concerns. Long-term concerns about being "overrun" by Chinese immigrants, for example, were mentioned by the Supreme Court near the end of the nineteenth century.[21] But if emergency were defined so broadly, then there would be few occasions on which an emergency did not exist. (Thus we offered a narrower definition of emergencies in chapter 1.) Overall, these policies were mainly peacetime policies adopted by the national government or the state governments with the acquiescence of the national government. The view that minorities are treated worse during emergencies glosses over the long record of democratic failure during normal times.

Treating these non–emergency deprivations as a baseline, we find it difficult to find examples of clear democratic failure during war or emergencies. We can generalize as follows. Consider cases where the targeted minority was associated in some way with the enemy. These cases include the treatment of Confederate sympathizers during the Civil War, ethnic Germans during World War I, Eastern European immigrants during the Red Scare, Japanese Americans during World War II, communist sympathizers during the early cold war, and Arab and Muslim Americans since 9/11. In most of these cases, the connection between the minority group and the enemy, not the political weakness of the minority group, is the most plausible explanation for the policies in question: without the benefit of hindsight, and acting in the fog of war, the government had reasonable grounds to fear that members of the targeted minority would be disloyal, and in some cases lacked the time or resources to sort out the loyal from the disloyal in a fine-grained way. In the cold war case, the minority was itself defined by the crisis—those who seemed sympathetic with the goals of the enemy, the Soviet Union—and not by ethnicity. The policies adopted during these emergencies may have been wrong, but, if so, they were of a piece with the numerous other policies adopted during emergencies that had nothing to do with the treatment of minorities.

Critics of the Japanese internment decision allege both that military officials on the West Coast acted with racist motives and that economic competitors of the Issei and Nisei acted opportunistically to expropriate their property or dampen competition.[22] There are two problems with all such claims. First, they do not explain why Roosevelt, who was neither a racist nor an economic competitor of the Issei and Nisei, issued the internment order.[23] His attorney general, Francis Biddle, ascribed the decision to Roosevelt's simple belief that "[w]hat must be done to defend the country must be done."[24] Second, they ignore the possibility that the internment decision was overdetermined, resting on more than one motive—either because the decision emerged from a coalition between those with disreputable motives and those with legitimate security concerns, or because some crucial actors held both motives simultaneously. Of course, we do not defend the internment order on the merits, because we lack the necessary expertise to judge, even in hindsight, whether the action was justified, all things considered. Our point is that both the civil libertarian commentators and the judges lack the necessary expertise as well. The former have often failed to recognize their own limited competence; the judges, burdened with real responsibility, usually do recognize their own limits during times of emergency.

If minority groups are usually targeted at least in part because of their possible connection with the enemy, why did the U.S. government target Japanese Americans, but not German and Italian Americans during World War II? Militarily, only the Issei and Nisei were geographically concentrated near a potential invasion front. Politically, German and Italian Americans were too numerous to intern or subject to legal disabilities and too well assimilated; by contrast, German Americans were targeted during World War I, when they were less assimilated. In addition, peacetime discrimination against Japanese Americans was greater than peacetime discrimination against German and Italian Americans. The differential treatment of these groups during World War II is not evidence for the proposition that an emergency increases the probability of political failure; rather, it is consistent with the view that the peacetime baseline holds (however good or bad that baseline was). A final point is that the failure to discriminate against German and Italian Americans during World War II is a problem for the failure theorists: it cuts against the claim that enhanced discrimination against emergency-relevant minorities is predictable during emergencies.

## Emergencies as a Progressive Force

Importantly, as we have discussed, the treatment of minority groups often improves during emergencies; historically, emergencies have often been engines of progressive government. Times of crisis demand good policy. During emergencies, the government needs the skills and loyalty of minority groups, on both the military and economic fronts, and is willing to pay for them. A large body of political theory and science emphasizes that the military and economic needs of the nation-state have tended, over time, to expand the scope of the franchise, reduce class privileges, and improve governmental accountability and the rule of law, because national governments have been constrained to offer an ever-broader range of groups political benefits commensurate with their political contributions.[25]

For example, consider Lincoln's decision, at the height of the Civil War, to proclaim emancipation for slaves behind enemy lines, with the hopes of enlisting their sympathies and assistance and of causing disruption to the enemy; the genesis of federal assistance for minorities in post–Civil War programs, such as the Freedmen's Bureau; the creation of national programs for poverty relief during the Depression and New Deal; the entry of women into the labor force during World War II; the desegregation of schools and workplaces during the cold war; and the integration of African Americans into the armed forces during World War II and the cold war. The last two developments occurred because a series of national governments saw improving the position of African Americans as an important part of the propaganda war against communism, and saw African Americans as an underutilized pool of capable workers and soldiers.[26]

This minority-protecting mechanism applies with equal force to emergency-relevant minorities—the minorities who have some connection to a perceived enemy and are thus conspicuous targets for scapegoating. Indeed, even while targeting Arab- and Muslim-American aliens after 9/11, the U.S. government poured prosecutorial resources into the enforcement of hate crime laws for their protection,[27] while in the United Kingdom, in the days immediately after the 7/7 attacks in London, the House of Commons passed a bill protecting Muslims from hate crimes.[28] The struggle against terrorism makes the skills and contributions of Muslim and Arab citizens more useful, not more dispensable.[29]

## Summary

We do not argue that invidious discrimination systematically tends to decline during emergencies, though it may. The minimum point we make is that the evidence is ambiguous: there is no systematic evidence that democratic failures occur more often during emergencies than during non-emergencies. If we are correct, there is no reason to believe that an emergency law that targets a minority, even a minority connected to the crisis, is more likely the result of democratic failure than is a non-emergency law that targets a minority. Democratic failure theorists typically acknowledge the judges' limited capacity for handling emergencies. But the critics resist the argument that limited capacity implies limited deference; to do so they argue that, as a result of scapegoating or the like, democratic failure is systematically more likely during emergencies. If that were true, judicial scrutiny might be justified as a way to protect minorities, despite the costs in reduced security. But it is not true.

The main difference between normal times and emergencies is that courts may have greater difficulty evaluating an emergency measure than a non-emergency measure, a point we expand upon below. The point for now is that there is no reason to think that democratic failure is more likely to occur during an emergency than during normal times. It might be the case that government error is more likely during an emergency, but error by itself is not democratic failure, and courts have no expertise advantage over the political branches. We now turn to the latter point—the problem of judicial capacities.

## DEMOCRATIC FAILURE: CITIZENS AND ALIENS

Above, we criticized the idea that democratic failure is more likely during emergencies than during normal times. We now turn to an improved version of the democratic failure theory. On this construal, the theory suggests that democratic failure is as likely and as damaging in emergencies as in normal times—no more, but certainly no less. On the remedial side, courts in times of emergency should, just as in normal times, ensure that laws are general and should strictly scrutinize laws that are facially discriminatory. *Carolene Products* applies to the same extent during emergencies as during normal times.

There is a third possibility, however, which we propose here: *Carolene Products* should not apply during emergencies, or only in weakened form. We argue that even if the *Carolene Products* theory justifies strict scrutiny of targeted or facially discriminatory laws during normal times, it does not justify strict scrutiny of such laws passed in response to emergencies (or, equivalently, strict scrutiny should be easier to satisfy in emergencies than in normal times). Thus, if courts should strike down statutes that target minorities during normal times, they should be far more deferential during emergencies. We then consider some distinctive problems concerning aliens and argue that the *Carolene Products* theory does not justify strict scrutiny of laws that burden aliens either during normal times or during emergencies.

## Citizens

The democratic failure theory holds that political dissenters and ethnic or racial minorities among the citizenry are exploited by the majority and therefore ought to be protected by courts in normal times. We assume, for the sake of argument, that this theory is correct and ask: to what extent does it justify strict scrutiny of targeted or facially discriminatory laws passed in response to emergencies? We argue that it does not justify strict scrutiny of such laws; alternatively, if strict scrutiny is adhered to as a nominal framework, claims of compelling governmental interest should be accepted more readily. Whatever the doctrinal framework, courts should defer heavily to nongeneral laws passed in response to emergencies.

A preliminary problem is the one we mentioned above. Democratic failure theories propose that courts should monitor and invalidate policies that impose excessive security regulation on minorities (defining "excessiveness" as above) in order to benefit the majority. No extant theory, however, suggests that courts can or should invalidate policies that provide excessive liberty or inadequate security. Presumably, democratic failure theorists shy from the latter problem because judicial review of inadequate security is infeasible; it would require affirmative judicial oversight of funding and regulatory decisions. Given this asymmetry in the structure of judicial review, however, a rational and ill-motivated government may simply substitute one type of exploitation for another. If courts block government from pandering to the self-interested majority by imposing security restrictions on minorities, or if courts make that form of pandering more costly, then government may switch instruments, pandering to the majority by spending too little on minorities' security, or by providing minorities with insufficient regulatory protection. Substitution of this sort is never costless, so the possibility does not show that judicial review of excessive security is pointless. The risk of substitution does, however, reduce the benefits to be gained from judicial review of policies that impose excessive security restrictions.

Let us now turn to the costs of minority-protecting judicial review; we argue that these costs rise in times of emergency. Imagine an official racial or ethnic profiling policy after 9/11: Arab Americans are stopped at airports and interviewed and searched at a higher rate than other Americans. The law that authorizes the profiling explicitly targets a discrete and insular minority. Under the *Carolene Products* approach, as normally understood, the court would apply strict scrutiny. Although it is conceivable that a court might find that the profiling system is a sufficiently tailored instrument for achieving a compelling state interest, we know from past experience that this is unlikely. Strict scrutiny usually means that the law is overturned.

As we noted in chapter 1, emergency policies adopted by the government balance the competing values of liberty and security. The racial profiling policy affects this balance in a special way: the reduction in liberty is suffered only by the minority group, while the benefits from enhanced security are enjoyed by all. The fact that the benefits and burdens are not equally shared, of course, hardly distinguishes this law from any other. In the case of ordinary regulatory laws, the numerical minority is outvoted, but the regulations are accepted because, in some rough sense, the benefits to the majority outweigh the losses to the minority, and the minority that loses in this case may participate in different majorities that win in other settings. The mere fact that a *particular* policy reduces the liberty of one group in order to enhance the security of another group does not show that it is the result of a democratic failure. What is special, under the *Carolene Products* theory, is not the presence of a law that benefits some and burdens others; it is the burdening of political dissenters or of a historically oppressed minority group. The concern is that such a group will repeatedly be on the losing end of the law-making transaction.

This implies that democratic failure is an aggregate theory. To set the benchmark against which failure is identified, the theory aggregates across a large set of laws and finds a democratic failure only if a persistent minority or minority group is repeatedly sacrificed for the benefit of a persistent majority. Courts, however, must proceed at retail, examining laws one at a time, and this makes it difficult for courts to implement the democratic failure theory in any straightforward way. The problem is that, in any given case, a law that targets some minority or subgroup may be justified by real security concerns. If it is, then in an aggregate sense there is no democratic failure, and the law just is "general" in the sense that the basis for the targeted classification would apply to *any* group that posed a similar security risk. Today's minorities will benefit from increased security just as will today's majority; future laws will be enacted by different coalitions, in which today's minority may participate, and those laws will place burdens on differently defined minorities.

Courts will often be hard pressed to evaluate whether these conditions hold. But in times of emergency, this problem of judicial capacity is especially acute. Consider a simple picture of the judges' position in normal times and of their dilemma in times of emergency. Courts review a law and either uphold it or strike it down. The law either reflects a democratic failure or it does not. If the court falsely believes that a law results from a democratic failure and strikes it down, then the court commits the type of error known as a *false positive*. The law is not the result of a democratic failure; the court falsely thinks that it is. If the court falsely believes that a law does not result from a democratic failure and upholds it, this is a *false negative*. The law is a democratic failure; the court falsely thinks it is not. The *rational basis test*, used for laws that do not target minorities or facially discriminate, assumes that the social cost of false positives (striking down legitimate laws) exceeds the social cost of false negatives (upholding illegitimate laws). Laws that are not targeted or facially discriminatory are presumed to be democratic successes. If courts were to frequently strike them down, then they would usually strike down politically valid laws while rarely interfering with a law that is the result of a democratic failure.

When the law targets dissenters or facially discriminates against a minority, the *strict scrutiny test* assumes that the social cost of false negatives exceeds the social cost of false positives. Laws that are targeted or facially discriminatory are presumed to be democratic failures. Courts frequently strike them down because in doing so they usually strike down democratic failures, while rarely interfering with a law that is democratically valid.

This is the standard *Carolene Products* picture, but its empirical premises fail in times of emergency. Both false negatives and false positives have an expected cost, which is a function of two quantities: the risk of error and the cost of the errors that occur. The expected cost of false negatives—erroneously upholding invalid laws—is the same in emergencies and in normal times. We argued above, and we assume here, that democratic failure is no more likely in emergencies than in normal times; the costs of democratic failures that do occur are also constant, because the harm to minorities is the same in either period. There is a ceiling on the amount of harm that can be imposed on minorities during both emergencies and normal times—deprivation of their lives and their property. This ceiling remains constant across the emergency and non-emergency settings. The level of actual deprivation in any case depends on the relative political power of the minorities, to be sure; but if our argument is correct that political constraints remain constant across settings, there is no reason to believe that deprivations accountable to democratic failure (as opposed to cost-justified security precautions) are likely to be greater during an emergency than during normal times. As we noted above, peacetime laws targeting African Americans, Mormons, and other minority groups have been just as severe as emergency regulations.

But the other side of the ledger is not constant. When an emergency occurs, the expected cost of false positives—erroneously striking down valid laws—increases. We begin by bracketing the risk of false positives and focusing on the social cost of the false positives that occur. In times of emergency, the law that is invalidated is no longer a law that makes it easier for police to arrest someone who may rob or kill; the law that is invalidated is a law that makes it easier for the police to stop a terrorist attack. The difference in the magnitude of the potential harm goes a long way toward justifying greater deference in the emergency case, but it is not the only important difference. Terrorism works not just by killing people but by frightening them, so that they urge governments to adopt policies that the terrorists want. Ordinary criminals, by contrast, do not have such a destructive impact on the political process. During an emergency, the social cost of emergency laws incorrectly struck down is so high that greater deference is justified.

In some circumstances, an erroneous invalidation will merely have a delaying effect. If an erroneous invalidation produces large costs, government may be able to adopt the needed measure again and receive deference from the now chastened judges. But delay is also a cost, a cost that rises during emergencies; indeed, the high cost of delay is a defining trait of emergencies, as we emphasize below. Moreover, delay is a problem even in a purely ex ante sense. Commentators sometimes suggest that we do not observe, as a historical matter, judicial protections of liberty that produce serious harms.[30] But this overlooks the law of anticipated reactions. If government must worry about whether its policies will survive judicial review, it will be slower at adjusting to the emergency; some necessary measures may be forgone altogether, and thus will never give rise to lawsuits. Fortunately, as we discuss below, the reason that we do not observe cases in which judicial protection of liberty produces serious harms is that the judges do not really protect liberty in times of emergency. If they did, they would start to produce harmful mistakes. The civil libertarian commentators who urge greater judicial vigilance extrapolate from the historical record of toothless judicial review to predict that judicial review with real bite would also prove harmless, but this is fallacious.

So much for the social cost of false positives; let us turn now to the *risk* of false positives. That risk will also be higher during emergencies (unless the judges recognize the risk and compensate by deferring, as we suggest below they actually do). Emergencies bring novel threats, and the novel security policies chosen by the government will be controversial and hard for judges to evaluate. An emergency calls for large-scale reorganization and a change in bureaucratic routines. These routines did not prevent the emergency and proved inadequate to cope with it; therefore, they must be changed. But if they must be changed, then the normal standards for evaluating existing bureaucratic processes will no longer apply. With hundreds of years of experience, we know how to determine the fairness of a trial of a person who is suspected of a routine criminal violation. We can complain if the crime rate goes up, police brutalize suspects, innocent people are convicted, or the police department consumes more resources than police departments in other cities. We are much less sure how to evaluate, say, the conduct of soldiers enforcing martial law. The soldiers are not expected to act like police; but how should they act? The policies of other countries do not provide a good basis of comparison because their positions are so different. They have different law enforcement systems, different levels of social homogeneity, different geopolitical stances, and so forth.

To be sure, the risk of false negatives will rise as well. If courts have trouble evaluating an emergency measure for evidence of democratic failure, they will just as often see success in a democratically invalid law as failure in a democratically valid law. The important point is that even if both risks increase by the same amount, the expected cost of false positives will exceed the expected cost of false negatives, because the social cost of error is higher for false positives (justified security measures struck down) than for false negatives (minorities unjustifiably harmed). That is why courts should be more deferential during emergencies than during normal times.

As we mentioned in chapter 1, constitutional lawyers concerned about democratic failure and government opportunism sometimes emphasize the principle of the *least restrictive alternative*. The idea is that if government's goal is to attain a security level of X, and if there are two policies for attaining X, one that requires sacrificing minorities' interests and one that does not, judges should force government to adopt the latter policy. The problem arises when government claims that, in light of the novelty of the threats and the lumpiness of the possible responses, the minority-respecting policy will only yield a security level of Y, much lower than X. In emergencies, judges will be hard pressed to evaluate this claim, and the cost of erroneously rejecting it may be large. The judges know that the government's claim may be opportunistic, but that knowledge is not useful, as they cannot distinguish opportunism from vigilance. In emergencies, the problem for courts is that they are more likely to make errors when they review emergency laws than when they review normal laws. This means that strict scrutiny brings with it a higher probability of false positives as well as a higher social cost when false positives occur.

*Carolene Products* and its successor decisions require strict scrutiny of laws targeting dissenters or ideological minorities, not merely those targeting racial and ethnic minorities; where dissenters are concerned, targeted laws may represent a governmental attempt to close off the channels of political change. But from the judges' standpoint, the problems are identical; everything we have said so far applies as well to judicial review of laws that target dissenters or reduce due process protections for narrowly defined classes of suspects. Consider, for example, a law that reduces process for all terrorist suspects, regardless of their race. People who might agree that courts should defer to the government in this case frequently argue that courts should not defer to the government if the antiterrorism law is facially discriminatory. But the two cases are exactly the same. In both cases, the standard of review will balance false positives (legitimate laws that are struck down) and false negatives (democratic failures that are upheld). In both cases, the false positive is more costly during an emergency than during normal times. And in both cases, the false negative is also of substantial concern (an unnecessary burden inflicted on a small group of people) but is constant across normal times and emergencies. We can think of no account of democratic failure that would explain why emergencies should cause courts to scrutinize facially discriminatory emergency laws more strictly than they scrutinize facially neutral emergency laws that impinge on some constitutionally protected value.

The upshot of this discussion is that courts should more readily uphold targeted or facially discriminatory security laws passed in response to emergencies than identical security laws passed during normal times. It is hard to say, in the abstract, how much more deferential courts should be. At the extreme, courts could simply apply deferential rational-basis review to all emergency legislation. There is a residuum of factual uncertainty here, and in chapter 1 we suggested that emergencies lie on a continuum or sliding scale, so that the judges will calibrate the deference they afford. What is not plausible is that courts should use the same approach in both emergencies and normal times.

Perhaps the best evidence for how the false positives and false negatives net out is that the judges often believe themselves incapable of evaluating governmental decisionmaking in times of emergency. Consider the notorious *Korematsu* case, which upheld the government's internment of Japanese aliens and Japanese-American citizens during World War II.[31] Note that the *Korematsu* majority employed nominally "strict" scrutiny yet upheld an explicit racial classification by the national government (in line with then-prevailing law, which allowed racial segregation in the armed forces and the District of Columbia public schools).[32] This illustrates our distinction between the nominal rules of judicial review and the operational level of judicial deference.

Democratic failure theorists often quote Justice Jackson's concern for generality and also his dissenting opinion in *Korematsu*, which expressed a concern about the ratchet effects of upholding governmental action during emergencies (a view we critique in chapter 4). Yet the core idea of his dissent was arguably different. The core idea was that courts are incapable of sorting justified from unjustified emergency measures, know themselves to be incapable, and thus have no real choice but to defer. As Jackson put it:

In the very nature of things military decisions are not susceptible of intelligent judicial appraisal. They do not pretend to rest on evidence, but are made on information that often would not be admissible and on assumptions that could not be proved. Information in support of an order could not be disclosed to courts without danger that it would reach the enemy. Neither can courts act on communications made in confidence. Hence courts can never have any real alternative to accepting the mere declaration of the authority that issued the order that it was reasonably necessary from a military viewpoint.[33]

Jackson perfectly captures the institutional dilemma that judges face. The issue is not only or primarily whether *Korematsu* was right or wrong. On our view, the fact is that decisions like *Korematsu* are inevitable. Ought implies can; because the judges can do little to evaluate the need for facially discriminatory policies in times of emergency, and because the judges know this, there is little point in asking them to apply genuinely strict scrutiny to such policies. The most that can be expected (whether for good or ill) is that judges will reassert themselves after an emergency decays, as they did in Youngstown and have recently done with respect to the Bush administration's post-9/11 policies. Beyond that is the possibility of ex post compensation when society decides, some generations later and with the full benefit of hindsight, that some emergency policy of an earlier day was unjustified.[34] Such compensation will often be accompanied by self-castigation or (what is even more pleasurable) the castigation of others, namely, the long-dead judges who, it will confidently be said, violated our commitment to civil liberties. The problem is that, when the next emergency comes around, the judges will defer again—not to the exact same policy, because circumstances will always be different, but to a new emergency policy whose justification the judges know themselves unable to evaluate.[35]

As we noted in chapter 1, American courts defer heavily to government in times of emergency. Given this history, we think the burden of factual uncertainty should be on those who urge courts to abandon this historical posture and adopt strict scrutiny. The burden is twofold. It is not only to show that genuine strict scrutiny is desirable because the expected harms of false negatives will exceed the expected harms of false positives. It is also to show that real judicial scrutiny of governmental action in times of emergency is feasible in a practical sense, given the institutional dilemma that judges face.

Indeed, we can go further: it may be affirmatively good that courts are more deferential during emergencies than during normal times. The reason is not only (as we argued above) that they believe that the executive branch has more information than they do about the nature of the threat. The reason is also that they think that the public is unified behind their political leaders, that the sort of political failures against which courts can usefully guard are not as likely to happen as they are during normal times, and that the change resulting from extraordinary political mobilization will often be beneficial. This flows from our argument, above, that emergencies have often been engines of progressive political change and increasing social justice. Emergencies expand the boundaries of political possibility, often for better, not worse. Judges know they should not stand in the way. We do not insist upon this point, however. We have suggested that deferential judicial review is desirable on error-cost grounds and is inevitable during emergencies in any event. This suffices to undercut the civil libertarian position that *Carolene Products* review should apply during emergencies.

## Aliens

The foregoing points apply to all kinds of *Carolene Products* review during times of emergency, whether conducted to protect resident aliens and other nonvoters or to protect political and ethnic minorities among the citizenry. Here, we round out our account by considering some distinctive problems that involve aliens. The connection to emergencies is that such problems, although always present, become more focal and more urgent during emergencies.

At first sight, the *Carolene Products* argument seems even stronger when applied to aliens than when applied to political or ethnic minorities. Since the end of Jim Crow, African Americans have had the right to vote, both de jure and de facto. Hispanics have significant and increasing political power. Even Arab Americans have substantial political power. Aliens, by contrast, have no general right to vote, although they may vote in a few categories of local elections. Because they cannot (usually) vote, they cannot directly affect political outcomes and thus would seem to be especially vulnerable to exploitation by the majority. Courts, on the *Carolene Products* theory, should offer aliens maximal protection by applying strict scrutiny to laws that discriminate against people on the basis of alienage. Such reasoning seems to have influenced the House of Lords, which recently struck down a British law that permitted the home secretary to detain without trial foreign nationals who pose a terrorist threat. The court singled out the law's facial discrimination against aliens; it did not apply to British nationals.[36]

There are several reasons for doubting the application of the *Carolene Products* theory to aliens. Initially, the argument raises the puzzle of why America's

duties to aliens are so much greater when the aliens reside in American territory than when they reside in their home countries. It is uncontroversial that
the U.S. government has much less responsibility over the welfare of aliens living in foreign countries than it has over American citizens, here and abroad. It
is also relatively uncontroversial that the U.S. government need not respect the
rights of foreign citizens living abroad to the same extent that it must respect
the rights of American citizens. And few people think that foreigners should
have the right to vote in American elections even though American foreign
policy heavily influences their interests. Thus, the question is: why should all
of this change merely because a foreigner crosses the American border?

One possible answer is that it is easier for the U.S. government to protect
people on its own territory than people who live abroad. But the U.S. government goes to great effort to protect Americans living abroad. Whatever the
practical and logistical differences, they are not extreme enough to justify such
a great difference between the treatment of aliens abroad and the treatment of
aliens on American soil.

Another possible answer is that the U.S. government does not have any
special duties toward aliens generally, but only for aliens who reside in the
United States for a sufficiently long period of time—resident aliens. We will
address this argument below. For now, it is important to note that if this view
implies that *Carolene Products* should protect resident aliens but not nonresident aliens, then much of the criticism of the U.S. government's 9/11 policy
loses its force. Except for the interviews, that policy did not target resident
aliens; its brunt was borne by nonresident aliens, who were rounded up and
deported if their papers were not in order.

The second reason for doubting the application of the *Carolene Products*
theory to alienage is that the treatment of aliens is not as bad as that theory
implies would be the case for a group that lacks the franchise. This is true
in the United States, even though constitutional protections of aliens are far
less than would be required by *Carolene Products*; and this is true in foreign
countries where there are no constitutional rights to speak of at all. During
normal times, aliens who are on American territory are not taxed any more
heavily than Americans are; they are not deprived of legal protections; they
are not mistreated or discriminated against in any overt way, unlike African
Americans during the Jim Crow era. The post-9/11 emergency did not lead
to discrimination against aliens qua alien; it led to discrimination against only
certain aliens—those with some connection to Afghanistan, Pakistan, Saudi
Arabia, and other countries with a significant al Qaeda presence. And although
aliens from these countries were subject to more discrimination than American citizens who share their national origin, that was surely because aliens are

assumed to be loyal to their home countries, whereas immigrants are assumed to be loyal to the United States. Whatever one thinks about ethnic or religious discrimination of this sort, it is clear that the government did not use 9/11 as a pretext to discriminate against alienage as such; for if it did so, it would not have limited discrimination to only these aliens.

Why don't states engage in greater discrimination against aliens? A fallacy in the *Carolene Products* view is to overlook that the welfare of aliens is itself a component of the welfare of the voting majority, so the self-interest of the majority need not produce exploitation of the minority. The welfare of aliens enters the welfare function of the voting majority in several ways.

First, the voting majority wants foreigners to come to its country—as tourists, who consume goods and services; as students, who pay tuition; and as employees, who bring needed skills. The voting majority hopes that some of these aliens will eventually settle and become citizens. States attract aliens by providing an environment in which discrimination against aliens is discouraged. If states regularly discriminate against aliens, people will be less likely to come. It is this exit option—or the option not to enter—that, as we will discuss shortly, ensures that aliens' interests are respected by governments.

Second, recent immigrants maintain family and ethnic ties to aliens and object when these aliens are subjected to governmental discrimination. Mexican Americans, for example, protested when the American government adopted harsh border control strategies that affected only Mexican nationals and not Mexican Americans. Clearly, Mexican Americans worried about the effect of these strategies on friends, relatives, and coethnics who had not been naturalized. Arab Americans objected to many of the 9/11 strategies that affected only Arab aliens, not Arab Americans. Its tradition of welcoming immigrants and its mosaic of ethnic groups ensure that, in the United States, aliens are treated quite well.

Third, many, if not most, resident aliens will eventually become citizens. Politicians thus have an incentive to treat them well; political parties bid against one another for their future support. Aliens cannot vote themselves, but their children, friends, and employers can, and these mechanisms of virtual representation give aliens a degree of political influence, despite their nominal disenfranchisement.

Fourth, members of the voting majority travel abroad, becoming aliens in other countries, and they know that their good treatment in foreign countries depends on the good treatment of aliens in the United States. If the United States wants to protect Americans abroad, it must promise to protect aliens on American soil. Thus, we can see the mechanism by which aliens obtain political power in the United States. The millions of Americans who enter foreign countries as tourists, students, and employees are members of the "majority" who, under the *Carolene Products* theory, have disproportionate influence on government policy. This majority lobbies the U.S. government to ensure that foreign governments do not engage in unreasonable discrimination against them. The foreign governments demand in return that the U.S. government not engage in unreasonable discrimination against aliens on American soil. These understandings are embodied in countless international conventions and treaties which oblige states to extend various protections to aliens on their soil, reflecting the simple reciprocal logic of alienage.[37] Thus, indirectly, aliens have quite substantial political influence in the United States.

A small but telling example of the power of reciprocation occurred in the wake of 9/11. In order to enhance control of migration, the U.S. government required that aliens entering American territory be fingerprinted. This was a small imposition, but enough to generate retaliation by states that believed that the American response was unreasonable. Brazil, for example, retaliated by requiring that Americans entering Brazil be fingerprinted.[38] Other states confined themselves to diplomatic protest, but even diplomatic protest cannot be ignored. The United States needed to decide whether fingerprinting was important enough that it would be willing to tolerate fingerprinting of Americans, or other intrusive security measures, when Americans entered other countries. Whatever the right decision, our point is that aliens do not lack influence on the American government despite their disenfranchisement. They have influence because Americans are disenfranchised in foreign countries.

There are many other examples of this phenomenon. The Mexican government has joined Mexican Americans in protesting America's treatment of Mexicans, including its border control policies and the application of the death penalty to Mexicans convicted of capital crimes. Indeed, Mexico brought proceedings against the United States in the International Court of Justice, arguing that the United States violated the Vienna Convention on Consular Relations by failing to notify several dozen Mexican nationals of their right to seek advice from the Mexican consulate after they were arrested for committing serious crimes.[39] Germany and Paraguay brought similar proceedings against the United States.[40] Conversely, the United States has protested when Americans are treated poorly in other states.

To sum up the argument so far, various factors ensure that governments do not treat aliens much more harshly than they do their own citizens. The most important, in our view, is the implicit contractual relationship between the alien and the host government—one that is enforced by the alien's exit option and the alien's own government. In order to attract and retain aliens who have valuable skills or resources, governments must treat aliens relatively well. This is not to say that this mechanism is perfect. Some governments might not bother to protect their citizens abroad; some governments may be unable to maintain a consistent policy toward aliens; and so forth. But ordinary politics are far from perfect also, and people who are in a political minority but not a suspect class entitled to special constitutional protections will often find that the government ignores their interests.

We mentioned above that one might make a distinction between a non-resident alien and a resident alien. Joseph Carens, for example, makes the apparently logical argument that a democracy exists only if government policy rests on the consent of the governed; resident aliens, unlike foreign tourists or students, are governed in their everyday lives by the law of the state in which they live; therefore, resident aliens ought to have all of the rights of citizens, including even the right to vote.[41] If they are nonetheless deprived of the right to vote, the *Carolene Products* theory would seem to provide a case for strict scrutiny of laws that discriminate against them.

This argument is flawed. A resident alien is simply at the midpoint between a nonresident alien and a citizen. Unlike a nonresident alien, the resident alien has numerous local ties (employers, friends, perhaps relatives) who will support the resident alien's interests in the political arena. This kind of virtual representation is not sufficient in itself, of course; but, in addition, the resident alien, unlike the nonresident alien, can expect to have the right to vote after the period of naturalization is over. A government that discriminates against resident aliens today takes the risk of negative votes tomorrow. Further, unlike a citizen, the resident alien retains the exit option, even if stronger local ties and weaker foreign ties make it less valuable for the resident alien than for the nonresident alien. And, unlike a citizen, the resident alien retains for the short term a "foreign" vote that, as long as the alien's government is democratic, can be used to cause the alien's government to influence the host government's policies toward aliens. Thus, the resident alien has three weak instruments for influencing the host government (exit option, future vote, current foreign vote), whereas the citizen has one strong instrument (vote); these three weak instruments may well be as good as one strong instrument. Finally, governments have an interest not only in attracting aliens, but also in encouraging some of them to become permanent residents. Aliens can choose for themselves whether they prefer to become residents or not. If the government unreasonably discriminates against resident aliens, then aliens—prior to becoming residents—can take this into account.

All of these considerations fade when our focus turns from resident aliens to the children of resident aliens. Children—especially children born and raised in the host state—will have strong ties with the host state, and thus their exit option will be weak. Once they become adults, they are in the position described by Carens: subject to regulation and therefore entitled to representation. Happily, in the United States, such children automatically obtain citizenship, so the *Carolene Products* problem does not come into existence. This leaves only the case of people who are born abroad, brought to the United States as young children, and then raised in the United States These people have strong ties to the United States, no ties to foreign nations, and no vote. This small class of people could potentially be brought under the *Carolene Products* umbrella, though again, as far as we know, they are not subject to the kind of intensive discrimination that motivates the theory of strict scrutiny.

Marginal cases aside, the extension of the *Carolene Products* theory from local minorities to aliens is unsound. Aliens, unlike ethnic or religious minorities, have an exit option and enjoy the protection of foreign governments. Although these advantages may not necessarily be more valuable than the right to vote in American elections (though they may be), the right to vote is not the appropriate baseline because aliens do not belong to the demos, or do so only in a limited and imperfectly understood fashion. In the terms we have used here, the strict review of laws and policies targeting aliens is unjustified.

## CONCLUSION

We began, in chapter 1, with a tradeoff thesis about security and liberty. This view suggests, as an expository device, that a rational and well-motivated government will balance the value of security and liberty, recalibrating the level at which both goods are provided as circumstances change over time. The democratic failure theory, whose legal corollary is *Carolene Products*, offers an internal critique of the tradeoff thesis, based on the failure of political representation to take all affected interests into account. Against this, we have argued, as a matter of comparative institutional performance, that democratic failure is no more likely during emergencies than during normal times, and that courts are less able to prevent democratic failure during emergencies. It follows that judicial deference should increase during emergencies. It is hard to say exactly how much deference is optimal, but we have argued that the historical level of deference, which has been quite high during the throes of emergency, is both desirable and predictable.

There is no need to repeat our criticisms of the democratic failure theory in any more detail, but we will underscore the consequences of rejecting it. A model judicial opinion for our view is *Dennis v. United States*, which applied first-order balancing of liberty interests and security needs to uphold the convictions of communists who advocated the overthrow of the U.S. government.[42] As in *Korematsu*, Justice Jackson's concurrence in *Dennis* explains the institutional dynamics that make deference predictable in this sort of case:

> If we must decide that this Act and its application are constitutional
> only if we are convinced that petitioner's conduct creates a "clear
> and present danger" of violent overthrow, we must appraise imponderables, including international and national phenomena which
> baffle the best informed foreign offices and our most experience[d]
> politicians. . . . No doctrine can be sound which requires us to make a
> prophecy of that sort in the guise of a legal decision.[43]

The Court later disavowed or limited *Dennis* by construing the relevant anticommunist statutes more narrowly,[44] and eventually by announcing a tighter constitutional test.[45] An important defense of this sequence portrays it as the development of a sort of second-order balancing, which places a libertarian thumb on the scales of the first-order balancing to compensate for predictable pressures toward deference.[46] In our view, the sequence is just part of the cycle of libertarian self-castigation that arises whenever the emergency has passed. Faced with a violent conspiracy of great but uncertain magnitude, governments will predictably strike, and judges will predictably allow them to do so, in part because they appreciate the institutional dilemma that Jackson outlines in *Dennis* and in *Korematsu*. The judges lack the information needed to evaluate government's claims, and know that they lack it.

This institutional dilemma makes judicial deference more and more likely as emergencies are more and more serious. In the limiting case, when the emergency is at its peak, judicial deference is inevitable, and those who counsel the judges to stand firm and to apply normal *Carolene Products* review are whistling in the wind. This sequence is neither irrational nor ill motivated, and it is largely unavoidable. Later generations will bemoan the violation of liberty, but that will not prevent yet later generations from doing the same when the hour of emergency comes 'round again.

## CHAPTER FOUR

# The Ratchet Theory and Other Long-Run Effects

So far, we have considered two internal critiques of the tradeoff thesis, which we have labeled the panic theory (chapter 2) and the democratic failure theory (chapter 3). In this chapter, we consider internal critiques of the tradeoff thesis that focus on the long-run consequences of governmental decision-making in emergencies. The common theme in these critiques is that governmental decisionmaking according to the tradeoff thesis—what we have called first-order balancing of security and liberty—will have long-run costs that the government in power at a particular time will fail to fully take into account. These critiques posit an intertemporal version of the democratic failure theory: even if government acts rationally, and even if government fully accounts for the welfare of persons affected by government policies in the current period, governmental decisionmaking may be distorted by a failure to consider the interests of those living in future periods. The government in place for the time being will externalize costs onto the future. On this account, the role of judicial review in times of emergencies would be to provide a long-run perspective that compensates for the shortsightedness of current governmental decisionmaking.

The most concrete version of these ideas is the *ratchet effect*, in which a succession of emergencies produces a unidirectional increase in some legal or political variable, an increase that is irreversible or at least costly to reverse. In the most common version of this claim, ratchets produce a long-term trend toward ever-greater security and ever-diminishing liberty, perhaps concluding in authoritarian oppression. We argue that the idea fails. The ratchet theory lacks a mechanism that permits governmental powers to expand and prevents them from contracting, and it makes implausible assumptions about the rationality of officials and voters who consent to legal changes during emergencies. Those who fear the ratchet's power point to constitutional trends—such as the rise of executive power—that are more plausibly the result of long-term technological and demographic changes, not of recurrent emergencies; they ignore the possibility of constitutional trends in the opposite direction, such as the rise of individual rights. (If there is such a trend, it is not a ratchet process either; we include below a critique of an optimistic variant of the emergency ratchet, in which a succession of emergencies causes government to display ever-increasing respect for civil liberties.)

We then critique some other long-run effects said to flow from emergency decisionmaking. The most important of these is the claim that offensive measures against *terrorism are counterproductive in the long run*. Here, the idea is that deterrence and other offensive measures against terrorism in one period will produce ever-greater levels of terrorism in subsequent periods, by increasing terrorist recruitment and delegitimating the deterring government. The idea fails to consider that a policy of *not* deterring terrorism in the current period creates an impression of weakness, which can itself increase terrorist recruitment and delegitimate the government that fails to deter. Governments should ignore these long-run speculations, which wash out in either direction, and do what makes sense in the short run. A fortiori, the speculative long-run effects of deterrence do not provide a basis for judicial intervention.

The discussion is structured as follows. We first provide a brief overview of ratchet accounts in legal theory, questioning their general utility, and then critique the most common version of the ratchet account, which holds that emergencies produce a *statist ratchet*: an irreversible trend toward increased state power and official suppression of civil liberties, free speech, and political association. We suggest that the statist ratchet account is implausible on conceptual, institutional, psychological, and normative grounds and provides no support for interventionist judicial review during emergencies. No more successful is the opposite account, which holds that emergencies produce a *libertarian ratchet* in the form of ever-increasing governmental respect for civil liberties. Generally, the ratchet idea has little utility for positive or normative arguments about emergencies, principally because ratchet accounts posit an implausible amount of friction in the law-making system. In our picture, by contrast, the law-making system adjusts fluidly, if unpredictably, to emergencies, exogenous shocks, and other changes in the political and social environment; few changes are unidirectional and irreversible in the strong sense that ratchet accounts suppose. Finally, we consider and reject the idea that offensive measures against terrorism are self-defeating in the long run and offer brief remarks on some other, vaguer appeals to the long-term costs of emergency policy.

## RATCHETS IN GENERAL

The *ratchet* (or, redundantly, the *one-way ratchet*) is a favored analytic tool of legal theorists. Too much so; ratchet accounts are invoked in a bewildering array of settings, ranging from the theory of regulation and bureaucratic behavior[1] to racial profiling[2] and sexual mores.[3] For a genuine ratchet to occur, however, highly specialized conditions must obtain. The essential features of a ratchet are *unidirectional* and *entrenched* change in some legal variable. First, the policy space in which the ratchet occurs is assumed to be one-dimensional, so that the ratchet produces ever-increasing values of a variable—more and more and more of something. Second, the incremental increases are wholly or partially fixed once they occur.

To be sure, the change need not be literally irreversible; although strong ratchet accounts posit irreversibility, weak ratchet accounts merely posit that change is sticky, because it is more or less costly to undo. Weak ratchet accounts seem more plausible than strong ones, but they also pack less punch: the less costly it is to undo a given change, the less important is that change. We will thus use the term *irreversible* as a shorthand that includes the idea of changes that are more or less costly to reverse and that are worrisome in proportion to the costs of reversing them.

Putting these conditions together, a well-formed ratchet account must have something like the following shape. At time 1, some legal rule or practice emerges endogenously from political processes, including the legal system; at time 2, the rule or practice is cemented by some mechanism and has become an exogenous constraint; at time 3, some dimension of the rule increases endogenously; at time 4, the increase is cemented into place; and the process repeats indefinitely. These conditions are rare, perhaps even nonexistent. The danger here is that the "ratchet" label is being bandied about too freely and is often confused with a simple trend or with endogenous but reversible change in some variable that would quickly revert to its original value if other legal or social conditions changed.

Despite the ubiquity of ratchet accounts, few such accounts are fully specified, and often there is no plausible way to cash them out. Take a popular idea, or intuition, in constitutional theory: if conservative judges respect precedent while liberal judges freely overrule precedents, and conservative courts alternate with liberal ones, then a ratchet effect is created, whereby the existing stock of precedents becomes increasingly liberal over time. But this account is either out of equilibrium, or arbitrarily assumes that the two camps have wildly disparate preferences. If the implicit picture is that both liberal and conservative judges are political, seeking to embody their preferences and attitudes in legal decisions, then conservative judges are myopic in refusing to overrule liberal decisions; they are repeatedly, and inexplicably, duped by the equally unprincipled but more cunning liberals. So the picture must instead be that liberal judges are political while conservative judges have a strong and principled preference for adhering to any past decision, whatever its political valence, but this seems arbitrary. Unsurprisingly, there is no real evidence that law systematically ratchets in liberal directions over time. If the Warren Court and early Burger Court pushed criminal law, criminal procedure, and the law of fundamental rights in liberal directions, the Rehnquist Court cut back a bit along the same margins and affirmatively pushed in conservative directions on other margins, such as federalism and executive power.

Perhaps history contains a few genuine ratchet processes. The gradual expansion of the political franchise in liberal democracies over the course of the nineteenth and twentieth centuries might qualify, although recent scholarship has shown that there were sustained reverses and contractions of the franchise even within that large-scale process.[4] Another example might be the alleged tendency of temporary taxes to become permanent, especially wartime taxes.[5] But this is belied by history: the U.S. government imposed an income tax during the Civil War and an excess profits tax during World War I, yet both were repealed afterward.[6] In general, ratchet arguments are methodologically suspect and are invoked with far greater frequency than is warranted by the evidence. This pattern holds true for ratchet arguments about emergency powers, to which we now turn.

## THE STATIST RATCHET

The statist ratchet identifies a putative tendency of emergency policies to "become entrenched over time and thus normalized and made routine. . . . The maintenance of emergency powers may be accompanied by expansion over time of the scope of such powers. At the same time, built-in limitations on the exercise of emergency authority and powers tend to wither away."[7]

As it turns out, however, the statist ratchet account has only a surface sheen of plausibility, and no core. It assumes that emergencies produce unidirectional and irreversible change in the direction of official intrusion on civil liberties. But there is no obvious reason to think that any such process occurs; the statist ratchet fails to supply a mechanism that would explain such a process if it did occur; and if there is such a mechanism, it is not clear that the resulting ratchet process is bad. We will organize these points into four critiques of the statist ratchet—conceptual, institutional, psychological, and normative—and then offer some remarks about ratchets and judicial review.

## Conceptual Problems

Proponents of the statist ratchet are vague about their assumptions, but tend to imagine a finite, one-dimensional policy space. In this space, government policies vary from minimally to maximally intrusive; the statist ratchet assumes that emergencies produce a continual increase that is unidirectional on this dimension, moving steadily from less official oppression to more.

But this picture is too crude. The policy space is not one-dimensional but multidimensional: official policies, whether instituted during an emergency or not, can intrude more (or less) on some margins while intruding less (or more) on others. At time T, the government policy for airport security is to search passengers who fit a given ethnic and religious profile. At time T + 1, the policy changes to random searches; the new policy, let us say, imposes a cost (at least in an expected sense) on a greater number of people, but reduces the stigma of being searched. Here, it is senseless to ask whether liberty has been increased or decreased; instead, it has been redistributed by imposing a smaller deprivation more widely. Second, there is the standard problem of conflicts or tensions among libertarian rights, which arise from budget constraints on the government that funds the institutions needed to protect those rights.[8] More money for airport searches may reduce the need for ethnic profiling, but it may mean less money for public defenders, or a longer court queue for citizens asserting constitutional liberties against the government.

These two problems—controversial choices about the distributive profile of libertarian rights and the interdependence of budgeting choices that affect rights—mean that officials face the difficult problem of trading off and aggregating liberties across different individuals. As discussed in chapter 1, in rare cases, Pareto-improving moves will enable greater security at a given level of official intrusion, or less intrusion with a constant level of security; but in most cases, more liberty for some means less liberty for others. Aggregative judgments are inescapable; the need to compare tradeoffs along different dimensions greatly complicates the simple ratchet picture.

To be sure, these conceptual problems are not dispositive in and of themselves. We might discover, empirically, a decrease of liberty on all dimensions, or on some suitably weighted or aggregated combination of dimensions. What is true, however, is that ratchet arguments must carefully specify the relevant dimensions and examine their interactions. The simple picture of unidimensional, unidirectional change embodied in the most common versions of the statist ratchet does not begin to engage these conceptual problems.

Finally, the boundaries of the policy space themselves change over time. Exogenous shocks arising from technological, economic, and social change can transform the policy arenas in which the balance between security and liberty is played out. Governments that had managed to assert some level of control over traditional media had to cope with the arrival of the Internet;[9] in a future era, perhaps personal teleporters will come into widespread use, making the government's struggle to control its physical borders seem hopeless as well. Unanticipated change undermines government's ability to control liberties. In place of the menacing picture drawn by the statist ratchet, which envisages a continuous increase of official power over information and personal conduct, we might imagine government as a rat on a treadmill, constantly struggling to keep pace with new forms of technology and new modes of citizen behavior. Technological change may also strengthen government's hand, but there is no basis for a presumption that it always or generally does so.

## Institutional Problems: Is There a Mechanism?

Statist ratchet accounts fail to specify any institutional mechanism by which legal and political measures intended to combat emergencies become irreversible. Why, exactly, do temporary measures stick after the emergency has passed? Although statist ratchet accounts usually gloss over this point, we can imagine several related mechanisms. First, judicial precedent developed in times of emergency might distend or spill over into the ordinary legal system, and precedent will be costly to overrule. Second, legal rules developed in times of emergency may be protected by the status quo bias built into the legislative system, or by the formation of bureaucracies and interest groups that coalesce around the new measures and block subsequent efforts to repeal them. We critique these ideas in turn.

**Precedent** The *locus classicus* for the argument from precedent is Justice Jackson's dissent in *Korematsu v. United States*, with its famous claim that

> once a judicial opinion rationalizes [an emergency] order to show that it conforms to the Constitution, or rather rationalizes the Constitution to show that the Constitution sanctions such an order, the Court for all time has validated . . . [a] principle [that] lies about like

a loaded weapon ready for the hand of any authority that can bring forward a plausible claim of an urgent need.[10]

Expanding upon (and modifying) Jackson's dissent, commentators such as Oren Gross and Mark Tushnet interpret him as saying that "it is better to have emergency powers exercised in an extraconstitutional way, so that everyone understands that the actions are extraordinary, than to have the actions rationalized away as consistent with the Constitution and thereby normalized."[11] We comment upon the idea that it is better for emergency powers to be exercised extraconstitutionally in chapter 5. Here we address the ratchet idea alone.

Jackson's ratchet idea is obscure. Suppose that, contra Jackson, judicial precedents explicitly uphold government actions in a time of crisis on the ground that the emergency justifies the order, even if a similar order would be invalid in ordinary times. Why must the precedent both (1) spill over into ordinary law and (2) remain entrenched "for all time," as Jackson puts it? As for the first condition, the precedent will itself have a built-in limitation to emergency circumstances. Presumably, the concerns are that precedents are extremely malleable and that the category of "emergency" is a fluid and unstable one. But if this is so, it is so in both directions; later judges may either distend the precedent to accommodate government power or else contract the precedent to constrain it. Jackson failed, in *Korematsu*, to supply an independent account to explain why the former possibility is more likely, and more harmful, than the latter.

The best stab at an account of this sort appears in another Jackson opinion. Institutional incentives will cause the executive to press the boundaries of the emergency category to ever broader extremes, and that will be possible because the category of emergency is extraordinarily nebulous and difficult to specify through legal formulations. Cognitive limitations will induce the courts to acquiesce in this expansion. Because the courts will be aware of the limits of their information and of the high risks of error if they frustrate executive action in a genuine emergency, they will adopt a deferential stance.[12] This reconstructed argument seems plausible as far as it goes, but rational judges who are aware of their cognitive limitations—and this account assumes self-awareness—can anticipate the slippage and forestall it by *initially* defining the category of emergency more narrowly than they otherwise would. The eventual expansion of the category will simply reinstate its optimal scope, rather than exceeding it.[13]

At bottom, the Jackson view must rest on a simple empirical conjecture: the expansion of emergency powers, once begun, will inevitably culminate in total executive domination. But this seems hysterical; there is no evidence for it in the study of comparative politics. Many constitutions contain explicit provisions for emergency powers, either in text or in judicial doctrine.[14] Sometimes, executive domination has overtaken the relevant polities; sometimes, it has not. Other variables probably dominate, such as the nation's stage of development, or its susceptibility to economic shocks, or the design of legislative and judicial institutions. Political scientists John Carey and Matthew Shugart find that "executive decree authority," a category that overlaps with executive emergency powers, lacks any systematic tendency to enable usurpation by the executive; rather, decree authority often serves the preferences of legislators.[15]

Recall the status quo position: judges typically defer to the executive in war and other emergencies, as we have emphasized. Civil libertarians seek to change this status quo, and thus they bear the burden of proof. They need to show that recognizing a legal category of emergency powers, or increasing the level of deference during judicially identified emergencies, will risk pushing the Constitution to the bottom of the slippery slope. A casual citation to a few salient examples, typically the emergency provisions of the Weimar Constitution, will not carry their intellectual burden.

As for the second condition, it is hard to see why precedents granting government emergency powers should be irreversibly entrenched, at least if precedents denying the government emergency powers are not. The force of precedent (*stare decisis*) will be either strong or weak. If it is weak, then past precedents granting emergency powers can be overruled, even if they cannot be cabined to emergency situations. If the force of precedent is strong, then courts will be unable to overrule precedents that previously denied government emergency powers in particular settings or that strongly entrenched liberties, as well as precedents that granted emergency powers. Here, too, the argument from precedent cuts in both directions. There is no ratchet mechanism that uniquely applies to precedents upholding government claims of emergency power; the general stickiness of precedent is a far broader point.

*Legislation (and Constitutional Amendment)* The argument from precedent points to the inertia built into the judicial system; there is a similar argument that points to the inertia of the law-making system, embodied in the costly procedures for statutory enactment and constitutional amendment. These design features partially entrench the legal status quo; the statist ratchet account might implicitly suppose that temporary legislation or constitutional provisions, enacted during emergencies, will thus stick after the emergency has passed. But rational and well-motivated legislators can anticipate this by inserting sunset provisions into emergency legislation (as Congress did in crucial sections of the PATRIOT Act); rational and well-motivated constitutional drafters can insert sunset provisions into constitutional rules.[16] Gross argues that "[t]ime-bound emergency legislation is often the subject of future extensions and renewals,"[17] but the existence of the sunset clause alters the status quo point: unless proponents of extension can surmount the costly hurdles to legislative action, the statute will lapse automatically. Thus, libertarian opponents of renewal still enjoy the advantage of legislative inertia.

The statist ratchet account must suppose that legislators either irrationally fail to anticipate the future termination of the emergency, perhaps because they are gripped by "panic," or else that legislators are motivated to use any and every emergency as a means to expand the permanent powers of government. We addressed panic in chapter 2. As for motivations, the idea that legislators desire to maximize permanent state power as against the individual is vivid, but it lacks microfoundations in the behavior of the individuals who occupy the legislature. Why, exactly, does it benefit legislators as individuals to expand the powers of government, when they possess only a fractional share even of congressional power, let alone of the whole government's power?[18] As members of a political party, they may or may not benefit from increasing government power. Even if legislators have a stake in the power of Congress as an institution, expanding government power in times of emergency usually benefits the executive most of all, and the executive is Congress's principal institutional rival. The statist ratchet fails to offer a plausible account of legislators' utility functions. We might posit that legislators strictly maximize their chances of reelection, but then the question just becomes why constituents demand legislation that (for lack of sunsetting) will outlive the emergency, and the picture must be that, during emergencies, constituents *irrationally* demand permanent legislation; so we are back to the panic idea again.

Even accepting the premise that legislators are frequently irrational or ill motivated, pointing to the status quo bias built into the law-making system proves too much. The status quo bias operates neutrally across different types of statutes and constitutional provisions. It not only (1) entrenches liberty-restricting laws (the only case the statist ratchet acknowledges), but equally (2) prevents enactment of liberty-restricting laws, and (3) entrenches liberty-protecting ones. As for case 2, the high costs of statutory enactment can weed out the most draconian proposals for controlling sedition and terrorism; an example is Senator John Chamberlin's 1918 proposal to enact legislation that would allow the government to punish spies by court-martial, which was killed by Wilson's opposition.[19] As for case 3, the costs of enactment protect from repeal any laws that protect liberties from infringement by later legislatures or the executive. Consider the Posse Comitatus Act,[20] which blocks the executive from using regular armed forces for domestic law enforcement, and thus embodies a traditional libertarian anxiety about "standing armies." The act is just as entrenched by the law-making process as the PATRIOT Act would be, had Congress not provided a sunset to the latter statute's most controversial provisions.

*Bureaucracies and Interest Groups* A related mechanism might posit that emergency policies generate bureaucracies that block the repeal of those policies. On this view, creating new agencies to cope with an emergency, perhaps by consolidation of old agencies (as with the Department of Homeland Security), creates a cadre of officials with vested interests in prolonging the new bureaucracy for as long as possible, even after the emergency has petered out. Those officials will use their influence in Congress and with client interest groups to block repeal of the agency's organic statute or diminution of the agency's power.

It is hardly clear that bureaucratic immortality is a real phenomenon; that sort of talk had more resonance before Congress abolished the Interstate Commerce Commission, deregulated the airlines, and reorganized and streamlined the security agencies. The same problems we have discussed—the underdeveloped account of officials' utility functions and the mismatch between the scope of the mechanism and the scope of the argument—persist here as well. It is unclear why rational legislators would fail to anticipate and block the future bureaucrats' strategy by inserting a sunset termination provision, a periodic review process, or some other device. And if bureaucratic inertia is a real phenomenon, it operates equally to block moves that would expand government power, restrict liberty, or permanently institutionalize a state of emergency. If an inefficient welter of competing security agencies hampers government's efforts to extend control over unpopular social groups, then those agencies will attempt to block congressional attempts to reorganize them into a more efficient, and more menacing, centralized department. If Congress nonetheless succeeds in doing so, as it recently has, why cannot a future Congress succeed in abolishing or curtailing the agency created to meet the emergency? The dilemma for the statist ratchet account is that either bureaucratic inertia is real, in which case it will block liberty-infringing moves as well as liberty-expanding ones, or it is not real, in which case liberty-infringing moves will not become entrenched.

Generally speaking, there is no reason to suppose that laws, policies, and bureaucratic institutions created during an emergency (1) systematically fail to change, or to change back, after a crisis has passed (2) because of institutional inertia and interest group pressure, rather than society's postenactment preferences. Condition 2 is as important as condition 1; ratchet proponents often overlook this point, neglecting the possibility that policies fail to change back because citizens and officials in later periods have simply decided, in light of their experience, that the policies are good. (Here, we assume that the postenactment preferences are not themselves an endogenous product of the enactment; we consider that possibility shortly.) Mark Tushnet notes that laws passed during emergencies may remain on the books partly from "legislative inertia," which he defines as "meaning, here, that repeal has a lower priority than other matters in light of voter and representative preferences."[21] Presumably, the idea is that the costs of repeal are positive and large enough to outweigh the gains, even if voters and officials would prefer the repeal were it costless. This is possible, but it does not distinguish policies adopted in and for emergencies from non-emergency policies, which frequently outlive their usefulness in this sense; consider outmoded statutes regulating blasphemy, fornication, and other morals offenses. The standard political mechanism for drawing the teeth from such laws is underenforcement by prosecutors and other bureaucrats, who choose enforcement levels in light of current political preferences and let outmoded statutes fall into desuetude.

Historically, it is rare that condition 1 and condition 2 are jointly satisfied. World War I produced a large new cadre of regulatory agencies that persisted into the New Deal and beyond.[22] But a plausible view is that the national economy was previously underregulated and that the new institutions satisfied social demand; so this example does not clearly satisfy condition 2. The quasi war with France in 1798 and partisan competition between Federalists and Republicans produced the Sedition Act, but the statute expired in 1801,[23] in violation of condition 1; why did the statist ratchet not operate there? The Enemy Aliens Act, also enacted in 1798, has persisted, but here again it is hardly clear that condition 2 was satisfied. Most strikingly, consider Lincoln's notorious suspension of habeas corpus—an action that was undone after the Civil War's end.[24] Why no statist ratchet?

These historical examples are impressionistic, but not more so than the examples adduced by proponents of the statist ratchet. Indeed, preliminary empirical work has now examined the ratchet thesis and finds that "[c]ontrary to widespread fear and speculation that doctrine created during wartime 'lingers' on in peacetime, the rights jurisprudence appears to 'bounce back' during peacetime."[25] As we discuss below, the best working presumption for constitutional law follows this finding. We should presume that no ratchet effects operate, in any direction. Institutional change displays no consistent trend or mechanism; is determined differently in different contexts by a complex mix of political, economic, and technological forces; and, as we shall discuss shortly, can be good or bad depending upon circumstances.

## Psychological Problems: Adaptive Preferences?

We will briefly look at the idea that the statist ratchet operates by virtue of a psychological mechanism. Proponents of the statist ratchet account say, rather vaguely, that government's emergency measures have a "tranquilizing effect . . . on the general public's critical approach toward emergency regimes."[26] The underlying picture here must be some sort of endogenous preference formation, which causes social preferences to conform to government policies, or the related idea of adaptive preferences, in which individuals limit their aspirations, not merely their actions, by reference to the set of feasible policies. Somehow, the intuition runs, society gets used to the postcrisis baseline of expanded governmental power; the ratchet operates not because temporary emergency measures block society's capacity to return to the status quo ante, but because society no longer desires to do so.

The implicit assumption here is that the postcrisis baseline is bad. If it is good—if the precrisis baseline represented a society underprepared for emergencies, in which law and institutions were supplying too much liberty and not enough order—then the endogenous formation of preferences for the postcrisis baseline would help to stabilize the new regime and would thus be good as well. At the very least, we would need a very strong account (welfarist or nonwelfarist) of the value of autonomous preference formation to say that the public's adaptation to the new social state is bad; the statist ratchet offers no such account. So the preference-based version of the statist ratchet is, like the institutional version, parasitic on a suppressed and wholly independent judgment that the status quo ante represents the correct balance between liberty and order; more on this below.

In any event, the evidence that endogenous or adaptive preference formation operates in this way is scant indeed. As we also discuss below, another view paints just the opposite picture of political and social psychology: in the postcrisis state, a widespread revulsion against the prevailing liberty-infringing policies sets in, and society judges, in hindsight, that the emergency measures were unnecessary. The stock example is the World War II–era internment of Japanese-American citizens, which is now widely described as an egregious mistake that inflicted unnecessary deprivations of liberty, due in part to racial animus. If this sort of post hoc revulsion operates consistently, then the right account would emphasize contrarian preference formation and hindsight bias, rather than the endogenous preference formation and confirmation bias posited by the statist ratchet. But we will claim that a third account—no ratchets operate systematically, in either a liberty-restricting or a liberty-expanding direction—is the most convincing of all.

## Normative Problems: Is the Statist Ratchet Bad?

Normatively, the statist ratchet account simply assumes that the status quo ante—the legal baseline prior to the emergency that produces an irreversible expansion of state control—already embodies the optimal balance between liberty and security. So the statist ratchet in effect makes two normative assertions: (1) the precrisis legal rules were optimally balanced for the precrisis state; and (2) the postcrisis rules are too restrictive for the postcrisis state.

Yet, in some settings, either or both of these assertions will fail to hold. We might deny 2 while affirming 1, if we think both that the precrisis rules were optimal for the precrisis state *and* that the postcrisis rules are optimal for the postcrisis state. If, for example, the crisis is the product of a permanent change in the polity's political circumstances, such that the value of security is higher after the crisis than before it, then the balance should be recalibrated after the crisis; failing to do so would constitute social paralysis, rather than a laudable respect for traditional liberties.

More interestingly, we might deny both 1 and 2, if we think that before the emergency society was, in some sense, unprepared for the emergency, underregulated, or excessively liberty protecting, while after the emergency society has attained the optimal balance. We might believe, for example, that as of September 10, 2001, American governmental institutions were supplying too much liberty and not enough security. Well-documented turf battles between uncoordinated, and arguably inefficient, security and intelligence agencies meant that government failed to anticipate and forestall a major terrorist attack, or even to plan sensibly for its aftermath.[27] On this view, the institutional puzzle would be to explain why government underreacted to the terrorist threat—the opposite of the puzzle for the statist ratchet account, which is to explain why government overreacts to threats. The point here is not to endorse this view of post-9/11 security reorganization, on the merits. But the possibility cannot be assumed away, a priori.

Proponents of the statist ratchet rarely consider these possibilities. Consider Dermot Walsh's argument that the expansion of law enforcement powers in the Republic of Ireland, from about 1970 to the present, has created a legal regime in which official powers to investigate and detain both suspected terrorists and ordinary criminals systematically trump civil liberties.[28] Walsh's account suggests that legal rules initially formulated to cope with terrorist campaigns and other security emergencies bled over into ordinary policing, resulting in a harsh regime of criminal procedure. Walsh disclaims any substantive evaluation of these developments, confining himself to the procedural objection that the developments never received adequate legislative deliberation. Oren Gross, however, cites Walsh's history in an argument that emergency powers of the sort initially granted to Irish officials will produce "insidious changes" by spilling over into non-emergency settings.[29]

But nothing in Walsh's history suggests any reason to condemn, on substantive civil libertarian grounds, the result of the developments he describes. Walsh notes that the initial impetus for expanded law enforcement authority was "[t]he escalation of subversive activity associated with Northern Ireland" (although he tendentiously calls this a "pretext") and acknowledges that the preexisting law was "so heavily biased in favour of the freedom of the individual that the task facing the prosecution could be described fairly as a very tricky obstacle course."[30] So an obvious alternative view is that in Ireland, circa 1970, the law of criminal procedure was too lax for an increasingly complex and polarized society—perhaps because the relevant law was initially impressed with the libertarian mold of nineteenth-century British procedure and had never been updated. The expansion of police powers after 1970, on this view, would just represent a belated adjustment toward the optimum balance of liberty and security, not a lamentable departure from that balance.

In like vein, Gross says that "emergencies have led to quantum leaps" in a process of "aggrandizement" of executive powers in America, France, and Great Britain after the two world wars.[31] "Aggrandizement" is meant to sound bad, but Gross never actually gives a straightforward normative argument to that effect. It is equally possible that quantum leaps occurred because war or emergencies liberated the polity from some institutional sclerosis, or entrenched equilibrium, that had held government power at an inadequately low level. Gross acknowledges that "[t]he growing complexity of modern society and the needs of its members have played an important role in the expansion of executive authority";[32] but this may be the whole story, not just part of it.

Why, exactly, is it bad if emergency or temporary measures spill over into the ordinary legal system? Spillover of this sort is, in itself, neither good nor bad. The only question is whether the new state of affairs is an improvement on the status quo ante or not; if it is an improvement, then the spillover was a benign event. Perhaps the war or emergency stimulated legal experimentation, spurred the development of new technology, or produced innovative policy mechanisms; in any of these cases, it might be wise, not foolish, to incorporate the new information or innovation into the ordinary law after the emergency has passed. The statist ratchet suffers from a virulent strain of the naturalistic fallacy: whatever complex of legal rules happens to exist at some status quo point is taken to be good, and any shift in the direction of greater security is taken to be bad. But if the status quo can embody too much liberty, rather than just the right amount, that picture is arbitrary.

## Ratchets and Judicial Review

These remarks suggest that the ratchet theory is useless as a prescription for judicial review. Judges lack the information necessary to determine whether ratchets are a legitimate concern in general; to know which particular governmental policies and institutional innovations are most likely to produce long-term ratchet effects; and to know whether ratchets would push policy, irreversibly, in bad directions or in good ones. It is not clear at all what judges worried about ratchets should do, because the relevant considerations are too speculative and inchoate. The ratchet concern would only have independent weight when a judge would otherwise uphold a policy adjustment or institutional innovation for the current emergency. In such a case, it would be bizarre for the judge to appeal to vague long-run concerns to strike down the policy adjustment, which by hypothesis the judges believe is a necessary emergency measure in the short run. In any event, it is hardly clear what judges could do about a ratchet-generating policy, even if judicial oversight were desirable. Political constraints will make it difficult for judges to appeal to long-run considerations to invalidate legislation or policies demanded by an aroused public concerned about short-run safety.

Perhaps for these reasons, even Justice Jackson did not suggest that judges concerned about ratchet effects should simply invalidate, on the merits, emergency policies they would otherwise sustain: Jackson's suggestion was that the court should in some obscure way declare the government's emergency action to be a nonjusticiable issue or "political question," thereby upholding it without approving it on the merits. Civil libertarians either take a similar tack or else suggest that ratchets should be constrained by institutional mechanisms other than judicial review—an example being Bruce Ackerman's proposal that governmental decisionmaking during emergencies should be regulated by a higher-order statute. We return to these ideas in chapter 5. Here, the point is just that the ratchet theory, even in the hands of its proponents, does not support substantive judicial oversight of governmental choices in times of emergency.

## THE LIBERTARIAN RATCHET

If the statist ratchet identifies a sustained and irreversible decline of civil liberties, a mirror image position—the libertarian ratchet—identifies a progressive and optimistic trend. In this camp are Chief Justice William Rehnquist's claim to discern a "generally ameliorative trend" in government's treatment of civil liberties during wartime;[33] an argument by Jack Goldsmith and Cass Sunstein that social evaluation, in hindsight, of government's performance during wars and other crises produces a "trend toward greater protection for civil liberties in wartime";[34] and similar arguments by Mark Tushnet, Seth Waxman, and David Cole.[35] Of these, Rehnquist, Tushnet, Waxman, and Cole seem to view the libertarian ratchet as good, while Goldsmith and Sunstein focus on explanation rather than normative assessment. Many of the preceding objections to the statist ratchet apply equally to the libertarian ratchet; we will confine ourselves to a few additional points.

The libertarian ratchet, like the statist ratchet, extrapolates a trend from an impoverished data set containing too few observations. In the case of America, proponents of the libertarian ratchet have little with which to work: the Civil War, World Wars I and II, the armed conflicts in Korea and Vietnam, perhaps the Red Scares of the 1950s, if "war" is defined capaciously. Many curves can be drawn through such a small set of points.

Goldsmith and Sunstein claim:

> Compared to past wars led by Lincoln, Wilson, and Roosevelt, the [George W.] Bush administration has, thus far, diminished relatively few civil liberties. Even a conservative Executive branch, it seems, is influenced by the general trend toward protections of civil liberty during wartime.[36]

Although the first point is indisputable—the Bush administration has not suspended the writ of habeas corpus, punished harmless dissenters, or interned large numbers of American citizens—the second point does not follow from the first and is methodologically infirm. To know whether the Bush administration would behave with greater respect for civil liberties than did the administrations of Lincoln, Wilson, or Roosevelt, we would have to observe similar conditions, and we do not. Would the Bush administration show as much restraint if enemy troops were within a short train ride of Washington, D.C. (Lincoln), if Europe exploded in armed struggle (Wilson), or if an American fleet had been wiped out by the surprise attack of a foreign state (Roosevelt)? It is not hard to imagine, even today, that civil liberties would be

extensively abridged in such circumstances. These are counterfactual speculations, but the libertarian ratchet itself rests on a counterfactual speculation—
that current administrations would behave with more restraint than past ones,
given like conditions.

The general claim is that a series of wars produces an ever greater respect
for civil liberties, but it is hardly obvious that the independent variable and
the dependent one are correlated, let alone causally linked. In many countries,
casual empiricism suggests that a series of wars and crises has not produced ever
increasing respect for civil liberties; consider the history of Prussia, and Germany as a whole, between 1871 and 1945. And in other countries, civil liberties
have increased over time periods when no wars occurred; Europe after World
War II is a large example. In the European case, and in other cases, national
wealth is a major confounding variable, one about which Goldsmith and Sunstein say little. A plausible hypothesis is that wealthier countries, whatever their
military history, show greater respect for civil liberties than poorer ones do.[37]

In a slightly different formulation, Goldsmith and Sunstein suggest that the
libertarian ratchet arises not merely from a series of wars, but from a series of
*successful* wars. Goldsmith and Sunstein say that "there is nothing inevitable"
about the ratchet effect they identify; it is a product of America's "remarkable
record of military success."[38] In this sense, Goldsmith and Sunstein suggest that
the libertarian ratchet is contingent—"an accident of America's distinctive
history."[39] (But what about America's military reverses, including the War of
1812, Pearl Harbor, the Vietnam War, and—arguably—Iraq?) If they mean that
the posited trend of increasing respect for civil liberties would be promptly
reversed by future military defeats, then it suggests there was no ratchet effect
in the first place; some form of stickiness or irreversibility is necessary for any
ratchet account.

To establish the libertarian ratchet, a much larger comparative study would
be necessary; confining the inquiry to one nation (America) and a few wars
tells us little. This is so even if there has been a constantly increasing respect
for civil liberties in America. To generate the general claim solely from the
American case is to commit the methodological mistake of selecting cases
on the dependent variable.[40] The claim that spring will come early whenever
the groundhog sees its shadow cannot be proved by looking solely at years in
which, in fact, spring came early.

Perhaps we should understand the libertarian ratchet not as advancing a
fully specified hypothesis of this sort, but simply as describing a causal mechanism that operates all else equal: after a series of wars, hindsight tends to produce
social judgments that past suspensions of civil liberties were unnecessary. But the
hindsight bias or social learning mechanism is underspecified; the level of gen-

erality at which hindsight operates makes a critical difference. Goldsmith and Sunstein seem to assume that the hindsight judgment operates to bar unnecessary future invasions of civil liberties, as a general class. But it may equally be true that hindsight condemns only the *specific* policies or programs instituted in past crises. New policies or programs will be categorized differently in the social cognition and will be assessed strictly ex ante. Tushnet puts it nicely:

> Judges and scholars develop doctrines and approaches that preclude the repetition of the last generation's mistakes. Unfortunately, each new threat generates new policy responses, which are—almost by definition—not precluded by the doctrines designed to make it impossible to adopt the policies used last time. And yet, the next generation again concludes that the new policy responses were mistaken. We learn from our mistakes to the extent that we do not repeat precisely the same errors, but it seems that we do not learn enough to keep us from making new and different mistakes.[41]

This is a version of the conceptual point we advanced against the statist ratchet: because the policy space changes over time, it is simplistic to ask whether wars or other emergencies cause an "increase" or "decrease" in governmental respect for civil liberties. As old forms of governmental control become disreputable and disappear (e.g., suspension of judicial process, suppression of political speech, and internment), new forms become technologically feasible and normatively freighted (consider sophisticated government monitoring of private communications, including Internet use, or of lawyers' conversations with clients). Here again, there just is no single dimension of greater or lesser respect for civil liberties—and thus no predicate for the unidirectional trend line that both the libertarian and statist ratchets assume, albeit in different directions.

Even putting aside these conceptual problems, the social learning hypothesis is implausible. The piece of wisdom that executive overreaching can occur if not prevented by courts or legislatures is centuries old—indeed, it was a central theme of the Glorious Revolution—not something that the courts and the American public have painfully learned crisis by crisis. Historical examples of possibly unjustified infringements of civil liberties by the executive branch have confirmed this wisdom and brought it up to date, but have not had straightforward implications for the much more difficult questions whether courts can and should try to constrain the executive during emergencies, and whether they could do so without interfering with justified action as well as unjustified action. And there is no evidence that courts have learned from the past that the answer to this question is that they should constrain the executive during emergencies.

Seth Waxman joins the social learning hypothesis with a further argument that courts today are more powerful than they used to be. Judicial prestige is higher today than in the past, so courts are confident that rulings that restrict the discretion of the executive branch will not be ignored, as happened when Lincoln disobeyed the ruling in *Ex parte Merryman*, or not result in retaliation, like FDR's court-packing plan in 1937.[42] Waxman reads the recent war-on-terror cases, such as *Hamdi*, as confirming this view: the Supreme Court was less deferential than during prior emergencies, and this is because it has learned from past executive branch mistakes. The most recent decision, *Hamdan*, provides further support for Waxman's view; overheated analyses have even called it a fundamental reassertion of congressional and judicial supremacy over the executive. We are skeptical, however. There is no reason to think that judicial prestige is high today; indeed, in some quarters, *Bush v. Gore* was supposed to have destroyed the prestige of the Supreme Court and revealed it as political body, and some polling data show this effect to be a serious one.[43] The current Supreme Court is no more powerful and self-confident than prior courts, such as, notably, the *Lochner* court, which struck down numerous New Deal programs at the height of a domestic economic crisis. And the war-on-terror cases have been notable for their caution, especially their de facto acquiescence—at least to date—to the president's claim that he can detain suspected terrorists indefinitely without charges. *Hamdan* is more limited than its celebrants claim, as we suggest in chapter 8, and represents nothing more than the usual reassertion of judicial power once the emergency has cooled. *Hamdan* was possible only because no attacks occurred in the homeland from 2001 to 2006; if another attack does occur in the future, the judges will pull *Hamdan*'s teeth. Far from providing a counterexample to the cycle thesis, *Hamdan* illustrates it.

## GOVERNMENT WITHOUT RATCHETS

There is a common premise underlying the libertarian and statist ratchets: both accounts assume that the history of civil liberties in America shows a constant trend, or at least that war and other emergencies have a constant, unidirectional ratchet effect on civil liberties. The two accounts simply disagree about the direction of the trend.

We favor a third view: there just are no systematic trends in the history of civil liberties, no important ratchet-like mechanisms that cause repeated wars or emergencies to push civil liberties in one direction or another in any sustained fashion. Although our interests are normative, not positive, a better positive thesis is that emergencies produce a cyclical pattern, in which civil liberties are restricted during an emergency and then reinstated when the emergency passes. Whatever the truth of the cycle thesis, there is no convincing reason to think that any political, social, or psychological ratchet operates, under which wars and emergencies have irreversible effects on future policies. The best available empirical work finds no ratchet effects, in either direction,[44] and the mechanisms said to create a ratchet are implausible or underspecified.

To be sure, as Tushnet notes, it is often the case with historical and comparative work that there are too few observations to produce a determinate and falsifiable causal theory.[45] For either the statist ratchet or the libertarian ratchet, our point is not that ratchet accounts should be dismissed just because they cannot be proven through a large-number study; we dismissed similar arguments about the cycle thesis chapter 1. But saying that the ratchet *might* nonetheless be true is just not a useful thing to say, either for judges and legislators deciding what course to pursue in times of emergencies or for constitutional designers and legal analysts concerned with evaluating and channeling the course of emergency policymaking. If both the statist ratchet and the libertarian ratchet are speculations, resting on no plausible mechanism and little in the way of plausible case study evidence, the most natural default view is that such speculations should be ignored. Proponents of ratchet theories bear the burden of uncertainty, in the sense that if their ideas are mere possibilities, the most obvious and sensible premise for emergency policymaking is to ignore the concern about ratchets altogether.

As a working presumption, then, we should approach each new social state—whether labeled war, emergency, or anything else—without worrying or hoping that our present choices will have systematic and irreversible effects on the choices made by future generations in unforeseeable future emergencies. The better question is just whether, given the circumstances as we know them to be at present, the policies that the government pursues are good ones, in light of whatever substantive theory of rights we hold and in light of the costs and benefits of alternative courses of action. This formulation is deliberately banal. What it rejects is any attempt to structure the inquiry into the merits of particular policies by worrying about the precedential effects of current policies or in some other way speculating on the irreversible system-level effects of those policies, over time, on future emergencies that future versions of our own society will face. That additional question is a strange attempt to get beyond or outside our own historical circumstances, and there is no reason to think that there are any such effects anyway.

## OTHER LONG-TERM EFFECTS

Here, we shall briefly canvass some other claims that governmental decision-making in emergencies will externalize long-term costs onto future periods. We begin with the most concrete of these: the worry that a policy of deterring terrorism has perverse or counterproductive effects in the long run. We then turn to the more nebulous idea that restricting civil liberties might cause a nation to betray its core values or even to lose its identity. Finally, we turn to the idea, most general and nebulous of all, that restricting civil liberties creates a slippery slope to authoritarianism.

### Terrorism, Offensive Measures, and Unintended Consequences

Emergency policy almost always rests on a complex mix, in varying proportions, of various policies. Among these are the deterrence of terrorists and the prevention of terrorism through military action, law enforcement, and judicial prosecution; hardening of targets through enhanced defensive security and through increased policing; intelligence activities; strategies for winning the hearts and minds of the populations from which terrorists arise; and a miscellany of other approaches. Among these, deterrence and prevention in their more aggressive forms—what we will loosely call "offensive measures"—come in for the sharpest academic criticism. The common theme is that an offensive response to terrorism ultimately produces more terrorism than it prevents, by delegitimating the deterring government and by inspiring resentments that increase terrorist recruitment.

Jon Elster, for example, writes that a "classical dilemma of deterrence is whether the *anger* it inspires may not in the end more than offset the *fear* it is intended to cause." The restriction or violation of civil liberties might increase terrorism by inflaming the populations that produce terrorists, and "we have no grounds for asserting that the primary effect of the [deterrent] measures (foiling attempts) will dominate the secondary effect (generating attempts)." The alternative is, seemingly, to maintain civil liberties at pre-emergency levels, because "in the long run respect for the rule of law and due process [is] likely to reduce the level of threats the government faces." Strictly defensive action is also justified, because "measures that aim at physical protection are not likely to have the side effect of generating more need for protection. . . . Although the cost of physical measures can be enormous, they do not impose costs on innocent residents, undermine respect for the law, or fuel resentment in groups with terrorist potential."[46]

This view, however, overlooks that if offensive measures can create resentment, the failure to undertake offensive measures can create contempt. A policy of static defense might create an appearance of weakness, by suggesting that the target government lacks the will or capacity to take the fight to the enemy, and thereby increase terrorist recruitment as much or more than does resentment. If resentment increases the number of those motivated to engage in terrorism, so might the appearance of weakness, for two reasons. Most obviously, a policy of forgoing offensive action reduces the expected costs of engaging in terrorist action, which in turn encourages self-selection into the terrorist career by those who would otherwise stick to less dangerous occupations. More broadly, people who are unsure whether to give their allegiance to the government or to terrorist organizations will often cast their lot with the stronger side. An appearance of weakness will then become self-fulfilling; the government that sticks to passive defense might, in the long run, lose adherents and become capable of nothing more than passive defense, whereas the government that resorted to strong offensive measures might see its strength increase.

To be sure, the long-run effects of weakness and the appearance of weakness are speculative. But so are the long-run counterproductive effects of deterrence, as Elster acknowledges. Faced with competing and offsetting long-run considerations of this sort, a sensible government will symmetrically ignore both speculations and will instead focus on adopting policies that make sense in the current period.

> In many, indeed most, decision problems there are associated with each of the options a number of unknown and essentially unknowable possibilities whose materialization depends on the future development of the universe. When trying to make up one's mind, one has to assume that those and other unknowable factors on each side cancel out, so that one can concentrate on the knowable ones. . . . The ensuing decision, although not ideally rational from the point of view of an omniscient observer, will at least be as rational as can be expected.[47]

To say that government should focus on what makes sense in the current period does not support any concrete conclusions. The optimal mix of deterrent and preventive policies vis-à-vis passive defense, propaganda, and other measures will vary with time and circumstances. This does not mean, however, that the alternatives to offensive measures are equally sensible; some of them have a fantastic air, which helps to explain why all governments include offensive measures as a principal component of their terrorism policies.

Here is an example. Bruno Frey criticizes deterrence-based policies as counterproductive in the long term. He argues instead for measures of governmental decentralization, which make a smaller target for terrorist attacks; for the use of carrots or positive incentives rather than sticks or negative sanctions, making alternatives to a terrorist career more attractive in order to raise the opportunity costs of terrorism; and for a governmental policy of obscuring terrorist groups' responsibility for attacks, in order to reduce the benefits of producing such attacks.[48] We take up the third of these suggestions, which is by far the most plausible, in chapter 7. The other two suggestions are inadequately defended, because the countervailing costs are so obvious, and it is not clear why Frey thinks that current policies are not optimal along these dimensions. Decentralization reduces the benefits of attacks but makes it harder for governments to function, raising the costs of implementing all other policies, including deterrence. Positive incentives might dampen terrorist recruitment, but might also encourage strategic behavior by terrorists; consider the risk of moral hazard, in which terrorists increase their attacks in order to induce target governments to offer larger and larger carrots. Frey is aware of these countervailing worries, but he gives no real reason to think that, on net, the marginal benefits of increasing decentralization and using more carrots will exceed the marginal costs, compared to the emergency policies that governments currently undertake.

To the extent that Frey is merely arguing that nondeterrent policies, including carrots as well as sticks, should be part of the mix of emergency policy-making,[49] he is entirely correct; indeed this is, already, what most governments faced with serious terrorist threats do most of the time, so to that extent Frey's point is a commonplace. But Frey and others want to go beyond this position to suggest that deterrence is systematically misguided, or at least has systematic costs that current-period governments will not adequately consider. This is but a one-sided speculation that governments should in fact ignore. A fortiori, it would be madness for judges to limit deterrence-based policies, through constitutional law, in order to minimize terrorism in the long run; nor do we read Frey, Elster, or others to suggest that judges should do so.

For completeness, we mention a variant of the view that deterrence or other offensive measures are counterproductive in the long run. The variant emphasizes not terrorist recruitment but rather the increasing disaffection of the deterring government's own citizens or of neutral publics. On this view, terrorism "trap[s] the authorities into brutal repression and over-reaction which then alienates the public and drives them into tacit or active collaboration with the terrorists."[50] The idea that deterrence measures will alienate the deterring government's own citizens, or other publics, is unconvincing.

It might be an ancillary benefit for terrorists that the government's repressive tactics make it unpopular, but in the normal course of things the government will choose appropriate measures, and the public will blame the terrorists for the government's repression. Terrorist tactics reflect the methods that are available, and terrorists succeed or not in obtaining public support to the extent that the public prefers the terrorists' goals to the government's; popular allegiance is fundamentally determined by the ends sought, not by the means used. Civil libertarians who object to their own government's use of repressive tactics are hardly likely to switch their allegiance to the terrorists who deliberately provoked them.[51]

## Civil Liberties and National Values

A vaguer and more ominous idea is that restricting civil liberties in order to increase security will eventually cause "us" to lose whatever it is that makes "our" society worth defending. In 2004, the House of Lords held that an antiterror statute authorizing the detention of foreign born suspected terrorists was inconsistent with the European Charter on Human Rights. The most widely praised opinion was that of Lord Hoffman, who said, "The real threat to the life of the nation . . . comes not from terrorism but from laws such as these." The statement has become notorious after the July 7, 2005, attacks in London, but it is merely an extreme exemplar of a common class. Consider Justice Sandra Day O'Connor's quotation, in the *Hamdi* case discussed in chapter 3, of a precedent stating that it "would indeed be ironic if, in the name of national defense, we would sanction the subversion of one of those liberties . . . which makes the defense of the Nation worthwhile."[52] In the narrowest interpretation of these statements, the worry is that terrorists will "win" if legal rules and policies are changed in ways that restrict the package of civil liberties in place before the terrorist threat emerged. In a broader interpretation, civil libertarians worry that restricting liberties to enhance security will change the society into something alien and unrecognizable; "we" will lose our very identity. As Martha Minow puts it, "[W]e must imagine our alternate destinies and fight to ensure that we do not become what we hate."[53] In either version, the concern might be combined with or might just amount to another expression of the statist ratchet theory, previously discussed; we will focus on what is distinctive in these statements.

As to the narrower version, whether restrictions on civil liberties count as a victory for terrorists depends on what terrorists are trying to achieve. Although al Qaeda's ultimate goals are to drive American troops from the

Middle East and, more broadly, to establish a Muslim caliphate in the region, its proximate goal is to kill ordinary people to bring pressure to bear on democratic governments. A change in policy that reduces the chance that more people will be killed does not hand the terrorists a victory; it frustrates their plans. A failure to alter any policies in response to a successful terrorist attack is, by contrast, a sign of weakness and paralysis, as we emphasized above.

The broader version is mysterious—does it suppose some organic national character or essential identity floating above the people who compose the citizenry at any given time?—and it is implausible where it has any concrete content. An incremental reduction in civil liberties is not equivalent to their elimination or to the establishment of an alien regime. British and American traditions are two-sided: they acknowledge that governments have an obligation to protect people's lives as well as their liberties. No nation preserves liberty atop a stack of its own citizens' corpses, but if one did, it would not be worth defending. Or, at least, many of that society's own members would not find it appealing or valuable. When civil libertarians talk about the risk to "our" values, they paper over the fact that there is serious disagreement about how much to value civil liberties; most people do not want to live in a society that protects civil liberties at an extremely high price.

The general assumption behind such arguments is that whatever package of civil liberties happens to exist at the time a terrorist threat arises must be maintained at all costs; adjustments that reduce liberty are bad even if they produce greater gains in security, potentially saving people's lives. As we argued in chapter 1, this is the fallacy that whatever policy happens to exist at the time of an attack is good and must be preserved for all time. In fact, the balance between security and liberty is constantly readjusted as circumstances change. A well-functioning government will contract civil liberties as threats increase, and does not jeopardize national values by doing so. As we said in chapter 1, a government that refuses to adjust its policies has simply frozen in the face of the threat. It is pathologically rigid, not enlightened, and that rigidity is at least as great a threat to national values or to the nation's existence.

## Slippery Slopes in General

More generally still, the arguments we have examined in this chapter are relatives of the timeworn argument that decisionmakers should beware a slippery slope. The statist ratchet theory is more specific than the slippery slope, but it partakes in a similar worry: that the policy choices that government makes now will inexorably produce disaster in the long run. The worry that restricting civil liberties poses a long-term threat to national values, or even to the nation's identity, is similar. These are deep conceptual waters, however. One might suggest that the slippery slope argument is analytically distinct from the ratchet argument; perhaps the crucial feature of the former is just that policy tends to move with accelerating speed in one direction, even if it is not costly to reverse course.[54] Consider the argument that "a single rights-violation by the government could remove a mental barrier to violations in general and increase the probability that more violations will follow."[55] This idea does not seem to posit or require a ratchet effect; the point does not seem to be that it would be costly to reverse course, but that no one would want to, because of the psychological effects of the initial rights violation.

Our analysis is institutional rather than conceptual, so the precise relationships among ratchet arguments, slippery slope arguments, and their other relatives are not crucial. What we do emphasize is that slippery slope arguments are cheap—easy to make but hard to make persuasively. In general, it is not persuasive to say that no lines can be drawn, when most legal rules and public policies rest on lines cut into continuous phenomena; such lines will often appear arbitrary, at least when the small area of policy space surrounding the line is viewed microscopically. At a minimum, slippery slope arguments require some reason to believe that the slope is slippery—some mechanism that makes one policy choice likely to produce an accelerating series of policy choices in the same direction—and also some reason to believe that falling down the slope would be a bad thing, as opposed to an improvement.[56] These critiques are a bit vague, because slippery slope arguments are themselves vague when stated in general terms, and they become more or less plausible according to context. We will examine such arguments in concrete settings in other chapters; in chapter 6, for example, we consider a slippery slope argument against legalizing coercive interrogation. For now, we merely seek to inoculate readers against mental infection by the slippery slope meme.

# PART II

## APPLICATIONS

**P**art I addressed some general reasons that courts and legislators should be more deferential during emergencies than during normal times, and that the security-liberty tradeoff shifts during emergencies so that policy should be less libertarian when emergencies occur. In this part, we narrow the focus and address a series of legal and policy controversies that has arisen since 9/11 with special emphasis on the role of courts.

Chapter 5 evaluates various alternatives to what we have called the *judicial deference thesis*. These approaches also reject the civil libertarian view and assume that the executive branch should be permitted to take extreme measures during emergencies with no or limited judicial interference; but they involve more elaborate methods for ensuring that the executive has proper incentives than the judicial deference approach does. We criticize these alternatives as unattractive and unworkable. Chapter 6 focuses on the controversy over coercive interrogation. We argue that, whatever its effectiveness, the type of institutional concerns invoked by its critics are not good reasons for preventing the executive branch from using coercive interrogation when it believes it to be necessary in emergency conditions. Chapter 7 addresses censorship and the reduction of process protections in trials of suspected terrorists. Censorship has not been advocated in the United States but has been implemented in Great Britain. Process reduction has been implemented in the United States and other countries. We argue that history and doctrine endorse censorship and process reduction during emergencies, that these measures are justified on the basis of the liberty-security tradeoff, and that historical judicial deference to the executive's balancing of these factors during emergencies is also justified. Chapter 8 addresses the military side of counterterrorism strategy, including the detention of terrorist suspects and their trial before military commissions, and argues that there are no strong international legal objections or constitutional objections to using military force or military processes in these settings.

We should be clear that we do not endorse or criticize any particular counterterrorism measure used by the Bush administration. One of our central points is that we, as lawyers, do not know enough about the underlying variables to be able to express an informed opinion; nor do the administration's vociferous critics, in many cases. What we do believe is that the government must make tradeoffs, that policy should become less libertarian during emergencies, and that courts should stay out of the way. Whether the Bush administration has made the right tradeoffs in any given case is a separate question. As we have emphasized throughout, government will inevitably make errors in formulating emergency policies, just as it makes errors in all other policy domains; the mistake is to assume that governmental error necessarily shows systematic bias, or shows that the political process or the governmental decisionmaking process has malfunctioned in a way that can be reliably corrected.

Apart from the merits of emergency policies, there is the separate question of whether the courts have reason to be skeptical of emergency policies in general, or the Bush administration's policies in particular—where "reason" refers to general psychological, institutional, legal, or political factors that indicate systematic bias against liberty rather than random error in any given case. Would the courts be justified in abandoning their historical stance of deference to the executive in times of emergency? The answer is, repeatedly, no. Courts have no reason to demand a more elaborate statutory mechanism governing emergency powers (chapter 5); no reason to reject the executive's claim that coercive interrogation is useful (chapter 6); no reason to prevent the executive from using censorship or reducing process rights during emergencies (chapter 7); and no reason to interfere with the government's military response (chapter 8). If the Bush administration's policies are wrong, the courts are not the place for correcting them.

# CHAPTER FIVE

# Institutional Alternatives to Judicial Deference

The civil libertarian approach is defective for the reasons we gave in prior chapters, but elimination of this approach from the field leaves a number of alternatives. The judicial deference approach is one of these alternatives, but there are others as well. In this chapter, we evaluate many of them and defend the judicial deference approach against the challengers.

Table 5.1 provides a way to organize the competition. There are two dimensions of disagreement. Some people believe that the president's emergency powers should be determined ex ante—prior to the emergency—and some people believe that the president's emergency powers should be determined ex post, or after the emergency begins. Thus, the first dimension concerns the timing of this determination. The second dimension concerns the identity of the decisionmaker who exercises the emergency powers or determines who exercises the emergency powers. There are three possibilities: the president exercises the emergency powers alone; the president exercises them with the consent of Congress; or—a special case—the president exercises them subject to the ex post consent of the public or some nonofficial decisionmaker, such as a jury.

The four main approaches that we consider are in boxes 2, 3, 4, and 6. Box 5 is not a coherent alternative, as we will explain. The executive order approach (box 1) is included for completeness, but we have found no adherents to this view. Let us explain each of the possibilities.

The *executive order approach* holds that the president may exercise any emergency powers that he provides himself in advance of the emergency, which would presumably be through an executive order. If the president tries to exercise powers that he has not given himself ex ante, then courts will interfere. One might imagine possible justifications for this approach; perhaps it

TABLE 5.1

| | president alone | president with Congress | president subject to popular approval |
|---|---|---|---|
| ex ante | (1) executive order framework | (3) framework statute (ex ante statutory authorization) | (5) |
| ex post | (2) judicial deference | (4) ex post statutory authorization | (6) outlaw and forgive |

would be helpful if the president were forced to state in advance how he would wield emergency powers. But we have found no one who advocates it; there is no reason to think that presidents can limit their own discretion with executive orders. The only question is whether the executive has complied with applicable statutes and the Constitution.[1]

The *judicial deference approach* holds that courts defer to the executive's exercise of emergency power (box 2). There is no requirement that the executive's powers be determined in advance, though of course there is no bar to an ex ante executive order or policy statement either. Thus, the judicial deference approach makes no distinction between emergency powers that are first claimed during an emergency and emergency powers that are exercised pursuant to a pre-emergency executive order: emergency actions are entitled to deference regardless of whether they are taken pursuant to an earlier executive order or to a policy statement.

The third approach has been advocated by Bruce Ackerman, who argues that Congress should pass a statute that provides the president with certain emergency powers that he can use as long as Congress acquiesces.[2] The crucial element of Ackerman's proposal, for our purposes, is that courts will not prevent the president from exercising these powers even if they would be unconstitutional during normal times. To curb executive abuse of power, a *super-majoritarian escalator* provides that, as time passes, congressional acquiescence is deemed to occur only if an increasingly large majority of Congress consents to further exercise of the emergency powers by the president.

The fourth approach has been advocated by several scholars, who argue that emergency actions deserve deference as long as Congress has authorized the executive to engage in them.[3] These scholars have focused on authorizations that occur during an emergency, but nothing about their argument would prevent them from embracing the ex ante approach as well. The emphasis is on congressional involvement; because emergencies always bring new problems and challenges, the historical examples that motivate the proposal emphasize ex post authorizations (box 4).

The fifth approach (box 6) has been endorsed by numerous scholars; it is what we call the *outlaw-and-forgive approach*.[4] This approach holds that executive officials are expected to violate the laws that prevent them from taking measures necessary for maintaining security and then to ask the public for forgiveness, which might come in the form of reelection, public support for amnesties, pardons, or jury nullification. Because it does not make any sense to talk of the public giving ex ante consent to emergency powers (except through legislation, which is redundant with box 3), box 5 is empty.

There are variations of these approaches that we will consider as well. But we put off the table proposals that would require that the U.S. Constitution be amended.[5] The constitutions of many nation-states grant special powers to the executive in times of emergency. In many European countries, the executive can declare an emergency, but the legislature must approve it; during the emergency, power shifts from local units to the national government and from the legislature to the executive; and judicial review is usually limited but not extinguished.[6] The frequency with which emergency provisions appear in foreign constitutions raises the question of whether a similar constitutional solution, presumably obtained through amendment, would work for the United States. However, the literature on emergency powers in foreign constitutions is inconclusive.[7] Further, there is no pressure for constitutional change in the United States today, perhaps because judicial deference during emergencies allows legal rules to change over time and thus makes such change unnecessary, or saps the motivation for it. Finally, by assuming that existing constitutional norms will remain in force for the foreseeable future, we keep our inquiry manageable.

## THE EX ANTE STATUTORY APPROACH

Bruce Ackerman argues that Congress should pass an emergency powers statute that authorizes the president to exercise broad powers in the case of emergency. We will not discuss all of the details of his proposal and instead will focus on its most important elements. First, the executive has the power to declare an emergency, and for a short period—one or two weeks—he has the power to act unilaterally. At the end of this period, the state of emergency expires unless a majority of Congress votes to sustain it. After another two or three months pass, the state of emergency expires unless 60% of Congress votes to sustain it. These periodic votes continue with the escalating supermajority requirement topping out at 80%.[8]

Second, the executive's power is largely but not completely unlimited. Ackerman's proposal is not clear in every detail, but he seems to grant the executive the power to detain people without permitting them to challenge the factual bases of their detentions. Torture is forbidden; limited rights to hearings and counsel remain. Detainees must be released after sixty days if the government cannot connect them to the emergency. Ackerman prohibits the executive from reorganizing the constitutional structure of government—for example, abolishing the judiciary—and from imposing censorship.[9]

Ackerman says that his scheme avoids the undesirable consequences of the civil libertarian and the judicial deference extremes. The civil libertarian view prevents the president from responding forcefully to an emergency. The judicial deference view, in Ackerman's opinion, risks the ratchet-like entrenchment of emergency powers. "Unless careful precautions are taken, emergency measures have a habit of continuing well beyond their time of necessity."[10] Ackerman's proposal allows the president to respond forcefully to an emergency without enabling him to maintain his emergency powers after the emergency ends.

Ackerman does not provide either a convincing diagnosis of a political problem during emergencies or a convincing defense of his proposed remedy. He refers at various times both to the panic and the ratchet theories, but he assumes the correctness of these theories without defending them, and as we dealt with those theories in chapters 2 and 4, we need not repeat our doubts here. As the quotation in the prior paragraph indicates, Ackerman largely assumes that executives will abuse their power and become dictators unless a statute such as his constrains them, but he provides no evidence for thinking that this is true. There are, of course, historical episodes in other countries when executives founded dictatorships by extending indefinitely powers that were granted temporarily, but no such episodes exist in American history, and it is hazardous to assume that what happened in ancient Rome or Weimar Germany will repeat itself in the United States. Even during emergencies, in the United States the national legislature and the judiciary retain substantial powers; America's federal system would complicate any attempt by a president to draw together all of the strings of power; media that are traditionally skeptical of executive power would need to be shut down; a robust civil society—religious institutions, clubs, universities, civic organizations—would need to be squelched. A dictatorship is not a serious possibility in the United States anytime soon; a statute designed to prevent such a dictatorship from occurring is quixotic.

And even if there is a serious risk that an American president would become a dictator as a result of an emergency, one must balance this risk against the gains from granting the emergency powers to the president, namely, the ability to address the threat swiftly and decisively and without compromising intelligence sources. Ackerman implicitly acknowledges these benefits, which is presumably why he advocates giving the president unilateral emergency power in the first weeks and then thereafter as long as Congress acquiesces. But Ackerman does not provide any details about the gains side of the ledger.

There are two reasons that constraining the president in the manner that Ackerman advocates may be unwise. First, the president's ability to entrench his power may decline over time rather than increase over time. People place their trust with him at the beginning of the emergency but not as they become accustomed to it or as the immediate need for action fades; the Bush administration has been an example. If this is the case, there is no reason to increase the threshold for congressional acquiescence over time.

Second, Congress's ability to obstruct may increase over time, or at least not decline over time. The supermajoritarian escalator implies that the likelihood of obstruction declines, but Ackerman does not explain why he thinks this is the case. As the initial shock wears off, national unity will fade, and normal political divisions will reassert themselves. And yet the need for secrecy and decisive action may remain as pressing as at the start of the emergency.

For present purposes, what is more interesting than the details of Ackerman's proposal or his defense of his proposal is his claim that an emergency powers statute is desirable. This claim raises the question whether the current form of judicial deference during emergencies is desirable, or whether it should be authorized, guided, and controlled by a statute.

Although we reject Ackerman's framework statute, we acknowledge that there are appealing reasons to support a statutory approach. The judicial deference view has evolved in a common law fashion and does not provide much guidance to judges. Consider the following ambiguities.

*Start of the Emergency.* The judicial deference view holds that courts should defer to the executive during emergencies, but it does not tell us whether courts should defer to the executive's declaration that an emergency exists. It might be appropriate for courts to refuse to acquiesce in emergency declarations that appear to be pretextual; that do not have the consent of Congress; that are not sufficiently public; and so forth. These questions have rarely arisen in the past—perhaps the *Youngstown* case,[11] where the Supreme Court implicitly rejected Truman's claim that a state of emergency justified his seizure of steel mills during a strike, is an example, although a borderline one, as we discussed in part I—and therefore we do not know what norms control or are likely to control the emergency declaration.

*Degree of Deference.* The judicial deference view does not tell us how much courts should defer. When Jackson said in *Korematsu* that "the military reasonableness of these orders can only be determined by military superiors,"[12] he was arguing that courts are in no position to insist that military orders exceed a threshold of reasonableness as they do when evaluating statutes and other executive actions. They must either defer to them or reject them. However, one can imagine deference that is intermediate rather than complete or strict; and one can imagine deference to some kinds of actions (for example, involving the military at home or the military overseas) and not others (for example, involving local police).

*End of the Emergency.* The judicial deference view also does not tell us when the emergency ends, or whether judges should stop deferring to "emergency" actions if they think the emergency has ended but the president says otherwise. For example, during the cold war, courts initially deferred to aggressive law enforcement measures against suspected communist spies and sympathizers, but by the 1960s they had become less deferential, even though the president never formally declared the end of any cold war emergency. It is impossible to point to a particular date when the emergency, as far as the courts were concerned, ended; it might be better if a mechanism existed that more clearly determined the end of an emergency.

This brings us back to Ackerman's proposal, which, whatever its defects, illustrates the possible contributions of a statute. Ackerman gives the president absolute authority to declare the start of an emergency, so it is clear that judges must defer to the emergency declaration even if it is arguably pretextual. He also provides for the end of the state of emergency at set intervals unless Congress votes to sustain it. Further, Ackerman distinguishes actions to which judges should defer (detentions, at least at the beginning) and actions to which judges should not defer (torture). Finally, he creates various other mechanisms that encourage power sharing and information sharing; these are designed to prevent the executive from exercising emergency powers on a pretextual basis.

But we see several problems with the ex ante statutory route. First, emergencies by their nature are not easily predicted: every emergency is different. Therefore, efforts to establish emergency protocols in advance are unlikely to succeed. One type of emergency, for example, might provide the president with exceptional opportunities for establishing a dictatorship in its first days; another type might be particularly vulnerable to congressional obstructionism months after it begins. Ackerman's scheme would neither prevent the dictator in the first case nor permit the president to exercise justified emergency powers in the second. Although law making often uses rules rather than standards despite this problem of over- and underinclusion, emergency powers are an especially bad area of law to subject to rules. Legal rules are best for routine areas of life where fact patterns repeat themselves, whereas emergencies are the opposite—unique and exceptionally hard to predict. Ackerman's scheme attempts to subject to rules an area of political relations where standards are far more appropriate.

Second, as Ackerman acknowledges, his statute is supposed to perform a constitutional function. It reorganizes governmental powers during an emergency, and then ensures that they return to normal after the emergency expires. A statute could, in principle, perform such constitutional functions by aligning the various parties' expectations about the future, which then provide a basis for objecting to usurpations or interference when the emergency occurs. However, history shows that statutory limitations are weak during emergencies. The War Powers Act, which limits the circumstances under which the president can use military force and imposes various reporting requirements when the president does use force, has repeatedly been ignored. The National Emergencies Act similarly imposes restrictions and reporting requirements on the president's power to declare emergencies, and the International Emergency Economic Powers Act limits the president's power to impose economic sanctions during emergencies. Neither of these statutes has had much of an impact on the behavior of executives.[13] The reason for the failure of statutory frameworks is plain. When an emergency arises, the executive needs flexibility; because statutory limitations determined in advance can only reduce flexibility, and do so in a way that does not anticipate the particular requirements of the new emergency, no one has any interest in insisting that these limitations be respected. Ackerman acknowledges the grim historical record but provides no reason to think that his framework statute might fare differently. Ackerman's statute is narrower than these others, but it is also more rigid, and thus more likely to break under stress.

Third, Ackerman's statute is a poorly designed cure for the ailment that he diagnoses. If his framework statute is needed to prevent panicking legislators from deferring to bad executive actions, then it seems unlikely that it can have that effect. A panicky Congress can simply ignore the supermajoritarian escalator and approve new statutory powers or a new statutory framework by majority rule; the PATRIOT Act, which Ackerman abhors, could have simply included one panicky section sweeping away any extant framework statutes limiting presidential power. Ackerman needs a stronger commitment mechanism than a statute; but he fails to supply one.

Fourth, even if we accept all of Ackerman's premises, there is a further danger that legislators will use his framework statute as a pretext for deferring to bad executive actions. They might acquiesce in the measures advocated by the executive on the grounds that executive power will expire shortly, and so they might agree to worse abuses than they would if Ackerman's statute did not exist and the legislators confronted the problem of expiration directly.[14] The statute might also encourage the president to act hastily and inconsiderately, while he has his freedom, rather than risk waiting until a point where a supermajority no longer extends the state of emergency. Indeed, if there are executive actions that can be taken during emergencies and that are costly to reverse afterward (a premise that we have questioned but that Ackerman accepts), then Ackerman's scheme gives the president every incentive to carry them out as soon as possible, before the legal hurdles escalate.

In sum, Ackerman's statute relies on elaborate procedures to deal with events that by their nature are unpredictable, fluid, and therefore unlikely to play out according to conceptions held years in advance. An instructive contrast is provided by the various emergency provisions in foreign constitutions, which are extremely vague. They are hardly clearer than the common-law version of judicial deference that exists in the United States. This convergence in vague standards rather than specific rules probably reflects an international consensus that emergency powers cannot be sensibly determined in advance because the requirements of future emergencies are so difficult to predict. It is better to provide that the executive may exercise emergency powers and then allow the political system, judges included, to come to a consensus about their appropriate scope once the emergency begins.

## EX POST STATUTORY AUTHORIZATION

The *ex post statutory authorization approach* holds that courts should defer to executive actions during emergencies as long as they have been authorized by Congress. As noted before, the ex post approach does not, strictly speaking, require that the authorization occur during the emergency; it could occur prior to the emergency as well. The approach emphasizes the general importance of congressional acquiescence in the president's emergency powers and does not make a fetish of its timing.

It is important to emphasize that this approach is not the same as the civil libertarian approach: courts might, for example, permit the executive with congressional authorization to detain suspected terrorists without charging them, which it would not permit during normal times.

Samuel Issacharoff and Richard H. Pildes have advocated this approach;[15] so has Cass Sunstein, based on his theory of judicial minimalism.[16] Issacharoff and Pildes argue that the ex post statutory authorization approach ensures that there is a political consensus behind the president's emergency powers. Sunstein takes the perspective of the courts and argues that, by demanding congressional authorization, the courts can permit security measures that infringe on civil liberties without violating deep constitutional commitments and legal understandings.[17]

We discussed and criticized the statutory authorization approach in chapter 1; here, we will briefly expand upon these criticisms as a way of further shedding light on the difference between ex ante and ex post approaches and the difference between unilateral executive action and executive action authorized by Congress.

One problem with the framework statute proposed by Ackerman was that Congress has little information about the nature of future emergencies, and thus has no basis for determining the rules that ought to govern the executive. The ex post approach avoids this problem through the simple expedient of having Congress authorize executive action after the emergency begins and its demands on the executive have become clear. For Ackerman, this is not good enough because Congress generally acts slowly, and indeed might not even be in session when the emergency begins, as was true at the start of the Civil War. But the most straightforward solution to this problem is not an ex ante framework statute; it is just to abandon any requirement of congressional involvement at all, which is the judicial deference view.

Another problem with the framework statute was that of time inconsistency: once the emergency begins, there is no way to force Congress to abide by the supermajoritarian escalator rule. In principle, courts could refuse to defer to executive action undertaken if the relevant supermajority rule is not obeyed, but in practice courts tend to obey subsequent majorities that override supermajority rules unless the latter are carefully drafted—and we expect that judicial deference would be especially likely during an emergency.[18] This problem suggests that the framework approach is infeasible, or close to it, and the only practical option for those who seek congressional involvement is the ex post approach.

A requirement of ex post statutory authorization thus seems more plausible than the ex ante statutory framework approach, but it does not seem better than the judicial deference approach. As we discussed in chapter 1, the involvement of Congress produces costs as well as benefits. On the cost side, congressional deliberation is slow and unsuited for emergencies. Congress has trouble keeping secrets and is always vulnerable to obstruction at the behest of members of Congress who place the interests of their constituents ahead of those of the nation as a whole. It is implicitly for these reasons that Ackerman gives the president the freedom to act unilaterally at the start of the emergency. But there is no reason to think that the problem of congressional obstruction and inefficiency will decline over time.

What are the benefits of congressional involvement? One possible benefit is that Congress has technical information about the advantages and disadvantages of various security measures and, relying on this information, will be able to block poorly considered security measures. But it is doubtful that Congress's information is better than the executive branch's, and in any event Congress can share this information with the executive branch if necessary. The modern national security system deprives Congress of useful information about threats to national security, and Congress by necessity must play a passive role.

The main possible benefit from congressional involvement is that Congress can prevent the executive from using the emergency as an opportunity to engage in self-aggrandizement, to obtain new powers, and to entrench them so that the executive will be more powerful even after the emergency ends. As we argued in chapter 1, however, it is not at all clear that executive aggrandizement during emergencies is a problem, and even if it is, congressional involvement might make things worse, not better. The value of congressional authorization is ambiguous as a theoretical matter. It slows down executive action, which is costly during emergencies, but may (or may not) block efforts by the executive to aggrandize its power. We also argued in chapter 1 that the historical evidence suggests that Congress is too weak an institution, during emergencies, to provide the asserted benefits. Congress defers to the executive during emergencies because it agrees that the executive alone has the information and the means necessary to respond to imminent threats. The added risk of executive abuse is a cost that Congress and voters have been willing to bear.

## OUTLAW AND FORGIVE

The *outlaw-and-forgive approach* is a defense of the form, but not the substance, of civil libertarianism. On the one hand, the defenders of the outlaw-and-forgive approach oppose judicial deference; they want courts to enforce constitutional norms during emergencies to the same extent as courts enforce these norms during normal times. Distinguishing themselves from the advocates of ex ante and ex post statutory authorization, the defenders of outlaw and forgive deny that congressional authorization releases courts from their obligation to enforce constitutional rights to their full extent.

On the other hand, the defenders of the outlaw-and-forgive approach want executive officials to disobey the law when doing so is justified by security needs. The example commonly used in the literature is torture; but the argument applies to any other aggressive measure, such as warrantless search, detention, and (we suppose) summary execution. The officials who use illegal security measures should, having violated the law, seek public vindication, including a pardon,[19] although some authors seem to want to adjust the status quo by, for example, encouraging elected officials to issue pardons when illegal actions are morally justified or creating special or expedited procedures for applying for pardons, and so forth. The latter approach begins to depart from civil libertarianism, but we will put this wrinkle aside and define *outlaw and forgive* as the view that the law should prohibit a broad class of actions with the expectation that officials will break the law when any particular action that falls within that class turns out to be sufficiently desirable.

Outlaw and forgive is not restricted to controversial law enforcement measures undertaken by low-level officials such as interrogators, police officers, and soldiers. The most famous example in American history occurred in a different context. When Lincoln suspended habeas corpus and declared martial law in the early months of the Civil War, he behaved illegally, most commentators agree. The U.S. Constitution, as normally interpreted, gives Congress, not the president, the power to suspend habeas corpus. But Lincoln himself argued that his actions were justified by military exigency and that the public could ultimately decide for itself at the next election. Although Lincoln did not exactly follow the outlaw-and-forgive protocol—which would have required him to acknowledge the illegality of his behavior and seek public forgiveness—one can interpret Lincoln's actions and subsequent electoral vindication as a rough example of the outlaw-and-forgive process. On this view, the absence of emergency powers in the Constitution protects civil liberties and the republican form of government from executive encroachment without at the same time undermining the security of the country because executives can be expected to violate the Constitution when the peril is great enough and then receive vindication at the polls.

The Lincoln example of outlaw and forgive is not wholly implausible. The president, at the apex of the government, is uniquely visible to the public and subject to intense scrutiny. We will say more about this version later in this chapter. For now, we will focus on the first example, where the outlaw-and-forgive approach is applied to lower-level officials. We will use coercive interrogation as our example because of its prominence in the outlaw-and-forgive literature, but what we say applies to any aggressive security measure, such as warrantless search. We will argue that this version of outlaw and forgive is wholly implausible.

Outlaw and forgive comes in two flavors. The first places the responsibility to forgive with political officials, such as prosecutors, governors, or presidents. The second places the responsibility with judges or juries.

## Popular Justice

The first version of outlaw and forgive holds that courts should convict government agents who use abusive or excessive security measures, but if their behavior was morally justified, then the defendant should be pardoned, or perhaps not tried in the first place via the exercise of prosecutorial discretion. One might even imagine the public taking matters in its own hands and hiding or protecting the defendant,[20] or electing him to office, or reelecting the defendant if he is already an elected official.

The peculiar feature of this argument is the assumption that public officials will act correctly if they are told that correct action is against the law. Why wouldn't they instead say to themselves, as they must every day: "I could get the truth out of this suspect by banging him up, but for whatever reason I'm not allowed to do this, so I won't"? The implicit assumption is that the public official will act correctly when enough lives are at stake,[21] but why should we assume that a police officer would be willing to risk his career and his freedom to save the lives of others? Of course, there are many heroes who would do this, but we don't normally design legal restrictions on the assumption that government agents will act heroically.

Let us try to think about this problem from the perspective of a police officer who has custody of a member of al Qaeda, a person who, the officer suspects, knows about plans for a major terrorist attack. Under outlaw and forgive, the officer should anticipate that if he uses coercive interrogation, he will be convicted of a crime, but there is a chance that the public will forgive him and that he will be not charged in the first place, acquitted by a jury, or, if convicted, later pardoned. But how will he know if the public will forgive him? The public might be grateful, but it might also be outraged. The public might make the correct moral calculus, or it might make the wrong moral calculus.

In general, there is no reason to think that outlaw and forgive will produce optimal incentives. Ex post politics will sometimes forgive coercive interrogation when it shouldn't be forgiven and sometimes punish coercive interrogation when it shouldn't be punished. If an outlaw and forgive regime does happen to produce optimal deterrence, it will be but a lucky coincidence, for there is no general mechanism that aligns the incentives produced by outlaw and forgive with optimal incentives. Moreover, even if the happy coincidence does occur, the optimal outlaw and forgive regime is unlikely to prove stable for very long, as we discuss below.

The argument against outlaw and forgive is identical to the argument in favor of the rule of law, an argument that appears to be decisive in every other setting, including the regulation of ordinary police practices, such as the use of deadly force. Although prosecutorial discretion, jury nullification, and the pardon power are important features of contemporary law enforcement, these phenomena are generally accepted as either unavoidable (in the case of prosecutorial discretion and jury nullification) or safety valves for correcting injustices that occur in anomalous cases, not as the chief tool for ensuring that people are given the right incentives against a background where desirable behavior is, for whatever reason, illegal. We need not rehash all of the rule-of-law arguments against such a system. It is sufficient to recall that there are good reasons of fairness and incentives to tell government agents in advance what they should do and what they shouldn't do. Regulating ex post through public opinion, even if mediated by political officials, such as prosecutors or elected leaders, makes officers dependent on their abilities to prognosticate the mood of the public, which can sometimes seize on factors that are irrelevant to the decision in question. Excessive caution is the most likely result.

Defenders of the outlaw and forgive approach argue that outlaw and forgive regimes can be found in other areas of criminal law, where they serve a valuable function.[22] Laws that prohibit sodomy, fornication, adultery, and euthanasia are frequently cited examples of laws that are on the books but that are not enforced or (in the case of euthanasia) are selectively enforced. But none of these examples provides support for an outlaw and forgive regime for coercive interrogation.

Most of these outlaw and forgive regimes—for example, sodomy and adultery laws—arose inadvertently, not as a result of deliberate policy. The regime is a by-product of changes in norms or behavior, changes that temporarily outrun changes in law; and the outlaw and forgive regime is precarious and often collapses in relatively short order, as the contradiction between official rule and actual practice becomes ever more widely understood. Indeed, "forgiveness" in these cases is automatic; people are almost never convicted for these crimes; and no one would claim that laws against sodomy cause people to engage in sodomy only in the limited (?) conditions when it is morally justified and not otherwise. Experience with these laws suggests that an outlaw and forgive regime for coercive interrogation would likely be infeasible, because unstable in the medium and long term, as it becomes widely understood that officials and juries are awarding ex post licenses to interrogators.

The best example of an outlaw and forgive regime that may seem functional is that of euthanasia. Many people acknowledge that mercy killing may be morally justified in narrow conditions, but they prefer to maintain an absolute ban on euthanasia, with the tacit understanding that doctors may be spared prosecution and punishment if circumstances are pressing enough. But, as a result, the practice of euthanasia is shrouded in secrecy. We know very little about euthanasia in the United States; perhaps doctors practice euthanasia at the right times, but perhaps they do not. When abortion outlaw and forgive regimes existed prior to *Roe v. Wade*, wealthier women could sometimes rely on their doctors, while poorer women resorted to back-alley abortions. Perhaps doctors today provide euthanasia to those who can afford high-quality health care, and others provide back-alley euthanasia to those who cannot.

Recent accounts from the Netherlands paint an unattractive picture of outlaw and forgive. There, consensual adult euthanasia is legal, but infant euthanasia is illegal and yet nonetheless practiced. "Behind the scenes paediatricians in the Netherlands have been making tacit deals with local prosecutors' offices for years, promising to report cases of 'life-ending treatment for newborns' in return for guarantees that the doctors will not find themselves hauled into the dock facing charges of murder."[23] Secrecy and lack of public accountability are the result. Doctors have recently demanded that the government issue regulations; despite the tacit deals, doctors fear criminal liability and are reluctant to continue the practice of infant euthanasia without an explicit legal license.[24] The Dutch outlaw and forgive regime for euthanasia, then, does not seem to provide good incentives, prevents public debate and accountability, and is unstable.

The euthanasia outlaw and forgive regimes, here and elsewhere, arose spontaneously, as a result of civil disobedience by doctors. No one proposed that these regimes be put in place. Accordingly, it is distinctive, and distinctly odd, to propose that coercive interrogation should *intentionally* and *avowedly* be regulated by means of an outlaw and forgive regime. The public statement of the proposal—after all, proponents of an outlaw and forgive regime publish their writings—gives it a self-defeating character, undermining the proposal itself. Outlaw and forgive regimes may often represent "states that are essentially byproducts,"[25] which can happen to come into being as the by-product of changes in norms outpacing changes in law, but which cannot be deliberately brought into being through intentional and publicly avowed policy choice. The publicity of the debate is crucial here. It is perfectly coherent for a group of legal elites secretly to approve of the twin facts that coercive interrogation is used and that the public does not generally understand that it is used; but presumably that is not the sort of conspiratorial position that the outlaw and forgive proponents mean to be defending.

## The Necessity Defense

Israeli law bans coercive interrogation, and yet Israeli security has used this measure, apparently because officials who use coercive interrogation may be shielded by the necessity defense (as well as by prosecutorial discretion that is predisposed in their favor).[26] Under the *necessity defense*, which exists in American law as well, an act that would otherwise be a serious crime—killing, torture—does not give rise to legal liability if it was necessary to prevent a greater harm. Now, in American law, the necessity defense would not typically be available to an official who engaged in coercive interrogation because the necessary act must usually prevent an imminent threat.[27] Shooting an armed suspect in order to prevent him from killing a hostage is justified;[28] using physical pressure on the suspect in order to extract the location of a hostage who is about to be killed is not justified. But in Israel, the necessity defense is, in practice, given greater scope.[29]

Critics of coercive interrogation who nonetheless believe it should be used in catastrophic scenarios sometimes see the necessity defense as a good compromise.[30] Coercive interrogation remains illegal, but the necessity defense can be used—either in its present form or broadened somewhat—in order to immunize the official who uses coercive interrogation to prevent a catastrophe. The rationale appears to be that the law's symbolic rejection of torture is maintained, while coercive interrogation can be used when it is justified. A closely related view is that judges should suspend the sentences of convicted torturers whose behavior does not meet the requirements of the necessity defense but which was nonetheless justified.[31]

This argument is puzzling. As Sanford Levinson remarks, reliance on the necessity defense would not avoid legitimating coercive interrogation;[32] it would avoid legitimating coercive interrogation only when it is not "necessary." The necessity defense is no more likely to maintain the illegitimacy of coercive interrogation than the doctrine of official immunity maintains the illegitimacy of the use of deadly force by police officers. The defense of necessity, like the defense of official immunity, renders legitimate those actions that fall within its scope.

The implicit theory of the advocates of the necessity defense is that a statute that creates liability sends a message to the public, while the statute that provides a defense against liability remains silent. But as the public does not usually pay attention to the law on the books—and when it does, never discriminates between statutes that create liability and statutes that provide defense—but instead observes police officers either being convicted of crimes or not being convicted of crimes, this theory is dubious. If the public is paying no attention to legal rules and only looks at outcomes, it will just see torturers going unpunished in a range of cases. If the public does pay attention to legal rules, why will it only pay attention to the ex ante prohibition and not the ex post license? Outlaw and forgive rests on arbitrary assumptions about the audience for law's expressions.

There is a further point, which is that if it really matters whether the power to use coercive interrogation is located in the statute that creates liability or in the defense, this can be easily handled; indeed, it already is. When a police officer kills a person, and a prosecutor charges him with murder, the officer's defense will be official immunity. Whether or not the police officer is convicted turns on the scope of the defense. If the killing was justified under the statute or doctrine that creates official immunity, then it was not murder. Coercive interrogation could be similarly handled, if these formal distinctions are thought to be important.[33]


## Presidential Outlaw and Forgive

Let us now return to the presidential case. We can focus the inquiry by considering President Lincoln's refusal to comply with Justice Taney's decision in *Ex parte Merryman*.[34] That case arose when Union forces detained Merryman on suspicion that he was involved in training Confederate soldiers. Merryman filed a writ of habeas corpus, which was granted by Justice Taney. If Justice Taney had followed the judicial deference view, he would probably have found a way to permit Lincoln's army to detain Merryman without a hearing.

Indeed, later courts would do just this.[35] Instead, Justice Taney issued the writ of habeas corpus, forcing Lincoln to decide whether to obey the law or not.

Lincoln disobeyed the writ. However, he did not follow the outlaw-and-forgive protocol in all of its rigor: he did not admit that he violated the law and ask the public to express its forgiveness by reelecting him. Instead, Lincoln claimed that he had the constitutional right to suspend the writ of habeas corpus.[36] Lincoln did win reelection and so, on the outlaw-and-forgive account, he was "forgiven" for violating the law, if that is the right word. Lincoln's dictatorial behavior was an issue in the presidential campaign, but apparently enough of the voters agreed with his view that the Constitution did not apply with full force in wartime.

Recall that the case for outlaw and forgive is that it ensures that officials respect civil liberties except in extreme circumstances, when they will violate the law in order to preserve the nation. We argued earlier that, as applied to ordinary officials, such as police officers or soldiers, the argument is not persuasive. We do not normally think that the way to give government employees the right incentives is to forbid them to engage in the desired conduct unless subsequently the public or a jury endorses their behavior. But the argument is not quite as unpersuasive when the president is the employee in question. The president is uniquely visible and is accustomed to maintaining his power by appealing for public support.

To understand the argument, we return to the idea expressed in Justice Jackson's opinion in *Korematsu*: a judicial opinion that approves a military order that violates civil liberties does long-term damage to the Constitution.

> But once a judicial opinion rationalizes such an order to show that it conforms to the Constitution, or rather rationalizes the Constitution to show that the Constitution sanctions such an order, the Court for all time has validated the principle of racial discrimination in criminal procedure and of transplanting American citizens. The principle then lies about like a loaded weapon ready for the hand of any authority that can bring forward a plausible claim of an urgent need. Every repetition imbeds that principle more deeply in our law and thinking and expands it to new purposes.[37]

In an interesting discussion of this passage, Mark Tushnet argues:

> Jackson does not quite make the point I extract from his opinion, which is that it is better to have emergency powers exercised in an extraconstitutional way, so that everyone understands that the actions

are extraordinary, than to have the actions rationalized away as consistent with the Constitution and thereby normalized. One might call this a claim that the actions have an extraconstitutional validity, one that the courts cannot endorse but that is consistent with the persistence of the constitutional regime.

Tushnet also argues that the extraconstitutional approach has another advantage: decisionmakers can then understand that they should regret that they find themselves compelled to invoke emergency powers. Once the emergency has passed, they should not only revert to the norms of legality that were suspended during the emergency, but should do what they can to make reparation for the actions they took. Here, too, Lincoln should be our guide, for among his observations in his second inaugural address, delivered in anticipation of a successful conclusion of the Civil War, was the injunction that we "strive on . . . to bind up the nation's wounds."[38]

There are two related arguments here. First, Jackson's argument is that if a court allows the president to violate the Constitution during an authentic emergency, a future president will be able to invoke the precedent to justify constitutional violations during spurious emergencies. Tushnet adds that by forcing presidents to act extraconstitutionally—that is, to disobey courts—the outlaw-and-forgive approach makes it clear to the public that the president is acting in an extraordinary fashion.[39] Second, the president will feel regret because he violated a constitutional norm, and this regret will cause the president both to make reparation for the violation and to resort to norms of legality once the emergency is over.

Neither of these arguments is persuasive. Jackson's argument, including Tushnet's variant, essentially claims that it is better for presidents to disobey a judicial order than for presidents to act with the acquiescence of the courts, even though the effect is the same, because the constitutional crisis that ensues will make clear to the public that what is happening is extraordinary. Perhaps. But Tushnet does not acknowledge the most likely consequence of such a practice, which is that the public will lose its trust in the presidency, in the judiciary, or in both institutions. And it is not clear why the publicity effect that Tushnet cares about could not be accomplished in a simpler and less risky manner through a rhetorical statement on the part of the judiciary: "we acquiesce in the president's act because of the extraordinary emergency that is upon us." To hope for a constitutional crisis during an emergency in order to publicize the unusual nature of the president's actions—a constitutional crisis that could result in the paralysis of government at a time when decisive, unified governmental action is of the highest importance—is idiosyncratic.

The second argument is also puzzling. Tushnet argues that the president will feel more regret if he is opposed by the judiciary than if he is not opposed by the judiciary, even though the action is the same. If the desire to avoid this feeling of regret (and the need to make reparation) is strong enough, however, then it will deter presidents from taking the needed action that Tushnet assumes is desirable. If the desire is not strong enough, then it will not deter them. The notion that a feeling of regret produces an intermediate level of disutility that would cause the president to act if and only if the action is justified, and return to the status quo after the emergency is over, is farfetched. That scenario may sometimes occur, but only fortuitously.

These arguments miss the most important difference between the outlaw-and-forgive approach and the judicial deference view. The main difference between these views is that the relevant decisionmaker—the entity that decides whether the president may engage in constitutionally proscribed conduct—is the public in the first case and the judiciary in the second. Put differently, the outlaw-and-forgive approach expects the public to evaluate the president's actions directly and to reward or sanction him at the ballot box; the president's exercise of emergency powers is carved out from his other powers and made the subject of direct democracy. The judicial deference view expects the public to retain its confidence in the judiciary, so that it may continue, as in normal times, to evaluate the president on political grounds as well as on legal or constitutional grounds.

The usual reasons for maintaining an independent judiciary explain why this limited reliance on direct democracy is a bad idea. Judges are accustomed to thinking about constitutional values and balancing the demands of security and liberty: they are therefore less likely to make errors than the public is. The public takes its cue from the judiciary, and if the judiciary declares that the president has acted unconstitutionally, then a constitutional crisis may ensue. It is this risk of a constitutional crisis, and the resulting loss of public confidence, that explains why presidents and other officials comply with the Constitution in the first place. The judicial deference view preserves this institutional structure, albeit commanding courts to be more deferential than they are during normal times. The outlaw and forgive approach undermines this structure, forcing the public to evaluate the president both on political and on constitutional grounds at the ballot box. This muddies the rules of the game, decreases political transparency, and is likely to embroil the government in constitutional crises and political uncertainties at the height of the emergency, when unity and clarity of purpose ought to prevail.

In the long term, the presidential outlaw-and-forgive approach is no more sustainable than the ordinary version. Ordinary people, like lawyers, reason from analogy and rely on precedent. If a president takes some action during emergency 1 in violation of a judicial order and is validated at the polls, then he or any future president will be able to cite this precedent to justify taking the same action during emergency 2. Popular precedents, just like legal precedents, lie around like loaded guns and can be picked up by anyone who might benefit from them; Jackson's *Korematsu* dissent does not take into account that the same arguments Jackson makes about formal legal rulings issued at time 1 can be made about any event that occurred at time 1. At time 2 or 3 or 4, the courts will be in the increasingly difficult position of insisting on constitutional understandings that have been rejected by the public, and, if history is any guide, eventually the courts will acquiesce. Their legitimacy is at stake also, after all; and if they insist that the president cannot do what the public thinks that he can and should do, then people will be less inclined to defer to courts' judgments about constitutional law. The outlaw-and-forgive approach, at bottom, relies on pretense—we will pretend that the Constitution forbids X even as we hope that officials will engage in X—even while removing the decisionmaking from an institution that could arguably maintain the pretense and placing it in the public arena, where pretense is impossible to maintain.

## CONCLUSION

It has been well known since the Greeks that a democracy, in order to survive an emergency, must place a great deal of power in the hands of the executive for the duration of the emergency. The challenge for a modern representative democracy is to ensure that the leader does not have too much power and can be made to relinquish it when the emergency is over. As far as history has shown, this problem has been solved in the United States. Under the judicial deference view, courts acquiesce in enhanced executive power for the duration of an emergency. Some lucky combination of congressional and judicial independence, political culture, civil society, and federalism has ensured that abuses of power for political gain have been relatively rare and that the status quo has been reestablished at the expiration of the emergency.

The ex ante and ex post statutory authorization approaches are undesirable and probably unsustainable efforts to limit the executive's power by forcing him to obtain authorization for emergency actions from Congress. The ex ante version is worse than the ex post version because it depends on the drafters of the framework statute being able to predict how emergency powers should be regulated long before the emergency occurs.

The outlaw and forgive approach eccentrically requires public deliberation and engagement about constitutional values and security threats during an emergency, when secrecy, decisiveness, and unity are all at a premium. It endorses pretense, but in a liberal democracy devoted to the rule of law and public deliberation, pretense will either be exposed and discredited or (in contradiction to itself) incorporated in the law. In the first case, we are back to civil libertarianism; in the second, we are back to judicial deference.

# CHAPTER SIX

# Coercive Interrogation

Coercive interrogation is now a live subject, thanks to 9/11 and to recent controversies about the use of coercive interrogation by the executive branch and by American allies. At one time, coercive interrogation played a role only in philosophical disputes about consequentialism, in which scholars asserted or denied that the police could coercively interrogate an individual in order to extract the location of a ticking nuclear bomb. None of the participants in those debates seriously considered the possibility that coercive interrogation could be justified except in extreme circumstances never likely to be met. Today, U.S. officials appear to engage in coercive interrogation or something very similar to it; so do other Western governments; and the possibility that coercive interrogation may be justified in nonremote circumstances has entered mainstream debate.[1] The task for legal scholars at this point is to understand how this practice fits into legal norms and traditions and how it ought to be regulated.

In earlier chapters, we distinguished two aspects of the theory of emergency powers: the theory of emergency policymaking, as to which we have defended first-order balancing, and the theory of constitutional judicial review during emergencies, as to which we have defended a strong version of judicial deference to the executive. In this chapter, we apply our views to the subject of coercive interrogation, meaning physically or mentally forceful interrogation used to extract information necessary to prevent future harms, such as terrorist attacks. We will argue that first-order balancing permits coercive interrogation under a range of emergency circumstances; that those circumstances should be regulated in roughly the same way that law regulates other harmful governmental tactics, such as the use of deadly force; and that judges should not invoke the Constitution to prohibit or constrict the resulting regulatory scheme.

Let us define some terms and delimit the topic. *Coercive interrogation*, we will say, involves (1) the application of force, physical or mental, (2) in order to try to extract information (3) necessary to prevent severe harms to others, such as terrorist attacks, suicide bombings, and the like.[2] Coercive interrogation can range from the mild to the severe. At some point of severity, coercive interrogation becomes a species of torture, which is flatly prohibited by domestic and international law;[3] even in its milder forms, coercive interrogation can amount to "cruel, inhuman and degrading treatment," which is also prohibited.[4] Coercive interrogation and torture are thus partially overlapping concepts; neither is a proper subset of the other. Sufficiently mild coercive interrogation does not amount to legal torture, which requires that a threshold of severity be met. And there are forms of torture that are not coercive interrogation—for example, when torture is used as a means of political intimidation or oppression, indeed for any purpose other than extracting information necessary to save third-party lives. Our interest is in the overlapping area of these two concepts: coercive interrogation that (by virtue of its severity) counts as torture or as cruel, inhuman, and degrading treatment. Henceforth, we will use *coercive interrogation* to denote this subset.

Given these stipulations, our inquiry is normative. We ask what legal regime should govern coercive interrogation. Should it ever be permissible? If so, what legal rules should be used to sort permissible from impermissible cases? Should judges place constitutional limits on the resulting scheme of coercive interrogation?

We argue that coercive interrogation should be legalized and subjected to regulatory oversight. Consider some analogous areas of law and policy. Police officers are allowed to use deadly force in order to prevent dangerous suspects from harming other people. Killing a person is, of course, also a serious harm to dignity and autonomy; although we will see arguments holding that coercive interrogation is worse than killing in some respects, there are other respects in which killing is worse than coercive interrogation. To prevent officials from engaging in unjustified killings, governments take the conventional route of enacting laws that describe the conditions under which a police officer may use deadly force, making the police liable only if they violate these rules in bad faith. Why shouldn't a similar system be used for coercive interrogation?

Or consider the use of force during war. The laws and usages of war permit soldiers to kill other soldiers, and sometimes civilians as well. Although the killing of civilians is generally regarded as a moral evil, it is justified and permitted when civilian deaths are not disproportionate, given a legitimate military target.[5] If governments authorize the killing of civilians in order to accomplish legitimate military objectives—which are all means to the end of national security—why shouldn't governments authorize coercive interrogation for the same purpose?

In short, the view that coercive interrogation should remain illegal assumes that coercive interrogation is special in a way that distinguishes it from police killings and other serious harms that officials are licensed to inflict. But what makes coercive interrogation special?

The answer, in our view, is that coercive interrogation is not special at all. If it is agreed that coercive interrogation is justified in certain realistic circumstances, even narrow circumstances, it should be made legal, albeit subject to numerous legal protections—again, in this way, like police shootings, wartime killings, preventive detentions, capital punishment, and other serious harms. The law should treat coercive interrogation the way it typically treats coercive governmental practices. Such practices are subject to a standard set of regulations defined ex ante: punishment of officials who use these instruments without a good justification; official immunity when they are used in good faith; various restrictions on the type of instruments that may be used; ex ante protections such as warrants;[6] and so forth. Our argument is that coercive interrogation should be treated in the same way.

The chapter begins with a brief and selective overview of the philosophical issues. Our purpose here is to delimit the topic in two critical ways. First, we bracket and ignore the claim that coercive interrogation is deontologically impermissible per se, whatever the facts. This is a view that few people hold; most mainstream philosophers—both consequentialists and deontologists—agree that coercive interrogation may be morally justified under certain conditions. Second, we outline the rule-consequentialist view that the harms of coercive interrogation are so great, the occasions for its justified use so infrequent, and the risks of decision-maker error so high that coercive interrogation should never be permissible. The rule-consequentialist view turns on empirical and institutional premises that we discuss subsequently. The only philosophical point is that, for either deontologists or consequentialists who believe that coercive interrogation can sometimes be permissible, there is no philosophical justification for thinking that coercive interrogation should be considered special and regulated differently from the other serious, coercive harms that government inflicts.

Having cleared some philosophical issues away, we then address empirical and institutional arguments for treating coercive interrogation as special in the legal system (that is, regulating coercive interrogation by a different legal regime than applies to other serious harms that government may inflict). These arguments rely on various tropes of second-order argument—

rules versus standards, slippery slopes, institutional failure, symbolism, and so forth—that, in this case, turn out to rest on implausible empirical premises. Our more precise point, however, is that if these arguments are accepted for coercive interrogation, then many other common practices would have to be prohibited as well—for example, the shooting of armed suspects and hostage takers.

Our institutional discussion will ignore the OAF (outlaw-and-forgive) position that coercive interrogation should be illegal in a nominal sense, but should be permitted through ex post mechanisms, such as pardons, jury nullification, or popular approval. In chapter 5, we argued that all of the reasons for creating a set of ex ante regulations that govern official conduct—rather than regulating official conduct ex post—apply as much to coercive interrogations as to other forms of law enforcement. Moreover, a regime of ex ante illegality and ex post license is unsustainable. If officials and citizens know that ex post defenses and forgiveness are available—and, in a liberal democracy, it is inevitable that the knowledge will become widespread—they will factor that knowledge into their understanding of what the law is, diluting the material and expressive effects of the "ban" on coercive interrogation.

Finally, we provide a proposed framework for regulating coercive interrogation. It emphasizes three elements: (1) rules that state what is permitted and what is not permitted; (2) immunity for officials who obey the rules and punishment for those who violate the rules; (3) internal regulatory oversight by executive branch officials. We also rebut some arguments that judges should prohibit coercive interrogation under the rubric of due process, freedom from unreasonable searches and seizures, or other constitutional provisions.

## COERCIVE INTERROGATION AND MORAL THEORY

Coercive interrogation is a stock subject in moral reasoning. We will outline some standard philosophical positions about coercive interrogation, put some off the table, and argue that the remainder turn crucially upon suppressed empirical and institutional premises, rather than the sort of conceptual claims that fall within the philosopher's distinctive expertise. Our aim is to set up the later discussion, in which we criticize the empirical and institutional premises necessary to sustain the view that coercive interrogation should be regulated differently from other serious coercive harms.

Let us begin by looking at the following standard views; we will offer some brief remarks on each.

## Absolutist Deontology

One might hold that coercive interrogation is absolutely impermissible, as a violation of rights rooted in human dignity or autonomy. This position is held by a very few moral philosophers. Here, the ticking-bomb hypotheticals are important: while it is possible to argue that such cases are so rare that they should be ignored by a rule-consequentialist calculus ex ante, an argument we consider below, it is fanatical to argue on deontological grounds that rights against coercive interrogation should not be overridden to prevent serious harms to others. That position denies that there can ever be such a thing as a justified violation of rights, or a necessary evil. Thomas Nagel seems to offer a brief defense of absolutism, saying that in standard cases where A sacrifices or harms B to save C, A can justify his conduct to B; but in the case of torture, no such justification is possible.[7] But this view is a nonstarter, even on its own terms, for Nagel is equivocating about what "torture" means. If coercive interrogation that aims to save lives, rather than sheer sadistic cruelty, is at issue, the structure of justification tracks the standard cases of harming B in order to save C.[8]

Put differently, coercive interrogation presents a "tragic choice."[9] A view holding that coercive interrogation is sometimes permissible need not deny that coercive interrogation is a grave moral evil; of course it is. But sometimes evils, even grave ones, are also necessary. The absolutist deontological view fails to come to grips with the inevitability of tragic choices. In what follows, then, we will put the absolutist deontological view off the table. Anyone who genuinely holds it may ignore our argument, but we do not think there are many such people.

## Deontology and Catastrophe

Charles Fried argues, as have many others, that it is permissible to kill an innocent person to save a whole nation from annihilation.[10] If so, coercive interrogation would be permissible a fortiori in those circumstances.

But why only *those* circumstances? Let us motivate the puzzle by imagining that a *catastrophe principle* governs the standard practice in which police officers may use necessary force, including lethal force, against persons who threaten harm to others. In this imagined regime, government officials may kill one person only to save (say) a thousand other people. No legal system adopts such a regime, nor is there any obvious reason to recommend it. Standardly, the permissible ratio[11] is one to one: where relevant restrictions are met, a government may kill A to save B, not merely a thousand Bs. Obviously, we can add further specification to either the coercive-interrogation case or the extrajudicial killing case: we might require that the threatened harm be "imminent," that the force used be no more than necessary, and so on. What is quite mysterious, however, is why the sheer catastrophic *size* of the threatened harm should matter. The obvious alternative is to say that the harm prevented must simply be greater than the harm inflicted. It will not do to say that "harms cannot be aggregated across individuals" or "we must take seriously the differences between persons." The catastrophe exception is already in the business of aggregating harms across persons. Oddly, however, the catastrophe exception builds in an arbitrary threshold below which the harms are of insufficient weight to override deontological restrictions and above which they are sufficiently weighty to do so.

Michael Moore responds to this point in the following way:

> [T]he worry may be that any point we pick for a threshold beyond which consequences determine the rightness of action may seem arbitrary. . . . [But] this is no more than the medieval worry of how many stones make a heap. Our uncertainty whether it takes 3, or 4, or 5, etc., does not justify us in thinking there are no such things as heaps. Similarly, preventing the torture of two innocents does not justify my torturing one, but destruction of an entire city does.[12]

Moore's point would be responsive if the question were a linguistic and conceptual one: how many stones make a "heap" and how many deaths make a "catastrophe." It is not responsive to the different question we raise: why, as a matter of substantive morality, should there be any such catastrophe threshold in the first place? Why exactly do the deontologists want to say that saving a mere, say, two or three lives does not justify a single act of coercive interrogation? Moore's final sentence restates the catastrophe view, but does nothing to justify it.

What typically animates a catastrophe exception is a complex of empirical and institutional considerations: the moral theorist is worried about the decisionmakers who will assess whether coercive interrogation is justified and about the collateral effects of licensing those decisionmakers to make those very decisions. In this sense, the deontologists who build in a catastrophe exception are often second-order consequentialists with particular institutional sensibilities. They do not want to prescribe fanatical respect for rights in scary cases, but they also worry that the exception will expand so as to swallow the rule; they are worried about institutional and empirical phenomena like slippery slopes and the effects on public attitudes of permitting coercive interrogation. Such worries are perfectly sensible in principle, although we will suggest below that they are much overblown in fact and cannot justify distinctive treatment of coercive interrogation. This complex of institutional concerns, moreover, is not one about which philosophers as such have anything distinctive to say.

Consider Henry Shue's famous argument against the moral permissibility of torture.[13] On this view, the central evil of torture—what makes it worse than the extrajudicial killing of a menacing criminal or (Shue's comparison case) the killing of enemy combatants—is that torture violates "the prohibition against assault upon the defenseless."[14] Torture is worse than killing, from the standpoint of a concern with dignity and autonomy, because torture "fail[s] . . . to satisfy even [the] weak constraint of being a 'fair fight.'"[15]

This is slippery moral philosophy, even without regard to the offsetting benefits of coercive interrogation. Torture is worse than, say, killing enemies or armed criminals, because the tortured captive is defenseless (ex post, at least). But killing enemies or armed criminals is worse than torture on another margin: killing, unlike torture, utterly extinguishes the victim and forever denies him any future possibility of exercising autonomy or enjoying human dignity. The victim of coercive interrogation may not get a fair fight, but at least he lives to fight another day. Shue has picked out the dimensions that put torture in the worst light so he can argue that it is worse than other, commonplace practices. The opposite tack would be to pick out the dimensions that put torture in a better light than other, commonplace practices. Neither approach seems obviously superior.

Still, what is of interest for our purposes here is that Shue is reluctantly willing to entertain exceptions. "[T]he avoidance of assaults upon the defenseless is not the only, or even in all cases an overriding, moral consideration."[16] Shue then adduces a string of brief empirical and institutional arguments against permitting coercive interrogation. First, it will be difficult to define the limited set of conditions under which coercive interrogation would be permitted. Second, such limiting conditions will predictably be violated even if they can be defined, because all torture has a "metastatic tendency."[17] "[A]ny practice of torture one set in motion would gain enough momentum to burst any bonds and become a standard operating procedure. . . . If it were ever permitted under any conditions, the temptation to use it would be very strong."[18] This is a slippery slope argument, and an unconvincing one, or so we will suggest below. The larger point is that Shue's slippery slope argument is untethered from moral theory, his area of presumptive expertise. The argument is entirely empirical, but Shue gives the reader little beyond a set of stylized assumptions about what the legal, political, and social effects of interrogation simply *must* be.[19]

We do not claim that only institutional considerations can justify a threshold-based approach, for example, a norm against killing that can be overridden to save a hundred lives, but not two lives. A strictly first-order moral justification for such thresholds might be that the deontological injunction not to kill does not have infinite weight, and at some point is overbalanced by other moral obligations.[20] Our narrower claim is just that Shue and many other opponents of coercive interrogation who subscribe to some sort of threshold-based approach tend to do so because of the second-order institutional and empirical concerns discussed below. Those concerns are not philosophical, and we will argue that they are also not plausible.

## Rule Consequentialism

The deontological parts of Shue's argument establish a moral presumption against coercive interrogation, subject to a consequentialist override; the subsequent move, one that Shue introduces on the quiet, is a prediction about the effects of coercive interrogation across a range of cases. Here, all views short of strict deontology—both ordinary consequentialism and the modified deontological position that admits a catastrophe exception—must assess the first-order and second-order consequences of coercive interrogation, comparing its costs with its benefits.

Two clarifications are in order here. First, here, as in other chapters, we mean nothing philosophically contentious by the terms *cost* and *benefit*. Any consequentialist view needs a value theory that labels some consequences as good, others as bad; we label the good consequences "benefits" and the bad consequences "costs." (Violations of rights might themselves count as bads, to be compared to other goods and bads.) In particular, we do not mean to invoke cost-benefit analysis in the technical sense; we do not suggest that costs and benefits must be monetized through a willingness-to-pay measure. Second, as we mentioned in chapter 1, the distinction between deontology and consequentialism does not track the distinction between rights-based and welfarist moral theories. One may hold a consequentialist view according to which the effects of actions on rights are themselves among the consequences to be evaluated, in which case the welfare consequences of actions are not the only consequences of interest.[21] This possibility is orthogonal to our discussion here, but nothing we say is inconsistent with it. The nonwelfarist consequentialist, who counts rights violations as bads, either does or does not admit some rate of tradeoff between the goal of avoiding rights violations and other goals. If the rate of tradeoff is zero, we will label the position "deontological," strictly to simplify our terminology. If there is some positive rate of tradeoff, we label the position "consequentialist," again for simplicity. In the latter case, rights violations count as a cost above and are folded into the cost-benefit calculus.

Putting aside Shue's modified deontological view, the assessment of consequences can proceed in either an act-consequentialist or a rule-consequentialist framework. There is also a possible motive-consequentialist approach, on which actors attempt to develop the character or disposition that will tend to produce the actions with the best overall consequences. We will ignore this variant in what follows. We also bracket the possible view that coercive interrogation is not merely morally *permissible* but indeed morally *required*, when lives are in the balance. Where coercive interrogation might save third-party lives, to fail to interrogate might be seen as itself a morally objectionable choice, a sort of moral squeamishness not justified by any plausible version of the distinction between acts and omissions.[22]

For act consequentialists, the important issue is whether the benefits of coercive interrogation exceed the costs in particular cases. Rule consequentialists, by contrast, ask which (set of) rules about coercive interrogation will produce the greatest net benefits. We have already seen the straightforward act-consequentialist argument for permitting coercive interrogation, especially in the standard ticking-bomb hypotheticals discussed above, so we will focus here on the rule-consequentialist alternative. We address here the second-order arguments for adopting a flat rule-consequentialist ban on interrogation, and find those arguments implausible. Subsequently, we ask whether there is any good reason to have a legal regime that differs from the moral regime. We suggest that there is none; the legal system should authorize coercive interrogation in some narrow range of circumstances, suitably defined and regulated ex ante.

The rule-consequentialist argument against coercive interrogation emphasizes second-order considerations. Perhaps, cases in which coercive interrogation is justified to prevent greater harms are in fact extremely rare; perhaps, frontline moral decisionmakers would be prone to commit errors by using coercive interrogation in cases where its costs outweigh its benefits; perhaps, there are important dynamic effects, such as the risk of a slippery slope from tightly regulated coercive interrogation to widespread casual torture. On this approach, coercive interrogation is declared morally impermissible on an ex ante cost-benefit calculus, not because there are no cases in which coercive interrogation would be justified from an ex post perspective—the rule consequentialist agrees that there are—but because it is predictable ex ante that licensing decisionmakers to attempt to identify such cases will do more harm than good. We comment on the empirical merits of similar second-order arguments below, suggesting that arguments for prohibiting all coercive interrogation because of concerns about the decisional capacities of officials in the legal system are unduly pessimistic. Here, we will confine ourselves to some remarks about the presuppositions of the rule-consequentialist approach.

It is important to acknowledge that a rule-consequentialist prohibition on coercive interrogation might turn out to be correct, in light of the facts. The great strength of this approach is that it cannot, by its nature, be ruled out of bounds in the abstract. Everything depends on the actual values of the second-order variables that the rule-consequentialist argument identifies.

Yet it is equally important to recognize that the rule-consequentialist approach purchases this immunity from abstract critique for a price: the rule-consequentialist approach is hostage to the facts as they actually turn out to be, in whatever empirical domain is at issue. Because the relevant facts vary over time and place, it is extremely implausible (although not logically impossible) that the rule-consequentialist calculus will counsel a flat prohibition on coercive interrogation always and everywhere. At some times, the harms that coercive interrogation might prevent will be greater and more likely to occur than at other times, and the rule consequentialist must take this into account. So too, in some polities, under some circumstances, coercive interrogation may be justified on this approach even if it cannot be justified in other polities under other circumstances. The faithful rule consequentialist cannot subscribe to any timeless and universal prohibition on coercive interrogation.

A related point is that, from the rule-consequentialist standpoint, a flat prohibition on coercive interrogation is a kind of extreme or corner solution and, as such, suspect. For any such rule, there will generally be a more permissive substitute, such as a rule-with-exceptions that permits some coercive interrogation under circumstances that can be clearly defined ex ante. Consider a rule-with-exceptions that bans coercive interrogation unless officials know to a certainty that a thousand people will imminently die. More generally, the rule consequentialist is obliged to consider a range of intermediate regimes short of a flat prohibition on coercive interrogation. The corner solution is salient but not superior, unless that salience itself produces some consequentialist benefit.

The final point is that the second-order arguments that support a prohibition on coercive interrogation risk proving too much. Those arguments are, in many cases, pitched at a level of generality that would also condemn other standard practices in which officials are legally licensed to inflict serious harms, such as extrajudicial killing. The rule consequentialist who subscribes to a prohibition on coercive interrogation bears the burden of confronting those practices, either by extending the prohibition to include them, or by offering some empirical consideration that makes coercive interrogation special. We subsequently argue that no such consideration can be shown to exist. Whatever the merits of our answer, however, the rule consequentialist cannot avoid the question.

To summarize the ground covered so far: we will bracket and ignore genuinely absolutist deontological arguments that coercive interrogation is impermissible per se. This position is very rarely defended, in light of cases suggesting that coercive interrogation is at least sometimes necessary to prevent third-party harms. Far more common are positions that incorporate consequences in some way. Of these, the two most prominent are (1) a modified deontological position that incorporates an exception or override to a baseline deontological prohibition, when coercive interrogation can prevent "catastrophic" harms, and (2) a rule-consequentialist prohibition. Both positions turn crucially upon empirical and institutional premises or assumptions, especially a set of predictions about the empirical and institutional effects of the possible legal regimes. We now turn to those second-order questions.

## EMPIRICAL AND INSTITUTIONAL CONSIDERATIONS

Here, we assume that the consequentialists and the nonabsolutist deontologists are right that, at least in limited circumstances, coercive interrogation is morally justified. This assumption, however, provides only a starting point for making policy choices. The further question is whether coercive interrogation can be justified in light of what we call second-order considerations about the legal system and about the institutional context in which coercive interrogation would take place. Some critics of coercive interrogation—even those who acknowledge first-order moral arguments for permitting coercive interrogation in catastrophic scenarios—argue that the second-order considerations are decisive with respect to real legal systems: they argue, in essence that even if a perfect government that made no errors should have the power to engage in coercive interrogation in extreme cases, no real-world government should have such a power. In the real world, government officials make mistakes, and actions that may be justified on a narrowly instrumental calculus have unforeseeable institutional or systemic effects that render them unjustified in general.

We address three groups of second-order considerations,[23] and argue that they are exceptionally weak. Second-order considerations do not justify a flat ban on coercive interrogation.

## Rules and Standards

The first argument is that catastrophic scenarios are too rare to justify authorizing the police to engage in coercive interrogation. Suppose that coercive interrogation can be justified only to save more than one thousand lives, and even then that coercive interrogation would be justified only if it were reasonably certain that the subject would provide the relevant information that could be used to save the lives. Outside of war, such scenarios are extremely rare; indeed, we can think of only one in the United States or any other Western country in recent history—the September 11, 2001, attacks—and even here it seems unlikely that the authorities would have been able to stop the attacks if they had had the power to engage in coercive interrogation.[24] Thus, the benefits of allowing coercive interrogation would be vanishingly small.

At the same time, the costs could be high. If officials are allowed to engage in coercive interrogation, then no doubt they will make errors and sometimes employ this measure against people who have no information about a pending terrorist attack or have information only about small-scale attacks whose seriousness does not justify the use of coercive interrogation. Unnecessary infliction of pain is an intrinsic cost, whether the suspects are innocent or guilty of some crime. If the benefits of permitting coercive interrogation are low in an ex ante sense and the costs are high because of unavoidable error, then a flat ban on coercive interrogation would be justified.[25]

This argument is a familiar point about rules and standards. Rules are simple and easy to administer but are overinclusive or underinclusive, and thus produce results that deviate from the normative optimum that the rules are supposed to approximate. Standards directly incorporate the normative ideal, or approximate it more closely than rules do, but because they are harder to understand are more likely to result in error by decisionmakers. Rules are likely to be better than standards when decision costs are high relative to error costs.

The rule-consequentialist argument against coercive interrogation amounts to the claim that a bright-line rule—a blanket prohibition on coercive interrogation—is superior to a standard that permits coercive interrogation in "extreme circumstances" or the like; or, for that matter, a slightly more precise rule such as one that permitted coercive interrogation "only when it is reasonably certain to save more than one thousand lives." The reason is that the standard would produce high costs—instances of unnecessary coercive interrogation—without producing large-enough benefits to justify these costs, given the rarity of extreme circumstances. This argument is conceptually coherent and superficially attractive, but we believe it to be flawed in point of fact.

*Does Coercive Interrogation Work?* Let us begin with the simplest question of whether coercive interrogation works (where by "works," we mean "produces information that prevents harms, in a nontrivial range of cases"). If coercive interrogation does not work, if it is all cost and no benefit, then there are no tradeoffs to be made, and both the moral and institutional questions are easy. This is a tempting view.[26] One can eliminate the need to address difficult moral and legal questions by insisting that coercive interrogation is either ineffective, because it produces no information, or counterproductive in the long run, because it radicalizes one's enemy. The latter argument is one that we rejected in chapter 4. The former argument is implausible on its face.

Many governments, liberal democratic as well as authoritarian, have used coercive interrogation in the past and use it today. To be sure, in some fraction of the cases, coercion is used to punish, or intimidate, or for other purposes than the prevention of harms, but those other purposes do not count as coercive interrogation as we have defined it, and it is clear that, in another fraction of the cases, many governments use coercion for strictly preventive aims. Perhaps, all of the officials and actors who use coercive interrogation to extract information on preventive grounds are acting immorally or imprudently; but to claim that coercive interrogation is entirely ineffective is to claim that those actors, all of them, are acting *irrationally*. (Of course, there is a separate question, which we take up below, about whether the costs of coercive interrogation exceed the benefits, and how the alternatives to coercive interrogation stack up. Interrogators may torture too easily or frequently, from the social welfare point of view, because they do not bear the costs; but we are here considering the more radical claim that the benefits to the interrogators are zero.) The claim that coercive interrogation is ineffective is a delusion, although it may be a morally pleasing one. It is either a form of wishful thinking or dissonance reduction that allows people to avoid conflict between their moral commitments and their prudential commitments, or a rhetorical turn that opponents of coercive interrogation use to advance their moral agenda.

But these are generalities. Let us focus on some evidence from Israel. Much of that evidence is anecdotal or impressionistic, but it strongly suggests that coercive interrogation saves lives. The Landau Commission found:

> [E]ffective activity by the [General Security Service, or GSS] to thwart terrorist acts is impossible without use of the tool of the [coercive] interrogation of suspects, in order to extract from them vital information known only to them, and unobtainable by other methods.

The effective interrogation of terrorist suspects is impossible without the use of means of pressure, in order to overcome an obdurate will not to disclose information and to overcome the fear of the person under interrogation that harm will befall him from his own organization, if he does reveal information.[27]

In a report submitted to the United Nations, Israel represented that GSS investigations had foiled ninety planned terrorist attacks, including suicide bombings, car bombings, kidnappings, and murders.[28] Although the Israeli Supreme Court later held that GSS practices of coercive interrogation violated rights of human dignity, and thus required clear legislative authorization, the Court acknowledged that coercive interrogation works. Here is one example the Court gave:

> A powerful explosive device [was found in the applicant's village] subsequent to the dismantling and [coercive] interrogation of the terrorist cell to which he belonged. Uncovering this explosive device thwarted an attack .... According to GSS investigators, the applicant possessed additional crucial information which he only revealed as a result of their [coercive] interrogation. Revealing this information immediately was essential to safeguarding state and regional security and preventing danger to human life.[29]

Many people are reluctant to believe that coercive interrogation works, not only because they convince themselves that morally bad practices must also be ineffective, but also because they have in the back of their minds a picture of rogue police officers beating suspects in a haphazard or indiscriminate effort to gain information. As the Israeli experience shows, however, coercive interrogation can be done well or poorly. GSS interrogators worked under elaborate guidelines concerning the amount and types of coercion that could be used, and under the constant supervision of superiors, who had to provide administrative approval for the application of particular methods.[30] Professionalism and training can increase the benefits of coercive interrogation, by increasing the chances of obtaining useful information, and thus decrease the harms to those interrogated.

In a sober-minded and useful treatment of the issue, Philip Rumney argues that coercive interrogation is indeed ineffective.[31] He discounts the testimony of the Israeli GSS and credits the assertions of Israeli human rights groups, which accuse the GSS of perjury; it is hard to know what to think of this dispute, and it is not obvious why Rumney discounts the claims of one side but not the other. The Israeli human rights advocates also say that there is not a "shred of evidence that physical force [i.e., coercive interrogation] is the only or the most effective means to prevent attacks."[32] But this is to change the subject from whether coercive interrogation produces reliable or useful information in some range of cases, to the larger question of whether it is cost justified, on net, relative to the alternatives; we take up that question shortly. Rumney's analysis is ultimately unconvincing because there are at least some clear cases in which coercive interrogation has worked, as Rumney acknowledges;[33] because it is hard to believe that many governments would use it if it were really ineffective; and because the doubters seem so often (although not in Rumney's case) to be the victims of wishful thinking or else to be pushing a moral agenda by mean of spurious empirical arguments.

*Costs and Benefits*   If coercive interrogation is effective in our sense, then the cost of a bright-line rule that bans it in all circumstances is the lives lost because information was not obtained before the bomb exploded, or before the suicide attack occurred, or before some other avoidable harm resulted. Against this cost, we must compare the benefit of the ban: the avoided cases where government agents would unjustifiably engage in coercive interrogation. And we must compare coercive interrogation with alternative measures that might yield the same benefits at lower cost. Let us begin by asking whether the error costs are so extreme that only a bright-line ban can be justified.

There are two main reasons for thinking that the answer to this question is no. First, the question, as posed, assumes an implausibly simple policy choice: either a flat ban or a vague standard that will be easily abused. But there are many alternatives that fall between these extremes. Coercive interrogation could be limited to cases where a certain number of lives are at stake—say, a thousand. It could be limited to cases where the subjects are known to be members of al Qaeda or another group that has proved its hostility and lethalness. It could be subject to special ex ante controls: its use could be limited to specially trained and monitored groups within the government; the type of coercive interrogation could be circumscribed so that only "moderate" measures are used; and so forth. We will discuss these design options in more detail below; for now, it is sufficient to point out that the policy choices are more nuanced than supporters of a complete ban allow.

Second, ordinary and rarely criticized law enforcement practices already assume that the cost of unjustified coercive interrogation is not extremely high. Existing policy—which permits light interrogation, but bans "cruel, inhuman and degrading treatment" and coercive interrogation that rises to the level of torture—already accepts the possibility that officials will err and use unjustified coercion. The distinction between coercive and noncoercive interrogation, or between harsh treatment and cruel, inhuman, or degrading treatment, is fuzzy and subject to much debate and litigation. Even a decision-maker acting in good faith can cross these lines and engage in coercion. If we cared so much about preventing torture that we were unwilling to tolerate even a single instance of it, then we could choose to restrict even noncoercive interrogations. A prophylactic ban on all interrogations, for example, would eliminate coercive interrogation.

But no government is willing to go so far; presumably, the reasons are that the benefits of noncoercive interrogation are high enough to justify a fuzzy rule or standard, even one that results in occasional erroneous decisions to coercively interrogate, and that the costs of coercive interrogation are, though high, not as high as people might initially claim. But then it follows that unless coercive interrogation is known to be ineffective—an implausible assumption, as we have argued—it may be appropriate to permit it with a fuzzy rule or standard that limits it to cases where the benefits exceed the costs.

The comparison with police shootings is again instructive. The costs of police shootings are extremely high—people are wounded or killed, unnecessarily when the police make errors, as they unavoidably do—but the benefits are also high: innocent lives are saved. Rather than banning police shootings because of the high costs of error, governments regulate them. And rather than using very clear rules, the regulations are replete with standards—references to "justified" force or force that the officer "reasonably believes to be necessary" are common.[34] Why shouldn't the government use the same system of regulation for coercive interrogations?

To be sure, it may be that the cost-benefit calculus is different for coercive interrogation and for extrajudicial killings. Perhaps extracting information is not as important as preventing immediate violence; extrajudicial killing will often save another life with high probability, while extracting information is a more speculative enterprise and will less frequently save lives. On the other hand, when coercive interrogation *does* save lives, it may often save more lives than does extrajudicial killing. The cost-benefit calculus must consider not only the probability of averting harm but the magnitude of the harms averted. Overall, then, it is hardly obvious that the net cost-benefit calculus is different in the two cases; and even if there is a difference, it is unlikely that the difference is great enough to justify a complete ban on coercive interrogation alone. We will return to the possibility of an empirical distinction between police killings and coercive interrogation below.

What we have said so far applies, with the same force, to the many subtle variations on the rules-standards argument that can be found in the literature. For example, it has been suggested that, if officials must balance the costs and benefits of coercive interrogation on a case-by-case basis, they will inevitably underestimate the costs and overestimate the benefits.[35] It is not clear why this would be true, though it is possible: maybe officials underestimate the costs because they don't sympathize with the subject; or because the officials themselves become dehumanized by their involvement in coercive interrogation and lose the ability to perceive the impact of their actions on the subject; or maybe they overestimate the benefits because they have personal or institutional reasons for exaggerating the likelihood of threats; or, most simple of all, perhaps officials estimate the costs and benefits accurately but just don't care about the costs, which are borne by those interrogated rather than by the officials themselves.

But, putting aside the fact that all of these worries are pure speculation unencumbered by serious empirical support, they apply with equal force to noncoercive interrogation; they are simply an aspect of much military and police work. If they are valid concerns, then they provide a general case for restricting executive agents, subjecting them to public oversight, and so forth; but they do not apply specially to coercive interrogation to justify a flat ban when other areas of police work seem appropriately governed by standards or soft rules. Part of the reason that such considerations are not taken seriously in any general way, and probably never will be, is that costs borne by those outside of the political community—a foreign terrorist suspect, for example—are not thought to count, or at least do not count equally with benefits to Americans, and it is a contentious question of political philosophy whether they should.

Taken together, these considerations suggest that the critics of coercive interrogation have not yet provided a justification for an absolute ban. Most law enforcement and intelligence work is governed by standards or soft rules; unless there is something special about coercive interrogation, the same approach should be used for that measure.

## Slippery Slopes

As we mentioned in chapter 4, the slippery slope argument holds that even if coercive interrogation survives a narrow assessment of its advantages and disadvantages—one that compares the immediate benefits from obtaining information and the harms to the subject of the interrogation—it is nonetheless unjustified because of its more remote effects. Once coercive interrogation is allowed in any circumstances, the argument goes, torture will come to be used casually, and a "culture of torture" will come into being.[36] The purposes for which officials use coercion will expand, from preventing harms to punishing convicted criminals, extracting confessions from suspects in routine criminal cases, and even intimidating political opponents.[37]

Slippery slope arguments identify a possible unintended negative consequence of a particular policy; if this consequence is likely enough, then it ought to count as a cost in the cost-benefit calculus used to evaluate the rule.[38] But the fact that bad consequences are possible is not itself a sufficient reason for banning an activity. Proponents of a slippery slope argument bear the burden of showing that the unintended consequence is likely enough that it should be included in the calculus; this involves (1) identifying a mechanism by which the initial policy choice might lead to the adverse consequence; and (2) providing some evidence that this mechanism operates in fact.[39] Proponents of a flat ban on coercive interrogation have not met this burden.

The first argument is that once the taboo against coercive interrogation is shattered, the psychological constraints against inflicting pain will fall away, brutalizing the law enforcement officials who use coercive interrogation and creating a broader culture of torture. Law enforcement, military, or intelligence officials who justifiably use coercive interrogation in one setting—the prevention of catastrophic terrorist attacks—will start using it to extract information or even confessions from petty criminals and even innocent bystanders who are thought to be withholding information about a crime that they have witnessed.[40] Alternatively, even if the shattering of the taboo does not itself increase official brutality, sadists may self-select into intelligence or police work at greater rates than they otherwise would.

These arguments are not supported by real evidence.[41] David Luban argues that "case-hardened torturers" will always go to extremes because of bureaucratic and social-psychological imperatives; as evidence, he cites tendentious anecdotes from human rights advocates in Israel, and examples of uncontrolled torture from liberal-democratic paradigms such as Algeria and Argentina.[42] Luban also alleges a "culture of torture" in the U.S. Department of Justice based on legal memoranda that supported a broad view of executive power to engage in coercive interrogation, which were later retracted by the Justice Department itself.[43] The problem here is that neither type of evidence, even if true, fits the story implicit in the slippery slope argument. The implicit story envisages a liberal-democratic nation that takes a first tentative step onto the path of coercive interrogation, only to descend into a netherworld of a torture culture. But nations like Algeria and Argentina were not liberal democracies to begin with, at the relevant times, and legal memoranda do not constitute a torture culture, whatever their content.

Proponents of the slippery slope argument point to the Abu Ghraib torture scandal as evidence for this view. They argue that, by authorizing the CIA to engage in torture or near-torture and by authorizing torture (or something close to it) against unlawful combatants at Guantanamo Bay, the Bush administration encouraged the military to regard torture as acceptable in Iraq as well. However, the evidence of a causal relationship at the time of this writing is thin. Some journalistic accounts suggest that some senior personnel in Iraq had also been involved at Guantanamo Bay, but they do not establish that these officials ordered soldiers to engage in torture. Indeed, most accounts suggest that lower-level soldiers acted on their own under inadequate supervision. The military began to investigate reports of torture even before the media scandal occurred, and several soldiers have been disciplined. Atrocities always occur during wars; to show that any particular atrocity is the result of a slippery slope mechanism, one needs evidence showing the mechanism at work.

It is unsurprising that the evidence here is weak and tendentious. One could make the same slippery slope argument about police shootings: if the government allows police to shoot people, then police will be morally corrupted and treat suspects with unnecessary brutality, and would-be Rambos will self-select into police work in large numbers. But this does not appear to have occurred, or, if it has, this adverse consequence of permitting the police to use deadly force is universally seen as justified by the need to protect crime victims. And if people who routinely inflict pain on others lose their capacity to sympathize with their subjects, there are a variety of institutional mechanisms (discussed below) that can be used to confine coercive interrogation to the appropriate setting, just as training, contractual incentives, criminal penalties, citizen oversight, and other institutional arrangements are used to prevent police shootings from slipping out of control.

Luban is quite right when he argues that ticking time-bomb hypotheticals are a distraction from the central issue, which is whether coercive interrogation can be controlled and managed successfully within an institutional and bureaucratic structure.[44] He goes wrong by having an excessively pessimistic, indeed cartoonish vision of how bureaucracies function. Police departments, military police, and intelligence services routinely manage the power to inflict deadly harms. Although there will always be cases in which bureaucratic controls fail, it is implausible to think that a slide into uncontrolled torture is inevitable.

A different, but related, argument is that society as a whole is brutalized if police engage in coercive interrogation. The shattering of the taboo against coercive interrogation would result in the public and the government acquiring a new enthusiasm not just for this measure, which could result in its routine use as an instrument of law enforcement, but also for torture as a device for punishing criminals, intimidating political opponents, and demonstrating the power of the state.

The problem with this argument is the same as the problem with the first: it is pure speculation, belied by our experiences with other measures. Take capital punishment. One could argue that killing convicted criminals is just as likely to brutalize society as torturing them. Yet the trend has been in the opposite direction. Historically, nations have cut back on capital punishment rather than expanding it; this has been driven by revulsion against its use against minor criminals or political opponents. In the United States today, there appears to be little pressure to expand the death penalty—to, say, ordinary murders or robbery or rape.

The argument recalls the various ratchet theories addressed in chapter 4, which hold that the adoption of new law enforcement measures that restrict civil liberties inevitably become entrenched, and thus the starting point when new emergencies generate pressure for aggressive law enforcement, so that there is always a downward pressure on civil liberties. These theories have never been adequately defended. In the context of torture, there have been many examples of Western countries adopting coercive interrogation and similar aggressive practices as temporary measures to deal with a particular emergency—France in Algeria, Britain against the Irish Republican Army—and then abandoning them when the emergency is over.[45] Israel uses coercive interrogation against suspected terrorists; as far as we know, this practice has not spread to other settings, such as the torture of suspected thieves or shoplifters. Far from desensitizing the public to violence and pain, the use of coercive interrogation and similar measures can inspire revulsion and a renewal of a commitment not to use them except in extreme circumstances.[46]

A related point, rarely mentioned by critics of coercive interrogation, is that dynamic effects, if they exist, may cause interrogation to work better. Once coercive interrogation is authorized, officials will, over time, become more and more expert in using it accurately, bureaucratic structures of control will become more fine-tuned and effective, and so on. As this happens, one of the main objections to coercive interrogation—that it is ineffective in general, or that it is often used even when it is ineffective—will disappear, and thus coercive interrogation, according to the cost-benefit calculus, will be more beneficial. This optimistic theory of institutional learning may be right or wrong; it is the flipside of the slippery slope theory and just as speculative. The point is that the critics of coercive interrogation should, but do not, consider it along with their pessimistic predictions. Consider too the idea that the permissibility of coercive interrogation will dampen police incentives to engage in the research and development of new technologies for discovering information. If coercive interrogation works well, and better than the alternatives, there is little reason for law to expend large resources stimulating such research and development. Any technique that works also dampens the search for substitute techniques, but that is no objection from a normative point of view; a dynamic of this sort would be another reason to favor coercive interrogation, not a reason to reject it.

Overall, the best presumption is that coercive interrogation, the use of deadly force against dangerous suspects, and similar law enforcement devices will be used, or not used, as circumstances warrant. It is possible that these devices have unpredictable second-order effects on public psychology, but we do not know the direction of those effects; the effects may run in different directions simultaneously, with unpredictable consequences on net; and the historical record does not support the claim that harsh police or intelligence tactics cannot be controlled but must inevitably become harsher. Here again, we emphasize that everything depends on what the facts turn out to be. Because arguments about policies such as coercive interrogation are hostage to what the facts show, in particular domains, there is no slope at all, just a series of discrete policy problems, all arrayed on a level. Support for coercive interrogation need not commit policymakers to support for punitive torture or torture of political opponents or other horrors.

## Symbolism

Several arguments in the literature can be placed under the heading of symbolism. These arguments often are hard to distinguish from slippery slope arguments, but we consider them separately because their force does not depend on slippery slope concerns being valid.

First, one might argue that coercive interrogation is in tension with the "symbolism of human dignity and the inviolability of the human body," in the words of Oren Gross.[47] We just don't understand this argument. Imprisoning criminals and using violence and deadly force against them when they threaten others also are inconsistent with human dignity and the inviolability of the human body, but they are nonetheless tolerated because of their benefits. Gross also argues that a flat ban on coercive interrogation gives "notice that fundamental rights and values are not forsaken."[48] But this giving of notice is, or ought to be, parasitic on the underlying cost-benefit decision. If it is justified to allow coercive interrogation, we don't want to give notice that we are not allowing coercive interrogation, or endorse values that are inconsistent with it.

Second, the ban on coercive interrogation might have an "educational function."[49] It teaches both Americans and foreigners about human dignity and the value of human rights. But if coercive interrogation—like imprisonment or police shootings—is justified, then we shouldn't want to teach people that coercive interrogation is wrong; quite the contrary. If coercive interrogation is justified, a ban on coercive interrogation might teach people to overvalue the avoidance of pain and undervalue human life.

Third, Jeremy Waldron argues that the ban on coercive interrogation is a "legal archetype" that expresses "the spirit of a whole structured area of doctrine, and does so vividly, effectively, publicly, establishing the significance of that area for the entire legal enterprise."[50] The policy expressed by the ban is that "*law is no longer brutal; law is no longer savage; law no longer rules through abject fear and terror.*"[51] Other legal archetypes, according to Waldron, are the writ of habeas corpus, the holding in *Brown v. Board of Education* that segregated schools are unconstitutional, the rule of adverse possession, and the doctrine of consideration.[52] As the last two examples make clear, Waldron holds that a legal archetype is a sort of heuristic device that helps people to organize a body of doctrine around its dominant principles.

Heuristics may have instrumental value, but Waldron overestimates their significance if he is claiming that the elimination of a heuristic will undermine or even result in serious confusion about an area of law or policy. Just as we could eliminate the doctrine of consideration without losing "contract law's commitment to market-based notions of fairness,"[53] we could eliminate a ban against coercive interrogation without losing the criminal justice system's commitment to avoiding brutality. The whole argument for coercive interrogation is that, if it is coercive, it is so necessarily, not unnecessarily. If it were important to do so, we could fall back on persuasive definition and say that cost-justified coercive interrogation is not "brutal" at all, precisely because it is justified. Here, Waldron errs by attempting to derive concrete conclusions from premises that are too general or abstract to cut between policy choices on the ground. The commitment to minimize law's brutality is on both sides of this argument. Where coercive interrogation can save lives, *not* engaging in it might seem the more brutal choice, especially to those whose lives are at stake. Those people might reasonably hold that there is a sort of brutal callousness, a self-absorbed moral preciosity, in the decision to preserve the law's archetypal integrity by permitting third-party deaths to go unprevented.[54]

Like many second-order arguments, Waldron's account trivializes the policies that he is trying to invest with significance. Consider how his argument might apply to the debate about capital punishment. The reason that critics oppose capital punishment is not that it expresses brutality; the reason is that it kills people. Similarly, the only strong argument against torture is that it causes pain. When we object to brutal laws, we object because they are brutal, not because they "express brutality." If we nonetheless tolerate them because they produce some good, or if we define them as nonbrutal precisely because they do more good than harm, their symbolic meaning falls by the wayside, in part because that meaning is qualified: a brutal law that does good no longer expresses brutality in unambiguous form. Indeed, such laws do no more than symbolize the government's willingness to produce the greatest possible good overall. On this view, a system of regulated coercive interrogation would have the same symbolic effect as the use of deadly force by police and the laws of war that permit the killing of civilians in the course of destroying a legitimate military target.

## International Opinion

There seems to be a strong feeling that if the United States abandons its ban on coercive interrogation, the rest of the world will imitate American policy—which, of course, is not objectionable if American policy is correct, as we are assuming for the sake of argument. But a concern is that the rest of the world will do worse; seeing that the United States endorses the infliction of pain for the purpose of interrogation, other countries will use it for punishment, show trials, and so forth.[55]

This argument rests on the assumption of American exceptionalism, the notion that, in Ronald Reagan's words, America is a "shining city on a hill" that the rest of the world looks up to and emulates.[56] Once America is shown to be a "normal" state, its ideals will cease to inspire others. There are many reasons for doubting this account. First, the United States is not as exceptional as it once was: there are many liberal democracies today; the United States is just one. Second, the United States increasingly has a reputation as a conservative, religious, punitive, and even militaristic country; its use of coercive interrogation in limited circumstances would have no more than a marginal effect when the United States is already heavily criticized for policies that will not change anytime soon—capital punishment, ungenerous social welfare policies, aggressive use of its military, reluctance to cooperate in international organizations, and so forth. Coercive interrogation is just one more item on this list, unlikely by itself to change the reputation of the United States. Third, the United States' reputation rests not only on its commitment to liberal principles, but on its lack of dogmatism about them, and especially the pragmatic way that it has relaxed them when necessary to counter internal or external threats. Liberal countries that collapse into chaos, that cannot protect their citizens, or that are bullied by authoritarian countries or terrorist organizations are not attractive role models.

Another argument that is sometimes made is that a ban on coercive interrogation "facilitates the government's claim to the moral high ground in the battle against terrorists."[57] This argument recalls the old cold war arguments that the United States should take the moral high ground in international relations in order to win the propaganda war against the Soviet Union.[58] These arguments had force then, and ought to have force now. Even if coercive interrogation is justified in some settings, its use will almost certainly be a public relations setback—just as the Abu Ghraib scandal was—and fodder for those who want to portray the United States as corrupt and immoral. Part of the problem for the United States is to persuade the undecided living in Muslim countries that they should throw in their lot with the West and not with Islamic radicalism. If the law enforcement methods of the United States are no more attractive than the law enforcement methods espoused by Islamic radicals, then a valuable propaganda tool is lost.

But there are countervailing considerations. The West must project an image of strength as well as virtue; undecided Muslims and Arabs will not cast their lot with governments that cannot protect themselves and their people, as we noted before. Polls suggest that large fractions of the populations of the United States and other countries approve of the use of coercive interrogation against suspected terrorists.[59] But whatever the force of these arguments, they only identify one cost that must be balanced against the benefits of coercive interrogation. The public relations effect of coercive interrogation is just one factor among many. It may justify restricting coercive interrogation more than the narrow instrumental calculus suggests; but it is hard to see how it could justify a flat prohibition.

## LEGAL REGULATION OF COERCIVE INTERROGATION

Given these considerations, how should legal rules on the subject of coercive interrogation be designed? We examine both the role of judicial review and the design of legal rules.

## Judicial Review

There is an ongoing argument about whether, and to what extent, coercive interrogation is permissible under existing constitutional doctrine. Alan Dershowitz argues that coercive interrogation is not subject to the Fifth Amendment's self-incrimination clause if the resulting statements are not introduced in a later criminal trial; that the Eighth Amendment does not apply, because coercive interrogation is not "punishment"; and that the requirements of the Fourth Amendment can be satisfied by the issuance of a "torture warrant" upon probable cause. Seth Kreimer and others dispute most of these points and emphasize that there is a constitutional fallback, which Dershowitz agrees is a potential obstacle to coercive interrogation: the catchall idea that government conduct that "shocks" the judicial conscience may violate the due process clauses of the Fifth and Fourteenth amendments.[60]

The legal materials here are both malleable and ambiguous; thus both sides support their positions with readings of the Court's fractured decision in *Chavez v. Martinez*,[61] which may or may not have settled the Fifth Amendment question (but in which direction?). Respected constitutional scholars can and do disagree not only about the import of the Constitution's more specific provisions, but also about catchall provisions like due process or the Fourth Amendment's reasonableness standard; moreover, the minimal case law that the courts have generated under those provisions is mostly limited to interrogation in law enforcement settings, not in national security settings.[62]

Given this pervasive ambiguity, the real question is whether judges should be sufficiently self-confident to override a judgment by other branches, should one be forthcoming, that some form of regulated coercive interrogation should be permitted. In our view, they should not. Nonjudicial politics may or may not strike the optimal balance between the costs and benefits of interrogation, but there is no reason to think that the judges will do better, no serious concerns about a slippery slope into unchecked torture absent judicial review, and no reason to worry that contrary views or interests will be insufficiently represented (given whatever baseline one uses to measure such things). One might worry about political failure on the ground that during emergencies national intelligence and law enforcement efforts will principally use interrogation against aliens who lack de jure representation in domestic politics. We have already addressed such arguments in chapter 3, however, and have suggested mechanisms of virtual or indirect representation of an alien's interests that mitigate such concerns. If anything, the relevant worry should be that nonjudicial politics will err in the other direction even during emergencies, licensing too little interrogation rather than too much, because of the enormous rhetorical power of charges that the government is engaging in torture, and because terror attacks or other harms prevented by successful coercive interrogation will by definition not occur and will thus be less salient than vivid stories of those coercively interrogated in error.

In any event, if a government is intent on engaging in interrogation to protect national security, there is little the judges can do about it anyway. This is just an extreme version of the point we make in chapter 3: judicial deference in matters of national security is inevitable, whether or not it is desirable. There is little reason to believe that a ringing judicial proclamation against coercive interrogation would have real-world effect, precisely because the national security settings in which coercive interrogation will be of greatest value and where it is most likely to be used are the very settings which are least amenable to judicial oversight. Coercive interrogation by officials in remote or secret facilities abroad—not in the fishbowl of Guantanamo Bay, but in Bagram in Afghanistan in the Central Intelligence Agency's "black sites"[63]—will not be checked by the threat of lawsuits, since the subjects of such interrogation will rarely have access to lawyers and will be nonpersons until released; and governments facing problems of judicial review may simply engage in "rendition," or the handing over of subjects to allied governments which enjoy a freer hand to conduct coercive interrogations, in return for a share of any information obtained. Overall, it is very dubious that constitutional doctrine relating to coercive interrogation can be made relevant where national security concerns are at issue.

## The Torture Warrant

Although Kreimer and others want judges to invoke the Constitution to prohibit coercive interrogation (they would say "torture," misleading semantics, in our view), that large-scale proposal is not the only possible role for judicial review. Alan Dershowitz proposes that coercive interrogation should be regulated by what might be called judicial review writ small: the proposal is that coercive interrogation should be permitted only after officials have obtained a "torture warrant" from a judge.[64] This proposal has been criticized on the ground that in the catastrophic scenario there will rarely be an opportunity to consult a judge,[65] but this criticism is overdrawn. The torture warrant is not meant as a panacea; when there is time to obtain a warrant, the involvement of the judiciary serves its purpose. When there is not time, then the warrant requirement could be waived—as in the case for ordinary search and arrest warrants when exigent circumstances exist. The torture warrant serves its purpose only when there are not time constraints, but there is no reason to think that this is the null set.

The more serious concern is that the torture warrant will simply be an empty formality even in the case where time is not of the essence. There is a real question whether warrants in ordinary law enforcement cases under the Fourth Amendment have an effect, as opposed to being a ritual of judicial rubber stamping. Whatever the truth in that setting, judicial oversight is likely to be far more pro forma in the national security settings that give rise to the strongest demand for coercive interrogation.[66] The Foreign Intelligence Surveillance Court grants more than 99% of warrant applications,[67] and although some of this generosity can be explained by ex ante anticipation by the officials applying for warrants, who will make sure that they do their sums correctly, there is still reason to think that any national security court will wield a strong presumption in the government's favor.

Even if judicial review writ small were effective, however, we do not think that the torture warrant is the end of the story. Just as in the case of searches, a warrant requirement can be only one piece of a much larger regulatory structure, which will principally feature legislative regulation through general rules and administrative self-regulation through ordinary bureaucratic processes.

## Administrative Oversight

In order to deter and investigate crimes, police employ a range of measures, including surveillance of public places; stops, interrogations, and pat-downs of people who are acting suspiciously; temporary detention; noncoercive interrogation that may, however, involve deception and mild intimidation; the use of force, including deadly force, to protect the lives of third parties, such as hostages and crime victims; searches of people and places; and wiretapping and the like. The measures range from the minimally intrusive (surveillance of public places) to the maximally intrusive (use of deadly force), and there are corresponding thresholds that limit the circumstances under which these measures may be employed. There is virtually no limit on surveillance of public places; reasonable suspicion is required before police can stop and question a person; probable cause is needed before a search warrant will be issued; and the threat of imminent harm to a third party is necessary if deadly force is to be used.

What happens when the police violate these rules? In some cases, nothing at all. In extreme cases, police officers may be sanctioned, fired, or convicted of crimes. For example, a police officer who kills a suspect who did not pose any immediate danger to the public is likely to be penalized and even fired; if the circumstances are egregious, the officer will be prosecuted for murder.

The reasons for this scheme of administrative oversight are straightforward. Police officers are agents, and as principal-agent models show, a bundle of carrots and sticks is necessary to provide them with the right motivations.[68] Ideally, police officers will use intrusive measures only when the gains to the public safety exceed the costs to the people who are subject to the measures (whether they are innocents who are misidentified or criminals). However, police officers, like ordinary people, do not necessarily have the right incentives to use these measures properly.

The basic problem is this. If police officers are paid a flat salary, and not rewarded for good work, then they may not work diligently to deter crime and capture suspects. The normal solution to this problem is fire or demote lazy officers and to reward the diligent officers—usually by retaining (and paying) them, promoting them at intervals, and giving them better working conditions (for example, day rather than night shifts). The problem with this simple scheme, however, is that police officers might act too aggressively. If they are rewarded for arresting a lot of people, then they may be tempted to arrest people who are not clearly guilty, or to use aggressive measures, such as searches, to find the guilty. In addition, zeal for law enforcement or sympathy for victims may result in excessively aggressive police tactics even in the absence of the normal reward mechanisms.

And so police departments and legislatures try to steer police officers away from tactics that externalize costs on innocents, or that offend our sense of how the guilty ought to be treated. This is why we have rules that prohibit police from shooting people who are unarmed, or engaging in high-speed chases through busy streets, or searching houses without warrants. These rules refine the incentives so that police officers aggressively pursue criminals without creating excessive costs for innocents or otherwise exceeding the bounds of civilized behavior.

Where does coercive interrogation fit in? Traditionally,[69] it was off-limits in the same sense as shooting unarmed criminals is; even if a useful police tactic in some cases, it exceeds the bounds of civilized behavior and thus is unacceptable. If philosophers are correct that coercive interrogation may be justified in limited cases, however, and if 9/11 and experience in Israel and elsewhere show that this set of cases may be nontrivial and realistic, then coercive interrogation ought to be added to the basket of permissible tactics, albeit subject to the same sorts of safeguards.

As we have already argued, we think that the regulation of the use of deadly force provides a model for regulating coercive interrogation. Just how coercive interrogation should be regulated depends on several factors. To take the extreme case, if coercive interrogation simply does not work or rarely works, or it is always inferior to the alternatives, then obviously it is sensible to ban it with no exceptions. In what follows, we sketch out a general framework that assumes that coercive interrogation is effective in a nontrivial range of cases; but the details of this framework will depend on just how effective it is and whether its effectiveness is limited to certain situations.

*Thresholds for Using Coercive Interrogation* It seems sensible to limit coercive interrogation in the same way that deadly force is limited. The rule might be: "police officers may use coercive interrogation only when they are reasonably certain that an individual possesses information that could prevent an imminent crime that will kill at least $n$ people," where $n$ is some number that reflects the balance of gains and losses from coercive interrogation (a thousand? a hundred? one?).[70] For the consequentialist, $n$ may be a relatively low number; for the deontologist, $n$ might be very high (the catastrophe scenario); but otherwise, both types of thinker should approve of our rule.

*Limits of Coercive Interrogation: Methods* Just as police are not generally allowed to carry bazookas, they should not generally be allowed to use methods of coercive interrogation that are excessive—that will cause too much harm relative to the benefits. The literature refers to "moderate" methods.[71] We do not know what methods these are; perhaps, a good starting point would be the methods already used by U.S. agents against high-level members of al Qaeda—sleep deprivation, disorientation, and the like.[72] In any event, a good rule would limit agents to the minimal amount of coercion that is necessary. Coercive interrogation might also be videotaped for review by administrative superiors, other legislative or bureaucratic overseers, or judicial tribunals considering warrant applications.

*Limits of Coercive Interrogation: Subjects* It seems reasonable to limit the use of coercive interrogation to known or suspected members of international terrorist groups known to use violent methods against American civilians. The obvious example today is al Qaeda, but al Qaeda might disappear and be replaced with some other group, or simply an even more diffuse network of terrorists. The benefit of such a limit is that it would prevent the use of coercive interrogation against ordinary criminals; the cost is that the limit would prevent the use of coercive interrogation when coercive interrogation would be justified—for example, against domestic terrorists, against members of new international terrorist groups, and against members of al Qaeda who are not known or suspected to be members of al Qaeda. It might be that these costs are too high and the subject limitations should be broader—to include, for example, kidnappers with a violent history who have been captured and refuse to disclose the location of the kidnapping victim.[73]

*Warrants*  As we have noted, Dershowitz's warrant idea might make sense when the harm is not imminent, so that there is time to involve a magistrate or judge, although there is a real chance it will devolve into an empty ritual. If the scheme is used, the magistrate or judge might be charged with issuing a warrant only when coercive interrogation will likely yield information that will prevent a crime that will kill $n$ people, or restrictions on other dimensions could be specified.

*Immunities and Punishments*  Police officers who employ coercive interrogation measures in violation of these rules should be punished in the same way that officers who violate the rules against deadly force are punished. Typically, police officers are granted immunity when they act reasonably, or in "objective good faith";[74] and this may be appropriate for coercive interrogation as well. Even so, administrative sanctions may be appropriate. When police officers do not act reasonably, the immunity should be withdrawn, and the police officer should be punished for violating laws against battery, torture, and similar uses of force.

*Training and Expertise*  Nearly all police officers are authorized to use deadly force. An important way of preventing error is through training. Similarly, one might argue that police officers should be trained in coercive interrogation. Alternatively, to the extent that coercive interrogation requires unusual skills, or may corrupt its practitioners, or lead them to use it in routine cases, and to the extent that it is not necessary to use it very often, it might make sense to have a special squad of officers who are trained in coercive interrogation and who are made available when circumstances warrant.[75] However, this can work only when there are minimal time constraints; otherwise, it is subject to the same objections as the warrant requirement.

*Administrative Review and Transparency* One important distinction between deadly force and coercive interrogation is that the first occurs frequently, and each instance is subject to public debate. The latter occurs much less frequently, and when it does, it is either concealed from the public or roundly condemned. As a result, the merits and demerits of coercive interrogation are much more poorly understood than the merits and demerits of deadly force. To correct this imbalance, we think that instances of coercive interrogation should always be carefully analyzed, by some combination of special commissions of experts, inspectors general and other regulatory overseers, and public interest groups.

This seems obvious, but we mention it because many people in the literature think that the symbolism is a good reason for banning coercive interrogation, or discouraging it; and this idea seems to drive the proposal that it should be kept illegal for symbolic purposes even though officials will sometimes be morally justified in violating the law.[76] As we discussed above, we don't think this argument makes much sense; a further problem with it is that it will encourage police officers to conceal their behavior. After the Israeli Supreme Court rejected the use of coercive interrogation, the GSS officially stopped using it. It is possible that now the GSS has found less objectionable ways to maintain security, but some reports suggest that the use of coercive interrogation has continued, albeit with greater secrecy.[77] If so, then the methods may be used with less political oversight and accountability. This would be unfortunate.

What is needed are legality and openness.[78] Explicit rules, which clearly prohibit some forms of pressure and permit others, can be easily evaluated; if outcomes are not acceptable, the rules can be adjusted.

## THE BURDEN OF UNCERTAINTY

A proposal for law reform of this kind can rarely be demonstrated to be correct. It remains possible for someone whose empirical estimates differ from ours to claim that coercive interrogation should be flatly prohibited, on rule-consequentialist grounds. Such a person might claim that there are raw empirical differences between coercive interrogation and other coercive practices that law addresses through ordinary ex ante regulation (as opposed to either strict prohibition or the scheme of ex post pardons, nullification, and the like). Perhaps, for example, extrajudicial killing is very often necessary, as a factual matter, while coercive interrogation is rarely so, again as a factual matter. Note also, however, that legal policy should take account of the *expected* costs and benefits of official action, which is a function not only of the frequency of relevant events but also of their costs and benefits when they do happen to occur. The expected benefits of coercive interrogation might be equal to or greater than those of extrajudicial killing, if coercive interrogation, while rarely useful, saves many more lives when it is useful.

Given the factual uncertainties, it is incumbent upon those who oppose coercive interrogation to explain why the right regime is either of the alternatives: a flat ban on coercive interrogation, which we have criticized as an implausible corner solution, or the outlaw-and-forgive regime of "prohibition" plus ex post relief, which we have criticized as both undesirable and unstable. Even if one believes that coercive interrogation is rarely warranted, the most-sensible approach, within the framework of our proposal, would simply be to tighten the relevant standards to the point where the benefits of licensing coercive interrogation exceed the costs. Coercive interrogation could be limited, for example, to known members of designated terrorist groups, such as al Qaeda, or limited to cases in which more than ten lives will certainly be saved if the information is extracted; penalties for officials who violate the rules in unreasonable or bad-faith ways, and who are thus stripped of immunity, could be made more severe.

In the face of empirical uncertainty, that is, the simplest starting point is to assume that law should regulate coercive interrogation within the same type of framework that law uses to regulate similar activities. There might indeed be a difference between coercive interrogation and other coercive practices, but there is no a priori reason to assume so, absent proof. Opponents of legalization—in our ordinary sense of legalization, as opposed to the self-undermining OAF sense—bear the burden of showing that coercive interrogation should be treated differently; and they have not carried that burden.


## CONCLUSION

Our aim in this chapter has not been to praise coercive interrogation, which is a grave evil on any reasonable moral view. All we suggest is that law should treat coercive interrogation in the same way that it treats other grave evils. Law has a typical or baseline regulatory strategy for coping with grave evils that sometimes produce greater goods. That strategy involves a complex regulatory regime of rules-with-exceptions, involving a prohibition on the official infliction of serious harms, permission to inflict such harms in tightly cabined circumstances, and an immunity regime that requires officials to follow the rules in good faith but protects them if they do so. Contrary to the academic consensus, we see no plausible reason for treating coercive interrogation differently.

In terms of our general themes, if the case for coercive interrogation during normal times is weak because the moral harms outweigh the benefits, the case dramatically strengthens during emergencies. During emergencies, the moral harms from coercive interrogation remain constant while the potential benefits rise. This is a simple application of the tradeoff thesis. At the time of this writing, proposals for explicitly permitting coercive interrogation have been defeated, but it appears likely that laws will permit relatively harsh interrogation methods—certainly harsher than those used against ordinary criminal suspects—albeit under ambiguous standards. Our judicial deference thesis suggests that courts should and will interpret these statutes broadly if any CIA interrogators are ever brought to trial.

## CHAPTER SEVEN

# Speech, Due Process, and Political Trials

During the cold war, law enforcement was used aggressively against suspected communists and Soviet spies. Although, in those days, people were not as concerned about surveillance and searches as they are today, people were deeply concerned about the fairness of the criminal trials of the cold war defendants and about the laws under which they were prosecuted. In retrospect, it is clear that many of the criminal defendants, including Alger Hiss and Julius Rosenberg, really were Soviet spies, but civil libertarians blamed the government for fomenting an atmosphere of hysteria in which fair trials were impossible. In addition, Smith Act prosecutions virtually illegalized membership in the Communist party, even though the decision to join one party or another is now thought to be protected First Amendment activity. These prosecutions, along with the McCarthy hearings, destroyed many lives and stifled intellectual and political debate.

After 9/11, the focus of civil libertarians has shifted from trials to investigations and surveillance. The post-9/11 terror trials so far have been relatively uncontroversial, at least compared to the cold war trials. The reason may be that Islamic fundamentalism simply does not have much of a following in the United States, and the public lacks even vague sympathy, unlike the situation with communism and the Soviet Union in the 1940s and 1950s. Most of the prosecutions so far have been straightforward affairs. Zacarias Moussaoui pled guilty to conspiracy charges in relation to the September 11, 2001, attacks, although the proceedings connected to his case often had a circus-like atmosphere. John Walker Lindh, an American, was jailed after he was discovered fighting on the side of Taliban forces in Afghanistan. Other prosecutions have targeted members of terrorist cells in Oregon, Virginia, and other states, and people who have tried to provide financial assistance to Islamic terrorist organizations. Recently, the United States transferred Jose Padilla from military to civilian custody and charged him with various terrorism-related crimes.

Still, these trials have raised concerns that are reminiscent of the criticisms of the cold war trials. The Moussaoui trial, in particular, raised national security issues when the government refused to provide the defendant with confidential materials that he claimed would exonerate him. Similarly, in the Rosenberg trial, the government refused to reveal confidential information about intelligence sources. Moussaoui also used the trial as a soap box to advance his extremist views, again recalling many of the cold war trials. And some trials of defendants accused of providing material support for terrorist organizations have raised concerns about whether the government is using excessively broad or vague laws to harass unpopular people who are essentially harmless.

The constitutional problems that arise when law enforcement is used against threats to national security—whether of the old cold war type of threat posed by citizens who lend aid to an enemy nation-state, or the modern type of threat posed by citizens or aliens who belong to a foreign terrorist organization—can best be understood against the baseline of criminal law enforcement during normal times. Simplifying greatly, this baseline can be described as "liberal legalism." *Liberalism* refers to the principle of political competition at the heart of modern liberal democracy: the government or party in power is forbidden to outlaw dissent or opposition. *Legalism* refers to the various rule-of-law or due process virtues, including the propositions that (i) people can be detained or punished only after they are convicted of committing a crime that has been identified in advance and incorporated in the law; (ii) surveillance, search, interrogation, and similar law enforcement techniques must comply with rules that ensure that they are used only when law enforcement agencies have reason to believe that subjects have committed a crime or will commit a crime; (iii) trials must be fair, which means that the defendant has the right to a hearing before an independent judge, has the right to a lawyer, can make arguments and interview witnesses, enjoys a standard of proof skewed in his favor, and (in the United States and a few other countries) has the right to demand a jury.

The first-order balancing view that we have defended implies that all of these rights should be relaxed during emergencies. Relaxed but not necessarily eliminated, of course: the degree of relaxation should reflect the magnitude of the emergency. The judicial deference view implies that the executive (and perhaps the legislature) should perform the tradeoffs during emergencies, and courts should defer to the political branches' judgments. This, again, does not mean that courts should exercise no scrutiny, just that they should intervene less than they do during normal times.

In extreme cases, these claims are uncontroversial. Everyone agrees that Congress has the power to suspend the writ of habeas corpus "when in cases of rebellion or invasion the public safety may require it,"[1] permitting the president to implement martial law. The military then may impose censorship, engage in surveillance without warrants, detain suspicious people without charging them, and punish suspects after summary trials. The constitutional limits on what the military may do are not clear, but it is clear that the military is not bound by the same rules that law enforcement agencies are, and that in any event courts, deprived of the writ of habeas corpus, are powerless to prevent the military from violating constitutional rights. Thus, in extreme cases, our thesis is embodied in existing constitutional understandings.

However, many people—and probably most academics—resist our claim that constitutional rights can be adjusted by degree in response to emergencies that do not provoke a suspension of the writ of habeas corpus. These academics agree with Justice Antonin Scalia who, in the *Hamdi* decision, argued that, unless the writ is suspended, the baseline criminal process must be used.[2] By contrast, we agree with the *Hamdi* majority,[3] which implicitly held that suspension of the writ of habeas corpus is one way to respond to an emergency, but it is not the only way. On this implied view, courts sensibly should and do relax constitutional rights and exercise greater deference to the actions of the political branches during emergencies, even when the writ has not been suspended by Congress.[4] In this chapter, we bolster this claim by examining the way that courts do this, both in American history and in foreign countries that share America's commitment to liberal legalism.

We examine two types of policy: censorship and what we will call *reduced process*. The latter term refers to the relaxation of the conventional rights enjoyed by defendants in criminal trials—the rights to independent judges and defense lawyers, the right to a jury, the right to cross-examine, and the right not to be detained or punished merely for being a threat to public safety. Our goal is to show that there is nothing exotic, special, or alarming about censorship and reduced process in response to threats to national security. There is a long history of such responses in the United States and in other liberal democracies. The history suggests that such responses are natural and largely unobjectionable. It also provides some clues about how courts and governments can best choose among the different avenues for reducing process. In chapter 8, we examine an even stronger form of process reduction: the substitution of executive detention and military tribunals for criminal courts.

Our argument begins with the assumption that there are two main philo-sophical justifications for liberal legalism: to minimize error and decision costs and to maintain political competition. We argue that the government has no worse incentives (and possibly better incentives) to minimize error and deci-sion costs during emergencies than during normal times. Because the cost of failing to convict or to detain national security threats is greater than the cost of failing to convict or to detain ordinary criminals, we should desire and expect process reductions (and possibly censorship) during emergencies. Further, as we argued in part I, courts are in a worse position to supervise the executive during emergencies than during normal times. Therefore, courts should be more deferential during emergencies than during normal times when the executive implements censorship or process-reduction policies.

We acknowledge that the government might be tempted during emer-gencies to use its heightened powers in order to reduce political competition. This is the dictatorship concern that we discussed in part I. But commentators mistakenly treat this danger as something special; it is not. Even during normal times, the party in power will use its control over the government to enhance its political power at the expense of the opposition—a standard and very seri-ous example is gerrymandering, a problem which is nonetheless largely tol-erated by courts because there is no plausible judicial remedy. Similarly, dur-ing emergencies, the party in power has special opportunities to enhance its power at the expense of opposition parties. It may take advantage of enhanced secrecy laws, for example, in order to engage in dirty tricks. This, too, is a cost intrinsic in government—technically, a problem of agency slack—that courts do not necessarily have the power to remedy. A reduction in political compe-tition is just a cost like any other cost and may be worth incurring in order to obtain the benefits of greater security, as long as the reduction in political competition is not too great. What is often overlooked, moreover, is that the government's incentive to use emergency powers to reduce political competi-tion is subject to a counterforce: its fear that it will lose the public's trust at a time when public trust is especially important as a result of high stakes and the need for secrecy. In some circumstances, governments may prefer to cooperate with opposition parties in order to strengthen the emergency response or war effort, as Roosevelt did when appointing Republicans to his cabinet during World War II. Thus, it is not clear that political competition is placed under greater stress during emergencies than during normal times.

Toward the end of the chapter, we will develop this idea by arguing that the U.S. government might tolerate and even welcome judicial independence during emergencies because judicial independence helps to reassure the pub-lic that the government is not acting out of partisan motives. However, for this process to function, the judges must also be flexible and allow the government to pursue people who would be protected by the judiciary during normal times.

## LIBERAL LEGALISM

Legalism is the view that courts should resolve social conflicts by applying previously enacted and publicly known rules to the conduct of individuals. The defendant has a right to make a defense, call witnesses, cross-examine witnesses, have an impartial judge and jury, and so forth. This package of rights is known collectively as the *right to due process*. Legalism can be understood as the view that the right to judicial process is paramount and should be violated only in the most unusual conditions.[5]

Legalism is not incompatible with laws against political opposition. A law that bans criticism of the state or government is such a law; a court could enforce the law without violating the right to judicial process as long as the defendant is given the opportunity to defend himself. Thus, an authoritarian state can have legalistic institutions, as Germany did prior to the Nazi era. The joint commitment to legalism and political tolerance is liberal legalism, which includes the idea that courts should not permit the government to ban political speech or opposition except when it causes immediate harm, for example, incitement to riot.[6]

## AN INSTRUMENTAL THEORY OF LIBERAL LEGALISM

Academic defenders of liberal legalism normally provide philosophical justifications for this system, arguing that liberal legalism—also called liberal democracy, or constitutional democracy, or the rule of law, depending on whether more emphasis is put on liberalism or legalism—promotes welfare or fairness, or ensures respect for human dignity, or maintains social peace more effectively than alternative systems do.[7] Without expressing a view on these approaches, we will take a different approach, which emphasizes rational choice on the part of individuals or groups with power. We approach liberal legalism not as a system of values imposed on the government, but as a reflection of the principles and attitudes that would be taken in a democratic system by a rational government, one that seeks to maximize its political support.[8]

A *government*, as we will use the term here, consists of the people who control the policies and activities of the state. In a parliamentary system, the government is typically controlled by a single party or a coalition of parties; the opposition, then, consists of the party or parties that are out of power. In a presidential system, the government is typically controlled by the president's party, but the president may be forced to share power with opposition parties if they control the legislature. In any event, we want to distinguish, very roughly, the "majority party" or "party in power" from the (mainstream) "opposition party." In liberal democracies, the various mainstream parties compete for power within a legal framework; the opposition party is never outlawed or forced to suffer legal disabilities. In some democracies, extremist parties may be outlawed or regulated; in others, they may be able to share power.

We assume that the government's main goal is to stay in power, and that a party's main goal is either to maintain power (if it has it) or to obtain power (if it does not). All political actors know that they cannot maintain power unless they implement policies desired by the general public, including (but not exclusively) their political base. One such policy is security, broadly conceived. Virtually every member of the public seeks security both against internal threats, such as those posed by criminal activity, and against external threats, such as invasion by hostile foreign countries.

It might seem that the best way to deter crime is to deny all rights to criminals, and simply seize and punish anyone who has committed a crime. Once the police satisfied themselves that a particular person committed a crime, they would punish him, without going through the risky and tedious business of a trial. The usual objections to this approach are that trials promote fairness and accuracy, and prevent the government from arresting and convicting people who are vulnerable but did not commit any crime, so as to make a show of responding to the public's fear of crime without having to expend resources on a criminal investigation. But these objections are not fully persuasive. If the government cannot keep criminal behavior at a low level, it will lose public support. If courts routinely convict the wrong people, then criminals will be encouraged rather than deterred. And if people care about the fairness of criminal procedure, then the government has no reason to use unfair procedures.

The main problem with denying procedural protections to criminal defendants is that without such protections the government can use its monopoly on force in order to harass, detain, or eliminate its political opponents. Authoritarian countries, in fact, frequently do this, but liberal democracies do not. Why not?

The tempting answer is the courts: independent courts prevent governments in liberal democracies from suppressing political opposition. The problem with this answer is that authoritarian countries have courts, and many liberal democracies do not have independent courts. The answer also begs the question of why governments bent on suppressing political opposition don't push courts out of their way; this is what happens in weak democracies. The question, then, can be reframed as follows: why do governments in liberal democracies with weak courts restrain themselves from suppressing political opposition, and why do governments in liberal democracies with strong courts restrain themselves from undermining the courts so that they can suppress political opposition?

The better answer is that a government that depends on the consent of the public cannot take the risk of allowing the public to think that the government eliminates political opponents who enjoy the support of at least some members of the public. Any particular criminal defendant may be an ordinary criminal, but he may also be an attractive political target because he leads or belongs to the opposition party, or he or his activities have symbolic importance for the opposition party. The public, especially the leaders and members of the opposition political party, will sometimes not know with confidence whether the government targets a particular criminal defendant because he has actually committed crimes or poses a threat to security, or because he poses a mere political (or partisan) threat to the government or party in power. If the public does not know whether the government uses its monopoly on power to target political opponents, or believes that it does, it may withdraw support from the existing government and look for alternatives. The reason is that a government that uses force against opponents rather than criminals is not providing maximum security, and indeed may be pursuing policies that benefit the government itself or its circle of supporters rather than the public at large. Thus, government tolerates (indeed, funds and supports) courts and all of the rules of legal process as a way of maintaining public confidence in its claim that it uses the police to deter crime rather than to harass political opponents.

This brings us back to liberal legalism. First, liberalism forbids the illegalization of political opposition, and its manifestation as formal law is freedom of speech, freedom of association, and the other basic political rights. A government that tolerates laws that protect opposition parties has taken the first step toward showing that it is a government that serves the public interest, a government that will maintain its power not by intimidating political opponents, but by creating good policies that please the public, which will reward the government by returning it to power.

Second, legalism ensures that the government will not circumvent the basic political rights through subterfuge. The judicial process forces the government to show that the defendant is an actual criminal or public threat and not just a political opponent. The government must show that the defendant has violated a law, that is, a rule with democratic credentials. The government must persuade an independent judge and jury. Rules of evidence and publicity ensure that the public can evaluate the government's case. Legalism prevents the typical subterfuge by which a government targets a political opponent not by eliminating him or outlawing his party but by convicting him of a crime that he did not commit, or a crime that is not generally enforced.

None of this suggests that a government will always adopt liberal legalism, or that liberal legalism is necessarily self-perpetuating. If a government believes that its political opponents are powerful and likely to win the next election, the government might think that it has little to lose by prosecuting them, especially if it believes that its opponents, once in power, will not permit the new opposition to reacquire it. In unstable democracies, this is a common occurrence. In the United States, this occurred only once—and while it was still an unstable quasi democracy—during the Sedition Act trials of the late eighteenth century, when Federalists used the judicial process to fend off political attacks by Republican newspapers.[9] In stable democracies, the reason that such trials do not occur more often than they do is that the reputational cost is so high: a government that prosecutes its political opponents will lose public support, and the party that controls it will find it difficult to obtain power again after power has been returned to the opposition. Indeed, in the United States, the Sedition Act prosecutions backfired, made martyrs of Republican writers and editors, and contributed to the defeat and extinction of the Federalists. The experiment would not be repeated.[10]

In sum, governments grant judicial process and refrain from banning political opposition as ways of showing that their policies are in the public interest. When this kind of self-restraint becomes entrenched in a society, we say that the state is both liberal and legalistic. A government that goes to the trouble of eliminating its political opponents does so only because it fears that these opponents are likely to attract followers, which can be the case only if a large segment of the public can be persuaded that the government's policies do not benefit it or are otherwise wrong or unjust. If this is the case, the elimination of political opponents—however attractive for narrow political reasons—is likely to give rise to the inference that the government's policies are bad and thus result in a loss of political support.

This theory is not incompatible with the philosophical view that political rights and judicial process are necessary because of fairness or the need to show respect for human dignity. Indeed, the instrumental theory of liberal legalism shows why a power-maximizing government will adopt liberal policies that many people find attractive on normative grounds. It thus shows why liberal legalism is politically robust, why governments sometimes voluntarily introduce liberal reforms, and why liberal legalism can be attractive to governments in societies (such as Japan) that do not have a long liberal tradition but instead emphasize communal values and the collective good. But the theory implies that liberal legalism faces limits, which are the subject of the next section.

## DEPARTURES FROM LIBERAL LEGALISM

If liberal legalism has instrumental value for governments in the way that we have described, then governments will be tempted to depart from liberal legalism under two conditions. First, the government faces an unusually dangerous threat that cannot be adequately addressed within the existing legal framework. Second, the government enjoys an unusually high level of trust among citizens, so that it need not worry too much about creating suspicions by denying process in selected cases.

As to the first point, a government knows that if it cannot protect the people, they will eventually withdraw their support. So it must take very seriously any threats to security. Threats to security can be purely internal but can also be external. The normal internal threat is everyday crime. Most governments can keep crime at tolerable levels without departing from liberal legalism. To be sure, the norms of liberal legalism are not rigid and are relaxed or tightened incrementally as circumstances warrant. When crime increases as a result of an exogenous shock—new drugs, new technologies— authorities almost always pass laws or take actions that depart incrementally from liberal legalism. The drug crisis stemming from the spread of crack cocaine led to a relaxation of liberal legalism across several dimensions: the government passed (i) vague laws that enabled prosecutors to target the most-dangerous criminals; (ii) broad complicity rules that enabled prosecutors to reach all members of a drug gang; and (iii) anti-association laws that enabled the police to prevent congregation of gang members on the street.[11] But the more significant test of liberal legalism is terrorism or domestic insurgency, and here most liberal states have departed much further from liberal legalism, usually for the duration of the crisis, by claiming broad powers to be exercised only against the terrorist or insurgent threat.

Even more important is the external threat. During wartime, virtually all legal protections may be suspended and military rule imposed, depending on the extent of the threat. In the United States, the Civil War resulted in the suspension of habeas corpus; World War I in aggressive sedition laws;

and World War II in martial law in Hawaii and the relocation of Americans of Japanese ancestry on the mainland.[12] Soviet-led international communism furnished ample reason, in the minds of American authorities, for relaxing liberal legalism in the 1920s and again in the 1950s. Today, Islamic terrorism is the chief external threat to American security and the reason for relaxing process protections.

As to the second point, when people believe that the government does not seek to eliminate its opponents, they are more likely to tolerate reductions in process. The reason is that, although reducing process may enhance error, it will not disadvantage opponents or entrench the existing authorities. One common method that governments use to enhance trust during emergencies is to invite political opponents into the government. Parliamentary systems often produce war cabinets with representatives from the party that is out of power. In the United States, the most famous example is the participation of the Republicans Henry L. Stimson and Frank Knox in Roosevelt's cabinet during World War II. Members of the opposition political party with knowledge of the internal workings of the government can be expected to raise a fuss if they discover that the government is using its emergency powers to persecute their colleagues and supporters.[13]

Let us put the argument in a more stylized form. Suppose that the possible defendant in a criminal trial—aside from ordinary criminals—may be either a "public threat" or a "political opponent" of the government. A *public threat* is a person, such as a terrorist, who is likely to harm the general public or the constitutional system; a *political opponent* is a person who poses a threat to an existing government but not to the public—the case of normal political opposition. Because the public threat has not committed any crime, he cannot be convicted of a crime if given normal, that is, "high" process. Assume that he can be convicted if given "low" process.

The dilemma faced by the government is that if it uses high process, then people who are public threats or who are suspected of being public threats are acquitted and set free; they engage in terrorist attacks or support subversion; and the public reacts by saying to the government, "if you cannot protect us, we'll find another (less scrupulous) government that will." The government might, with the acquiescence of the courts,[14] rationally grant a low amount of process in response so that it can convict more public threats. At the same time, the government knows that if it uses low process, the public will begin to suspect that the government may be targeting political opponents. And as long as the public assumes that the government is using low process in order to eliminate political opponents, the government has nothing to lose and much to gain from actually doing so.[15] Still, the public might rationally tolerate low process if the public threat is serious enough. It may be willing to give government a free hand to defeat the public threat even if the government will use the same powers to weaken its political opposition. If the government goes too far, however, it risks a withdrawal of public support.

There may be other ways for government to finesse these difficulties. Instead of granting low process to all criminal defendants, it can offer high process to "ordinary" criminals and low process to a class of people whom the public believes is more likely to pose a real threat. The American government, in fact, has done this quite frequently, granting lower process to aliens, people who openly identify themselves with extremist groups (communists, Islamic fundamentalists), and enemy soldiers.[16] These people may also be subject to greater surveillance than ordinary citizens are. The government can also grant higher than normal process to people who belong to mainstream opposition parties; this helps to avoid the inference that the government's motives are narrowly political.

To summarize the argument thus far, we can imagine the following sequence of events. First, some emergency or apparent emergency occurs, and the public demands protection against the real or imaginary threat. Second, the government responds by reducing procedural protections. At one extreme, it might suspend habeas corpus and declare martial law. But the reduction of procedural protections can take subtler forms: the enactment of new laws, or the invocation of long-dormant laws, that target seditious, disloyal, or dangerous behavior; reliance on newly broad interpretations of existing laws so that they may be used against the perceived threats; refusal by judges and juries to give certain types of defendants the benefit of the doubt; relaxed evidentiary standards; restrictions on defense lawyers' access to their clients; and so forth. Third, the government now has greater freedom of action, which it can use against political opponents as well as the people who pose the new public threat. A rational, power-maximizing government will use its freedom of action to pursue both types of person. Fourth, the public realizes that the government can use its freedom of action against partisan opponents as well as public threats. The public may partially or fully withdraw support from the government because it fears political persecution of marginal or even mainstream political opponents of the government; but it also may accept this reduction in political competition as an acceptable price to pay for enhanced security. Defendants in criminal trials will exploit this public unease and claim to be political opponents (when such a claim is plausible), whether or not they in fact are. Critics of the government will call these trials "political trials."

Whether they are rightly called political trials or not, these sorts of ambiguous trials—which may both counter a public threat and produce narrowly partisan benefits—are different from the extreme type, the show trial. Show trials were conducted by Nazi Germany, the Soviet Union, and many Soviet satellites. Defendants were tortured or threatened off-stage, then at trial would confess to whatever crimes the government charged them with, so as to avoid being tortured or shot afterward, and to spare their families the same fate. The defendants were, in effect, unpaid actors in a propaganda film. Show trials cut the Gordian knot: governments eliminate partisan opponents as well as public threats without losing public support through the simple expedient of pretending that they grant process protections when they are doing nothing of the sort. If the public believes the government, the government's problems are solved.[17] But the pretense cannot be maintained indefinitely even in an authoritarian state, and show trials usually stop after a few years. Show trials are not an option in an open society because they would require the collaboration of people with different political views and goals—prosecutors, judges, lawyers, juries—or else the wholesale destruction of existing institutions, which itself would alert people to the government's intentions.[18]

## SOME EVIDENCE

Liberal legalism is an instrumental strategy used by governments to maximize political support in societies that have a general interest in security but tolerate normal political opposition. Liberal legalism enables the government to minimize internal threats to public security to the largest extent possible, consistent with the need to reassure the public that it will not maintain its power by harassing political opponents. When security threats increase, governments depart incrementally from liberal legalism because the public now is willing to tolerate a marginal increase in the harassment of (usually extreme) political opponents in return for greater security. If the gain in security is large enough so that the public as a whole benefits even though the government itself can increasingly use trials with reduced process to enhance its own power, then erosion of liberal legalism is likely to be tolerated, at least for the duration of the emergency.[19]

American history supports the thesis that, in a liberal democracy, political trials—that is, trials with reduced process—are more likely to be (politically) successful when defendants are extremists than when they are mainstream opponents. The Sedition Act trials of Jeffersonian Republicans were a spectacular failure: rather than destroy the Republicans, they destroyed the Federalists. Another example is the failed impeachment of U.S. Supreme Court justice Samuel Chase in 1805, this time at the instigation of Republicans against a Federalist justice.[20] These failures helped to establish the legitimacy of political competition between mainstream parties in the United States:[21] the implicit bargain—that the judicial process will not be used against mainstream partisan opponents—has held, more or less, for 200 years.

Subsequent political trials can be divided into two categories. First, there were trials of people who had virtually no mainstream political support: anarchists, Nazi sympathizers, and communists. Although the trials of these people often took place in a circus-like atmosphere, the evidence suggests that the public approved of the trials and convictions, and that the political standing of the government improved as a result of them.[22] Second, there were trials of people whose views were somewhere between moderate and extreme: opponents of the Civil War, World War I, and the Vietnam War. These trials were only moderately successful, as one might expect. Civil War–era military trials of dissenters may have maintained order but were highly controversial and politically damaging.[23] World War I–era espionage and sedition prosecutions were popular and may have helped the war effort, but they also enhanced the prestige of radical politicians like Eugene Debs.[24] Vietnam War–era prosecutions like the Chicago 8 trial seem to have discouraged violent protests but also to have weakened support for the national government and its policies.[25]

The refusal to use political trials as a routine weapon against political opponents, reserving their use for serious public threats, can evolve in a decentralized fashion and need not be imposed by third parties, such as courts. The history of Britain supports this proposition, as does self-restraint in the use of the impeachment power in the United States,[26] and for that matter the self-restraint of executive branch officials even when there has been short-term public support for political trials. However, in the United States, the judiciary has great prestige, and it can interfere with political trials that the government is inclined to pursue. Thus, it is useful today to take the perspective of the judge, and ask how a judge should manage a criminal trial that is, or might be, motivated by the political goals of the government.

Before we do so, however, we discuss the most powerful tool in the government's arsenal—censorship, including laws against political dissent or opposition. As noted above, if the Constitution and public opinion permit the government to enact such laws, then the judiciary can participate in the suppression of threats to national security without relaxing due process protections.

## CENSORSHIP

A traditional way to counter public and political threats is through the use of censorship and other political laws that prohibit the formation of opposition parties or parties committed to dangerous or extreme ideologies. No one today thinks that such laws are necessary in the United States to counter Islamic terrorism, but some European countries do have such laws, and in 2005 the United Kingdom took steps to arrest or deport those who advocate violent Islamic fundamentalism.[27] The U.K. effort is based on the premise that mullahs who advocate terrorism do influence their followers; if the mullahs are silenced, less terrorism will occur. This premise is plausible, though of course it is the sort of argument that American legal academics reflexively deny. Censorship may serve other purposes in the war on terror. Antigovernment speech may demoralize soldiers and civilians. The disclosure of secrets may interfere with security and military operations. Hate speech directed against Muslims may strengthen the hand of terrorist organizations. In a more speculative vein, Bruno Frey argues that because terrorists depend on media organizations to convey their message, deliberate government obfuscation might usefully reduce the value of terrorist activity.[28] We do not express an opinion on the value of censorship but claim only that it is not too soon to think about whether the United States will need to follow Britain's lead, though the United States, unlike the European countries, does not have a hostile Muslim population. Indeed, other European countries have long-standing censorship laws that do not reflect concerns about al Qaeda in particular. Turkey—whose democratic credentials are solid but not perfect—bans fundamentalist Islamic parties. Germany prohibits parties that oppose its constitutional system.[29] Other democracies have similar bans on extremist parties and subversive activities that endanger the constitutional order.[30] Thus, they make a distinction between mainstream political dissent, which is tolerated, and extreme dissent that reflects opposition to the constitutional order, which is not tolerated.

In the United States, there have been four overt attempts to suppress political dissent. The Sedition Act of 1798, which prohibited "false, scandalous and malicious" statements about the government, was interpreted broadly so that it could be used to prosecute mainstream Republican opponents of the John Adams administration. That statute expired in 1801. Martial law during the Civil War permitted the military to try and punish people who criticized the Lincoln administration's conduct of the war.[31] The Espionage and Sedition Acts of 1917–1918, which prohibited the obstruction of recruitment and interference with the military, was broadly interpreted to prohibit criticism of American participation in World War I. The Smith Act of 1940 prohibited advocacy of the violent overthrow of the government and was also interpreted broadly until 1957.[32] The Internal Security Act of 1950 and the Communist Control Act of 1954 "effectively criminalized the Communist party."[33] Of these cases, only the Sedition Act of 1798 was, as interpreted by judges, a clear effort to suppress dissent by a mainstream group. The Espionage and Sedition Acts and the Smith Act targeted extremists, although these extremists did include prominent people (such as Debs) who had large followings. The Civil War case is ambiguous.

Why would a government prosecute members of fringe parties or people with idiosyncratic political beliefs? By assumption, these people do not pose a threat, or much of a threat, to the political dominance of the government. One reason is that such people may be dangerous to the public. The U.S. government prosecuted communists not because they posed an electoral threat, but because they were loyal to America's enemy, the Soviet Union.[34] The U.S. government currently pursues al Qaeda sympathizers because an al Qaeda sympathizer might provide money, shelter, or other support to actual terrorists. If the evidence of criminal behavior is not strong, the government moves against these people based on an assessment of the risks. A communist ideologue might be a spy, or know a spy.[35] An al Qaeda sympathizer—especially one with a great deal of wealth and ties to fundamentalist Islamic groups—is a risk even if he has not committed a crime, or cannot be proven, given the standards of criminal law, to have committed a crime. Such a sympathizer may also demoralize the public by cheering on terrorist attacks, and create an atmosphere of insecurity. Thus, people with extreme antigovernment beliefs are more likely to be public threats than people without such beliefs—even ordinary criminals—and for this reason governments may seek to prosecute them.

To prosecute such people without violating due process, the government needs to rely on laws that directly prohibit such activity. As we have seen, there are, and have been, many such laws—against subversion, conspiracy to violate the law, and the like—but these laws have proven to be unpopular in the United States. The problem with criminalizing membership in a particular organization, like the American Communist party, is that members can easily evade the law by disbanding the proscribed organization and setting up a new one. If broader laws are used, and all seditious organizations or activities are prohibited, then mainstream organizations can too easily be swept within the laws' net, a possibility that inevitably provokes widespread political opposition.[36] Still, if the United States ever develops problems similar to those of Britain, where radical Muslim preachers urge their followers to engage in terrorism with apparent success, we are likely to see efforts by the government to censor such preaching and other forms of advocacy of terrorism.

In American constitutional law, courts have alternated over time between two broad types of free speech decisions, where security concerns are at issue. One type is deferential to governmental regulation of speech that presents security threats; another type is not deferential and attempts to erect barriers to the content-based regulation of speech. These poles are represented by *Dennis v. United States*, decided in 1951, and *Brandenburg v. Ohio*, decided in 1969.

*Dennis* upheld the convictions of members of the Communist party for conspiring to advocate the overthrow of the government by force. Following Judge Learned Hand, the lead opinion relied on a cost-benefit test that asked "whether the gravity of the 'evil,' discounted by its improbability, justifies such invasion of free speech as is necessary to avoid the danger."[37] As we saw in chapter 3, Jackson's concurrence in *Dennis* added that judicial deference to government's weighing of these factors would be both inevitable and desirable where large-scale conspiracies, such as the Communist party, were at issue, because the existence of such a conspiracy would create emergency circumstances in which judges would simply lack the knowledge or capacity to second-guess governmental policies.

*Brandenburg*, by contrast, overturned the conviction of a Ku Klux Klan leader for advocating violent means of political change. Under the *Brandenburg* test, government may not censor speech on law-and-order grounds unless there has been express advocacy of imminent law violation. A generation of academics with a strong commitment to speech protection has taken *Brandenburg* as the gold standard of free speech law, justifying it by the claim that free speech law should adopt a "pathological perspective." On this view, "the overriding objective at all times should be to equip the first amendment to do maximum service in those historical periods when intolerance of unorthodox ideas is most prevalent and when governments are most able and most likely to stifle dissent systematically."[38]

The contrast between *Dennis* and *Brandenburg* has both normative and positive dimensions. Normatively, the issue common to both cases is the question of preemptive action against threats. The issue is the same one posed, *mutatis mutandis*, in the private law of self-defense and in the international law of preemptive warfare.[39] When can one actor (either a government or an individual) take offensive action against another actor who threatens to inflict harm? On *Dennis*'s expected cost-benefit test, the question is one of first-order balancing, with judicial deference to governmental policies. *Brandenburg*, by contrast, restricts the first-order weighing of probabilistic harms through an imminence requirement, just as does the conventional formulation of the self-defense test for governmental use of force in the international sphere.

On the theory we have laid out in previous chapters, *Dennis* is the better test for times of emergency.[40] The *Brandenburg* approach must rest on a claim that during emergencies either government or judges or both will not accurately weigh the *Dennis* factors; errors will be systematically biased against speech rather than randomly distributed. Why might this be so? One idea is that decisionmakers will suffer from cognitive or emotional distortions—the "pathology" induced by emergencies. Orthodox free speech theorists also tend to worry that dissenters' interests will not be taken into account by decisionmakers; here, the idea is one of motivational failure, in which the decisionmaker applying the cost-benefit calculus is rational but fails to internalize the harms to dissenters (or the social benefits of free speech, which need not be the same thing).

Neither idea is very persuasive, as we have already suggested in earlier chapters. The pathological perspective view makes something like an argument for cognitive or emotional distortions, but it is a mishmash of imprecise ideas. One strand is a straightforward panic theory, of the sort discussed in chapter 2. A related strand, with a different emphasis, is the idea that

> when the collectivist thinking that is necessary for a war effort takes hold, officials, judges, and the public at large tend to overestimate dramatically either the level of cooperation required to effectuate the goals of the community or the extent to which the achievement of sufficient cooperation requires the stifling of dissent.[41]

We are not sure what to make of this vague picture, which looks something like a cognitive panic, or herding based on cascades and other social influences; these are also discussed in chapter 2. As for the motivational theory, it is a species of democratic failure argument, discussed in chapter 3.

Most important is a positive rather than normative point: the alternation between *Dennis* and *Brandenburg* is predictable and probably inevitable in a political system that faces a recurrent series of emergencies. In times of emergency, when the government alleges with any degree of plausibility that a large-scale conspiracy to overthrow the government or to inflict serious damage is afoot, it is hard to imagine that the judges could or would stand in the way. Even after *Brandenburg*, a federal court enjoined the publication in a progressive magazine of information about how to build a hydrogen bomb,[42] basically because the possible harms, although not imminent, were rather large, even discounted appropriately. The episode suggests that *Dennis* lives on because, as the judges are quite aware, the consequences of taking *Brandenburg* seriously during an emergency would be intolerable.

A complementary point is that the Communist party leaders, suppressed in *Dennis*, were more dangerous to the government and nation than the Klan, which was no longer an effective force by the time of *Brandenburg*. Where government can plausibly claim harms of the scale at issue in *Dennis*, public sentiment will weigh irresistibly in the government's favor; the little bulwarks of free speech law that libertarian judges have erected in prior periods, out of a concern for future "pathologies," will be swept away like so many sand castles. As we emphasized in chapters 2 and 3, there is no tenable mechanism for precommitment against the relative shift from liberty to security during emergencies, even assuming such precommitment is desirable.

If a government cannot enact laws against political opposition, then it will find itself hampered in its efforts to prosecute public threats who have not engaged in clearly illegal or violent acts. Its best hope is to bring charges under a general law against disorderly or subversive behavior or even unrelated laws against, say, wire fraud or extortion,[43] and then persuade the judge to acquiesce in restrictions on process. These restrictions are the hallmark of political trials in liberal democracies and the focus of the next several sections.

## PROCESS REDUCTION

Our argument so far can be understood as an application of the tradeoff thesis to problems of speech and process. During normal times, the regulation of speech reflects a balance between liberty and security. In the United States, more so than in other countries, the law reflects a conviction that speech has a great deal of value, and so it should be censored only in narrow cases. Nonetheless, there are many security-related cases in which censorship is permitted—including speech that is likely to produce imminent harm or non-imminent but enormous harm. The balance shifts during emergencies, when "loose lips sink ships." Laws restricting dangerous speech are more likely to be enacted, and courts will enforce them. Similarly, during normal times, judicial process reflects a balance between liberty and security. Ordinary crime is a serious problem, but locking up innocent people is undesirable, so process protections are exacting. During emergencies, locking up innocent people is still undesirable, but the security threat is greater, so process is reduced. Again, courts are willing to acquiesce. Censorship and process reduction during emergencies raise the concern that the government will suppress political competition, but in the United States, governments have taken this concern seriously since the Sedition Act debacle of 1798–1801 and have tried hard to reassure the mainstream political opposition that it is not the target of emergency measures. We now examine more closely some of the ways that government can reduce process during emergencies without at the same time alarming the political opposition and losing its loyalty.

## Charges, Defense, and Evidence

Legalism requires that defendants be charged with the violation of an existing law; that defendants be informed of the charges against them, so that they may prepare a defense; and that defendants be given access to evidence, so that they may prove their case.

All of these elements of normal process interfere with the prosecution of public threats. If the government does not have laws against political or ideological opposition, then it will not be able to apply generally applicable rules against criminal behavior to people who have not yet caused a harm or who are not on the verge of doing so. If the government must candidly inform the defendant that it has no legal case against him, then he will be able to make a plausible argument that the trial is political. And the government may not be able to reveal evidence that the defendant is a public threat without compromising intelligence assets and revealing information that will harm security. In the trial of Julius and Ethel Rosenberg for espionage, for example, some of the government's evidence came from secret cable intercepts that, if revealed, would have permitted the Soviet Union to destroy valuable intelligence sources.[44] The problem for the government is that, if it denies process—say, it tries the defendant in secret in order to determine whether he is a public threat or not—then it risks losing its credibility.

The government reduces these tensions in several ways.

*Selective Prosecution* First, the government prosecutes public threats, when possible, for violating generally applicable laws—laws against conspiracy, disorderly conduct, subversion, trespass, incitement to riot, material support, and so forth—that are not usually enforced against ordinary people who do the things that the actual defendant did. This approach is very much a compromise. On the one hand, the public will be suspicious of the government because selective prosecution can be used against political opponents. On the other hand, the harm to the government's reputation is mitigated by the fact that the generally applicable laws have received public approval, and political opponents can maintain their freedom by complying with these laws. There may be a special hardship in complying with nanny taxes, sodomy laws, and conspiracy laws to which no one else pays attention, but that is not as bad as prosecution that is unconstrained by the law. In addition, general laws often have lower sentences, precisely because they can be applied to so many people; so the corresponding risk to political opposition is lessened.

For example, discussing the trial of LeRoi Jones in 1967, one scholar notes, "[I]t was uncertain whether Jones was on trial for a stated or implied charge— for having possessed [two revolvers], or for having been responsible, in some mysterious way, for the riots that had engulfed Newark."[45] The Chicago 8 were tried for conspiracy to incite riots, but the real motivation was to suppress the defendants' vigorous opposition to government policy and to make an example of them.

An extreme example comes from the Haymarket trial. The defendants had advocated violent revolution, but no evidence linked them to the bomb thrower (never caught) who killed the police officers. The judge instructed the jury that the defendants could be convicted if they "by print or speech advised, or encouraged the commission of murder, without designating time, place or occasion at which it should be done."[46] The government sought to disrupt the anarchist movement, and the murders became the occasion for eliminating several of its leaders and frightening its members.

Governments can rarely be completely candid in trials that target public threats because they do not want to admit that the trial violates due process even if the violation is justified for reasons of public security. Instead, governments accuse the defendant of violating a general law, while also arguing that the acute danger posed by the defendant justifies a harsh sentence. Defendants might complain that if they do not know the real reason that the government is prosecuting them, they cannot mount an effective defense. LeRoi Jones could argue that he cannot defend himself if he thinks that the government is prosecuting him for gun possession when in fact the judge and jury will convict him if they think that he caused the Newark riots. We will say more about this concern below.

Today, critics have made similar arguments about the Bush administration's reliance on material support laws. Under 18 U.S.C. 2339B:

> Whoever knowingly provides material support or resources to a foreign terrorist organization, or attempts or conspires to do so, shall be fined under this title or imprisoned not more than 15 years, or both, and, if the death of any person results, shall be imprisoned for any term of years or for life. To violate this paragraph, a person must have

knowledge that the organization is a designated terrorist organization
. . . , that the organization has engaged or engages in terrorist activity
. . . , or that the organization has engaged or engages in terrorism.

This statute was used against seven American citizens who never engaged in
a terrorist attack but did receive training from al Qaeda in Afghanistan. These
people were certainly public threats, but in the absence of the material support
statute, they would never have violated a law until they committed a terrorist act, if that was what they planned to do. The FBI could not have arrested
them for being Muslims, or being descendants of people from the Middle East,
or being sympathetic to the aims of Osama bin Laden. The material support
statute allowed the authorities to lock them up for many years.[47]

Prosecutors have argued in favor of a broad definition of the statute, broad
enough so that mere membership in a foreign terrorist organization would
be a violation, even if the defendant did not engage in any particular crime,
as long as the defendant is under the control of the leaders of the organization. One can imagine even broader readings—nominal affiliation with the
charitable arm of a terrorist organization, for example—that would sweep in
large numbers of people. Such an interpretation would raise First Amendment
concerns, but courts could ignore them as they did during the early period of
the cold war.

The advantage of such a broad interpretation is that it permits the government to arrest and imprison people who are merely terrorist threats. Given
resource constraints, the government would most likely target the most dangerous people—those who trained in Afghanistan, not those who for ideological reasons merely associate themselves with a terrorist group—but there
is no guarantee. Conceivably, the government could target partisan political
opponents as well. But in the current political climate, that seems unlikely.
The Bush administration does not gain any partisan benefit from imprisoning
innocent Muslims—nor would a Democratic administration. And imprisoning harmless people in order to show that progress is being made in the war
on terrorism risks a backlash, because people do not feel safer when harmless
people are imprisoned.

*Partial Sharing of Evidence* Second, the government may be willing to
reveal classified evidence to the judge or to the defense lawyer as long as it is
not shared with the defendant. The defendant can legitimately object that he
will not be able to mount a sufficient defense without having access to the
information; he may not be able to reveal relevant mitigating evidence to his

lawyer or the judge unless he knows about the apparently inculpatory evidence that is classified.

The upshot is that the government gains the power to use classified evidence but also may incite the distrust of members of the public, who might believe that the evidence is not inculpatory and the defendant is merely a political opponent. The solution is to shift the burden to the judge (and/or the defense lawyer) in the hope that the public will believe that the judge will evaluate the evidence impartially and can evaluate it correctly without hearing the response of the defendant. The solution can be effective—in the sense of maintaining the government's credibility while allowing it to convict the defendant—only if the public believes that the judge is impartial and that the defendant's inability to respond to the evidence does not undermine his ability to defend himself. But then the question is: why should the public trust the judge? We return to this question later.

*Political Defenses* Third, the court, with or without the government's acquiescence, may allow the defendant to mount a political defense. Ordinary criminal defendants are rarely permitted to argue that their crimes were justified because the government is evil. There is no reason for an ordinary criminal trial to become a forum for evaluating the government's policies. But when the public suspects that the defendant is being prosecuted for his political views, it may make sense to allow the defendant to mount a political defense. If his views are extreme—for example, he is an anarchist who thinks that terrorism is justified—then the public will be more likely to support the prosecution. If his views are moderate, then it will be more likely that the government's motives are partisan. The defendant may be constrained to tell the truth, at least partially, as he will want both to persuade the public that he does not pose a threat and to reassure his supporters that he has not betrayed them. Thus, by allowing defendants to make political statements, governments may be able to show that prosecution is appropriately directed toward a public threat rather than motivated by partisanship.

The judge in the *Debs* case permitted the defendant to make a speech defending his actions—opposition to American participation in World War I—on political grounds.[48] The judge in the *Dennis* case prevented the defendants from arguing that the Communist party had an appealing political program and limited them to the question of whether the party had ever advocated violent revolution.[49] Both trials were successes for the government and the judge, though the *Debs* trial was less disruptive even though Debs was a more politically popular figure.

The problem with allowing defendants to mount a political defense is that they may persuade the public to take their side; and, even if they do not, they may be able to undermine the public's confidence in the justice system by converting the trial into theater, preferably farce. Mockery of the judge, disruption, grandstanding, and delay become the defendant's most powerful tools. Disruption provokes the judge to take harsh measures against the defendants, which further show that the judge is complicit in the government's effort to suppress political dissent.

This strategy succeeded spectacularly in the trial of Elizabeth Dilling and her codefendants—a group of Nazi sympathizers prosecuted under the Smith Act during World War II—whose lawyers objected to every act of the prosecutor and disputed every ruling of the judge. The trial dragged on for months and then ended abruptly with the death of the trial judge—from exhaustion, it is said. A retrial more than a year later was dismissed.[50]

To deal with these problems, judges need great skill and patience. The judges in the trial of Edward Dennis and other members of the American Communist party in 1949 and in the trial of the Chicago 8 in 1969 were considerably less tolerant of courtroom theatrics than the *Dilling* judge was. The *Dennis* judge frequently cut off the defendants and their lawyers. The Chicago 8 judge jailed defendants and their lawyers for contempt. In taking these steps, the judges opened themselves up to the accusation that they were depriving the defendants of a fair trial. Numerous rulings of the Chicago 8 judge were reversed on appeal. Although both judges survived the ordeal,[51] the *Dennis* judge was far more successful; and the reason was almost surely that Dennis was a less sympathetic figure at the time than the Chicago 8 defendants were. America was unified in its opposition to the Soviet Union, and therefore Dennis was unpopular; America was divided over Vietnam, and thus the Chicago 8 defendants, although politically extreme, enjoyed some mainstream support for their stand against American militarism.

Judges can interrupt defendants who do not follow the rules and hold defense lawyers to be out of order, but the defendants can complain of this, and so jurors and other witnesses might conclude that the government's motives are partisan, the judge is complicit, and the defendants are political opponents rather than public threats. Thus, like the other devices we have discussed, limiting the defense can have ambiguous effects. It can increase the probability of convicting a public threat by depriving the defendant of a defense, but it can also cause the jury to acquit the defendant, or the public to withdraw support from the government, because they suspect that the defendant is merely a political opponent.

## The Judge

Judges are supposed to be impartial: they enforce the rules without bias toward the prosecution or the defense. For ordinary criminal trials, the ideal of the impartial judge is attainable because judges, whatever their hostility toward criminals, can enforce the rules of due process and ensure that people likely to have committed crimes are locked up in jail. Generally, applicable criminal laws are uncontroversial; the judges can enforce those laws; and the ordinary rules of process function mainly to ensure that innocent people are not inadvertently convicted.

Normal process no longer functions smoothly when the defendant is a public threat who has not committed any crime. If no law against political dissent or opposition exists, then the judge can ensure conviction of the public threat only by relaxing the rule of law. In this way, the judge must be complicit in the government's effort to selectively apply vague, general laws against particular defendants, or even in the trumping up of charges when no such laws can be used.

This leads to our familiar dilemma. If judges relax process when they think that a defendant is a public threat, then governments may take advantage of this opportunity and bring charges against partisan opponents. Eventually, the public, including the mainstream opposition, will realize that process protections have been relaxed, and the government will lose its credibility. If people believe that the government targets its political opponents by persuading judges that they are public threats, they will—on the theory we have advanced—withdraw their support from the government. They would likely withdraw their trust from the judiciary as well.

Several institutional features of the judiciary mitigate this tension. We divide them into two categories: the selection of judges and the incentives of judges.

*Selection of Judges* In the United States, virtually every judge is a member of one of the two major political parties and is selected on the basis of two criteria: competence and proved partisan loyalty. In most other liberal democracies, judges are members of the government bureaucracy but are trained as, and treated as, experts rather than partisans.

The American system functions properly as long as the parties alternate in power and/or government is occasionally divided, so that judicial appointments are, individually or in the aggregate, the product of compromise between the two parties.[52] As most judges are the product of the patronage system, they will refuse to allow the other party in power to convict members of their own party on trumped-up charges. To be sure, frequently a (say) Republican government will be able to bring a case before a Republican judge, but then there is the chance that the appellate panel will be dominated by Democrats, who will be sure to draw attention to partisan elements in the trial, if there are any. By contrast, neither a Republican judge nor a Democratic judge will have much sympathy for a radical who seeks to destroy the constitutional system under which the judges exercise power. Thus, they are more likely to relax the rules of process in such cases.

The selection system in foreign countries is not quite as effective. Judges are trained as technocrats, and therefore they are more likely than their American counterparts to apply process rules in a mechanical fashion, regardless of the political views of the defendant. This may explain why legislatures in some of these countries—especially Germany—are more likely to pass laws that prohibit extreme political dissent inconsistent with the constitutional underpinnings of the state.

*Incentives of Judges*  But the civil law systems make up for the weak selection mechanism with more powerful incentives. Judges are bureaucrats, and while they have some civil service protections, they are vulnerable to sanctions meted out by the government. In Japan, for example, judges who displease the government may be assigned to remote, rural districts.[53] To avoid such sanctions, judges may be willing to relax process rules when the defendant is a public threat.

But then why wouldn't such judges also permit convictions of partisan opponents? The answer is likely that the judges must fear that the mainstream opposition party of today will be the party in power tomorrow and then be armed with the power to exile the judge to remote districts or to show their displeasure in other ways. Thus, the alternation of parties maintains an incentive to enable the prosecution of people whom both parties dislike—genuine public threats—and not the prosecution of people whom only one party dislikes, namely, members of the other mainstream party.

By contrast, it is harder for the American government to punish judges who fail to relax process in trials of public threats. Federal judges have independence under the Constitution, which, as a practical matter, makes punishment impossible. Still, the government can reward compliant judges by elevating them. Indeed, the judges in the *Rosenberg* and *Dennis* cases were elevated to the court of appeals.[54] Judge Hand, who ruled against the government in an Espionage Act case during World War I, was subsequently denied elevation to the court of appeals, which may have been his due.[55]

As a practical matter, then, the American and foreign systems have the same effect. They either select judges, or give them incentives, such that process rules are likely to be maintained for trials of mainstream partisan political opponents, but not for trials of public threats or people with fringe views. Judges might expect to be rewarded when they conduct trials that lead to convictions of people who are widely regarded as public threats—either with popular acclaim or elevation or similar benefits. In the first week after the *Dennis* case concluded, the presiding judge received 50,000 letters from grateful citizens, who urged him to run for office.[56] And, of course, judges may share the public's fear of public threats and be willing to relax process rules in order to convict them.

*How Judges Relax Process* How do judges relax process without destroying the rule of law as a device for maintaining political peace between mainstream groups? The key has been to relax process only for the trials of suspected extremists and only during times of emergency.

As to the first point, there are only two historical episodes in American history when mainstream political opponents were prosecuted. The first episode involved the prosecutions under the Sedition Act of Jeffersonian opponents of the Federalists. These prosecutions were extremely unpopular and contributed to the massive electoral defeat of the Federalists in 1800, and their elimination as a viable political party.[57] Consistent with our thesis, the Federalists only made themselves more unpopular—less trustworthy for most voters—by prosecuting their political opponents.

The second episode was the Civil War, when military rule enabled authorities in the North to prosecute people who expressed political sympathy with the Confederacy. These trials sometimes led to significant political disturbances in the North, and Lincoln, who was more politically sophisticated than the generals to whom he had to delegate military rule, was not happy with them.[58] However, to avoid the obstructionist efforts of mainstream judges like Justice Roger B. Taney,[59] Lincoln had to rely on military rule, and with it the attendant risks.

Since then, there have been no American political trials against mainstream political opponents. All political trials have targeted extremists, for example, communists, anarchists, Nazis, KKK members, members of Islamic fundamentalist groups. When the government prosecutes extremists, we are not as likely to assume that it is trying to obtain partisan advantage—these extremists are just too weak and unpopular, and are feared because of their tendency toward violence—except, of course, when the prosecution takes advantage of public fears or misunderstandings for political gain.

This is not to say that trials of extremists have been uncontroversial. Political views fall along the spectrum, and trials of extremists alarm people who are between the extreme and the mainstream. But the point, for now, is that American judges have allowed these trials to proceed, and they have been politically possible and even advantageous.

Indeed, some judges have enthusiastically facilitated political prosecutions. The Federalist judges in the Sedition Act cases instructed juries in such a way that much of the burden of proof was shifted onto the defendants.[60] Most judges in Espionage Act cases during World War I read the statute broadly, so that the government would not need to provide evidence that the defendant's statement caused a direct harm, such as the obstruction of military recruitment.[61] The judge in the Haymarket case allowed the bailiff to stack the jury with middle-class, mostly native-born citizens hostile to the anarchist, working-class, foreign-born defendants.[62] The judge in the Chicago 8 case jailed many of the defendants and their lawyers for contempt, errors that were reversed on appeal.[63] The judge in the LeRoi Jones case made clear, by his questioning and demeanor, that he believed that Jones was guilty.[64]

An abiding concern for judges is that if they identify too closely with the government, they will lose their reputation for impartiality. If they are not considered to be impartial, or at least as some sort of constraint on the government, they will lose both much of their public support and the support of the government itself, which benefits from judges who constrain it somewhat, rather than too much or too little. Judges preserve their integrity while allowing governments leeway in two main ways.

First, judges relax process mainly during wartime and other emergencies. In doing so, they ensure that normal political competition will occur during normal times, at which time judges will enforce normal process protections. This is not altogether satisfactory, however, because the government can use emergencies, or pretextual emergencies, as opportunities to consolidate power. In addition, if judges are seen as toadies of the government during an emergency, they may not be able to shake off this reputation during normal times.

Second, judges encourage governments to create specialized courts that are not operated by regular (Article III) judges. Military courts and commissions are examples; notice that these tribunals do not eschew process altogether but reduce it. Military judges and lawyers are loyal to the military, but are expected to act with some independence and can be trusted to keep secrets.[65] Allowing the government to use the military does not protect partisan opponents, but it does preserve the integrity of the judiciary (except to the extent that permitting military trials undermines it), so that the judiciary can credibly reassert its impartiality between the mainstream parties when the emergency ends.

We have seen these two factors at work in the Bush administration's creation of military commissions to try al Qaeda members and Taliban soldiers.

The establishment of these commissions has not hurt the government politically[66] because the public appears to believe that emergency conditions justify a relaxation of due process and, at the present time, it is not plausible to think that these commissions are being used against mainstream partisan opponents. We will say more about military commissions in chapter 8.

## The Jury

Scholars today usually think of juries as fact-gathering institutions or as representatives of the community. Because jurors bring diverse experiences and expectations to the trial, they can combine their perspectives, enabling them to sift evidence more effectively than even a highly experienced judge. The assumption that juries are necessary for accuracy has stimulated a large literature that investigates the extent to which jurors really do make correct decisions about guilt and innocence. Although this literature has not come to firm conclusions, evidence suggests that cognitive biases and social influences may cause jurors to make worse decisions than judges do.[67]

This scholarly focus has obscured another function of juries, which is not so much to contribute to the accuracy of the fact-gathering process as to present a barrier against government oppression with judicial connivance. The jury's entrenchment in American jurisprudence is due to its success prior to the American Revolution, when jury nullification derailed prosecutions of revolutionaries and other critics of the British government. The judges, who owed their position to British authorities, took the side of the prosecution and were frustrated by the recalcitrant juries. This history implanted in the American mind the conviction that juries, not judges, are the bulwark against political prosecutions.[68]

The history suggests that the jury could be an ideal device for permitting political prosecutions against public threats but not against partisan opponents. After the American Revolution, the jury could no longer regard the government as a presumptively hostile force. And if the government can make a plausible case that a particular defendant poses a public threat, the jury may be willing to convict even though the legal basis of the conviction is weak. In addition, as long as the jury is politically diverse—in the sense of having at least one or two members who belong to, or sympathize with, the opposition party—the unanimity rule ensures that partisan convictions will not be possible. To be sure, extremists who find their ways onto juries may be able to block the conviction of a public threat, but judges and lawyers are careful to prevent such people from being assigned to the jury. Thus, as a general matter, juries ought to be able to hinder partisan prosecutions but not prosecutions of public threats.

American history provides only ambiguous evidence for this hypothesis. Juries have tended to return convictions, whether the defendant belonged to an extremist or mainstream group. Thus, although it is true that Wobblies, members of the Communist party, and foreign spies have been routinely convicted,[69] juries also returned convictions almost without exception under the Sedition Act of 1798, which targeted mainstream opponents of the government.[70] Juries did not interfere with Sedition Act prosecutions because jurors were selected by political appointees, such as marshals,[71] and many of the judges, at that time, instructed the juries in an aggressive fashion. However, jury manipulation became a political issue that was exploited by the Republicans.[72] And perhaps the fear of jury nullification explains why there were not more trials in the Republican-dominated South.[73]

The best evidence for the hypothesis that juries could block political convictions comes from the indirect case of the Civil War. We cannot directly prove this argument because, with the suspension of habeas corpus and military rule, political opponents could be tried without a jury or, for that matter, without an independent judge. But it seems clear that the reason that Lincoln and then Congress suspended habeas corpus was that they expected juries to acquit southern sympathizers and others who were conspiring to impede troop movements or engage in sabotage but who had not committed a provable crime.[74]

Thus, although juries have not in practice interfered with many political trials, the costs and visibility of manipulating them in order to ensure that a conviction will be obtained may prove to be too high for many governments. The more mainstream the political opponent, the more difficult it will be to manipulate the jury—because it is more likely that a member of the opponent's party will end up on the jury unless manipulation takes place. And even if manipulation is successful, it may be blatant and thus good fodder for the defense. It might be that there have been fewer partisan trials than there would have been if there had been no jury right.

## The Defense Lawyer

Good legal process grants criminal defendants the right to competent and independent defense counsel. Competence is a straightforward requirement; independence is more complex. Defense lawyers are officers of the court, and they are not permitted to help the defendant engage in perjury. But, even if paid by the government, they are, as a matter of custom, law, and professional self-understanding, antagonistic to the prosecution, to the point that obtaining an acquittal of a guilty client may seem to be a positive duty and a badge of honor. And, of course, defense lawyers attract clients by obtaining acquittals.

When the defendant is a public threat, the independence of the defense counsel may create problems. At one extreme, defense lawyers may belong to groups that share the subversive goals of the defendant. If so, revealing classified information to defense lawyers becomes an unacceptable risk for the government. Even allowing defense lawyers to have private contact with defendants may pose unacceptable risks, as defense lawyers may carry messages between defendants and their organizations.[75] Even if the defense lawyer does not share the defendant's goals, he may inadvertently reveal sensitive information.

At the other extreme, the defense lawyer's good-faith zeal on behalf of his client may hinder the prosecution of a public threat. Defense lawyers demand process; if the government relaxes process, the defense lawyer will draw attention to the government's efforts, cause public embarrassment, and perhaps persuade the jury to acquit. All of this may be tolerable but far from ideal.

But denying the defendant a lawyer is hardly a solution, as it encourages the public to think that the government believes that the defendant is being tried because he is a partisan opponent rather than a criminal or public threat.

Various intermediate mechanisms have been developed. First, the weakest constraint is to require defense lawyers to abjure any connection with, or sympathy for, extremist groups. In the United States, this constraint arose in a decentralized way when bar associations decided that their members may not belong to the Communist party.[76]

Second, governments may replace civilian defense lawyers with military lawyers. This requires a suspension of habeas corpus, as in the Civil War, or else the classification of the defendant as an enemy combatant.[77] Military procedure supplies defendants with lawyers; but the defense lawyers are soldiers and therefore can be assumed to be more loyal to the state than ordinary defense lawyers are.

Third, governments can give more or less assistance to lawyers; more or less access to their clients; and so forth. In some of the recent enemy combatant cases, the defendants were initially denied access to a lawyer and then given limited access under supervision.

To the extent that defense lawyers feel loyalty to the government or have internalized norms of judicial process—so that they will attack the prosecutor but not the system—they may have limited value for the political defendant. The American Communist party instructed its members not to use lawyers, or to limit them to the technical aspects of the case, and trained members to use the courtroom as a platform for espousing their opposition to capitalism. The goal was not to persuade the jury to acquit the defendant—though that would have been welcome—but to persuade workers that the capitalist justice system could not do justice.[78]

## CONCLUSION

This chapter has focused on history and not on the current challenges posed by Islamic fundamentalist terrorism, but the lessons of history can be applied to the current challenges, and indeed we will say more about current American efforts in the next chapter. For now, we emphasize some more general theoretical conclusions.

Our main point is that the principles of liberal legalism evolved to ensure that governments would not use law enforcement to suppress partisan political opposition, and the various rules that reflect these principles—rules requiring general laws, hearings, and so forth—were never supposed to prevent the government from countering a serious threat to public safety. These rules work well enough during normal times because they reflect the balance between liberty and security appropriate for those times. During emergencies, judges and other decisionmakers do and should relax the rules to the extent that they are no longer consistent with the theory that animates them.

According to this theory, the normal rules of liberal legalism reflect a tradeoff between public safety and political competition. The freer the hand of the government to address concerns of public safety, the greater is its power to suppress political opposition. During normal times, a large amount of crime is tolerated for the sake of political opposition, but during emergencies, the balance shifts, and courts rationally acquiesce when governments demand greater power to address the new threat. In extreme cases, the government can legitimately demand the right to censor or suppress dangerous political organizations. But, in more ordinary situations, the government demands only somewhat greater control over what can be revealed at trial, the type of defense counsel the defendant can have, and so forth. So far, courts have sometimes but not always acquiesced.

Still, there are ways that courts and governments can reassure the public so that the public will not lose its confidence in the government, which would hamper its ability to respond to the emergency. Some of these ways are already built into American institutions. The tradition of partisan judges ensures that courts will, on average, be hostile to prosecutions of members of mainstream parties, but not necessarily hostile to prosecutions of extremists. The jury, which will normally have members from both mainstream parties, is likely to have a similar attitude.

Other methods are discretionary. Judges can, and should, facilitate prosecutions of threats to security by relaxing publicity rules, defining crimes broadly, and in other ways limiting process on the margin—as long as they believe that the government has made a good case that the defendant belongs to the class of people who pose a threat to security. However, to prevent the government from abusing these powers too much, judges might permit defendants to make political arguments in court.

# CHAPTER EIGHT

# Military Force

The Bush administration's reaction to the 9/11 attacks combined law enforcement, administrative, and military strategies. As we discussed in the introduction, the law enforcement strategies mainly took advantage of the enhanced search, surveillance, and information-sharing provisions of the USA PATRIOT Act, as well as earlier laws against material support, conspiracy, and terrorism. Federal authorities have arrested, tried, and convicted a number of people involved in terrorist activities on American soil. The administrative strategies have focused on immigration control; numerous aliens were detained and deported in the wake of the September 11 attacks, and since then standards for permitting entrance into the United States have been tightened. The military strategies have raised the most far-reaching and challenging issues, and they are the subject of this chapter.

The military operates under a set of procedures and expectations different from those that constrain law enforcement. The military has the right to shoot and kill anyone on the battlefield who looks like an enemy soldier and has not surrendered; the police may shoot and kill only a person who is immediately threatening others. The military can use overwhelming violence even when doing so kills innocent civilians as long as the destruction of innocent lives is not "disproportionate," given the military target; police are much more strictly regulated. The military engages in search, surveillance, and interrogation as required by military necessity and labors under few restrictions; the police must respect strict constitutional and legal restrictions on these activities. The military can detain soldiers who surrender until the end of hostilities; the police can detain suspects only for a limited time, and then they must either be released or charged and tried. The military can try prisoners of war (POWs) and enemy combatants for war crimes, but the due process requirements are low; the police must turn over suspects to courts, which observe the full package of due process requirements.

One difference between the military and law enforcement is frequently overdrawn. The military usually operates on foreign territory (or the high seas), and police usually operate at home. But the military can and does operate on home territory, as it did during the War of 1812, the Civil War, and World War II, when Hawaii was under martial law. And when fugitives escape overseas, American police rely on the assistance of foreign law enforcement agencies, and if the fugitive is captured, complex and legalistic extradition procedures are used.

The Bush administration's counterterrorism policies gave rise to a brief debate in the legal literature about whether reliance on military force is lawful or appropriate.[1] Critics argued that the 9/11 attacks were a "crime," not an "act of war," because al Qaeda is not a state, and only states can make war. Al Qaeda is simply a foreign criminal organization, and its behavior is not different, from a legal perspective, from a mob hit on American territory by agents of a Sicilian Mafia organization or a narcotics offense on American territory by a Colombian drug lord. The appropriate response is thus a law enforcement response, not a military attack.

The debate rests on a misunderstanding. There is no constitutional rule that forbids the government to use military force against ordinary criminals; indeed, the United States used military force against pirates soon after its founding, and has used military force against illegal drug organizations in Latin America and elsewhere over the past several decades.[2] When riots occur, state governments call up the National Guard; when state governments defy federal orders, as they did during the 1950s, the federal government relies on military force. There is no legal or constitutional requirement to classify the al Qaeda attack as either a military invasion or a criminal act, and then to respond with military forces or law enforcement in a manner that is consistent with the classification.

Whether and how to use military force and law enforcement, whether to do so separately or in combination, whether to use military force at home or law enforcement abroad—these are all important policy questions that turn on the specific advantages and disadvantages of each approach. The tradeoff, crudely put, is that the military can bring much greater firepower against an enemy than the police can, but it is not nearly as effective at deterring ordinary criminal behavior in a manner that civilians are willing to tolerate. The military is not a fine-tuned instrument; in bringing to bear greater force against the enemy or threat, it causes greater collateral damage to civilians. Military force is usually used abroad because civilians in foreign countries are not American voters; it is rarely used at home because voters find military government to be intolerable except in extreme cases when the alternative is riot or insurrection. But the extent to which the challenge posed by al Qaeda requires a new mixture of military and law enforcement strategies, at home and abroad, cannot be determined on the basis of past practices, though the latter may provide helpful information. The right mixture is a policy question that depends on the unique characteristics of the conflict between the United States and Islamic fundamentalist terrorist organizations.

The particular military tactics used by the Bush administration include the conventional military invasion and occupation of Afghanistan. More important from a legal perspective has been the decision to treat members of al Qaeda and related groups, including American citizens, as enemy combatants who can be detained indefinitely under the laws of war; who have forfeited many of the protections of the Geneva Conventions; and who can be tried by military commissions that operate under relaxed rules of due process.

In the remainder of this chapter, we discuss the constitutional and international law implications of these practices.

## CONSTITUTIONAL AND STATUTORY RESTRICTIONS

We will look first at the scope and limits of the president's power, under domestic law, to use military force in domestic settings (including some brief remarks on settings whose classification as "domestic" or "foreign" is ambiguous and contested, such as Guantanamo Bay). Here, some of the most critical questions are shrouded in uncertainty. This uncertainty is a chronic feature of emergency law. Because emergencies pose novel issues and threats, the precedents of earlier eras tend to be of limited value; rather than prescribing detailed rules before the fact, Congress often relies on the executive to react after the fact, or passes general framework legislation that makes large, although nebulous, delegations of authority. We will review some of the major open questions and indicate how they should be resolved under the tradeoff thesis.

### Domestic Law Enforcement

The Posse Comitatus Act restricts the use of military forces to perform law enforcement functions. The act is perforated with exceptions and loopholes, however. Its terms permit a large degree of military assistance to local law enforcement, which means that federal military officials can often control matters from off-stage. And there is a range of explicit statutory exceptions, created by the Insurrection Act, the Stafford Act, and the PATRIOT Act.[3] The president has authority to use military personnel to suppress insurrection or to overcome obstructions to or interference with the enforcement of federal or state law,[4] and a network of provisions authorizes the military to prevent attacks on American civilians with weapons of mass destruction, or to restore order in affected areas after such an attack. Overall, there is ample statutory authority for the president to use military forces in terrorism-related operations within the United States. The tradeoff thesis suggests that this is a sensible set of rules, to which judges should and will defer, but other approaches would also support this broad authority. Those who emphasize statutory authorization of emergency powers, for example, should have no quarrel with the law in this area.

## Detention of Enemy Combatants

Another critical question is whether the president may detain either citizens or noncitizens, captured either within the United States or on foreign battlefields, on the ground that they are enemy combatants, rather than civilians. We must distinguish two issues: the authority to detain enemy combatants, and the process that is due in determining whether a detainee is in fact an enemy combatant. Separate from these is the further issue of whether some subset of alleged enemy combatants may be tried for war crimes before military commissions. We discuss that issue at the end of the chapter, although some of our discussion of detention applies to military commissions as well.

As to the first question: the baseline constitutional restriction, stemming from the Civil War era decision in *Ex parte Milligan*, is that the executive may not detain civilians and try them according to military process, so long as the civilian courts remain open. Where enemy combatants are concerned, however, the rules are different. The governing rule, stemming from the *Ex parte Quirin* decision during World War II, is that the president may detain enemy combatants and either hold them while hostilities continue or have them tried by military commissions, at least if Congress has authorized the detention. In the recent *Hamdi* decision, a majority of the justices held that the Authorization for Use of Military Force enacted after 9/11 authorizes the president to detain citizens in some unclear range of circumstances. Although Justice Scalia, joined by Justice Stevens, suggested that the only constitutionally permissible options are suspension of habeas corpus or the ordinary criminal process, seven other justices rejected this proposition as irreconcilable with *Quirin*,[5] in which

Roosevelt detained, tried by military commission, and executed Nazi sabo-
teurs (one of whom was an American citizen). *Hamdi* left open whether the
statutory authorization to detain enemy combatants extends to noncitizens,
but the logic of the decision suggests that it does. The District of Columbia
Circuit drew that conclusion in the *Hamdan* decision, which we discuss below.
Although the Supreme Court later reversed on other grounds, it continued to
leave this question open.[6]

However, a majority of the justices in *Hamdi* also rejected Justice Clarence
Thomas's position that the president's determination of enemy combatant status should govern so long as there is "some evidence" in support. Rather, the
majority adapted the due process balancing test of *Mathews v. Eldridge*,[7] under
which an additional component of procedure is mandated if the accuracy
benefits outweigh the harm to the government's interests.[8] The Court did
not determine what process this test actually demanded, in the circumstances.
*Hamdi* leaves open all of the critical questions, including whether judicial
review is required or whether review by military tribunals is enough, and
whether there is a right to counsel in such proceedings and what the precise
scope of such a right might be. Subsequently, the Defense Department set up
a system of combatant status review tribunals to process alleged noncitizen
enemy combatants held at Guantanamo Bay, in Iraq and in Afghanistan; their
legal status is unclear as of this writing.[9] Overall, *Hamdi* is compatible with—
neither requires nor forbids—future decisions that give the government most
or all of the policies it desires, simply through deferential rulings on the merits.[10] As of the present, it is simply not clear what the consequences of *Hamdi*
are, or even whether it is a consequential decision at all.

## Detention in General

Much of *Hamdi* is consistent with our approach, although some of it is not.
We will begin with the authority-to-detain issue, and then turn to due process. Under the tradeoff thesis, the authorization analysis of *Hamdi* is clearly
correct, insofar as the justices said that the president has the authority to
detain enemy combatants. Indeed, we suggested in chapter 1 a more ambitious view: to the extent that the justices emphasize statutory rather than
constitutional authorization in such decisions, the authorization holding is
rarely a real issue or a moving part, because the courts strain to find statutory
authorization to uphold executive action taken in emergency circumstances,
in order to avoid large constitutional questions and to create a legislative fig
leaf for emergency action by the executive. Whether or not *Hamdi* is itself an

example of strained statutory interpretation, the point is that the result of the decision, as far as authorization is concerned, is just what the tradeoff thesis counsels courts to say.

## Indefinite Detention?

A separate sub-issue in *Hamdi*, under the heading of authority to detain, was the question of whether the president has the authority to detain *indefinitely*, while hostilities last. The plurality opinion by Justice O'Connor interpreted Hamdi's objection to be

> not to the lack of certainty regarding the date on which the conflict will end, but to the substantial prospect of perpetual detention. . . .
> If the Government does not consider this unconventional war won for two generations, and if it maintains during that time that Hamdi might, if released, rejoin forces fighting against the United States, then . . . Hamdi's detention could last for the rest of his life.[11]

The plurality concluded, narrowly, that Congress had authorized detention so long as active combat operations continued in Afghanistan, but combined this with a vague warning that "[i]f the practical circumstances of a given conflict are entirely unlike those of the conflicts that informed the development of the law of war, that understanding may unravel."[12]

This passage casts a cloud over the government's authority to detain for the duration of hostilities. This uncertainty is a cost, and for what benefit? The plurality does not explain, exactly, what would be wrong or even troubling with holding Hamdi for the rest of his life, if hostilities last that long. (We use Hamdi's name as a placeholder; in fact, Hamdi has already been released.) If the laws of war authorize the detention of enemy combatants for the duration because there is a risk that they will return to the battlefield, and there is a risk that Hamdi will return to the battlefield, then he should be detained—or at least there is no reason to override the government's judgment that the benefits of doing so outweigh the costs. (We bracket the separate possibility that Hamdi might be detained not preventively but for interrogation, as to which the plurality issued the bald dictate that "indefinite detention for the purpose of interrogation is not authorized.")[13]

Implicit in the plurality's treatment of preventive detention must be one of two theories, or assumptions. The first is that, over time, government officials will overestimate (in good faith) or exaggerate (in strategic bad faith) the risk that Hamdi poses; rather than conduct periodic reviews of particular cases, the government will simply throw Hamdi and others similarly situated down a black hole and forget about them. This is possible, but speculative and unlikely. If Hamdi no longer poses a threat, because the conflict has evaporated, from age, or for some other reason, it is not obvious why the government will want to detain him; detention is costly, and it offends foreign governments. Indeed, the United States has released numerous detainees, including Hamdi himself, as it has become clear that they no longer have intelligence value, or no longer pose a threat, or can be adequately monitored by their own governments. The plurality seems to be assuming a systematic governmental bias in favor of excessive detention, without articulating any mechanism that would produce such a bias. Enemy combatants were promptly released after earlier conflicts concluded or petered out.[14] Although Hamdi was a U.S. citizen (who surrendered his citizenship as a condition of release), where the far larger class of noncitizen detainees at Guantanamo Bay is concerned, the government has instituted annual reviews of detention for those previously found to be enemy combatants. In the first round of reviews, some 26% of detainees were transferred to the custody of another nation-state, while 3% were released outright.[15]

But, it has often been said, the war on terror is not like earlier conflicts, and this is the second concern that seems implicit in the plurality's treatment. Perhaps it is not only unclear when the war on terror will end, but also whether it ever will. But those things might have been said in 1941 just as easily; perhaps World War II might have degenerated into the sort of indefinite stalemate of superstates that Orwell imagined in 1949.[16] In World War II, it might also be said, at least there was a theory about what would *count* as an ending—a formal surrender by one sovereign state or another, or the collapse of one of the combatant states—whereas with the war on terror the very concept of an "ending" is obscure, because there is no organized entity who can surrender on behalf of terrorism.[17] This seems overly demanding, however. In the national struggle to defeat polio, or the Mafia, or the Ku Klux Klan, it is hard to say exactly when victory occurred, and hard to be clear even about what counted as victory. But it is clear that the problem is in a real sense no longer a live one; we know that it has been solved or at least contained. Someday, the same may be true of terrorism.

At bottom, the *Hamdi* plurality's idea that there is something troubling with the lifetime detention of an enemy combatant, while hostilities continue, smacks of the sporting theory of justice—in a temporal version that requires each particular combatant to get a chance to return to play sometime, even if the war on terror continues. This is an inadequate basis for judicial intervention. In any event, for current purposes, the upshot of the plurality's discussion is obscure. The *Hamdi* plurality did not, in fact, override the government's judgment about detention, indefinite or not. The plurality's treatment of indefinite detention remains just another question mark, exacting a cost in legal uncertainty, but not (yet?) amounting to a concrete restriction on government power. Here, too, the Court (or the effective coalition on the Court) ducked a confrontation with executive power in a time of emergency, as judges tend to do.

## Detention and Due Process

What about the due process component of *Hamdi*? Normatively, the majority's[18] due process analysis is half right, given our theory. The *Mathews* test is a marginal cost-benefit test for additional process, and thus fits comfortably with the cost-benefit test of *Dennis* (for censorship cases) and the general tradeoff thesis we have defended. The problem with the *Hamdi* majority's approach,[19] however, is that it does not explain why the judges should apply the balancing test themselves, rather than simply deferring to the balance the government had previously struck. One needs a theory to explain why the government will weigh the relevant factors with systematic bias, as opposed to random error, as we discussed in chapter 1. If there is no such theory, or no valid one, then the judges can do no better than the government on average, and will probably do worse from lack of information and expertise.[20]

One such theory, which is crude but grips the minds of many civil libertarians, is that the government will just want to detain in perpetuity or convict before a military commission everyone the president alleges is an enemy combatant, so the procedural cost-benefit analysis will be distorted; the government will afford too little process. The theory is mystifying. There is no reason to think that the executive would benefit from an excessive detention or conviction rate, or that political constraints would permit the executive to implement such a preference in any event.

As to preferences, the government has an interest in accuracy in its own right; thus the *Mathews* test is mistaken to the extent that it opposes accuracy to the government's interests. The government's interest in accuracy is that it benefits from a process that sorts out real enemy combatants from those who are swept up in the fighting by mistake. The government seeks to incapacitate and deter terrorists and attackers, but if the probability of detention or conviction bears no relationship to the individual's actions, then there is no incapacitation and no deterrence—just as there would be no incapacitation or deterrence if the government tried to fight terrorism by randomly detaining people. Perhaps the theory is that the government will weigh erroneous releases more heavily than erroneous detention, erring on the side of detaining the innocent. It is not at all clear, however, that this is objectionable. If there is an asymmetry in the harms from erroneous releases and erroneous detentions—the former being more harmful, because it puts active enemy combatants back into the field to pursue terrorist activities, while the latter merely deprives individuals of liberty for the time being—then there should be a corresponding thumb on the procedural scales.

As for the political constraints, the alleged enemy combatants are not citizens, but the government is constrained by domestic politics, which is responsive to citizens, including citizens with civil libertarian views. If the national political process is driven by constituents who do not want to allow the government to detain people willy-nilly, or to convict everyone in sight before military kangaroo courts, then the government will not be able to do so. Consider the parallel case of coercive interrogation, in which senators of President Bush's own party have taken the lead in prohibiting coercive interrogation and protecting the legal and procedural rights of foreign detainees.[21] Executive behavior is constrained by constituent preferences and the partisan tug-of-war; there is no reason to believe that such forces will systematically tend to push the executive toward more and more draconian behavior. Overall, although the cost-benefit approach to due process is congenial to our view as a first-order approach, the Court gave no valid second-order institutional reason for substituting its own judgment on the due process issue for the government's. There is no valid theory of panic, democratic failure, or ratchets that supplies such a reason.

As a descriptive matter, *Hamdi* does not contradict our running claim that there are powerful pressures for judicial deference during emergencies. The decision declares in ringing tones that judges can review government's actions, even during emergencies, on due process grounds. But the decision also says nothing, concretely, about what process is due; it remains entirely possible that the judges will give the government some, most, or all of what it wants, by holding on the merits that military tribunals for determining combatant status, military commissions for trying war crimes, and the other components of the government's policy satisfy due process.[22] As mentioned before, the judicial declaration has not yet had any real consequences, so *Hamdi* was at most a cheap victory for civil liberties. To be sure, however, it is part of the cyclical pattern of emergencies that judges will reassert themselves after they perceive that the emergency has ended. The recent *Hamdan* decision illustrates this tendency, as we discussed in chapter 1. We return to *Hamdan* at the end of the chapter.

## Jurisdiction and Extraterritoriality

A final line of decisions is even murkier than those we have already discussed. In *Johnson v. Eisentrager*,[23] decided in 1950, the Court seemed to hold that individuals detained as enemy combatants outside the United States—or at least in a zone of active combat—could not file a petition for writ of habeas corpus in a court within the United States. In *Rasul v. Bush*,[24] decided in 2004, the Court held, very dubiously, that *Eisentrager* had in effect been overruled in part by an intervening decision (which did not even mention *Eisentrager*).[25] The upshot was that noncitizens alleged to be enemy combatants and detained in Guantanamo Bay, a U.S. territory leased from Cuba and thus of ambiguous status, could file habeas petitions to challenge their enemy combatant status.

*Rasul* is quite narrow; it removes the apparent procedural barrier of *Eisentrager*, but leaves open myriad other questions. The scope of the resulting habeas law is unclear: did the Court mean to distinguish between detainees held in active combat zones and those in other territories outside of the United States? Surely such a distinction must be drawn—the Court presumably cannot mean that enemy combatants detained and held in combat zones may seek relief, with resulting disruption to ongoing military operations—but the opinion does not speak clearly to the question. Another critical point is that the writ of habeas corpus does not, by itself, provide any grounds for relief; a constitutional or statutory violation must also be shown. It remains open, even after *Rasul*, for courts to say that the Guantanamo detainees simply have no relevant constitutional or statutory rights that can be enforced on habeas; some lower courts have said just that, while others have disagreed.[26]

Like *Hamdi*, then, *Rasul* is consistent with great deference to government on the merits of the succeeding cases. Our discussion of citizenship, alienage, and judicial deference in chapter 3 entails that courts have especially powerful reasons to defer to executive action outside the core homeland of the United States. *Rasul* leaves open whether such deference will occur, and it is simply unclear, for now, whether there is anything objectionable in the Court's approach to such issues from the standpoint of the tradeoff thesis.

## A NOTE ON THE DETAINEE TREATMENT ACT OF 2005

As of this writing, an additional layer of uncertainty has been introduced by the Detainee Treatment Act of 2005. The act makes two significant changes. One part—the McCain amendment—prohibits coercive interrogation that rises to the level of "cruel, inhuman and degrading treatment." Another part—the Graham-Levin amendment—specifically overrides the jurisdictional holding of *Rasul*; gives the District of Columbia Circuit Court exclusive jurisdiction to "determine the validity of any final decision of a Combatant Status Review Tribunal that an alien is properly detained as an enemy combatant," but only for aliens detained at Guantanamo Bay; and limits the circuit court's review to claims that the review tribunal did not follow its own announced procedures, or that the procedures were themselves illegal or unconstitutional. The act mandates the same arrangement for military commissions.[27]

The Detainee Treatment Act poses many difficult questions. One is an issue of retroactivity; does the statute apply to pending habeas petitions brought by aliens at Guantanamo Bay under the holding of *Rasul*? Beyond this, what review does the statute authorize of combatant status review tribunals or of military commissions, and are the restrictions (if such they are) constitutional?

One part of the answer is already clear, but is narrower than many have assumed. The *Hamdan* decision held that the jurisdiction-restricting provisions of the act do not apply to pending habeas petitions. However, this holding quite explicitly applies only where the petition challenges the legality of a military commission before a final decision of the commission has occurred.[28] This covers only a handful of cases, and it differs from the more common situation, in which Guantanamo detainees seek to challenge the completed decision of a Combatant Status Review Tribunal finding the detainee to be an enemy combatant. Even after *Hamdan*, courts might still find that the act does apply to pending habeas petitions challenging the latter sort of determination—by far the largest category of cases.

These and other questions are currently under consideration by federal courts at various levels. They add to the legal haze that currently surrounds the war on terror. The effects of this uncertainty are not neutral. Legal uncertainty and indecision amount to deference to the executive, because the executive sets the status quo unless and until overridden by other institutions.[29] Courts that are unwilling to defer conspicuously may defer to the executive inconspicuously, by temporizing, by obscurity on the merits (as in *Hamdi*), by delay through inconclusive litigation, and by ducking cases that would present awkward choices. In our view, that is all to the good. What matters from the institutional and social point of view is that the executive be given free scope for action during emergencies. If another round of litigation ensues over the Detainee Treatment Act, with courts leaving the interim status quo as it currently is, this will be deference by another name.

## INTERNATIONAL LEGAL RESTRICTIONS
## ON MILITARY TACTICS

The Bush administration's counterterrorism strategy arguably has violated several provisions of international law; indeed, *Hamdan* said that the administration's procedures for military commissions violated the Geneva Conventions, as incorporated by reference in domestic law. Critics have made the following claims:

- The invasion of Afghanistan was a violation of the UN Charter. The UN Charter permits a state to use military force in self-defense, but only against another state. Al Qaeda is not a state, nor did it act as an agent of Afghanistan when it launched the September 11, 2001, attacks.
- The denial of POW status to members of al Qaeda and Taliban soldiers who were detained in Afghanistan during the hostilities violated the Geneva Conventions, which require that POW status be given to enemy soldiers.
- The failure to provide hearings to determine whether a detainee is an enemy combatant or not prior to classifying him as such is a violation of international humanitarian law. This has since been corrected, but critics argue that the hearings do not meet due process requirements under the Geneva Conventions.
- Torture or cruel treatment of detainees violates the Geneva Conventions, whether or not they are POWs; it also violates the Convention Against Torture as does rendition of detainees to foreign countries known to engage in torture.
- Detentions and targeted killings of al Qaeda suspects outside the battlefield violate the International Covenant on Civil and Political Rights, which imposes due process requirements.
- Trials by military commissions violate the Geneva Conventions and the International Covenant on Civil and Political Rights because POWs are entitled to the same level of process that American soldiers receive, and, even if the detainees are not classified as POWs, they are entitled to more process than they have received.

Some of these arguments are strong; others are weak. For now, we assume that they are strong arguments and focus on the more important question of whether the United States should comply with international law that interferes with valuable counterterrorism operations—or, what is roughly the same thing, whether the United States should insist on narrow interpretations of international law such that its counterterrorism tactics would not be barred.

In the following, we argue that the question *whether* the United States should comply with international law is inseparable from the question *why* it should (or should not) comply with international law. Our running example will be the laws of war (that is, what is also called international humanitarian law, which includes the Geneva Conventions). For reasons of space, we do not address the other claims in the list above. We argue that the United States should comply with the laws of war in its battle against al Qaeda only to the extent that these laws are beneficial to the United States, taking into account the likely response of other states and of al Qaeda and other terrorist organizations. At the present time, there is no strong reason for the United States to grant members of al Qaeda the protections of the laws of war, but that could change if the character of the war against terror changes.

## The Laws of War

The laws of war can be divided into general principles and specific rules.[30] The principles hold that soldiers may target only enemy soldiers and other military objectives, and not civilians or civilian property; that incidental damage to civilians and their property should not be disproportionate to the value of the military target; and that weapons and tactics used even against military targets should not cause unnecessary suffering.

These principles are reflected in various specific rules. An early rule against the use of dumdum bullets was based on the premise that their military objective—stopping a soldier—could be accomplished with an ordinary bullet, and the dumdum bullet caused unnecessary bodily damage. A similar idea underlies rules against the use of poison gas, blinding laser weapons, and explosives that produce microscopic projectiles that cannot be detected by doctors. Recent efforts to outlaw land mines rest on the argument that these weapons' harm to civilians outweighs their military value. Rules against the destruction of military hospitals and the mistreatment and execution of POWs reflect the principle that suffering should be limited to what is necessary for achieving legitimate military objectives.

The traditional statement in favor of the laws of war is that they serve humanitarian principles.[31] Wars are brutal; it would be better to minimize the suffering by requiring soldiers to follow rules. It is better for soldiers to take prisoners than to execute enemies who surrender; it is better to treat

POWs well than to starve and torture them; it is better to spare civilians than to kill them.[32]

As attractive as these ideas are, they are vulnerable to diverse criticisms. One problem is that, if the laws of war are enforceable, why limit them to the scope of the principles described above? Why not outlaw war altogether, or limit it to a duel between chosen representatives of each side, as was tried (unsuccessfully) by the Greeks and the Trojans in the *Iliad*? And if this is unrealistic, then why think that the existing laws of war can exert any force in the first place? The implicit assumption of the laws of war is that the evils of war can be lessened but cannot be eliminated. However, the idea of humanitarianism is too vague to provide an explanation for the lines that are drawn.

A second problem with the humanitarian theory is that the laws of war apply equally to both (or all) sides of the dispute, and thus indifferently to the aggressor and its victim. In theory, the French should have complied with the laws of war to the same extent as the Nazi invaders, but if aggression was initiated by the Nazis, why shouldn't the prospect of foreign occupation and Nazi tyranny justify the use of all means necessary to resist the invasion, including the mass killing of German civilians? Indeed, by the end of the war, the British and the Americans had concluded that the mass killing of enemy civilians was justified for ending the Axis menace, even if it was formally a violation of the laws of war.[33]

Third, a more humane war may be one that is more likely to occur, and more likely to persist once it begins. One argument in favor of area bombing during World War II was that it would demoralize German citizens and end the war earlier. Thus, the short-term costs would be high, but in the long term fewer soldiers and citizens would die than if targeted bombing were used. This was also one justification for dropping atom bombs on Hiroshima and Nagasaki. And during the cold war, reliance on nuclear weapons was justified for their deterrent value: no war would occur because the weapons were so inhumane.

These considerations suggest that the humanitarian contribution of the laws of war is ambiguous. The laws may make war more humane by depriving soldiers of destructive weapons and tactics; but they may make war less humane by prolonging it, and they may make the world less secure by making war more attractive. How these tradeoffs should be evaluated is a difficult question that one of the authors has addressed elsewhere.[34] Note only that if the laws of war are intrinsically bad, the United States should not only violate those that interfere with the war on terrorism: it should advocate the abolition of all laws of war. Instead of making this argument, we will assume that a proper evaluation of the tradeoff would not indicate that the laws of war are undesirable. We will assume that some laws of war—moderate or expansive—are optimal, assuming that they are complied with.

Our focus from now on is this issue of compliance. Many proposed laws of war, though desirable in the abstract, are not created because states will not agree to them or because they are not enforceable.

## Symmetry and Reciprocity

As noted earlier, the ideal of humanitarianism does not explain why some weapons and tactics are outlawed and others are not. The ideal has no natural stopping point: it suggests that all weapons and tactics should be outlawed, which in turn implies that war itself should be outlawed. But the premise of the laws of war is that wars themselves are going to occur, whether or not they are outlawed. So we have an empirical and normative puzzle. The empirical puzzle is why some weapons and tactics are outlawed but not others, even though they are all inconsistent with humanitarianism. The normative puzzle is: why should humanitarianism stop short of the abolition of war?

To answer these puzzles, we need to understand what the laws of war accomplish from the perspective of the states. Suppose that two nation-states, A and B, are at war; expect the war to end some day; and, in the meantime, prefer to minimize their own losses. Everything else being equal, the ultimate winner would rather win at less expense of blood and treasure than at greater expense; the ultimate loser would also rather lose at less expense than at greater expense. Thus, even though the states are at war, they share an interest in minimizing their losses. The problem for each state is that it can minimize its own losses only by persuading the other state to use less, rather than more, destructive weapons and tactics. But, given that the states are at war, how can one state persuade the other to use less force?

The answer is that, in theory, the states can implicitly agree on joint limits on the use of force as long as the limits make both states better off, as long as each state can credibly threaten to retaliate against the other state for violating the limits, and as long as they care enough about the future. The strategic problem is similar to the prisoners' dilemma, and the solution is the same: mutual threats of retaliation.[35] But there must be limits to cooperation; why, otherwise, have the war in the first place, or not end it early rather than merely limit the use of weapons?

This brings us to what we will call the *symmetry* and *reciprocity* conditions. These conditions are probably necessary for self-enforcing laws of war; we doubt they are sufficient, however.

The *symmetry* condition says that a law of war can be self-enforcing, and indeed possible in the first place, only if it gives an advantage to neither state in the conflict. It must be neutral as between them.

Consider two examples. Prior to World War II, the great powers discussed banning submarine warfare and certain kinds of sea mines. Britain favored such a rule, but other nation-states—including France and Germany—opposed it.[36] The great powers also discussed banning poison gas, did so, and (for the most part) did not violate the rule.[37] What accounts for this difference?

The best answer is that a ban on submarine warfare and sea mines would have provided an advantage to one state; the ban on poison gas did not. Because every major state had the capacity to manufacture and deploy poison gas, gas was extremely destructive, and the ban benefited all while not clearly providing an advantage to any state. Thus, a ban was possible and turned out to be self-enforcing during World War II, as between the major belligerents.[38] By contrast, although Germany and Britain both would have benefited from a ban on submarine warfare because such a ban would have protected their commercial shipping, Britain would have benefited much more than Germany would have, and this would have given Britain an advantage over Germany in a war. In the poison gas case, the gains were equal, giving no one a *relative* gain; in the submarine warfare case, the gains, while positive for both sides, would have been unequal, giving Britain a relative gain vis-à-vis Germany.

These examples are relatively clear, but symmetry is always a matter of context, and often the relative gains of a rule are hard to identify and vary between different pairs of belligerents. Requiring humane treatment of POWs, for example, may seem symmetrical, but in practice it may not be for various reasons. For example:

1. Some states have, for internal reasons, a long history of treating POWs well, so a new rule does not require any changes to practice or culture; other states do not. The rule benefits the first group more than the second.
2. Some states turn out to have logistical advantages. If one state captures POWs in its territory, for example, it may be easier to treat them humanely than a state that captures them on hostile territory at the end of long supply lines. The rule benefits the first state more than the second.
3. Some states might believe that treating POWs well is a good way to encourage them to surrender, while other states might believe that treating POWs poorly is a good way to demoralize the belligerent

state and persuade it to surrender. The rule benefits the first state by not requiring it to act differently from the way that it thinks is military appropriate; the rule hurts the second state.[39]

As a result, one finds a complex pattern in the treatment of POWs, reflecting all of these factors. We will say more about this in a moment.

Let's turn to the second condition for self-enforcing laws of war, which is *reciprocity*. By this, we mean that if a belligerent nation-state violates the laws of war, the opponent both has the capacity and an interest in retaliating by violating the same rule or some other rule. Reciprocity exists only when a war is ongoing, the outcome is unclear, all belligerents share an interest in keeping the war limited, and all belligerents have the ability to constrain those who fight under their flag.

Reciprocity requires that each state maintain an effective military authority that can ensure both that its own soldiers obey the laws of war and that an appropriate response—generally, retaliation—can be made if the other state violates the laws of war. When a war is about to end, and the enemy is in disarray, the other state has less reason to obey the laws of war because the losing state is powerless to retaliate: thus, pillage and looting are more likely to result than otherwise. And when one state violates all of the laws of war—if it adopts a scorched-earth policy—then it loses the ability to retaliate against the other state when that state violates the laws of war, as it cannot adopt less restrained tactics than those that it already uses. In a limited war, both states exercise self-restraint so that they have a way of retaliating if the other state fails to restrain itself in kind.

Reciprocity helps to explain why the law of occupation is so ineffective. In only one case since World War II has a state declared that the laws of occupation are applicable to a particular occupation—the only exception being America's current occupation of Iraq.[40] The reason is that a conquered state has no power to retaliate against the conqueror for violating the laws of war. There is no reciprocity.

Reciprocity is intuitive but frequently misunderstood. One often hears the following complaint about a particular violation of the laws of war, say, the American abuse of detained Iraqis during the recent war in Iraq: "Because the United States has violated the laws of war by torturing POWs and civilians, we can expect that in its next war the United States' enemy will torture American POWs." The logic here is dubious. Suppose that the United States' next war is with North Korea. There is no reason to believe that North Korea will torture American POWs *because* U.S. forces tortured Iraqis. After all, if North Korea tortures American POWs, it can expect the United States to retaliate in some way. North Korea has no interest in vindicating the rights of Iraqis; its interest is in limiting (or not) its war with the United States.

What is true is that, if the United States and North Korea are at war, the United States may want to treat North Korean POWs humanely in the hope that North Korea will reciprocate and treat American POWs humanely. This is the true sense in which reciprocity may function to the benefit of both sides.[41]

The symmetry condition and the reciprocity condition overlap somewhat, but they are intended to capture distinct phenomena. The symmetry condition says that the law must give an advantage to no party. The reciprocity condition says that one party must be able to retaliate if the other party violates the law. If it can't, this is usually because it has already been defeated (as in the case of occupation) or is not a well-organized army (as in the case of civil wars involving guerrillas and irregulars, in some cases).

## The War on Terror

As noted earlier, there are two polar responses to the problem of applying the laws of war to international terrorism. One response is that the laws of war apply with full force against terrorists. This view is reflected in the 1977 protocols to the Geneva Conventions, which many states, but not the United States, have ratified. Under the 1977 protocols, nearly everyone picked up in a theater of combat is entitled to the protection of the laws of war.[42] People guilty of war crimes—including terrorists who blow up civilians—would, under these laws, be entitled to various procedural protections. They could be punished for their crimes, but not otherwise treated any differently from regular soldiers.

The opposite response is that no laws of war should apply to a state's military operations against terrorists because terrorist groups are criminal organizations and not states, and lacking state capacity cannot be (and, of course, are not) signatories of the relevant international treaties. The deeper point here is apparently that terrorist groups do not act like states, either, so it would not make sense to apply the law to them. But this view rests on two misunderstandings. The first is that terrorism is purely destructive and has no political aim. Most terrorist groups have a specific political aim: in the case of al Qaeda, the elimination of American military forces from Muslim and Arab lands, and possibly the elimination of Western influence in the Middle East.[43] This is a coherent political aim, and it could be satisfied if the United States adjusted its strategic priorities. The second misunderstanding is that terrorists are not amenable to reason and unable to exercise self-discipline. Terrorist groups frequently respect certain rules, or enter modi vivendi with particular governments.[44] Often, terrorists seek to force governments into negotiations, and they respect certain ground rules the violation of which would make negotiation impossible.[45] In many cases—including in Spain, Italy, Northern Ireland, and South Africa—terrorist organizations ultimately (albeit in some cases, only partially) evolved into political organizations that reached settlements with the nation-states' governments.[46]

It is true that terrorist groups do not act like most states, but states themselves are highly diverse, and sometimes the governments of states and terrorist organizations are hard to distinguish. Many such states do comply with many rules of international law, even as they sponsor or engage in terrorism. If ordinary states can be expected to comply with the laws of war while fighting each other, then quasi states, terrorist states, rogue states, and state-like terrorist organizations may be too.

Laws of war are possible between states and terrorist organizations for the same reason that they are possible in interstate disputes. Although each side has an interest in defeating the other side (which, again, need not be extinction but could be a limited political defeat, such as secession of a region), each side also has an interest in minimizing its own losses prior to victory or defeat, as the case may be. When each side can curtail its use of destructive tactics against the other side, can benefit from the other side doing the same, and does not, in doing so, confer a military advantage to the other side, then self-enforcing limitations on conduct are possible.

But there is a difference between saying that the laws of war *can* apply to states fighting terrorists and saying that the existing laws of war—those that have evolved to deal with limited wars between roughly equal states—*will* apply. The premise of acknowledging a body of laws of war is that the belligerents have a reason to comply with them; but one expects that the body of laws that two ordinary states would respect would be different from the body of laws that a state and a terrorist organization would respect in their violent dealings with each other.

Indeed, one might argue that the dealings between governments and different terrorist organizations are too heterogeneous to be covered by a single code of law. We might prefer to refer to, and describe, the various conventions that evolve, or should evolve, between one government and one terrorist organization, and another such pair, and so on, rather than a broad code. This is reasonable, but one could say the same thing about the relationships between states that engage in limited war; these are surely just as heterogeneous. What matters is not the label one uses but the substance of the laws, or conventions, or modi vivendi, that arise or ought to arise as states and terrorist organizations struggle with each other.

The question is: given that terrorism exists, what rules should govern the military conflict between terrorists and governments?

The first point to recall is the constraint of symmetry. Any rule that provides an advantage to government or terrorist will not be respected. The outlawing of terrorist methods is the extreme example: governments can outlaw terrorism but cannot expect terrorists to pay attention.

As another example, consider the prohibition on the coercive interrogation of POWs. This rule has not always been respected during regular wars, but it has been respected sometimes. When each belligerent benefits more from the humane treatment of its soldiers by the enemy than it loses from being deprived of the fruits of coercive interrogation, and when—crucially— they can monitor each other's performance either through intermediaries like the Red Cross or through reports from escaped or rescued POWs, the rule is, in principle, self-enforcing. And even if each state may cheat a little on the margins, it does seem that the laws of war have improved the treatment of POWs during some wars.[47]

But now, we must ask ourselves whether the United States could benefit from a similar implicit deal with al Qaeda. The answer is probably not. Al Qaeda does not currently hold American soldiers as prisoners, and if it ever does, it seems highly unlikely that it would refrain from torturing and killing them, regardless of how the United States treats captured al Qaeda members. The problem is that, at the present time, al Qaeda would not gain by sparing Americans: it believes (as far as we can tell) that it gains large dividends, perhaps in terms of recruiting new people and motivating its agents, when it beheads prisoners and records their beheadings. If al Qaeda stopped beheading its prisoners, it would not receive any benefit from the United States, which does not behead al Qaeda members and probably would see little benefit from treating al Qaeda prisoners more humanely than it does now. The al Qaeda–U.S. conflict is not symmetrical in the way that an ordinary war is: the United States cannot expect to gain any benefits from al Qaeda by treating al Qaeda prisoners in a humane manner, given al Qaeda's demonstrated ferocity in its treatment of enemy captives.

Thus, the symmetry condition is violated; it may be that the reciprocity condition is violated as well. Suppose that both the United States and al Qaeda believed that both would be jointly—and equally—better off if they agreed (implicitly) to treat prisoners humanely. The question now is whether each party can credibly promise to comply with the deal as long as the other party does. We know that the United States could; but we do not know if al Qaeda could. It depends on whether the al Qaeda leadership can exercise discipline over all those who see themselves as carrying its banner. On one hand, some view al Qaeda as a relatively coherent organization, and it may be that Osama bin Laden and other leaders can control the activities of its members. If so, reciprocity is met; al Qaeda could engage in self-restraint in return for American self-restraint. On the other hand, many people think that al Qaeda has dissolved into local splinter groups or loose affiliates, and that Islamic terrorism is now a more diffuse phenomenon, in which no one person or organization controls the activities of members. If so, reciprocity is not met. The practical problem is that al Qaeda's leaders would not be able to prevent members from treating prisoners inhumanely; if so, then the United States has no incentive to enter into a deal with al Qaeda.

This discussion is only illustrative, but one clear implication is that the laws of war between states and terrorist organizations are likely to be highly context specific.

We conclude that it is theoretically possible that some terrorist organizations are similar enough to states—they have enough power and organization, and they have political goals that the target state may be willing to accommodate—that it makes sense for a government and the terrorist organization to try to limit the violence through the application of the laws of war, even as they try to work out a political solution in the context of an ongoing military conflict. It is not clear that there are real examples of such limited cooperation; perhaps the PLO-Israel conflict could be cited. But whatever the case, the conflict between al Qaeda and the United States has not reached this stage, though it may in the future.

In the meantime, the United States should not consider itself governed by the laws of war, as they are normally understood, in its conflict with al Qaeda, but it should be alert for opportunities for creating implicit norms of conduct that serve the American interest.[48] If such opportunities arise, the traditional laws of war may serve as a useful source for creating these norms.

The U.S. courts have said little, so far, about whether international law constrains the president's counterterrorism tactics. The only major case that addresses this issue involves Salim Ahmed Hamdan, who was captured in Afghanistan in November 2001 and placed under detention at the Guantanamo Bay naval base. The U.S. government alleges that Hamdan served as bin Laden's chauffeur and bodyguard, transported weapons for al Qaeda, and trained at an al Qaeda facility. He was charged with terrorism and related crimes and was to be tried before a military commission when he filed a writ of habeas corpus with a federal district court. The district court granted the writ.

The appellate court reversed the district court's judgment.[49] Several of the appellate court's arguments are of interest here. First, the appellate court argued that the Geneva Convention does not create a private right of action. A state party's obligation to comply with the Geneva Convention is directed toward other states, not toward individuals. If the United States' treatment of Hamdan violated the Geneva Convention, then Hamdan's home state has a right to protest, but Hamdan has no domestic legal right to obtain relief. The court's decision was based on an interpretation of a treaty and did not reflect any larger theoretical approach to counterterrorism or military activities. Nonetheless, we note that the court's approach is consistent with our discussion of international law. Whether and how the United States complies with international law should depend on whether and how other countries comply with that law; the determination that it is in America's interest to comply or not should be made by the president, not by the courts.

Second, the court argued that even if the Geneva Convention creates private rights of action, Hamdan would not benefit from its protections. The protections that Hamdan seeks are available only for two types of armed conflicts: international conflicts and armed conflicts "not of an international character occurring in the territory of one of the" state parties.[50] International armed conflicts can occur only between states and al Qaeda is not a state, or between a state and a "power" that accepts the Geneva Conventions as binding and al Qaeda is not such a power. Hamdan's argument that the conflict is "not of an international character" is stronger. Hamdan participated in an armed conflict on the territory of Afghanistan, which is a state party. However, the appellate court rejected this argument because President Bush declared that the conflict was "international in scope." Bush drew a distinction between Afghanistan's civil war and the conflict between the United States and al Qaeda. Although al Qaeda operatives also participated in Afghanistan's civil war, and were detained on Afghan territory, they were at the same time part of an international conflict with the United States.

The lower court's conclusions were squarely rejected by the controlling opinion of the Supreme Court, which held (as relevant here) that Common Article 3 of the Geneva Conventions is part of the law of war incorporated by reference in domestic statutes. This is potentially a significant holding, with implications in many domains of national security law, but only potentially; future decisions may read *Hamdan* for all it is worth but could also cabin it rather tightly. In important respects, the lead opinion by Justice Stevens is rather narrower than some triumphant critics of the Bush administration have suggested. The opinion does not say that there is a freestanding private cause of action to enforce Common Article 3; the treaty issue entered the case only indirectly, through interpretation of domestic statutes. On the issue of statutory authorization for military commissions, the controlling opinion acknowledges such authorization in a potentially broad range of cases, finding only that conspiracy charges were prohibited. The opinion acknowledged, as it had to do given *Quirin*, that domestic statutes do authorize military commissions (not complying with court-martial procedures) in many settings and for many offenses other than conspiracy, so long as traditionally sanctioned by the law of war. Furthermore, as we have mentioned, it is not even clear that the decision helps detainees challenging enemy-combatant determinations by Combatant Status Review Tribunals. As to that subset of pending cases, the lower courts can still say that the Detainee Treatment Act's restrictive provisions do apply.

However, we are less interested in the legal merits of these arguments than in the question whether courts should defer to the president's interpretation of treaties, especially treaties bearing on national security, because that is "the sort of political-military decision constitutionally committed to him."[51] Quite remarkably, the lead opinion in *Hamdan* does not so much as mention the principle of deference to presidential interpretations of treaties; nor does it argue that the president's interpretation was clearly incorrect, as opposed to incorrect all things considered. Under the traditional deference approach, the former determination would be required, because a reasonable presidential interpretation prevails in the face of ambiguity.

*Hamdan*'s approach to this issue is thus lawless. Fortunately it is also probably unsustainable in the medium and long term. The standard practice of deference to the president in treaty interpretation reflects persistent institutional pressures. The president is in a better position than are judges to determine how narrowly interpreting or violating treaty obligations will be received by other states and thus whether the benefits outweigh the costs. Indeed, we have seen this balancing process at work. Many Guantanamo Bay detainees have been released to friendly nations that have objected to the detentions and can plausibly guarantee that they will keep an eye on the former detainees. No doubt the decision to release also depends on an independent judgment of a detainee's dangerousness and intelligence value. These are judgments that should not be made by courts, and in practice they will not be made by courts, whatever the nominal state of the law on judicial deference after *Hamdan*.

## CONCLUSION

*Hamdan* is just the latest in a line of cases that shows the importance of judicial deference. The Supreme Court's refusal to afford any deference to the president on matters of treaty interpretation, bearing on national security, is simply untenable in the long run. The court of appeals' approach is no longer the law, but it is the only approach with a realistic future. Although the appeals court justified its deference on the basis of the president's foreign relations authority, it also no doubt reflected the court's concern about giving the president flexibility to respond to an emergency. To be able to respond to international crises, the president cannot be hemmed in by international treaties and constitutional limitations, as interpreted by judges.

This is not to say that international law and constitutional law do not matter. The president, when deciding whether to comply with, narrowly interpret, or violate international law, should look at the practical consequences of taking these actions. Some critics argue that America's reputation, in some general sense, is harmed when it violates international law and for that reason the United States should scrupulously follow it. However, there is no evidence that this is true. The practical politician is not interested in such second-order, long-term possibilities in any event, and cares—properly so, in our view—only whether a violation of international law will result in some measurable harm to the national interest. What could that harm be? Normally, it is retaliation by the state that is a victim of the violation. Fear of such retaliation explains why the United States and other countries comply with international law in many cases outside of the terrorism context. When the laws of war operate in normal conditions, fear that the other side will abuse one's soldiers causes belligerents to treat their own POWs humanely. However, there is no reason to think that al Qaeda will treat Americans better if Americans treat members of al Qaeda better.

For this reason, the Bush administration has acted properly in refusing to apply the Geneva Conventions rigorously to the conflict with al Qaeda, and until the Supreme Court decided *Hamdan* courts acted properly in exercising deference to the president's judgment. On this view, *Hamdan* is just a typical reassertion of judicial muscle after an emergency has run its course. Also quite typically, future decisions will in turn gut *Hamdan* when the institutional pressures that give rise to judicial deference again become insistent.

# CONCLUSION

# Emergency Powers and Lawyers' Expertise

We have laid out an affirmative theory of emergency powers and terrorism in chapter 1; criticized competing theories in chapters 2, 3, and 4; criticized some institutional alternatives in chapter 5; and laid out the implications of our view in chapters 6, 7, and 8. Rather than review these arguments in detail, we will take up a theme that runs throughout our discussion, which is the limited ability of lawyers, as lawyers, to contribute anything of value to the theory and practice of governmental decisionmaking in emergencies.

Lawyers' training gives them confidence in their abilities to contribute to the working of government. Yet the principal contribution that lawyers can make is to engineer process; the lawyer's occupational hazard or professional deformation is the belief that more process is always better, a distortion caused by neglect of the costs of process, including the opportunity costs of governmental action that is delayed or forgone while the wheels of legal liberalism turn ponderously. In normal settings, involving the bureaucratic and judicial regulation of the small-scale claims that are the everyday stuff of the legal system, lawyers' proceduralism is often beneficial or, if it is bad, is rarely very damaging. In emergencies, however, where the stakes are high and time is of the essence, procedural excess can be disastrous.

Fortunately, however, as we have emphasized throughout, those in power when emergencies actually occur tend to recognize the limits of their expertise. Legislators defer to the executive, enacting statutes that delegate sweeping power to the president or that ratify presidential actions already undertaken. Such statutes supply material to process-minded lawyers who hope that statutory authorization means something and that legislatures play an important role in emergencies; but in fact the statutes are often epiphenomenal products of the emergency rather than moving parts in the government's response to the crisis. Judges, too, facing a real risk that their procedural complaints will hamper the nation's emergency policies, overwhelmingly tend to defer to the executive in a crisis, although they may pretty up the pig by straining to find statutory authorization for the executive's acts.

Not so with academic lawyers, a majority of whom are reflexively hostile to executive power in matters of national security (as opposed to administrative regulation of the economy), and who are not made responsible by actually having to make decisions that are consequential in the short term. The liberal legalist urge to turn everything into a question of process explains the oddly indirect character of the arguments from civil libertarian lawyers canvassed in chapters 2, 3, 4, and 5. These lawyers know that substantive arguments on the merits of emergency policies fall outside of their domain of competence or, at a minimum, will be rhetorically unconvincing to an audience that knows that lawyers often lack the information necessary to evaluate the choices made by national security experts. The temptation for civil libertarians is then to abandon substance in favor of sophisticated second-order arguments about the government's decision-making processes and its long-term institutional consequences. We have tried to meet these arguments on their own ground, by suggesting that these second-order tropes are in most cases far too speculative, precious, or implausible and that the corresponding solutions proposed by liberal legalists are gimmicky and infeasible—the prime example being Bruce Ackerman's proposal for emergency governance through a framework statute with a supermajoritarian escalator, discussed in chapter 5. For the most part, governments react rationally to emergencies (although perhaps mistakenly; it is hard for outsiders to evaluate), and things return to normal at the emergency's end. The most interesting and consequential second-order possibilities remain mostly academic.

Our emphasis on the limits of lawyers' expertise does not entail that some other discipline can stand in. Philosophers are experts in clarifying matters at the conceptual level, but emergencies do not occur at the conceptual level, and the hard questions about emergency policy are mostly institutional and empirical. As we saw in chapter 6, where we discussed arguments against coercive interrogation by Henry Shue and others, philosophers have a proclivity to slide rather quickly and quietly outside of their domain of professional competence, into institutional and empirical arguments that are the province of security experts in government and on which the philosophers lack critical information. There is no reason for officials or interested publics to afford their arguments special weight as philosophical argumentation, rather than the weight that the opinion of any person in the street deserves on matters of emergency policy.

As lawyers, our contribution has been negative, deliberately so. What lawyers can contribute, and what we have tried to do, is to restrain other lawyers and their philosophical allies from shackling the government's response to emergencies with intrusive judicial review and amorphous worries about the second-order effects of sensible first-order policies. We hope merely to clear the ground for government to react to emergencies, enabling it to adopt whatever policies survive review by national security experts and the political process. Such policies will often be mistaken, but it is very hard for lawyers to know which ones are mistaken, and in any case nothing in the lawyer's expertise supplies the necessary tools for improving on the government's choices.

# NOTES

## Introduction

1. We do not mean emergencies in a technical legal sense. The president has declared approximately forty emergencies under the National Emergency Act since 1976, but these were all of a relatively technical nature, for example, to impose an embargo on a hostile state. *See* HAROLD C. RELYEA, CONGRESSIONAL RESEARCH SERVICE, NATIONAL EMERGENCY POWERS 13–16 (2005).

2. Authorization for Use of Military Force Joint Resolution, Pub. L. No. 107–40, 115 Stat. 224 (2001).

3. *See* Alan Cowell, *Britain Lists Offenses in Effort to Bar or Deport Foreign Militants*, N.Y. TIMES, Aug. 25, 2005, at A7.

## Chapter 1

1. *See, e.g.,* MARTIN S. SHEFFER, THE JUDICIAL DEVELOPMENT OF PRESIDENTIAL WAR POWERS (1999); WILLIAM H. REHNQUIST, ALL THE LAWS BUT ONE: CIVIL LIBERTIES IN WARTIME (1998); John C. Yoo, *Judicial Review and the War on Terrorism*, 72 GEO. WASH. L. REV. 427 (2003); Christina E. Wells, *Interdisciplinary Perspectives on Fear and Risk Perception in Times of Democratic Crisis*, 69 MO. L. REV. 897 (2004); Mark Tushnet, *Controlling Executive Power in the War on Terrorism*, 118 HARV. L. REV. 2673, 2679 (2005); CLINTON ROSSITER, CONSTITUTIONAL DICTATORSHIP: CRISIS GOVERNMENT IN THE MODERN DEMOCRACIES (1948). In an effort to test this view, Lee Epstein and coauthors created a data set consisting of 3,344 civil rights cases decided by the Supreme Court from 1941 to 2001. *See* Lee Epstein et al., *The Supreme Court During Crisis: How War Affects Only Non-War Cases*, 80 N.Y.U. L. REV. 1 (2005). The results of the study are puzzling. For the entire data set, the Court favored the government more during wartime than during peacetime. But for cases involving war-related laws, the Court was no more likely to rule for the government during wartime than during peacetime. *Id.* at 70–74. These results support neither the deference view nor the alternative, the civil libertarian view. Neither view implies that the Court would, during wartime, defer to the government's actions that are unrelated to war, but at the same time would not extend such deference to government actions that are related to the war. Both the deference view and the civil libertarian view

imply that the Court would not defer to non-war-related actions during wartime. Thus, the Epstein et al. study provides no reason for doubting the conventional wisdom.

2. *Korematsu v. United States*, 323 U.S. 214 (1944).

3. CASS R. SUNSTEIN, ONE CASE AT A TIME: JUDICIAL MINIMALISM ON THE SUPREME COURT (1999).

4. Cass R. Sunstein, *National Security, Liberty, and the D.C. Circuit*, 73 GEO. WASH. L. REV. 693, 693 (2005).

5. Cass R. Sunstein, *Minimalism at War*, 2004 SUP. CT. REV. 47 (2005).

6. Although one of us has argued for extremely limited judicial review of national law making—*see* ADRIAN VERMEULE, JUDGING UNDER UNCERTAINTY: AN INSTITUTIONAL THEORY OF LEGAL INTERPRETATION (2006)—we bracket that view here, assuming instead that some form of robust judicial review obtains during normal times.

7. Richard A. Posner, Not a Suicide Pact: Constitutional Rights in Time of National Emergency (Jan. 2, 2006) (unpublished manuscript); WALTER ENDERS & TODD SANDLER, THE POLITICAL ECONOMY OF TERRORISM (2006); W. Kip Viscusi & Richard J. Zeckhauser, *Recollection Bias and the Combat of Terrorism*, 34 J. LEGAL STUD. 27 (2005).

8. Jon Elster, "Fear, Terror and Liberty: A Conceptual Framework" (unpublished draft 2006) at 20–21.

9. Detention, Treatment, and Trial of Certain Non-Citizens in the War Against Terrorism, 66 Fed. Reg. 57, 833 (Nov. 13, 2001).

10. 524 U.S. 507 (2004).

11. The text of the legislation maybe found at www.opsi.gov.uj/acts/acts2006.

12. *See* Racial and Religious Hatred Bill, H.L. Bill 31 (2005) (Gr. Brit.).

13. *See* Anti-Terrorism, Crime and Security Act, c. 24, §§ 37–42 (2001), *at* http://www.opsi.gov.uk/ACTS/acts2001/20010024.htm.

14. *See* Don Van Natta, Jr., *Cleric Convicted of Stirring Hate*, N.Y. TIMES, Feb. 8, 2006, at A1.

15. *See* Dave Eberhart, *New FBI Rules Open Mosques to Scrutiny*, NEWSMAX.COM (May 30, 2002), *at* http://www.newsmax.com/archives/articles/2002/5/30/64029.shtml.

16. Adam B. Cox, *Citizenship, Standing, and Immigration Law*, 92 CAL. L. REV. 373, 413–14 (2004).

17. *See* Laurie Goodstein, *A Nation Challenged: Civil Rights; American Sikhs Contend They Have Become a Focus of Profiling at Airports*, N.Y. TIMES, Nov. 10, 2001, at B6.

18. Foreign Intelligence Surveillance Act, Pub. L. No. 95–511, 92 Stat. 1783 (1978) (codified as amended at 50 U.S.C. § 1801 et seq. (2000)).

19. *See* L. Brett Snider, *Intelligence and Law Enforcement*, in U.S. INTELLIGENCE AT THE CROSSROADS: AGENDAS FOR REFORM 243, 245–48 (Roy Godson, Ernest R. May, & Gary Schmitt eds., 1995); RICHARD A. POSNER, PREVENTING SURPRISE ATTACKS: INTELLIGENCE REFORM IN THE WAKE OF 9/11, at 31 n.23 (2005).

20. This account follows NATIONAL COMMISSION ON TERRORIST ATTACKS UPON THE UNITED STATES: THE 9/11 COMMISSION REPORT 78–80 (2004) [hereinafter 9/11 COMMISSION REPORT]. For the legal complexities, *see In re Sealed Case*, 310 F.3d 717 (FISA Ct. Rev. 2002).

21. 9/11 COMMISSION REPORT, *supra* note 20, at 353.

22. *Id.* at 386.

23. *Id.* at 383–87.

24. Detainee Treatment Act of 2005 § 1003, Pub. L. No. 109–148, 119 Stat. 2739 (2006).

25. Douglas Jehl, *Questions Left by C.I.A. Chief on Torture Use*, N.Y. TIMES, Mar. 18, 2005, at A1.

26. Quan Li, *Does Democracy Promote Transnational Terrorist Incidents?* 49 J. CONFLICT RESOL. 278 (2005).

27. 9/11 COMMISSION REPORT, *supra* note 20, at 127.

28. *See* Alan Cowell, *Britain Sets Militants' Boundaries*, INT'L HERALD TRIB., Aug. 25, 2005, at 1 (noting that the British government feared that "firebrand Muslim clerics and scholars" were "igniting violent militancy among British Muslims").

29. ROBERT PAPE, DYING TO WIN: THE STRATEGIC LOGIC OF SUICIDE TERRORISM (2005).

30. William L. Eubank & Leonard B. Weinberg, *Does Democracy Encourage Terrorism?* 6 TERRORISM & POL. VIOLENCE 417 (1994); Leonard B. Weinberg & William L. Eubank, *Terrorism and Democracy: What Recent Events Disclose*, 10 TERRORISM & POL. VIOLENCE 108 (1998); Li, *supra* note 26.

31. Viscusi & Zeckhauser, *supra* note 7.

32. COST-BENEFIT ANALYSIS: ECONOMIC, PHILOSOPHICAL, AND LEGAL PERSPECTIVES (Matthew D. Adler & Eric A. Posner eds., 2006).

33. *See* Neil K. Komesar, *Imperfect Alternatives: Choosing Institutions in Law, Economics and Public Policy* (1994).

34. *See Ashcroft v. American Civil Liberties Union*, 542 U.S. 656, 666 (2004).

35. Geoffrey R. Stone, *What's Wrong with the Patriot Act?* LEGAL AFF. DEBATE CLUB, Oct. 3, 2005, *at* 8, http://www.legalaffairs.org/webexclusive/debateclub_patact1005.msp.

36. Jeremy Waldron, *Security and Liberty: The Image of Balance*, 11 J. POL. PHIL. 191 (2003).

37. *Id.* at 197.

38. *Id.* at 210.

39. *Id.* at 209.

40. *Id.* at 203.

41. *Id.* at 205 ("Reducing liberty may prevent an action taking place which would otherwise pose a risk of harm. But it necessarily also increases the power of the state, and there is a corresponding risk that this enhanced power may also be used to cause harm.").

42. *See* William Scheuerman, *Emergency Powers and the Rule of Law After 9/11*, J. POL. PHIL. 14, NO. 1 (2006).

43. Amartya Sen, *Rights and Agency*, 11 PHIL. & PUB. AFF. 3 (1982).

44. Jon Elster, *Comment on the Paper by Ferejohn and Pasquino*, 2 INT'L J. OF CONST. L. 240 (2004).

45. *Ex parte Merryman*, 17 F.Cas. 144 (1861).

46. For details, see www.yale.edu/opa/newsr/01-12-13-03.all.html.

47. *Cf.* Cass R. Sunstein & Edna Ullmann-Margalit, *Second-Order Decisions*, 110 ETH-ICS 5 (1999).

48. *Home Building & Loan Ass'n v. Blaisdell*, 290 U.S. 398 (1934).

49. *See Block v. Hirsch*, 256 U.S. 135 (1921); *Woods v. Cloyd W. Miller Co.*, 333 U.S. 138 (1948).

50. Samuel Issacharoff & Richard H. Pildes, *Between Civil Libertarianism and Executive Unilateralism: An Institutional Process Approach to Rights During Wartime*, 5 THEORETICAL INQUIRIES L. 1 (2004); Sunstein, *Minimalism at War, supra* note 5.

51. Cass R. Sunstein, *Deliberative Trouble? Why Groups Go to Extremes*, 110 YALE L.J. 71 (2000).

52. For some examples, *see* chapter 2.

53. *See, e.g.*, Authorization for Use of Military Force Joint Resolution, Pub. L. No. 107–40, 115 Stat. 224 (2001); 10 U.S.C. § 821 (2000); Gulf of Tonkin Joint Resolution of Aug. 10, 1964, Pub. L. No. 88–408, 78 Stat. 384 (1964); International Emergency Economic Powers Act (IEEPA), 50 U.S.C. §§ 1701–6 (1976); National Emergencies Act (NEA), Pub. L. No. 94–412, 90 Stat. 1255 (codified at 50 U.S.C. §§ 1601–51 (2000)); Emergency Detention Act, Pub. L. No. 81–831, 64 Stat. 987 (codified at 50 U.S.C. §§ 811–26 (1950)) (repealed 1971).

54. Sunstein, *Minimalism at War, supra* note 5, provides the best and most comprehensive version of this account.

55. This problem also renders untestable Epstein et al.'s conjecture that the authorization requirement may explain their puzzling finding that courts hold for the government more often during wartime than during peacetime, but no more in wartime war-related cases than in peacetime war-related cases. See Epstein et al., *supra* note 1. To test this conjecture, one would need to compare cases that review authorized executive actions and cases that review unauthorized executive actions. The problem is that virtually none of the 134 war-related cases in Epstein et al.'s data set involved a unilateral executive action. If all of the cases involve statutes, then one cannot test a theory that makes outcomes turn on whether a case involves a statute or not.

56. *See* Exec. Order No. 9066, 7 Fed. Reg. 1407 (Feb. 19, 1942); Act of Mar. 21, 1942, Pub. L. No. 77–503, 56 Stat. 173 (1942).

57. DANIEL FARBER, LINCOLN'S CONSTITUTION (2003).

58. The plurality's reading is ably defended by Curtis A. Bradley & Jack L. Goldsmith, *Congressional Authorization and the War on Terrorism*, 118 HARV. L. REV. 2047 (2005).

59. *See Hamdi v. Rumsfeld*, 542 U.S. 507, 540–46 (2004) (Souter, J., concurring in part, dissenting in part).

60. *Ex parte Quirin*, 317 U.S. 1, 44 (1942).

61. *Dames & Moore v. Regan*, 453 U.S. 654 (1981). In the same vein is *Regan v. Wald*, 468 U.S. 222 (1984). Here is Professor Tribe's assessment of *Regan*: "[F]ive Justices purported to find, in a factual situation that should probably have been deemed at best ambiguous, clear congressional authorization for the Reagan administration's summary ban on travel to Cuba." LAURENCE H. TRIBE, AMERICAN CONSTITUTIONAL LAW, 677 n.30 (3d ed. 2000).

62. *See Loving v. United States*, 517 U.S. 748 (1996) (the authority delegated to the president by the Uniform Code of Military Justice implicitly included authority to proscribe aggravating factors in death penalty sentencing); compare *Kent v. Dulles*, 357 U.S. 116 (1958) (invalidating a State Department regulation that denied passports for communists in light of administration practice before the relevant statute), with *Zemel v. Rusk*, 381 U.S. 1 (1965) (holding that the same statute implicitly authorized such area restrictions); *Haig v. Agee*, 453 U.S. 280 (1981) (reading the statute to allow revocation of a passport where the holder's activities abroad would compromise national security).

63. Terry M. Moe & William G. Howell, *The Presidential Power of Unilateral Action*, 15 J.L. ECON. & ORG. 132, 152, 174 (1999). *See also* William G. Howell, POWER WITHOUT PERSUASION: THE POLITICS OF DIRECT PRESIDENTIAL ACTION 147–50 (2003); Joel Fleishman & Arthur Aufses, *Law and Orders: The Problem of Presidential Legislation*, 40 L. & CONTEMP. PROBS. 1 (1976). A comprehensive overview of case law, coming to the same conclusions we reach here, is SHEFFER, *supra* note 1.

64. 323 U.S. 214.

65. *Id.* at 223–24.

66. *See Duncan v. Kahanamoku*, 327 U.S. 304 (1946). Although *Ex parte Endo*, 323 U.S. 283 (1944), is sometimes offered as another example of the statutory authorization requirement, *Endo* involved an executive agency that exceeded its authority under the relevant executive order and the statute. *See* 327 U.S. at 297–304. *Endo*, then, is at best an ambiguous precedent on the statutory authorization question.

67. Bradley & Goldsmith, *supra* note 58.

68. *Youngstown Sheet & Tube Co. v. Sawyer*, 343 U.S. 579 (1952).

69. *See also New York Times v. United States*, 403 U.S. 713 (1971) (Marshall, J., concurring) (government lacks necessary statutory authorization to seek an injunction). However, the majority did not consider the statutory authorization issue and decided the case directly on free speech grounds.

70. *See* Neal Devins & Louis Fisher, *The Steel Seizure Case: One of a Kind?* 19 CONST. COMMENT. 63 (2002). The political science literature emphasizes that "divided government, interest group opposition, and public approval ratings have statistically significant impacts on the probability that the president wins [a] court case." Howell, POWER WITHOUT PERSUASION, *supra* note 63, at 164.

71. Seth P. Waxman, *The Combatant Detention Trilogy Through the Lenses of History*, in TERRORISM, THE LAWS OF WAR, AND THE CONSTITUTION: DEBATING THE ENEMY COMBATANT CASES 1 (Peter Berkowitz ed., 2005).

72. Benjamin Wittes, *Judicial Baby-Splitting and the Failure of the Political Branches*, in TERRORISM, THE LAWS OF WAR, AND THE CONSTITUTION: DEBATING THE ENEMY COMBATANT CASES 101 (Peter Berkowitz ed., 2005).

73. Bill Myers, *Prof: Terror Cases Could Let Court Demonstrate Independence*, CHI. DAILY L. BULL, Apr. 1, 2004, at 2, *at* http://www.law.uchicago.edu/news/stone_terrorism.html.

74. As with *Hamdi*, there are complexities here about vote-counting, because Justice Kennedy declined to join portions of the lead opinion, authored by Justice Stevens.

However, these complexities are irrelevant to our analysis. For simplicity, we take the Stevens opinion to be controlling.

75. *In re Debs*, 158 U.S. 564 (1895).

76. Daryl J. Levinson, *Empire-Building Government in Constitutional Law*, 118 HARV. L. REV. 915 (2005).

77. *Id*. at 928–29.

78. *Id*.

79. Li, *supra* note 26.

80. *Id*.

81. On the tradeoffs inherent in increased delegation to the executive, both generally and during emergencies, see Philippe Aghion, Alberto Alesina, and Francesco Trebbi, *Endogenous Political Institutions*, 2004 QUARTERLY JOURNAL OF ECONOMICS 565–611. The intuition is that delegation to the executive should and does increase during emergencies, despite the risk of abuse, because there is a greater anticipated benefit if the executive uses its enhanced discretion to adopt utility-improving policies. See id. at 594–96.

82. *See* "Panels Say Britain Underrated Threat Before July Attacks," *New York Times* (May 12, 2006).

83. Michael J. Klarman, *What's So Great About Constitutionalism?* 93 Nw. U. L. REV. 145, 160–63 (emphasizing that judicial review does not serve a countermajoritarian function, including the protection of civil rights and liberties).

84. John M. Carey & Matthew Soberg Shugart, *Institutional Design and Executive Decree*, in EXECUTIVE DECREE AUTHORITY 274, 296 (John M. Carey & Matthew Soberg Shugart eds., 1998).


## Chapter 2

1. MICHAEL IGNATIEFF, THE LESSER EVIL: POLITICAL ETHICS IN AN AGE OF TERROR 58–61 (2004); GEOFFREY R. STONE, PERILOUS TIMES 531 (2004); Bruce Ackerman, *The Emergency Constitution*, 113 YALE L.J. 1029, 1072 (2004); David Cole, *Their Liberties, Our Security: Democracy and Double Standards*, 31 INT'L J. LEGAL INFO. 290, 304 (2003); Richard H. Kohn, *Using the Military at Home Yesterday, Today, and Tomorrow*, 4 CHI. J. INT'L L. 165 (2003); Christina E. Wells, *Questioning Deference*, 69 MO. L. REV. 903 (2004); ROBERT E. GOODIN, WHAT'S WRONG WITH TERRORISM? (2006); Jon Elster, *Fear, Terror, and Liberty* (unpublished, 2006).

2. *See* Chisun Lee, *Civil Rights Rollback: The Spread of Racial Profiling Since 9–11*, VILLAGE VOICE, Aug. 3, 2004; Anthony Lewis, *Bush and the Lesser Evil*, N.Y. REVIEW OF BOOKS, May 27, 2004, *at* http://www.nybooks.com/articles/17111; Aryeh Neier, *The Military Tribunals*, N.Y. REVIEW OF BOOKS, Feb. 14, 2002, *at* http://www.nybooks.com/articles/15122.

3. Mark Tushnet suggests that the fear thesis is just a metaphor, and that its advocates may have some mechanism in mind, such as another emotion like depression or anxiety, or rational updating by risk-averse individuals. Mark Tushnet, *Issues of Method in Analyzing the Policy Response to Emergencies*, 56 STAN. L. REV. 1581, 1587 & n.23 (2004). Perhaps;

but we cannot construct these arguments on behalf of the advocates; they are dubious at first glance (depressed people do not overreact, they underreact); and we have the more-modest ambition of criticizing arguments that have been made rather than all possible arguments on the other side.

4. Paul Wilkinson, Terrorism and the Liberal State 81 (1977). *See also* Bruno Frey, Dealing with Terrorism: Stick or Carrot? 29–36 (2004).

5. Parenthetically, we find this view, which has made its way into the legal literature (*see* Cole, *supra* note 1; Oren Gross, *Cutting Down Trees: Law-Making Under the Shadow of Great Calamities, in* The Security of Freedom: Essays on Canada's Anti-Terrorism Bill 39, 43 (Ronald Daniels, Patrick Macklem, & Kent Roach eds., 2001)) unconvincing. It might be an ancillary benefit for terrorists that the government's repressive tactics make it unpopular, but in the normal course of things the government will choose appropriate measures and the public will blame the terrorists for the government's repression. Terrorist tactics reflect the methods that are available, and terrorists succeed or not in obtaining public support to the extent that the public prefers the terrorists' goals to the government's. Liberals who object to their own government's use of repressive tactics are hardly likely to switch their allegiance to the terrorists who deliberately provoked them. For a more measured discussion, see Clive Walker, The Prevention of Terrorism in British Law 1–3 (1986).

6. For a survey of the psychology literature on fear, *see* Arne Ohman, *Fear and Anxiety as Emotional Phenomena: Clinical Phenomenology, Evolutionary Perspectives, and Information-Processing Mechanisms, in* Handbook of Emotions 520 (Michael Lewis & Jeannette M. Haviland eds., 1993); for discussions of the psychology literature on emotion and its relation to legal regulation, *see* Jeremy A. Blumenthal, *Law and Social Science in the Twenty-First Century*, 12 S. Cal. Interdisc. L.J. 1 (2002); Ward Farnsworth, *The Economics of Enmity*, 69 U. Chi. L. Rev. 211 (2002); Dan M. Kahan & Martha C. Nussbaum, *Two Concepts of Emotion in Criminal Law*, 96 Colum. L. Rev. 269 (1996); Eric A. Posner, *Fear and the Regulatory Model of Counterterrorism*, 25 Harv. J.L. & Pub. Pol'y 681 (2002); Eric A. Posner, *Law and the Emotions*, 89 Geo. L.J. 1977 (2001). There is not much other work on this relationship. Kuran and Sunstein's examination of the legal response to environmental panics, for example, treats these panics as though they were purely cognitive phenomena. *See* Timur Kuran & Cass R. Sunstein, *Availability Cascades and Risk Regulation*, 51 Stan. L. Rev. 683 (1999); Posner, *Law and the Emotions, supra*, at 2002–6.

7. Ohman, *supra* note 6, at 520.

8. Kuran & Sunstein, *supra* note 6, at 400, 700–703, 742.

9. *See* Albert O. Hirschman, The Passions and the Interests: Political Arguments for Capitalism Before Its Triumph (20th anniversary ed. 1997).

10. *See* Anthony R. Damasio, Descartes' Error: Emotion, Reason, and the Human Brain (1994); Ronald de Sousa, The Rationality of Emotion (1987).

11. *E.g.*, Damasio, *supra* note 10.

12. Martha C. Nussbaum, Upheavals of Thought 117 (2001).

13. *See* William Ian Miller, The Anatomy of Disgust (1997).

14. Nussbaum, *supra* note 12, at 394.

15. Moran argues that psychologists distinguish these phenomena. *See* Rachel F. Moran, *Fear Unbound: A Reply to Professor Sunstein*, 42 WASHBURN L.J. 1, 10–11 (2002). Ohman, however, does not distinguish these phenomena. *See* Ohman, *supra* note 6. One might distinguish the classic flight response associated with fear, and say that an anxious person is primed to have that response. But the special cognitive and motivational characteristics of fear seem to carry over to the analysis of anxiety.

16. This may be true of some people, but does not seem to be generally true about all people.

17. GREG ROBINSON, BY ORDER OF THE PRESIDENT: FDR AND THE INTERNMENT OF JAPANESE AMERICANS 75 (2001).

18. For such an argument, see Wells, *supra* note 1.

19. *See* Kuran & Sunstein, *supra* note 6.

20. *E.g.*, Wells, *supra* note 1, at 923–24.

21. *See* W. Kip Viscusi & Richard J. Zeckhauser, *Hindsight-Choice Bias in Combating Terrorism*, HARVARD LAW AND ECONOMICS DISCUSSION PAPER NO. 458 (2004); *see also* W. Kip Viscusi & Richard J. Zeckhauser, *Sacrificing Civil Liberties to Reduce Terrorism Risks*, 26 J. RISK & UNCERTAINTY 99 (2003); W. Kip Viscusi & Richard J. Zeckhauser, *Recollection Bias and the Combat of Terrorism*, 34 J. LEGAL STUD. 27 (2005).

22. An intrapersonal analogy can be found in a favored technique of anger management: when one feels angry, one should take a deep breath and count to ten before acting. If one trains oneself to respond in a Pavlovian fashion to an event or condition, and the response is likely to restore or improve judgment, then anger-inspired actions can be avoided. Note, however, that this outcome is achieved through the use of a technique by which one's judgment can return to normal; few people think that fear can go away after a deep breath.

23. We have not found in the psychology literature any studies on whether fearful individuals can mentally compensate for biases introduced into their judgment by their own fear. The cognitive psychology literature suggests that individuals can avoid the effect of their own cognitive biases or their reliance on misleading heuristics in limited cases: for example, their judgments can improve through unbiased feedback, or they can choose to rely on outside experts. However, there are severe cognitive and motivational impediments to learning. *See* Jeffrey J. Rachlinski, *The Uncertain Psychological Case for Paternalism*, 97 Nw. U. L. REV. 1165, 1211–24 (2003).

24. *Cf.* THOMAS SCHELLING, *Epilogue: Rationally Coping with Lapses from Rationality*, in GETTING HOOKED: RATIONALITY AND ADDICTION (Jon Elster & Ole-Jxrgen Skog eds., 1999).

25. Martha Minow, *What Is the Greatest Evil?* 118 HARV. L. REV. 2134, 2140 (2005) (reviewing MICHAEL IGNATIEFF, THE LESSER EVIL: POLITICAL ETHICS IN AN AGE OF TERROR (2004)) (emphasis added).

26. *See* CLINTON ROSSITER, CONSTITUTIONAL DICTATORSHIP: CRISIS GOVERNMENT IN THE MODERN DEMOCRACIES 39, 139–50 & 215–17 (1948) (describing historical examples).

27. DAVID BONNER, EMERGENCY POWERS IN PEACETIME 286 (1985).

28. *See Woods v. Cloyd W. Miller Co.*, 333 U.S. 138, 146 (1948) (Jackson, J., concurring) (describing the federal government's war power as "dangerous" because "[i]t usually is invoked in haste and excitement [and] . . . is interpreted by judges under the influence of the same passions and pressures. Always, [the] Government urges hasty decision to forestall some emergency or serve some purpose and pleads that paralysis will result if its claims to power are denied or their confirmation delayed.").

29. *See* Mark Tushnet, *Defending* Korematsu? *Reflections on Civil Liberties in Wartime*, 2003 WIS. L. REV. 273, 289 (2003).

30. ROBINSON, *supra* note 17, at 99–100, 102–3.

31. Samuel Issacharoff & Richard H. Pildes, *Between Civil Libertarianism and Executive Unilateralism: An Institutional Process Approach to Rights During Wartime*, 5 THEORETICAL INQUIRIES L. 1, 53 (2004).

32. This appears to be the general conclusion of Elster, who expresses skepticism about the claim that constitutional constraints can be relied on to counteract popular passions. *See* JON ELSTER, ULYSSES UNBOUND: STUDIES IN RATIONALITY, PRECOMMITMENT, AND CONSTRAINTS 157–61 (2000). In this book, Elster qualifies his earlier work; *see* JON ELSTER, ULYSSES AND THE SIRENS: STUDIES IN RATIONALITY AND IRRATIONALITY (rev. ed. 1984). *See also* JEREMY WALDRON, LAW AND DISAGREEMENT (1999) (criticizing the commitment argument).

33. The Weimar government had strong emergency powers, but they were used more against the Left than against the Right. *See Rossiter, supra* note 26, at 39–41.

34. BERNARD BAILYN, ORIGINS OF THE AMERICAN REVOLUTION 95 (1992).

35. *Id.* at 99.

36. Not, however, the Constitution or the Bill of Rights, which were framed several decades after the events Bailyn describes.

37. CNN.com, *Poll: Fifth of Americans Think Calls Have Been Monitored*, Feb. 14, 2006, *at* http://www.cnn.com/2006/POLITICS/02/14/poll.wiretaps/index.html.

38. *See* List of Communities That Have Passed Resolutions, *at* http://www.aclu.org/SafeandFree/SafeandFree.cfm?ID=11294&c=207.

39. *See, e.g.*, Jennifer C. Evans, *Hijacking Civil Liberties: The USA Patriot Act of 2001*, 33 LOY. U. CHI. L.J. 922 (2002); Patria Mell, *Big Brother at the Door: Balancing National Security with Privacy Under the USA Patriot Act*, 80 DENV. U. L. REV. 375 (2002); Jeremy C. Smith, *The USA Patriot Act: Violating Reasonable Expectations of Privacy Protected by the Fourth Amendment Without Advancing National Security*, 82 N.C. L. REV. 412 (2003); William E. Zieske, *Demystifying the USA Patriot Act*, 92 ILL. B.J. 82 (2004); Elaine Scarry, *Acts of Resistance*, HARPER'S, May 2004, at 15.

40. *See, e.g.*, Vermont Legislature Resolution, *at* http://www.aclu.org/SafeandFree/SafeandFree.cfm?ID=12734&c=207; Community Resolution for Lowell, MA, *at* http://www.aclu.org/SafeandFree/SafeandFree.cfm?ID=17189&c=207; Community Resolution for Kansas City/Wyandotte County, KS, *at* http://www.aclu.org/SafeandFree/SafeandFree.cfm?ID=17190&c=206; Community Resolution for Westchester, NY, *at* http://www.aclu.org/SafeandFree/SafeandFree.cfm?ID=16526&c=207; Community Resolution for Richmond, VA, *at* http://www.aclu.org/SafeandFree/SafeandFree

.cfm?ID=15549&c=207; Community Resolution for Homer, AK, *at* http://www.aclu .org/SafeandFree/SafeandFree.cfm?ID=13243&c=206; *see also*, the ACLU draft resolution, which many of the resolutions copy in some form or another, Model Local Resolution to Protect Civil Liberties, *at* http://www.aclu.org/SafeandFree/SafeandFree .cfm?ID=11267&c=207 (saying that the PATRIOT Act "expand[s] the authority of federal agents to conduct so-called 'sneak and peek' or 'black bag' searches").

41. *How the USA-Patriot Act Expands Law Enforcement "Sneak and Peek" Warrants, at* http://www.aclu.org/Privacy/Privacy.cfm?ID=9769&c=39.

42. *Dalia v. United States*, 441 U.S. 238, 247–48 (1979).

43. The noisiest of the groups making such claims includes the ACLU; *see* http://www .aclu.org/SafeandFree/SafeandFree.cfm?ID=12263&c=206; and the Electronic Frontier Foundation, *at* http://www.eff.org/Privacy/Surveillance/Terrorism/PATRIOT. City and state resolutions have also criticized the surveillance power authorized under the PATRIOT Act as an invasion of rights, *see, e.g.*, Minneapolis's resolution, *at* http://www .aclu.org/SafeandFree/SafeandFree.cfm?ID=12291&c=207; the Alaska State Legislature's Resolution, *at* http://www.aclu.org/SafeandFree/SafeandFree.cfm?ID=12707&c=207; and the State of Maine Resolution, *at* http://www.aclu.org/SafeandFree/SafeandFree .cfm?ID=15294&c=207.

44. Eric A. Posner & John Yoo, *The Patriot Act Under Fire*, Wall St. J., Dec. 9, 2003, at A26.

45. James Risen & Eric Lichtblau, *Bush Lets U.S. Spy on Callers Without Courts*, N.Y. TIMES, Dec. 16, 2005, at A1.

46. *See In re Sealed Case*, 310 F.3d 717 (FISA Ct. Rev. 2002).

47. Richard W. Stephenson & Adam Liptak, *Cheney Defends Eavesdropping Without Warrants*, N.Y. TIMES, Dec. 21, 2005, at A36 (quoting Geoffrey R. Stone saying, "The president's authorizing of N.S.A. to spy on Americans is blatantly unlawful.").

48. *See* STONE, *supra* note Error! Bookmark not defined. (*passim*).

49. *See* Cass R. Sunstein, *Fear and Liberty*, 71 SOCIAL RESEARCH (forthcoming) (manuscript at 17).

50. *See United States v. Dennis*, 183 F.2d 201, 212 (2d Cir. 1950) (Hand, J.). This is a slight *lapsus linguae*; Hand meant "discounted by its probability."

51. *See Brandenburg v. Ohio*, 395 U.S. 444 (1969).

52. Proposed and discussed with more nuance than we can do justice to here by STONE, *supra* note 1.

53. STONE, *supra* note 1, at 539.

54. *Id.* at 540.

55. *Id.*

56. *See* Adrian Vermeule, *The Constitutional Law of Congressional Procedure*, 71 U. CHI. L. REV. 361, 432–33 (2004). Stone acknowledges this problem. STONE, *supra* note 1, at 540.

57. Jacob E. Gersen, Temporary Legislation 20–21 (Sept. 2005) (unpublished manuscript).

58. *See, e.g.*, RICHARD A. POSNER, PREVENTING SURPRISE ATTACKS: INTELLIGENCE REFORM IN THE WAKE OF 9/11 (2005). Elster, similarly, points out that there is a difference

between "panic" and "urgency." *See* Jon Elster, Terrorism and Civil Liberties (Minerva Lecture, 2005) (unpublished manuscript).

## Chapter 3

1. GEOFFREY R. STONE, PERILOUS TIMES 531 (2004). Other versions of this position include Jeremy Waldron, *Security and Liberty: The Image of Balance*, 11 J. POL. PHIL. 191, 194 (2003); David Cole, *Their Liberties, Our Security: Democracy and Double Standards*, 31 INT'L J. LEGAL INFO. 290, 304 (2003); MICHAEL IGNATIEFF, THE LESSER EVIL: POLITICAL ETHICS IN AN AGE OF TERROR 58–61 (2004).

2. *See Stephen Holmes & Cass R. Sunstein, The Cost of Rights* 50 (1999).

3. *United States v. Carolene Products Co.*, 304 U.S. 144 (1938).

4. *E.g.*, JOHN HART ELY, DEMOCRACY AND DISTRUST: A THEORY OF JUDICIAL REVIEW (1980).

5. Adam B. Cox, *Citizenship, Standing, and Immigration Law*, 92 CAL. L. REV. 373, 413–14 (2004).

6. *See* Vincent Blasi, *The Pathological Perspective and the First Amendment*, 85 COLUM. L. REV. 449 (1985).

7. *Railway Express Agency v. People of State of New York*, 336 U.S. 106, 112 (1949) (Jackson, J., concurring).

8. Cole, *supra* note 1, at 304.

9. *Nixon v. Administrator of General Services*, 433 U.S. 425, 472 (1977). *See also Village of Willowbrook v. Olech*, 528 U.S. 562 (2000) (holding that a homeowner may claim that village arbitrarily treated her as a "class of one").

10. JOSEPH RAZ, THE AUTHORITY OF LAW 216 (1979).

11. For a critique, *see* DONALD A. WITTMAN, THE MYTH OF DEMOCRATIC FAILURE (1995); for a brief but lucid critical survey, *see* Bryan Caplan, *Rational Irrationality and the Microfoundations of Political Failure*, 107 PUB. CHOICE 311 (2001) (emphasizing the importance of irrationality).

12. *See* GERRY MACKIE, DEMOCRACY DEFENDED (2003). For responses, *see* Don Herzog, *Dragonslaying*, 72 U. CHI. L. REV. 757 (2005); Saul Levmore, *Public Choice Defended*, 72 U. CHI. L. REV. 777 (2005).

13. Saul Levmore & Kyle Logue, *Insuring Against Terrorism—and Crime*, 102 MICH. L. REV. 268, 319 (2003).

14. Robin Wolpert & James Gimpel, *Self-Interest, Symbolic Politics, and Public Attitudes Toward Gun Control*, 20 POL. BEHAV. 241 (1998).

15. Wikipedia, *Gun Politics*, at http://en.wikipedia.org/wiki/Gun_control.

16. Dean E. Murphy, *Security Grants Still Streaming to Rural States*, N.Y. TIMES, Oct. 12, 2004, at A1; Keven Diaz, *Pork-Barrel Security: Federal Money to Protect Americans from Terrorism May Not Be Going to States That Need It the Most: Formulas and Politics Are Behind the Disparities*, STAR TRIB. (Minneapolis–St. Paul), Sept. 11, 2004, at 1A; Elizabeth Shogren, *More Federal Aid Sought for Cities at Risk of Attack: Under the Current Rules, a Large Chunk*

*of Such Funds Goes to Less Vulnerable Areas: Efforts to Redirect Money Have Stalled in Congress*, L.A. TIMES, Aug. 10, 2004, at A21.

17. *United States v. Carolene Products Co.*, 304 U.S. 144, 152 n.4 (1938).

18. Mark Tushnet, *Issues of Method in Analyzing the Policy Response to Emergencies*, 56 STAN. L. REV. 1581 (2004).

19. *Id.* at 1591.

20. *See* PETER GOUREVITCH, POLITICS IN HARD TIMES: COMPARATIVE RESPONSES TO INTERNATIONAL ECONOMIC CRISES (1986); STEPHEN HAGGARD & ROBERT KAUFMAN, THE POLITICS OF ECONOMIC ADJUSTMENT (1992); RUDIGER DORNBUSCH & SEBASTIAN EDWARDS, REFORM, RECOVERY, AND GROWTH: LATIN AMERICA AND THE MIDDLE EAST (1995).

21. *Chae Chan Ping v. United States*, 130 U.S. 581, 595 (1889).

22. *See, e.g.*, STONE, *supra* note 1, at 286–96.

23. Exec. Order No. 9066, 7 Fed. Reg. 1407 (Feb. 19, 1942).

24. FRANCIS BIDDLE, IN BRIEF AUTHORITY 219 (1962).

25. *See* Stephen Holmes, *Lineages of the Rule of Law*, in DEMOCRACY AND THE RULE OF LAW 19 (José María Maravall & Adam Przeworski eds., 2003); Eric A. Posner & Adrian Vermeule, *Emergencies and Political Change: A Reply to Tushnet*, 56 STAN. L. REV. 1593, 1595 (2004). We have profited from Mark Graber's excellent historical overview. See Mark A. Graber, *Counter-Stories: Maintaining and Expanding Civil Liberties in Wartime*, in THE CONSTITUTION IN WARTIME: BEYOND ALARMISM AND COMPLACENCY (Mark Tushnet ed., 2005).

26. *See* MARY L. DUDZIAK, COLD WAR CIVIL RIGHTS (2000).

27. *See* James Zogby, *Arab-American Rights Still Intact One Year Later*, GULF NEWS, Sept. 2, 2002, *at* http://www.aaiusa.org/wwatch/090202.htm (after 9/11, "the DOJ and the FBI . . . have made an unprecedented effort to find and punish those who committed crimes of hate against Arab Americans").

28. Patrick Goodenough, *Religious Hate Law Aimed at Protecting Muslims Passes UK Vote*, CNSNEWS.COM, July 12, 2005, *at* http://www.cnsnews.com/ViewForeignBureaus.asp?Page=%5C%5CForeignBureaus%5C%5Carchive%5C%5C200507%5C%5CFOR2 0050712a.html.

29. Douglas Zehl, *C.I.A. Reviews Security Policy for Translators*, N.Y. TIMES, June 8, 2005, at A1.

30. STONE, *supra* note 1, at 544 ("[T]here is not a single instance in which the Supreme Court has *overprotected* wartime dissent in a way that caused *any* demonstrable harm to the national security. The argument that courts cannot be trusted because they will recklessly shackle the nation's ability to fight is simply unfounded.") (emphases in original).

31. *Korematsu v. United States*, 323 U.S. 214 (1944) (Jackson, J., dissenting).

32. Not until 1954 did the Court squarely hold that racial segregation by the federal government was unconstitutional. *See Bolling v. Sharpe*, 347 U.S. 497 (1954).

33. *Id.* at 245.

34. *See, e.g.,* Civil Liberties Act of 1988, 50 App. U.S.C. § 1989 (1988) (granting reparations to Japanese Americans interned during World War II).

35. Mark Tushnet, *Defending* Korematsu? *Reflections on Civil Liberties in Wartime*, 2003 WIS. L. REV. 273 (2003). This is the "cycle thesis," defended by Justice William Bren-

nan and Chief Justice William Rehnquist, among others. For a thoughtful account of the cycle thesis, *see* Seth P. Waxman, *The Combatant Detention Trilogy Through the Lenses of History*, *in* TERRORISM, THE LAWS OF WAR, AND THE CONSTITUTION: DEBATING THE ENEMY COMBATANT CASES 1, 3–10 (Peter Berkowitz ed., 2005). However, as we discuss in chapters 7 and 8, Waxman takes the *Hamdi* decision too seriously when he describes it as a counterexample to the cycle thesis. *See id.* at 12.

36. *A and Others v. Sec. of State for the Home Dept.*, 2 A.C. 68 (2004).

37. *See, e.g.*, Vienna Convention on Consular Relations, Apr. 24, 1963, 21 U.S.T. 77, 596 UNTS 262 (entered into force Mar. 19, 1967).

38. Larry Rohter, *Brazil Fingerprints Americans (to U.S. Dismay)*, INT'L HERALD TRIB., Jan. 10, 2004, at 1.

39. Case Concerning Avena and Other Mexican Nationals (Mexico v. United States), 2004 I.C.J. 12 (Mar. 31).

40. Case Concerning the Vienna Convention on Consular Relations (Paraguay v. United States), 1998 I.C.J. 248 (Apr. 9); LaGrand Case (Germany v. United States), 2001 I.C.J. 466 (June 27).

41. Joseph H. Carens, Immigration, Democracy, and Citizenship 8 (2005) (unpublished manuscript), *at* http://ptw.uchicago.edu/carens01.pdf.

42. *Dennis v. United States*, 341 U.S. 494 (1951).

43. *Id.* at 570 (Jackson, J., concurring).

44. *Yates v. United States*, 354 U.S. 298 (1957); *Scales v. United States*, 367 U.S. 203 (1961).

45. *Brandenburg v. Ohio*, 395 U.S. 444 (1969).

46. CASS R. SUNSTEIN, LAW OF FEAR: BEYOND THE PRECAUTIONARY PRINCIPLE, ch. 9 (2005).


## Chapter 4


1. Larry F. Darby & Joseph Fuhr, *Investment Incentives and Local Competition at the FCC*, 9 MEDIA L. & POL'Y 1, 18 (2000); Bruce Yandle & Andrew P. Morriss, *The Technologies of Property Rights: Choice Among Alternative Solutions to Tragedies of the Commons*, 28 ECOLOGY L.Q. 123, 148 (2001).

2. Bernard E. Harcourt, *The Shaping of Chance: Actuarial Models and Criminal Profiling at the Turn of the Twenty-First Century*, 70 U. CHI. L. REV. 105, 124–25 (2003).

3. Amy L. Wax, *Against Nature: On Robert Wright's The Moral Animal*, 63 U. CHI. L. REV. 307, 340–41 (1996) (book review).

4. See ALEXANDER KEYSSAR, THE RIGHT TO VOTE: THE CONTESTED HISTORY OF DEMOCRACY IN THE UNITED STATES 225–55 (2000).

5. John Donne wrote, "And though each spring do add to love new heat / As princes do in action get / New taxes, and remit them not in peace / No winter shall abate the spring's increase." JOHN DONNE, POEMS OF JOHN DONNE, 1 (E. K. Chambers ed., London: Lawrence & Bullen, 1896), 34–35. Thanks to Jon Elster for this reference.

6. *See* JOHN WITTE, POLITICS AND THE DEVELOPMENT OF THE FEDERAL INCOME TAX (1985).

7. *See* Oren Gross, *Chaos and Rules: Should Responses to Violent Crises Always Be Constitutional?* 112 YALE L.J. 1011, 1090 (2003). See also Terry M. Moe & William G. Howell, *The Presidential Power of Unilateral Action*, 15 J.L. ECON. & ORG. 132, 157 (1999) (analyzing "the ratchet effect of expansion of accepted authority in the office of the president with each new emergency"); JOHN E. FINN, CONSTITUTIONS IN CRISIS: POLITICAL VIOLENCE AND THE RULE OF LAW 54 (1991) ("[d]esperate measures have a way of enduring beyond the life of the situations that give rise to them"); Jules Lobel, *Emergency Power and the Decline of Liberalism*, 98 YALE L.J. 1385, 1397–1421 (1989) (attempting to show that successive wars and crises have steadily expanded executive authority, at the expense of civil liberties); George J. Alexander, *The Illusory Protection of Human Rights by National Courts During Periods of Emergency*, 5 HUM. RTS. L.J. 1, 26–27 (1984) (emergency decisions may "infest law long after the emergency has passed").

8. *See* generally STEPHEN HOLMES & CASS R. SUNSTEIN, THE COST OF RIGHTS (1999) (explaining that rights are implemented by affirmative government decisions to fund protection for those rights).

9. *See* Jack Goldsmith & Timothy Wu, *Digital Borders*, 2006 LEGAL AFF. 40 (Feb. 2006).

10. *Korematsu v. United States*, 323 U.S. 214, 246 (1944) (Jackson, J., dissenting).

11. Mark Tushnet, *Defending* Korematsu? *Reflections on Civil Liberties in Wartime*, 2003 WIS. L. REV. 273 (2003); for Gross's similar view, *see supra* note 7, at 1125. Tushnet is quite explicit that Jackson "does not quite make the point I extract from his opinion."

12. See *Woods v. Cloyd W. Miller Co.*, 333 U.S. 138, 146 (1948) (Jackson, J., concurring) (describing the federal government's war power as "dangerous" because "[i]t usually is invoked in haste and excitement [and] . . . is interpreted by judges under the influence of the same passions and pressures. Always, [the] Government urges hasty decision to forestall some emergency or serve some purpose and pleads that paralysis will result if its claims to power are denied or their confirmation delayed").

13. For an account of *Youngstown Sheet & Tube Co. v. Sawyer*, 343 U.S. 579 (1952), that explains Black's opinion as an example of this strategy, see Adrian Vermeule, *The Judicial Power in the State (and Federal) Courts*, 2000 SUP. CT. REV. 357, 404–5 (2001).

14. *See* ERGUN ÖZBUDUN & MEHMET TURHAN, EMERGENCY POWERS (1995) (report of the European Commission for Democracy Through Law) (providing an overview of legal provisions on emergency powers from thirty-two nations); COPING WITH CRISES: HOW GOVERNMENTS DEAL WITH EMERGENCIES (Shao-chuan Leng ed., 1990) (detailed case studies of emergency law from Israel, Northern Ireland, Italy, South Korea, and Taiwan).

15. John M. Carey & Matthew Soberg Shugart, *Institutional Design and Executive Decree*, in EXECUTIVE DECREE AUTHORITY 274, 296 (John M. Carey & Matthew Soberg Shugart eds., 1998).

16. *See, e.g.*, U.S. CONST. art. I, § 9, cl. 1; U.S. CONST. art. V.

17. Gross, *supra* note 7, at 1090.

18. For a skeptical analysis of the claim that legislators and other officials generally seek to expand their institutional powers, *see* Daryl J. Levinson, *Empire-Building Government in Constitutional Law*, 118 HARV. L. REV. 915 (2005).

19. Jack Goldsmith & Cass R. Sunstein, *Military Tribunals and Legal Culture: What a Difference Sixty Years Makes*, 19 CONST. COMMENT. 261, 285–86 (2002); Arthur Krock, *When Martial Law Was Proposed for Everybody*, N.Y. TIMES, July 14, 1942, at 18.

20. 18 U.S.C. § 1385 (2003).

21. *See* Mark Tushnet, *Issues of Method in Analyzing the Policy Response to Emergencies*, 56 STAN. L. REV. 1581, 1583 n.7 (2004).

22. Larry D. Kramer, *But When Exactly Was Judicially Enforced Federalism "Born" in the First Place?* 22 HARV. J.L. & PUB. POL'Y 123, 132 (1998).

23. *See* Wayne D. Moore, *Reconceiving Interpretive Autonomy: Insights from the Virginia and Kentucky Resolutions*, 11 CONST. COMMENT. 315, 323 (1994).

24. *See Ex parte Milligan*, 71 U.S. 2 (1866).

25. Lee Epstein et al., *The Supreme Court During Crisis: How War Affects Only Non-War Cases*, 80 N.Y.U. L. REV. 1, 81 (2005).

26. Gross, *supra* note 7, at 1093–94.

27. *See* U.S. GENERAL ACCOUNTING OFFICE, REPORT TO CONGRESSIONAL COMMITTEES: COMBATING TERRORISM 10–17 (2001) (prepared before 9/11 and released afterward; the GAO gives government preparedness a mixed review, finding important failures of accountability and of coordination, both among federal agencies and between the federal government and the states).

28. Dermot P. J. Walsh, *The Impact of the Antisubversive Laws on Police Powers and Practices in Ireland: The Silent Erosion of Individual Freedom*, 62 TEMP. L. REV. 1099, 1102 (1989).

29. Gross, *supra* note 7, at 1072.

30. Walsh, *supra* note 28, at 1128–29.

31. Gross, *supra* note 7, at 1095–96.

32. *Id.* at 1095.

33. WILLIAM REHNQUIST, ALL THE LAWS BUT ONE: CIVIL LIBERTIES IN WARTIME 221 (1997).

34. Goldsmith & Sunstein, *supra* note 19, at 262.

35. Tushnet, *Defending Korematsu? supra* note 11, at 294–95; Seth P. Waxman, *The Combatant Detention Trilogy Through the Lenses of History*, *in* TERRORISM, THE LAWS OF WAR, AND THE CONSTITUTION 1, 17–25 (Peter Berkowitz ed., 2005); David Cole, *Judging the Next Emergency: Judicial Review and Individual Rights in Times of Crisis*, 101 MICH. L. REV. 2565, 2571–77 (2003).

36. Goldsmith & Sunstein, *supra* note 19, at 288.

37. For discussions of the evidence, see Steven C. Poe & C. Neal Tate, *Repression of Human Rights to Personal Integrity in the 1980s: A Global Analysis*, 88 AMER. POL. SCI. REV. 853 (1994); Steven C. Poe, C. Neal Tate, & Linda Camp Keith, *Repression of the Human Right to Personal Integrity Revisited: A Global Cross-National Study Covering the Years 1976–1993*, 43 INT'L STUD. Q. 291 (1999).

38. Goldsmith & Sunstein, *supra* note 19, at 285.

39. *Id.* at 262.

40. GARY KING, ROBERT O. KEOHANE, & SIDNEY VERBA, DESIGNING SOCIAL INQUIRY: SCIENTIFIC INFERENCE IN QUALITATIVE RESEARCH 129 (1994).

41. Tushnet, *Defending* Korematsu? *supra* note 11, at 292.

42. Waxman, *supra* note 35, at 25–33.

43. *See* Joseph Carroll, Gallup Organization, *Americans' Confidence in High Court Declines: Current Rating Among Lowest Ever*, June 21, 2005, *at* http://institution.gallup.com/content/default.aspx?ci=17011.

44. *See* Epstein et al., *supra* note 25, at 53–54.

45. *See* Mark Tushnet, *Issues of Method in Analyzing the Policy Response to Emergencies*, 56 Stan. L. Rev. 1581 (2004).

46. Jon Elster, *Responses to Uncertainty: Terrorism and Civil Liberties* (2005), *at* http://economics.uchicago.edu/download/Responses_to_uncertainty.pdf. For similar arguments, see Bruno Frey, Dealing with Terrorism: Stick or Carrot? (2004); Robert Pape, Dying to Win: The Strategic Logic of Suicide Terrorism (2005).

47. Jon Elster, *Solomonic Judgments: Against the Best Interests of the Child*, 54 U. Chi. L. Rev. 1 (1987).

48. Frey, *supra* note 46.

49. *Id.*

50. Paul Wilkinson, Terrorism and the Liberal State 81 (1977). See also David Cole, Enemy Aliens 183–208 (2003); Oren Gross, *Cutting Down Trees: Law-Making Under the Shadow of Great Calamities, in* The Security of Freedom: Essays on Canada's Anti-Terrorism Bill 39, 43 (Ronald Daniels, Patrick Macklem, & Kent Roach eds., 2001); Oren Gross, *Are Torture Warrants Warranted? Pragmatic Absolutism and Official Disobedience*, 88 Minn. L. Rev. 1481, 1505 (2004).

51. For a measured discussion, *see* Clive Walker, The Prevention of Terrorism in British Law 1–3 (1986).

52. *Hamdi v. Rumsfeld*, 524 U.S. 507, 532 (2004) (quoting United States v. Robel, 389 U.S. 258, 264 (1967)).

53. Martha Minow, *What Is the Greatest Evil?* 118 Harv. L. Rev. 2134, 2169 (2005) (book review).

54. Thanks to Fred Schauer for suggesting this view in conversation.

55. Elster, *Responses to Uncertainty*, *supra* note 46, at 15.

56. The best overview of slippery slope arguments is Frederick Schauer, *Slippery Slopes*, 99 Harv. L. Rev. 361 (1985); for emphasis on the need to identify a concrete slippery slope mechanism, *see* Eugene Volokh, *The Mechanisms of the Slippery Slope*, 116 Harv. L. Rev. 1026 (2003).

## Chapter 5

1. *Whitman v. American Trucking Ass'ns*, 531 U.S. 457 (2001).

2. Bruce Ackerman, *The Emergency Constitution*, 113 Yale L.J. 1029 (2004).

3. Samuel Issacharoff & Richard H. Pildes, *Between Civil Libertarianism and Executive Unilateralism: An Institutional Process Approach to Rights During Wartime*, 5 Theoretical Inquiries L. 1 (2004); Cass R. Sunstein, *Minimalism at War*, 2004 Sup. Ct. Rev. 47 (2005).

4. For the most comprehensive recent discussion, *see* Oren Gross, *Are Torture Warrants Warranted? Pragmatic Absolutism and Official Disobedience*, 88 MINN. L. REV. 1481, 1520 (2004). We will discuss other sources below.

5. *See* Mark Tushnet, *Controlling Executive Power in the War on Terrorism*, 118 HARV. L. REV. 2673 (responding to Bradley & Goldsmith).

6. *See* ERGUN ÖZBUDUN & MEHMET TURHAN, EMERGENCY POWERS (1995) (report of the European Commission for Democracy Through Law).

7. *See, e.g.*, CLINTON ROSSITER, CONSTITUTIONAL DICTATORSHIP: CRISIS GOVERNMENT IN THE MODERN DEMOCRACIES (1948); John Ferejohn & Pasquale Pasquino, *The Law of the Exception: A Typology of Emergency Powers*, 2 INT'L J. CONST. L. 210 (2004).

8. Ackerman, *supra* note 2, at 1047.

9. *Id.* at 1056–59, 1070–76.

10. *Id.* at 1030.

11. *Youngstown Sheet & Tube Co. v. Sawyer*, 343 U.S. 579 (1952).

12. *Korematsu v. United States*, 323 U.S. 214, 248 (1944) (Jackson, J., dissenting).

13. *See* Jules Lobel, *Emergency Power and the Decline of Liberalism*, 98 YALE L.J. 1385, 1412–31 (1989).

14. *Cf.* Jacob E. Gersen, Temporary Legislation (2004) (unpublished manuscript).

15. Issacharoff & Pildes, *supra* note 3.

16. Sunstein, *supra* note 3.

17. We criticized this argument in chapter 1.

18. Eric A. Posner & Adrian Vermeule, *Legislative Entrenchment: A Reappraisal*, 111 YALE L.J. 1665 (2002). We do not think that there is a constitutional barrier to entrenching legislation, but it may sometimes be difficult as a practical matter because of the ways that prior rules can be circumvented.

19. Henry Shue, *Torture*, 7 PHIL. & PUB. AFF. 124, 127 (1978); Gross, *supra* note 4, at 1520; Sanford Levinson, *"Precommitment" and "Postcommitment": The Ban on Torture in the Wake of September 11*, 81 TEX. L. REV. 2013, 2048 (2003). A related view can be found in Eyal Benvenisti, *The Role of National Courts in Preventing Torture of Suspected Terrorists*, 8 EUR. J. INT'L L. 596 (1997).

20. *Cf.* ROBERT COVER, JUSTICE ACCUSED (1984) (describing protection of fugitive slaves in the North).

21. *See* Gross, *supra* note 4, at 1529–34.

22. They have a family resemblance to the notion of acoustic separation. *See* Meir Dan-Cohen, *Decision Rules and Conduct Rules: On Acoustic Separation in Criminal Law*, 97 HARV. L. REV. 625 (1984).

23. *See* Ian Traynor, *Secret Killings of Newborn Babies Trap Dutch Doctors in Moral Maze*, GUARDIAN, Dec. 21, 2004, *at* http://www.guardian.co.uk/uk_news/story/0,,1377808,00.html.

24. *Id.*

25. *See* JON ELSTER, SOUR GRAPES (1983).

26. ISRAELI GOVERNMENT PRESS OFFICE, COMMISSION OF INQUIRY INTO THE METHODS OF INVESTIGATION OF THE GENERAL SECURITY SERVICE REGARDING HOSTILE TERRORIST ACTIVITY (1987), *reprinted in* 23 ISR. L. REV. 146 (1989).

27. *See* WAYNE R. LAFAVE, SUBSTANTIVE CRIMINAL LAW § 10.1(d) at 129–131(2003) (one must wait until there is absolutely no other option and "the hope of survival disappears").

28. *See id.* § 10.5 at 161.

29. Although the Israeli Supreme Court denied that the necessity defense authorizes coercive interrogation, it, at the same time, said that officials could use the necessity defense if they are charged. H.C.J. 5100/94 *Public Comm. Against Torture in Israel v. State of Israel*, 38 I.L.M. 1471, 1486–88 (1999) (Isr.). This distinction is a rather subtle one, but may have led to a reduction in the use of coercive interrogation by Israeli security. John T. Parry & Welsh S. White, *Interrogating Suspected Terrorists: Should Torture Be an Option?* 62 U. PITT. L. REV. 743, 760 (2002).

30. Parry & White, *supra* note 29, at 764–65. Shue also seems to suggest that the necessity defense may be appropriate. Shue, *supra* note 19, at 123.

31. *See* Shue, *supra* note 19.

32. Levinson, *supra* note 19, at 2045.

33. This approach would allow the legislature to decide the standard for using coercive interrogation, rather than relying on a doctrine that was never understood to have this purpose (at least, in American law) and would need to be revised. *See* Alan Dershowitz, *Is It Necessary to Apply "Physical Pressure" to Terrorists—and to Lie about It?* 23 ISR. L. REV. 192 (1989) (discussing problems with using the necessity defense in these circumstances); Mordechai Kremnitzer, *The Landau Commission Report: Was the Security Service Subordinated to the Law or the Law to the "Needs" of the Security Service?*, 23 ISR. L. REV. 216, 237–47 (1989).

34. *Ex parte Merryman*, 17 F.Cas. 144 (1861).

35. *Rumsfeld v. Padilla*, 542 U.S. 426 (2004).

36. DANIEL FARBER, LINCOLN'S CONSTITUTION 158–59 (2003). Perhaps, he implicitly acknowledged the law violation in his famous rhetorical question of whether the government should permit "all the laws but one" to be violated so as not to violate that one, but this was not the basis of his argument.

37. *Korematsu v. United States*, 323 U.S. 214, 246 (1944) (Jackson, J., dissenting).

38. Mark Tushnet, *Defending* Korematsu? *Reflections on Civil Liberties in Wartime*, 2003 WIS. L. REV. 273, 305–7 (2003) (footnotes omitted).

39. This seems to be the thrust of Oren Gross's argument as well; he emphasizes that the outlaw-and-forgive approach forces the executive to be candid about the reasons for his actions. Oren Gross, *Chaos and Rules: Should Responses to Violent Crises Always Be Constitutional?* 112 YALE L.J. 1011, 1023–26 (2003).

## Chapter 6

1. *See* Sanford Levinson, *"Precommitment" and "Postcommitment": The Ban on Torture in the Wake of September 11*, 81 TEX. L. REV. 2013 (2003) [hereinafter *"Precommitment" and "Postcommitment"*]. Levinson's important paper supplies evidence for the first two claims in the text and constitutes evidence for the third. For other recent debate about torture,

*see* TORTURE: A COLLECTION (Sanford Levinson ed., 2004) (collecting major essays on the practical, philosophical, and moral considerations surrounding the historical and contemporary use of torture). For a recent media report, *see* Eric Lichtblau, *Justice Dept. Opens Inquiry into Abuse of U.S. Detainees*, N.Y. TIMES, Jan. 14, 2005, at A20.

2. The last clause excludes the use of coercive interrogation to extract confessions to be used in later prosecution. We define coercive interrogation strictly as a military or law enforcement practice used to prevent harm to others, rather than as a prosecutorial tool.

3. The principal legal sources of the prohibition on torture are the United Nations Convention Against Torture and Other Cruel, Inhuman and Degrading Treatment or Punishment, G.A. Res. 39/46, Annex, 39 U.N. GAOR, Supp. No. 51, at 197, U.N. Doc. A/39/51 (1984), *reprinted in* 23 I.L.M. 1027 (1984), *modified in* 24 I.L.M. 535 (1985); the U.S. Senate reservations to the convention, which adopted a more restrictive definition of "torture," U.S. Reservations, Declarations, and Understandings and Convention Against Torture and Other Forms of Cruel, Inhuman or Degrading Treatment or Punishment, II(1)(a), 136 Cong. Rec. S17491–92 (1994); 18 U.S.C. § 2340(1)–(2) (criminalizing torture committed outside the United States by U.S. nationals and persons later found in the United States); Torture Victim Protection Act, 28 U.S.C. § 1350 (providing a civil remedy against torturers acting under color of the law of a foreign nation); and U.S. Supreme Court decisions holding that "police interrogation practices that severely infringe on a suspect's mental or physical autonomy violate the due process clause regardless of whether they produce statements that are admitted against the suspect," John T. Parry & Welsh S. White, *Interrogating Suspected Terrorists: Should Torture Be an Option?* 62 U. PITT. L. REV. 743, 751 (2002). In sum, "[t]orture is prohibited by law throughout the United States." U.S. DEPT. OF STATE, INITIAL REPORT OF THE UNITED STATES OF AMERICA TO THE U.N. COMMITTEE AGAINST TORTURE (1999), *at* http://www.state.gov/www/global/human_rights/torture_articles.html (quoted in Parry & White, *supra*, at 753). A complication, which we will ignore, is the claim by some Bush administration officials that statutory and treaty restrictions on certain forms of coercive interrogation should be narrowly construed and might even be unconstitutional to the extent that they prohibit the president from using coercive interrogation in the exercise of the commander-in-chief power. Memorandum for Alberto R. Gonzales, Counsel to the President, Re: Standards of Conduct for Interrogation under 18 U.S.C. §§ 2340–2340A, Part V, 31–39 (Aug. 1, 2002), *at* http://news.findlaw.com/hdocs/docs/doj/bybee80102mem.pdf; WORKING GROUP REPORT ON DETAINEE INTERROGATIONS ON THE GLOBAL WAR ON TERRORISM: ASSESSMENT OF LEGAL, HISTORICAL, POLICY, AND OPERATIONAL CONSIDERATIONS (Mar. 6, 2003), *at* http://www.ccr-ny.org/v2/reports/docs/PentagonReportMarch.pdf.

4. Department of Defense Appropriations Act § 1003, Pub. L. 109–148, 119 Stat. 2739 (2006).

5. *See* GEOFFREY BEST, WAR AND LAW SINCE 1945, at 323 (1994).

6. The idea of ex ante warrants for torture is taken from Alan Dershowitz. *See* ALAN DERSHOWITZ, WHY TERRORISM WORKS: UNDERSTANDING THE THREAT, RESPONDING TO THE CHALLENGE (2002).

7. Thomas Nagel, *War and Massacre, in* WAR AND MORAL RESPONSIBILITY 3, 17 (Marshall Cohen et al. eds., 1974).

8. Levinson, *"Precommitment" and "Postcommitment," supra* note 1, at 2032.

9. Martha Nussbaum, *The Costs of Tragedy: Some Moral Limits of Cost-Benefit Analysis,* in COST-BENEFIT ANALYSIS: LEGAL, ECONOMIC, AND PHILOSOPHICAL PERSPECTIVES (Matthew D. Adler & Eric A. Posner eds., 2001). Where tragic choices are involved, Nussbaum suggests, decisionmakers should at a minimum take pains to commemorate the values or rights or interests that are overridden in the service of other commitments. That commemoration can presumably occur in a variety of ways, from compensatory payments to public apologies and memorials. Nussbaum also suggests that decisionmakers should think dynamically, with a view to anticipating and reducing the number of future occasions that present tragic choices. We fully agree, and see nothing inconsistent with our views in that insight.

10. CHARLES FRIED, RIGHT AND WRONG 10 (1978).

11. We bracket the question of whether the catastrophe threshold is best understood as a ratio, as opposed to some other sort of function. *See* Larry Alexander, *Deontology at the Threshold,* 37 SAN DIEGO L. REV. 893, 898–900 (2000).

12. Michael S. Moore, *Torture and the Balance of Evils,* 23 ISRAEL LAW REVIEW 280, 332 (1989).

13. Henry Shue, *Torture,* 7 PHIL. & PUB. AFF. 124, 127 (1978). For a somewhat different philosophical account, according to which the central evil of torture is that it makes the torture victim "actively complicit in his own violation," see David Sussman, *What's Wrong with Torture?* 33 PHIL. & PUB. AFF. 1 (2005). For our purposes, this account need not be separately considered.

14. Shue, *supra* note 13, at 125.

15. *Id.* at 130.

16. *Id.* at 137.

17. *Id.* at 143.

18. *Id.* at 141.

19. For his large propositions about the nature and effects of torture, Shue cites two documents from Amnesty International. *See id.*

20. *See* Moore, *supra* note 12 (arguing that consequences always count, even below the catastrophe threshold, but that consequences are outweighed by the deontological prohibition unless and until the threshold is reached—just as a buildup of water will eventually overspill a dam); SHELLEY KAGAN, NORMATIVE ETHICS 78–84 (1998). For acute first-order criticisms of this sort of justification for the threshold approach, *see* Alexander, *supra* note 11.

21. *See* Amartya Sen, *Rights and Agency,* 11 PHIL. & PUB. AFF. 3 (1982).

22. *See* Jean Bethke Elshtain, *Reflection on the Problem of "Dirty Hands," in* TORTURE: A COLLECTION, *supra* note 1, at 86–87 ("Far greater moral guilt falls on a person in authority who permits the deaths of hundreds of innocents rather than choosing to 'torture' one guilty or complicit person."); Winfried Brugger, *May Government Ever Use Torture? Two Responses from German Law,* 48 AMER. J. COMP. L. 661, 669–71 (2000) (arguing that under

the German constitution, which requires the government to aid individuals, torture may be constitutionally obligated).

23. They have been recently summarized by Oren Gross, though he sees six; several, though, are versions of others. Oren Gross, *Are Torture Warrants Warranted? Pragmatic Absolutism and Official Disobedience*, 88 MINN. L. REV. 1481, 1501–11 (2004).

24. *See* NATIONAL COMMISSION ON TERRORIST ATTACKS UPON THE UNITED STATES: THE 9/11 COMMISSION REPORT 254–77, 339–57 (2004) (indicating that the problem was not that the authorities could not extract information from suspects, but that they were unprepared for the type of terrorist activity that would occur on 9/11).

25. *See, e.g.*, Parry & White, *supra* note 3, at 762.

26. *See, e.g.*, PHILIP HEYMANN, TERRORISM, FREEDOM AND SECURITY: WINNING WITHOUT WAR 109–12 (2004); Philip N. S. Rumney, *Is the Coercive Interrogation of Terrorist Suspects Effective?* 40 U.S.F. L. REV. (forthcoming 2006).

27. ISRAELI GOVERNMENT PRESS OFFICE, COMMISSION OF INQUIRY INTO THE METHODS OF INVESTIGATION OF THE GENERAL SECURITY SERVICE REGARDING HOSTILE TERRORIST ACTIVITY 78 (1987), *reprinted in* 23 ISR. L. REV. 146, 184 (1989) [hereinafter Landau Report].

28. U.N. Comm. Against Torture, *Consideration of Reports Submitted by States Parties Under Article 19 of the Convention, Second Periodic Reports of States Parties Due in 1996*, Addendum, Israel, 7 U.N. Doc. CAT/C/33/Add.2/Rev.1 (1997) [hereinafter U.N. Report].

29. H.C.J. 5100/94 *Public Comm. Against Torture in Israel v. State of Israel*, 38 I.L.M. 1471, 1474 (1999) (Isr.) [hereinafter Public Committee Against Torture in Israel].

30. U.N. Report, *supra* note 28, at 3–4.

31. Rumney, *supra* note 26.

32. *Id.* at 12 (quoting B'TSELEM, LEGISLATION ALLOWING THE USE OF PHYSICAL FORCE AND MENTAL COERCION IN INTERROGATIONS BY THE GENERAL SECURITY SERVICE 52–53 (2000)).

33. *See id.* at 36 & n.149.

34. While state statutes list some specific circumstances when deadly force is allowed, such as acting as the executioner at the orders of a competent court, they also create more general standards for when force is "justified." *See, e.g.*, Ala. Code § 13A-3–27 (2004) ("A peace officer is justified in using deadly physical force upon another person when and to the extent that he believes it necessary . . . (2) To defend himself or a third person from what he reasonably believes to be the imminent use of deadly force."); 720 Ill. Comp. Stat. Ann. 5/7–5 ("[A peace officer] is justified in the use of any force which he reasonably believes to be necessary to effect the arrest and of any force which he reasonably believes to be necessary to defend himself or another from bodily harm while making the arrest."); Utah Code Ann. § 76–2–404 (2004) ("A peace officer . . . is justified in using deadly force when: . . . (c) the officer reasonably believes that the use of deadly force is necessary to prevent death or serious bodily injury to the officer or another person."). State statutes are not the last word, of course. In *Tennessee v. Garner*, 471 U.S. 1 (1985), the Court found unconstitutional a statute that authorized deadly force against a flee-

ing suspect who was neither armed nor dangerous. Most state statutes, however, already comply with *Garner's* rules.

35. Gross, *supra* note 23, at 1507.

36. David Luban, *Liberalism, Torture, and the Ticking Bomb*, 91 VA. L. REV. 1425, 1446 (2005).

37. Gross, *supra* note 23, at 1508–9; Seth Kreimer, *Too Close to the Rack and the Screw: Constitutional Constraints on Torture in the War on Terror*, 6 U. PA. J. CONST. L. 278, 278 (2003); Parry & White, *supra* note 3, at 763; Mordechai Kremnitzer, *The Landau Commission Report: Was the Security Service Subordinated to the Law or the Law to the "Needs" of the Security Service?*, 23 ISR. L. REV. 216, 254–57, 261–62 (1989).

38. Frederick Schauer, *Slippery Slopes*, 99 HARV. L. REV. 361 (1985).

39. Eugene Volokh, *The Mechanisms of the Slippery Slope*, 116 HARV. L. REV. 1026 (2003).

40. Kremnitzer, *supra* note 37, at 260–61.

41. One scholar argues that the CIA contributed to the destabilization of the Philippines and the overthrow of the shah of Iran by training officers in the techniques of psychological torture. *See* Alfred W. McCoy, *Cruel Science: CIA Torture and U.S. Foreign Policy*, 19 NEW ENG. J. PUB. POL'Y 209, 228–31 (2005). But his evidence is exceedingly weak and consistent with the opposite conclusion: that the Philippines would be less stable and the shah's government would have collapsed earlier had they not used torture. As McCoy concedes that these countries would have used torture even without the CIA's help, and as he argues only that the CIA's contribution consisted of training foreign police in the techniques of *psychological* torture, his evidence does not support the claim that the use of torture by the CIA "metastasized," resulting in unintended injury to friendly governments.

42. Luban, *supra* note 36, at 1446.

43. *Id.* at 1453.

44. *Id.* at 1440–41.

45. *See* BENJAMIN STORA, ALGERIA: 1830–2000: A SHORT HISTORY 49–51 (Jane Marie Todd trans., 2001) (describing the use of torture by French forces to defeat an insurrection in Algiers). Kreimer, *supra* note 37, at 280 n.10 (discussing the British use of coercive interrogation in Northern Ireland in the 1970s).

46. *See* STORA, *supra* note 45, at 87–93 (describing the reactions of the French public to the use of torture in Algeria).

47. Gross, *supra* note 23, at 1504.

48. *Id.*

49. *Id.; see also* Parry & White, *supra* note 3, at 763.

50. Jeremy Waldron, *Torture and Positive Law: Jurisprudence for the White House*, 50 COLUM. L. REV. 1681, 1723 (2005). Waldron actually casts his argument as a condemnation of "torture," but he focuses almost exclusively on what we call coercive interrogation, and we address his argument only to that extent.

51. *Id.* (emphasis in original).

52. *Id.*, at 42.

53. *Id.*, at 43. The consideration doctrine does not exist in civil code countries, which are just as committed to market principles as are the United States and the United Kingdom.

54. *See* Moore, *supra* note 12, at 329; Elshtain, *supra* note 22.

55. Levinson, *"Precommitment" and "Postcommitment,"* *supra* note 1, at 2052–53; Parry & White, *supra* note 3, at 763.

56. Ronald Reagan, *Farewell Address to the Nation* (Jan. 11, 1989), at http://www.reagan.utexas.edu/archives/speeches/1989/011189i.htm he was quoting John Winthrop.

57. Gross, *supra* note 23, at 1505.

58. *See* Mary L. Dudziak, Cold War Civil Rights: Race and the Image of American Democracy (2000).

59. *See* MSNBC.com, *Poll Finds Broad Approval of Terrorist Torture*, Dec. 9, 2005, *at* http://msnbc.msn.com/id/10345320.

60. *Rochin v. California*, 342 U.S. 165 (1952).

61. *Chavez v. Martinez*, 538 U.S. 760 (2003).

62. But see *A and Others v. Sec. of State for the Home Dept.*, U.K.H.L. 71 (2005) (holding that information extracted by torture of terrorist suspects is inadmissible).

63. *See* Dana Priest, *CIA Holds Terror Suspects in Secret Prisons: Debate Is Growing Within Agency About Legality and Morality of Overseas System Set Up After 9/11*, Wash. Post, Nov. 2, 2005, at A1.

64. Dershowitz, *supra* note 6, at 158–59.

65. Gross, *supra* note 23, at 1536.

66. Richard A. Posner, *Torture, Terrorism, and Interrogation, in* Torture: A Collection, *supra* note 1, at 296.

67. In 2004, the court approved 1,754 of 1,758 submitted applications. Ninety-four of those applications were approved subject to FISA court modifications. *See* Letter from William E. Moschella, Assistant Attorney General, to J. Dennis Hastert, Speaker of the United States House of Representatives, 2004 Annual FISA Report to Congress (Apr. 1, 2005), *at* http://www.usdoj.gov/oipr/readingroom/2004fisa-ltr.pdf. For reports from previous years, all of which show similarly high approval rates, *see* Office of Intelligence Policy Reviews: FOIA Reading Room Records, *at* http://www.usdoj.gov/oipr/readingroom/oipr_records.htm.

68. Eric A. Posner, *Agency Models in Law and Economics, in* Chicago Lectures in Law and Economics 225 (Eric A. Posner ed., 2000).

69. That is, since the Supreme Court invalidated these measures just prior to World War II. *See* Parry & White, *supra* note 3, at 748–54.

70. Or a vaguer standard might be used, such as that of the Model Penal Code § 3.07:

1. Use of Force Justifiable to Effect an Arrest. Subject to the provisions of this Section and of Section 3.09, the use of force upon or toward the person of another

is justifiable when the actor is making or assisting in making an arrest and the actor believes that such force is immediately necessary to effect a lawful arrest.
. . .

(b) The use of deadly force is not justifiable under this Section unless:
    (i) the arrest is for a felony; and
    (ii) the person effecting the arrest is authorized to act as a peace officer or is assisting a person whom he believes to be authorized to act as a peace officer; and
    (iii) the actor believes that the force employed creates no substantial risk of injury to innocent persons; and
    (iv) the actor believes that:
        (A) the crime for which the arrest is made involved conduct including the use or threatened use of deadly force; or
        (B) there is a substantial risk that the person to be arrested will cause death or serious bodily injury if his apprehension is delayed.

71. U.N. Report, *supra* note 28, at 2 (referring to the type of pressure used to obtain information from terrorists as being moderate).

72. *See* Levinson's survey of media accounts; Levinson, *"Precommitment" and "Postcommitment," supra* note 1, at 2017–28.

73. *See* Amnesty International, *Germany's Torturous Debate, at* http://web.amnesty.org/web/wire.nsf/April2003/Germany (describing an incident in which a kidnapper disclosed the location of the victim—a child, whom he had killed—after a police officer threatened to use force against him).

74. *Harlow v. Fitzgerald,* 457 U.S. 800 (1982).

75. The Investigators Unit, the GSS unit that uses coercive interrogation, is a small minority of the total GSS personal. *See* Landau Report, *supra* note 27, at 148.

76. Gross, *supra* note 23, at 1486–87, 1504–5.

77. *See* Human Rights Watch, *Israel, the Occupied West Bank and Gaza Strip, and Palestinian Authority Territories,* WORLD REPORT 2003, *at* http://www.hrw.org/wr2k3/mideast5.html ("On September 4, the Public Committee Against Torture in Israel reported that there appeared to be a 'gradual reversion to the use of torture' despite the September 1999 High Court decision outlawing its use. While the extent of their use was unclear, methods outlawed by the High Court but reportedly used during interrogation included exposure to extremes of temperature, sleep deprivation, the requirement to remain in an enforced position for extended periods, and intense psychological pressure.") The report mentioned above can be found at http://www.stoptorture.org.il/eng/publications.asp?menu=5&submenu=1.

78. *See* Alan Dershowitz, *Torture Without Visibility and Accountability Is Worse Than with It,* 6 U. PA. J. CONST. L. 326 (2003); *cf.* Eyal Benvenisti, *The Role of National Courts in Preventing Torture of Suspected Terrorists,* 8 EUR. J. INT'L L. 1, 4 (1997) (arguing that a nominal ban on coercive interrogation could have perverse effects by driving interrogation underground).

## Chapter 7

1. U.S. CONST. art. I, § 9.

2. *Hamdi v. Rumsfeld*, 524 U.S. 507, 554 (2004) (Scalia, J., dissenting).

3. As to the point we discuss in text, this majority was composed of a four-justice plurality, led by Justice Sandra Day O'Connor, plus Justices David Souter, Ruth Bader Ginsburg, and Clarence Thomas.

4. *Hamdi*, 524 U.S. at 533–34 (describing the process that the Court believes to be required in such circumstances).

5. *Legalism* is more or less synonymous with the notion of the rule of law. On this, *see* the essays collected in DEMOCRACY AND THE RULE OF LAW (José María Maravall & Adam Przeworski eds., 2003).

6. With respect to the domestic setting, this seems to be Shklar's view, which puts great weight on the harm principle. JUDITH SHKLAR, LEGALISM: LAW, MORALS, AND POLITICAL TRIALS 60–70 (1964).

7. See the essays in ETERNALLY VIGILANT: FREE SPEECH IN THE MODERN ERA (Lee C. Bollinger & Geoffrey R. Stone eds., 2002).

8. This is roughly the approach of Stephen Holmes, *Lineages of the Rule of Law, in* DEMOCRACY AND THE RULE OF LAW, *supra* note 5, at 19; and Adam Przeworski, *Why Do Political Parties Obey Results of Elections? in* DEMOCRACY AND THE RULE OF LAW, *supra* note 5, at 114.

9. *See* JAMES MORTON SMITH, FREEDOM'S FETTERS: THE ALIEN AND SEDITION LAWS AND AMERICAN CIVIL LIBERTIES (1956).

10. *Id.* at 431. Smith provides specific examples that show that defendants convicted of Sedition Act violations often became heroes; in one case, the defendant was an elected official who was rewarded with reelection after he was released from prison. *See, e.g., id.* at 238, 241, 244, 274, 395.

11. There is a large literature on this. *See, e.g.,* Harry Litman, *Pretextual Prosecution*, 92 GEO. L.J. 1135 (2004) (vague laws); Dan M. Kahan & Tracey L. Meares, *Foreword: The Coming Crisis of Criminal Procedure*, 86 GEO. L.J. 1153 (1998) (gang loitering laws).

12. *See* GEOFFREY R. STONE, PERILOUS TIMES (2004), for a recent discussion.

13. In the United States, the executive branch might also seek broad support from Congress, as emphasized by Samuel Issacharoff & Richard H. Pildes, *Between Civil Libertarianism and Executive Unilateralism: An Institutional Process Approach to Rights During Wartime*, 5 THEORETICAL INQUIRIES L. 1, 161 (2004), and by Cass R. Sunstein, *Minimalism at War*, 2004 SUP. CT. REV. 47 (2005). However, given that the problem of distrust is partisan rather than institutional, we would argue that it was more important for Roosevelt to appoint the Republicans Knox and Stimson to his cabinet than for him to obtain the acquiescence of the Democratic Congress.

14. We will discuss later the extent to which governments can expect judges to acquiesce in this way. For now, assume that judges will do what they think the government wants them to do.

15. *See* John E. Finn, *Electoral Regimes and the Proscription of Anti-Democratic Parties, in The Democratic Experience and Political Violence* 51, 66 (David C. Rappaport & Leonard

Weinberg eds., 2001). "It is a fact that almost immediately after the beginning of World War I people of the political right used the war as an excuse to attack people of the left. They did so by accusing leftists of being disloyal." H. C. Peterson & Gilbert C. Fite, Opponents of War, 1917–1918, at 45 (1957). *See also id.* at 213–21.

16. This was Justice Jackson's argument in *Dennis. See Dennis v. United States*, 341 U.S. 494, 570 (1951) (Jackson, J., concurring).

17. Some people might argue that the purpose of show trials is to instill fear and intimidate the public, which is supposed to know that the defendant's confession was the result of torture, and thus that torture is the punishment for political opposition. This is, at best, a small portion of the truth: disappearances or, for that matter, overt violence against political opponents would serve the purpose of intimidation. The great show trials in the Soviet Union had the specific purpose of discrediting Stalin's opponents and were intended for foreign as well as domestic audiences (foreign journalists were invited to attend the trials). The trials did not fool everyone in the West, as the charges were often absurd, and some of the facts asserted in the trials could be checked out and disproved; but they did fool many influential people in the West, including politicians, journalists, artists, and intellectuals. *See*, e.g., Robert Conquest, The Great Terror 91 (1990) (describing foreign observers at the trial of the old Bolsheviks); *id.* at 105–8 (describing the Western reception of the trial); *id.* at 463–76 (describing the Western reaction to all of the trials of the 1936–1938 period).

18. There is a sliding scale, and some devices used in a political trial can make it hard to distinguish from a show trial. In France, the "amalgam" was a device for associating a political opponent with ordinary criminals with whom he never conspired but shared some superficial similarity. One trial in 1894 brought together some anarchists whose offense was only political with ordinary criminals who justified their crimes using anarchist rhetoric but who otherwise had no association with the political defendants. *See* Otto Kirchheimer, Political Justice: The Use of Legal Procedure for Political Ends 196 & n.40 (1961). The fiction here was more than the court could tolerate.

19. A complementary philosophical treatment can be found in John E. Finn, Constitutions in Crisis: Political Violence and the Rule of Law (1991), in which he argues that during emergencies the commitment to constitutionalism can be maintained, even as a particular constitution's requirements are evaded, as long as certain elemental requirements of constitutionalism—reason, deliberation, etc.—are satisfied.

20. A more ambiguous example is the trial of Aaron Burr for treason in 1807. *See* Ron Christenson, Political Trials: Gordian Knots in the Law 47–50 (1986). Burr was a political enemy of Jefferson, but by 1807 he probably could not be considered to be a part of the mainstream opposition; Justice John Marshall, however, who derailed the trial by defining "treason" narrowly, was. But see Robert K. Faulkner, *Justice Marshall and the Burr Trial*, 53 J. Legal Hist. 247 (1966).

21. *See* Richard E. Ellis, The Jeffersonian Crisis: Courts and Politics in the Young Republic 278–79 (1971).

22. *See, e.g.*, Paul Avrich, The Haymarket Tragedy 280–85 (1984) (anarchists);

Michal R. Belknap, Cold War Political Justice: The Smith Act, the Communist Party, and American Civil Liberties 113 (1977) (communists). However, it is important to note that these trials created a political backlash. Several of the Haymarket defendants were ultimately pardoned, and the trial radicalized many workers. Avrich, *supra*, at 307–12 (after trial), 409–14 (after executions), 433–36 (long-term effect).

23. During the U.S. Civil War, a large number of northerners suspected of southern sympathies were detained by the military, with no judicial process. The precise number is unknown, but it was probably in the hundreds (if one limits oneself to the clearest cases) or thousands (especially if one includes draft resisters, unexplained arrests, and so forth). *See* Mark E. Neely, Jr., The Fate of Liberty: Abraham Lincoln and Civil Liberties 51–65, 113–38 (1991). Detainees did receive military hearings, which involved regular procedures. *Id*. at 162–75.

24. Harold Josephson, *Political Justice During the Red Scare: The Trial of Benjamin Gitlow*, *in* American Political Trials 181 (Michal R. Belknap ed., 1981).

25. See James W. Ely, Jr., *The Chicago Conspiracy Case*, *in* American Political Trials, *id*. at 249–50.

26. *See* Peter Charles Hoffer & N. E. H. Hull, Impeachment in America, 1635–1805 (1984).

27. *See* Alan Cowell, *Britain Lists Offenses in Effort to Bar or Deport Foreign Militants*, N.Y. Times, Aug. 25, 2005, at A7.

28. Bruno Frey, Dealing with Terrorism: Stick or Carrot? (2004).

29. *See* Finn, *supra* note 15, at 56 (quoting article 21(2) of the German Constitution: "Parties which, by reason of their aims or the behavior of their adherents, seek to impair or abolish the free democratic basic order or to endanger the existence of the Federal Republic of Germany, shall be unconstitutional . . . ").

30. *Id*. at 70–74 (describing laws of Chile, Estonia, France, Germany, Ireland, Israel, Italy, Portugal, Romania, and Rwanda).

31. *See* J. G. Randall, Constitutional Problems under Lincoln 177–85 (1926).

32. *See Yates v. United States*, 354 U.S. 298, 338 (1957).

33. Finn, *supra* note 15, at 60.

34. Stone, *supra* note 12, at 410.

35. The Soviets preferred agents with ideological motivation because they were more reliable than paid agents. *See* Allen Weinstein & Alexander Vassiliev, The Haunted Wood: Soviet Espionage in America: The Stalin Era 29 (1999).

36. This is one of the distinctive problems in the current pursuit of terrorists. *See* William J. Stuntz, *Local Policing After the Terror*, 111 Yale L.J. 2137 (2002).

37. *Dennis v. United States*, 341 U.S. 494, 510 (1951).

38. Vincent Blasi, *The Pathological Perspective and the First Amendment*, 85 Colum. L. Rev. 449 (1985).

39. John Yoo, *Using Force*, 71 U. Chi. L. Rev. 729 (2004); Eric A. Posner & Alan O. Sykes, *Optimal War and Jus Ad Bellum*, 93 Geo. L.J. 993 (2005); Alan Dershowitz, Why Terrorism Works: Understanding the Threat, Responding to the Challenge (2002).

40. Other scholars have taken this view, *e.g.*, Richard A. Posner, Not a Suicide Pact: Constitutional Rights in Time of National Emergency (Jan. 2, 2006) (unpublished manuscript).

41. Blasi, *supra* note 38.

42. *United States v. Progressive, Inc.*, 467 F. Supp. 990 (W.D. Wis. 1979).

43. That many federal (and state) laws are so broad and vague that they can be used to criminalize almost any tort or even breach of contract has been noted by many scholars. *E.g.*, John C. Coffee, Jr., *Does "Unlawful" Mean "Criminal"? Reflections on the Disappearing Tort/Crime Distinction in American Law*, 71 B.U. L. REV. 193, 202–13 (1991). The effect of these laws is to give prosecutors a great deal of discretion. *See* Daniel C. Richman, *Federal Criminal Law, Congressional Delegation, and Enforcement Decision*, 46 UCLA L. REV. 757 (1999); William J. Stuntz, *The Pathological Politics of Criminal Law*, 100 MICH. L. REV. 505 (2001).

44. RONALD RADOSH & JOYCE MILTON, THE ROSENBERG FILE xv–xxii (2d ed. 1997) (discussing the Venona project).

45. Kenneth M. Dolbeare & Joel B. Grossman, *LeRoi Jones in Newark: A Political Trial? in* AMERICAN POLITICAL TRIALS, *supra* note 24, at 227–32.

46. Avrich, *supra* note 22, at 277.

47. *See* Robert M. Chesney, *Civil Liberties and the Terrorism Prevention Paradigm: The Guilty by Association Critique*, 101 MICH. L. REV. 1408 (2003). The material support statute has been heavily criticized by civil libertarians. *See, e.g.*, DAVID COLE, ENEMY ALIENS: DOUBLE STANDARDS AND CONSTITUTIONAL FREEDOMS IN THE WAR ON TERRORISM (2003).

48. Peterson & Fite, *supra* note 15, at 252–54.

49. PETER L. STEINBERG, THE GREAT "RED MENACE": UNITED STATES PROSECUTION OF AMERICAN COMMUNISTS, 1947–52, at 161 (1985).

50. BELKNAP, *supra* note 22, at 196.

51. For the *Dennis* trial, see *id.* at 77–116; STEINBERG, *supra* note 49, at 157–77; for the Chicago 8 trial, *see* Daniel J. Danelski, *The Chicago Conspiracy Trial, in Political Trials* 178–80 (Theodore L. Becker ed., 1971).

52. *Cf.* J. Mark Ramseyer, *The Puzzling (In)Dependence of Courts: A Comparative Approach*, 23 J. LEGAL STUD. 721 (1994); Matthew C. Stephenson, *"When the Devil Turns . . .": The Political Foundations of Independent Judicial Review*, 32 J. LEGAL STUD. 59 (2003).

53. *See* Ramseyer, *supra* note 52, at 727–28.

54. Irving Kaufman, who presided over the *Rosenberg* case, and Harold Medina, who presided over the *Dennis* case, were both elevated to the Second Circuit Court of Appeals.

55. *See* STONE, *supra* note 12, at 168–70. His elevation was delayed several years. Other judges who acted similarly were attacked in the press and ostracized.

56. BELKNAP, *supra* note 22, at 113.

57. *See* SMITH, *supra* note 9.

58. *See* RANDALL, *supra* note 31, at 179 & n *.

59. As shown in *Ex parte Merryman*, 17 F.Cas. 144 (1861); see also *Ex parte Milligan*, 71 U.S. 2 (1866).

60. *See, e.g.*, SMITH, *supra* note 9, at 326–27 (instructions for Thomas Cooper's trial).

61. Peterson, *supra* note 15, at 17.

62. *See* Avrich, *supra* note 22, at 262–67.

63. *Id.* at 78.

64. *See* Dolbeare & Grossman, *supra* note 45, at 232–34.

65. For the Supreme Court's views of the tradeoffs involved, see *Johnson v. Eisentrager*, 339 U.S. 763, 778–79 (1950) (upholding conviction by military tribunal of nonresident enemy aliens).

66. Democratic candidate John Kerry did not make an issue of them during the 2004 presidential election campaign.

67. *See, e.g.*, CASS R. SUNSTEIN ET AL., PUNITIVE DAMAGES: HOW JURIES DECIDE (2003).

68. *See* Akhil Reed Amar, *The Bill of Rights as a Constitution*, 100 YALE L.J. 1131, 1149 (1991).

69. But not always; trials of some prominent radicals during World War I under the Espionage Act resulted in hung juries. *See* STONE, *supra* note 12, at 170 & n ★. Some Vietnam era trials also ended in acquittals or hung juries. *Id.* at 483.

70. *See* SMITH, *supra* note 9, *passim*; for one exception, *see id.* at 282.

71. *See id.* at 422–23; and *see, e.g., id.* at 235–36 (trial of Lyon), *id.* at 321 (trial of Cooper), *id.* at 348 (trial of Callender).

72. *See, e.g., id.* at 321, 348.

73. *Id.* at 187. The preponderance of trials in the northern and middle states was due to the greater influence of Federalists in those areas. *Id.* at 177.

74. DANIEL FARBER, LINCOLN'S CONSTITUTION (2003).

75. *See* Julia Preston, *Lawyer Is Guilty of Aiding Terror*, N.Y. TIMES, Feb. 11, 2005, at A1 (lawyer for al Qaeda member convicted of providing material aid to a terrorist).

76. *See* KIRCHHEIMER, *supra* note 18, at 253–54 (citing *Konigsberg v. State Bar of California*, 353 U.S. 252 (1957)). *See also Sacher v. United States*, 343 U.S. 1 (1951).

77. It remains unclear whether defendants must be given civilian lawyers. *See Hamdi*, 542 U.S. at 539 (O'Connor, J., plurality).

78. BELKNAP, *supra* note 22, at 13–17.

## Chapter 8

1. *E.g.*, Peter Spiro, *Not War, Crimes*, FINDLAW, Sept. 19, 2001, *at* http://writ.news.findlaw.com/commentary/20010919_spiro.html; Noah Feldman, *Choices of Law, Choices of War*, 25 HARV. J.L. & PUB. POL'Y 457 (2002).

2. The Posse Comitatus Act forbids the government to use military forces for law enforcement on American territory under certain conditions, but it does not forbid all use, and, as a statute, it can be repealed if necessary. Subsequent laws have provided that military forces can be used to assist domestic law enforcement in certain circumstances.

3. *See* 10 U.S.C. §§ 331–33; 42 U.S.C. §§ 5170b(c); 18 U.S.C.A. § 2332e.

4. *See* 10 U.S.C. §§ 331–33.

5. *Ex parte Quirin,* 317 U.S. 1, 44 (1942).

6. *Hamdan v. Rumsfeld,* 415 F.3d 33 (D.C. Cir. 2005), *cert. granted,* 126 S. Ct. 622 (2005), reversed on other grounds, 126 S. Ct. 2749 (2006).

7. 424 U.S. 319 (1976).

8. *Id.* at 334–35.

9. Compare *In re Guantanamo Detainee Cases,* 355 F. Supp. 2d 443, 467–68 (D.D.C. 2005) (determining that the CSRT procedures do not afford due process) with *Khalid v. Bush,* 355 F. Supp. 2d 311, 323 n.16 (D.D.C. 2005) (noting that the CSRTs comport with due process).

10. Benjamin Wittes, *Judicial Baby-Splitting and the Failure of the Political Branches, in* TERRORISM, THE LAWS OF WAR, AND THE CONSTITUTION: DEBATING THE ENEMY COMBATANT CASES 101 (Peter Berkowitz ed., 2005); Bruce Ackerman, *The Emergency Constitution,* 113 YALE L.J. 1029 (2004).

11. *Hamdi v. Rumsfeld,* 542 U.S. 507, 520 (2004).

12. *Id.* at 521.

13. *Id.*

14. Typically, at the conclusion of a war, POWs are exchanged.

15. *See* Press Release, U.S. Dept. of Defense, Guantanamo Bay Detainee Administrative Review Board Decisions Completed (Feb. 9, 2006), *at* http://www.globalsecurity.org/security/library/news/2006/02/sec-060209-dod01.htm.

16. GEORGE ORWELL, 1984 (Irving Howe ed., 2d ed. 1982) (1949).

17. Thanks to Jeremy Waldron for emphasizing this point.

18. Here, the O'Connor plurality was joined by Justices Souter and Ginsburg, who had dissented on the statutory authorization issue.

19. The plurality, led by Justice O'Connor and joined by Chief Justice Rehnquist and Justices Anthony Kennedy and Stephen Breyer, held that, although detention of U.S. citizen enemy combatants is permissible, due process requires that the detainee have an opportunity to contest the factual basis for his detention. *Hamdi,* 542 U.S. at 533. In their concurrence, Justices Souter and Ginsburg agreed that Hamdi should be given a meaningful opportunity to contest his detention on remand although they believed that his detention was not authorized. *Id.* at 553. Justices Scalia and Stevens found it unnecessary to rely on the due process clause at all because they determined that the lack of congressional authorization or action under the suspension clause was determinative. *Id.* at 575–76. Justice Thomas's dissent was the only opinion that agreed both that the government could detain Hamdi and that he need not be given an opportunity to challenge the factual basis for his detention. *Id.* at 589.

20. Our argument here is similar to that of John Yoo, *Enemy Combatants and the Problem of Judicial Competence, in* TERRORISM, THE LAWS OF WAR, AND THE CONSTITUTION, *supra* note 10, at 69; John Yoo, *Courts at War,* 91 CORNELL L. REV. 573 (2006).

21. *See* Eric Schmitt, *President Backs McCain on Abuse,* N.Y. TIMES, Dec. 16, 2005, at A1.

22. *See* Wittes, *supra* note 10.

23. 339 U.S. 763 (1950).

24. 542 U.S. 466 (2004).

25. *Id.* at 478–79 (discussing *Braden v. 30th Judicial Circuit Court of Ky.*, 410 U.S. 484 (1973)).

26. Compare *In re Guantanamo Detainee Cases*, 355 F. Supp. 2d 443, 467–68 (D.D.C. 2005) with *Khalid v. Bush*, 355 F. Supp. 2d 311, 323 n.16 (D.D.C. 2005).

27. *See* Detainee Treatment Act of 2005, § 1003, Pub. L. No. 109–148, 119 Stat. 2739 (2006), *at* http://jurist.law.pitt.edu/gazette/2005/12/detainee-treatment-act-of-2005-white.php.

28. See *Hamdan*, slip op. at 18 n. 14.

29. *See* Terry M. Moe & William G. Howell, *The Presidential Power of Unilateral Action*, 15 J.L. Econ. & Org. 132 (1999); William G. Howell, Power Without Persuasion: The Politics of Direct Presidential Action (2003).

30. On the history, see generally, Geoffrey Best, War and Law Since 1945 (1994); Geoffrey Best, Humanity in Warfare (1980); and the essays in The Laws of War: Constraints on Warfare in the Western World (Michael Howard, George J. Andreopoulos, & Mark R. Shulman eds., 1994).

31. *See* Christopher Greenwood, *The Law of Weaponry at the Start of the New Millennium, in* The Law of Armed Conflict: Into the Next Millennium 185 (Michael N. Schmitt & Leslie C. Green eds., 1998).

32. *See*, generally, Best, War and Law Since 1945, *supra* note 30.

33. The issue arose again during the Kosovo intervention, when human rights groups complained that NATO's use of high-altitude bombing protected pilots at unreasonable expense to civilians, who were killed or injured by errant bombs. *See, e.g.*, Amnesty International, *"Collateral Damage" or Unlawful Killings? Violations of the Laws of War by NATO During Operation Allied Force* 13–16 (June 2000). The relevant question is, if you think that the Kosovo intervention was justified on humanitarian or security grounds, but think that American public opinion would not have tolerated an air campaign that resulted in nontrivial casualties to American pilots, should the American government have chosen not to intervene in order to avoid violating international humanitarian law?

34. Eric A. Posner, *A Theory of the Laws of War*, 70 U. Chi. L. Rev. 297 (2003).

35. The actual strategic setting is more complicated. There must probably be asymmetric information—for why would the states go to war unless there were some kind of bargaining failure?—and the asymmetric information problem that results in war may explain why states are unable, during the war, to make deals limiting the kinds of weapons and tactics they can use. Agreeing to laws of war prior to the war makes such bargaining unnecessary, but then asymmetric information may interfere with the threat of retaliation in case of violation of the laws, which then makes cooperation difficult. We are assuming that the decision to go to war is a rational choice. *See* James D. Fearon, *Rationalist Explanations for War*, 49 Int'l Org. 379 (1995).

36. *See* Jeffrey W. Legro, Cooperation Under Fire: Anglo-German Restraint During World War II, at 37 (1995).

37. *See* Best, War and Law Since 1945, *supra* note 30, at 206–7.

38. Germany used poison gas in its death camps, but those murdered were mostly German civilians.

39. For a discussion of these and related factors, see James D. Morrow, *The Institutional Features of the Prisoners of War Treaties*, 55 INT'L ORG. 971 (2001).

40. *See* EYAL BENVENISTI, THE INTERNATIONAL LAW OF OCCUPATION (1993).

41. Note that there will often be divergence between the formal laws of war agreed to in advance of war, and the "law in action," as the war progresses. This happens because, during wars, weapons and tactics evolve quickly and unpredictably, rendering earlier judgments irrelevant. For example, during World War I, when the British imprisoned German U-boat crews for war crimes, Germans responded by imprisoning a group of British officers. Eventually, the British gave in: they could not deter the Germans from their U-boat tactics because they valued the humane treatment of their captured soldiers more than any gains from imprisoning U-boat crews. GARY JONATHAN BASS, STAY THE HAND OF VENGEANCE: THE POLITICS OF WAR CRIMES TRIBUNALS 61–62 (2000).

42. Protocol Additional to the Geneva Conventions of Aug. 12, 1949, and Relating to the Protection of Victims of International Armed Conflicts, Dec. 12, 1977, art. 48, 1125 UNTS 3 (entered into force Dec. 7, 1978).

43. *See* STEPHEN STRASSER, THE 9/11 INVESTIGATIONS (2004).

44. Religious terrorists may be undeterrable because they are motivated by religious duties. *See* BRUCE HOFFMAN, INSIDE TERRORISM 168 (1998). They are also more violent. *Id.* at 93. But they have aims that they are pursing using rational means; and this is true for terrorists generally. *Id.* at 183.

45. Hoffman provides some examples. Israel and the Palestine Liberation Organization exchange prisoners, *id.* at 67; so have other states and terrorist organizations, *id.* at 133–35; and terrorist organizations sometimes try to avoid civilians, focusing on soldiers and officials instead, *id.* at 164.

46. *See* MICHAEL VAN TANGEN PAGE, PRISONS, PEACE AND TERRORISM 164–68 (1998).

47. *See* Morrow, *supra* note 39.

48. It might be politically sensible to evade the laws of war through aggressive interpretation of their provisions, rather than declaring as a matter of policy that the United States will not regard them as conferring protections on members of terrorist organizations even if, under a proper interpretation of the laws, they do. Alternatively, the United States could declare that they do not apply to terrorist organizations unless those organizations commit to respecting their substantive provisions regarding the treatment of prisoners, civilians, etc., which is highly unlikely. We take no position on this question.

49. *Hamdan v. Rumsfeld*, 415 F.3d 33 (D.C. Cir. 2005), reversed in part, 126 S. Ct. 2749 (2006).

50. Geneva Convention Relative to the Treatment of Prisoners of War, Aug. 12, 1949, common art. 3, 6 U.S.T. 3316, 75 UNTS 135.

51. *Hamdan*, 415 F.3d at 42.

# INDEX